European Police Systems

PATTERSON SMITH REPRINT SERIES IN
CRIMINOLOGY, LAW ENFORCEMENT, AND SOCIAL PROBLEMS

A listing of publications in the SERIES *will be found at rear of volume*

PUBLICATION NO. 54: PATTERSON SMITH REPRINT SERIES IN
CRIMINOLOGY, LAW ENFORCEMENT, AND SOCIAL PROBLEMS

European Police Systems

BY

RAYMOND B. FOSDICK
Former Commissioner of Accounts, City of New York

With a New Introduction by
DONAL E. J. MacNAMARA

Montclair, New Jersey
PATTERSON SMITH
1969

363.2
F748e

SBN 87585-054-5

Library of Congress Catalog Card Number: 69-14926

75-1023

INTRODUCTION TO THE REPRINT EDITION

The map of Europe is much changed since Raymond B. Fosdick visited London, Paris, Berlin, Rome, Vienna, and other of its major cities in 1913-14. No longer reign the Hohenzollerns, Hapsburgs, and the house of Victor Emmanuel, then arrogant in their majesty and splendor and much concerned with the effectiveness of their police in suppressing popular dissent and in ferreting out conspirators. Nevertheless one has a strong feeling of *déjà vu* as one reads Fosdick's descriptions of the police apparatus in these cities, some now under different sovereignties and nearly all under quite different forms of government. Certainly the more things have changed in the police field, the more they have remained the same.

Fosdick is an admirer, although not a wholly uncritical one, of the continental police systems. He sees them as having higher standards of integrity, more flexible organizational and operational patterns, and (despite inadequacies in pay, prestige, and general education) far more effectiveness in meeting their police responsibilities than their American counterparts. To some extent Fosdick was an "innocent abroad," overimpressed by the charming manners, pre-war courtesy to the visiting student, and the European policing methods which though superficially "scientific" consisted largely of lip service to the teachings of Hans Gross and limited application of the techniques of Alphonse Bertillon, Salvatore Ottolenghi, Juan Vucetich, and L. W. Atcherley (of *modus operandi* fame). To one whose previous observations were limited to the New York police department, which at that time was neither progressive nor particularly courteous (*vide* contemporary newspaper and periodical accounts), the European police forces were understandably impressive.

Fosdick did recognize however that the homogeneity of the populations policed, the more stringent registration and identification controls, and the relatively low population mobility and transiency were factors favorable to crime repression. But he was unaware, at least so far as is evident from his comments, of the rather direct relationship between the diminished individual freedom which characterized most of the societies he studied and the effectiveness of their police apparatus (his brief discussion of the Royal Irish Constabulary and the Dublin Metropolitan Police makes no mention of their reinforcement by large numbers of regular British troops nor of Ireland's stringent penal code, perhaps more repressive than any other in history, which was designed to keep a rebellious populace in check). In a cross-cultural study (particularly one made before World War I) comparing the police of other countries with that of the United States, such variations in political freedom can be highly significant.

When I first taught a course in Comparative Police Administration at the University of Southern California some twenty years ago, *European Police Systems* was the only available English-language text. Since then James Cramer's very useful *The World's Police* (1964) has been published, whose three-page bibliography lists Fosdick's work as the only predecessor dealing with the police system of more than one country and one of only a few describing any national police system other than the British. The extensive bibliography in *European Police Systems* is itself of great interest and value, even at this late date, to the student of police and criminological development.

In the Summer of 1968, I had occasion to visit Copenhagen, Stockholm, Amsterdam, Berlin, Leningrad and Moscow. Certainly the police systems in these continental metropolitan centers have undergone many changes in the years since 1914, but the ratios of police to population are today, as in Fosdick's time, still much higher than those usually prevailing in American municipalities of similar size. Furthermore, the uniforms, insignia, rank and section designations, and more importantly the traditions and operating techniques remain strikingly similar to the descriptions in Fosdick's monograph. The Volkspolizei of the German Democratic Republic (East Germany), for example, reflect more closely the patterns of their West German brother police agencies and officers than those of their ideological co-professionals of the Soviet law enforcement apparatus.

Cross-cultural studies of government institutions and agencies, their development, their problems, and above all the manner in which they interact with other elements within their socio-economic systems are of great importance today. Fosdick's *European Police Systems*, particularly, retains its relevance to our new and heterogeneous culture, which numbers among its population millions of immigrants and descendants of immigrants whose concepts of justice and attitudes toward the agencies of law enforcement have been molded or conditioned by direct or indirect exposure to European patterns.

—DONAL E. J. MACNAMARA

John Jay College of Criminal Justice
City University of New York
January, 1969

CONTENTS

CHAPTER I

THE PURPOSE AND FUNCTION OF THE POLICE

CHAPTER II

THE PLACE OF THE POLICE DEPARTMENT IN THE STATE

CHAPTER III

THE ORGANIZATION OF THE POLICE DEPARTMENT

Contents

CHAPTER IV

THE COMMISSIONER

CHAPTER V

THE ASSISTANT COMMISSIONERS AND THEIR DEPUTIES

CHAPTER VI

THE UNIFORMED FORCE

Contents

CHAPTER VII

THE UNIFORMED FORCE (*Continued*)

CHAPTER VIII

THE DETECTIVE FORCE

CHAPTER IX

METHODS OF CRIME DETECTION

Contents

CHAPTER X

THE INTEGRITY OF THE EUROPEAN POLICE

APPENDICES

Contents

CHARTS

INTRODUCTORY NOTE.

The object of this book, the third of a series published by the Bureau of Social Hygiene, is to describe and to discuss critically the essential features of the police systems of the larger European municipalities. The material presented was drawn from extended personal inquiry and observation in the chief cities of England, Scotland, France, Germany, Austria-Hungary, Italy, Holland and Belgium.[1] To the investigation of the subject and the preparation of the book almost two years were devoted.

It affords me genuine pleasure to make the fullest acknowledgment of the aid given to me by governmental officials, police officers and others all over Europe. To mention by name those to whom my thanks are due is manifestly impossible. But I may at least be permitted to testify to the uniform and unwearied courtesy and helpfulness which I encountered everywhere. Reports and documents were freely placed at my disposal; unhampered facilities for observation were furnished;

---

[1] The cities visited included London, Liverpool, Manchester, Birmingham, Glasgow, Edinburgh, Paris, Lyons, Berlin, Hamburg, Bremen, Dresden, Munich, Stuttgart, Cologne, Vienna, Budapest, Rome, Brussels, Amsterdam and Rotterdam.

Introductory Note

abundant opportunity for discussion was given, and finally the manuscript was read and criticized. To those to whom I am indebted for these services I can never be sufficiently grateful.

RAYMOND B. FOSDICK.

New York City,
    December 15, 1914.

EUROPEAN POLICE SYSTEMS

EUROPEAN POLICE SYSTEMS

CHAPTER I

THE PURPOSE AND FUNCTION OF THE POLICE

Definition of police.— Common purpose of all police bodies.—
Varying tasks.— Police task modified by economic conditions.— By
a city's size and the character of its industries.— By relative
homogeneity of population.— By national traits and characteristics.
— Comparative criminality of European states.— Varying concep-
tions of the police.— British and Continental conceptions contrasted.
— Different functions of the police.— British and Continental
functions contrasted.— German police ordinances and penalties.—
Unwieldiness of the German system.— The common problem of the
European police.

THE English word "police" as a term to signify an
organized body of constabulary is of comparatively modern origin. When Sir William Blackstone published his
celebrated *Commentaries* in 1765, he gave it a much
broader meaning. "The public police and economy,"
he said, "must be considered as the due regulation and
domestic order of the kingdom, whereby the individuals
of the state, like members of a well-governed family,
are bound to conform to the rules of propriety, good
neighborhood, and good manners " [1]— a definition wide
enough to include the entire domestic policy of a nation.
Not until the Parliament Act of 1787, which provided

[1] *Commentaries,* Tenth edition, London, 1787, Vol. IV, p. 162.

for a constabulary system in Ireland,[1] did the word come to be used officially in its modern and somewhat limited sense. To-day we mean by police the primary constitutional force for the protection of individuals in their legal rights, or — to use M. Louis Lépine's definition — "an organized body of officers whose primary duties are the preservation of order, the security of the person and the safety of property."[2] To the study of the organization and operation of such bodies in European municipalities this book is devoted.

The definition just given indicates the general purpose of all police bodies. It is at once evident, however, that in fulfilling this purpose, the task of the police can in no two communities be exactly the same. The police problem is a variable problem, not only as between different countries, but as between different cities in the same country, and even as between different periods of time in the same city. The Italian police are confronted with a situation unfamiliar to the English police; Stuttgart and Königsberg, two typical German cities, require in the way of police activity, somewhat different treatment; Vienna presents to-day a police problem quite distinct from that of twenty years ago.

So many factors are responsible for these variations that it is possible to mention only the more important. Alterations in economic conditions, for example, inevi-

---

[1] 27 Geo. III c. 40. This act laid the foundation for the subsequent formation, in 1836, of the Royal Irish Constabulary. See *History of the Royal Irish Constabulary*, Curtis, Dublin, 1871; and the *Report of the Committee on Inquiry*, appointed by the Chief Secretary for Ireland, Dublin, 1902.

[2] *La Police (Extrait du "Répertoire du droit administratif")* Paris, 1905, p. 4.

The Purpose and Function of the Police

tably produce changes in the kind of activity required of the police. Three hundred thousand paupers settled in Liverpool during the four years that followed the Irish famine of 1849, with consequences visible even to-day in the peculiarly difficult problems which face the police authorities of that city. " I have no hesitation in saying," wrote the former Head Constable in 1910, " that by far the greater part of the crime of Liverpool is due to poverty." [1] In Dresden, a German city of approximately the same size, the police problem is far less acute. For this condition a variety of causes may be assigned, but prominent among them is the absence of a pauper class. " We have no real poverty here," the police president of Dresden told the writer.

Again, the task of the police varies with the size of a city and the character of its industries. A large manufacturing center such as Birmingham or Manchester is, from a police point of view, decidedly more difficult to handle than smaller, quieter cities like Worcester and Lincoln. Not only is the total volume of crime smaller in the latter cities, but the number of crimes per thousand of population is smaller, while in point of variety the crimes themselves have a comparatively limited range. Moreover, the proportion of serious crimes, such as murder and burglary, is not so large in the smaller towns as in cities of complex industrial development.[2]

[1] *Report to the Watch Committee on the Police Department of Liverpool for the year 1910.*

[2] These conclusions are borne out in striking fashion in the following table (compiled from *Judicial Statistics of England and Wales,* 1911, published by the British Home Office), in which a comparison is made between the crimes of the thirty-three English

5

European Police Systems

The simple social and economic environment of the less important municipalities produces a comparatively simple police problem.

Similarly, the police problem varies according as the population of a city is homogeneous or heterogeneous. A population made up of different elements, each with its own traditions, habits and racial peculiarities, is not so easily directed or controlled as one having a common heritage and uniform customs. European cities show a somewhat surprising homogeneity. Of the more than seven million people living within the Metropolitan police district of London, only 211,000 were born abroad. Of this number, 45,000 are Russians, 42,000 are Germans, 27,000 are Poles, 14,000 are Italians, while the remainder consists of smaller numbers of various nationalities.[1] In other words, less than three per cent. of London's population is of alien birth. Similar condi-

boroughs which exceed 100,000 population each and the twenty-nine which fall below that figure.

	33 Boroughs over 100,000 population	29 Boroughs under 100,000 population
Average population	239,530	68,436
Total number of crimes *....	34,136	5,628
Number of crimes per 10,000 population	43.19	28.36
Varieties of crimes..........	25.70	15.80
Proportion of serious crimes (crimes against the person and crimes against property with violence) to total number of crimes............	16.8%	11.4%

* By "crimes" is meant indictable offenses known to the police.

[1] *Census of 1911.* Vol. 9. This volume does not give the figures for the Metropolitan police district as a whole. These statistics have been obtained by adding the figures given in the census for the administrative County of London to those of the other boroughs and districts that make up the Metropolitan Police District.

tions exist in Berlin. Of a population numbering 2,071,257, German is the mother tongue of all but approximately 60,000. Only 2.9 per cent. of the population speak a foreign tongue either in addition to, or to the exclusion of, German.[1] In Paris, 170,000 out of 2,720,000 represent other nationalities than French, approximately 6 per cent., a figure somewhat higher than that of Berlin or London.[2] In Vienna, less than 1 per cent. of the 2,031,498 inhabitants come from beyond the bounds of the Dual Monarchy. The population of the Austrian capital is, nevertheless, heterogeneous to a degree not indicated by this figure.[3] The Empire embraces a number of widely divergent and antagonistic races, and the population of Vienna is steadily recruited not only from Hungary but especially from the Czech provinces of Bohemia and Moravia. This concentration of discordant elements threatens ominously the peace of the city described by Bismarck as the German capital of a Slavic empire. With the exception, however, of Vienna and other cities of Austria, the populations of European cities are remarkably homogeneous, and the task of the

[1] *Statistisches Jahrbuch der Stadt Berlin,* 1913, pp. 40, 41. The 60,000 of whom German is not the mother tongue are made up of 31,000 Poles, 3,600 Czechs, 3,000 Hungarians, 2,400 Russians, 1,860 English, 1,557 Italians, and other nationalities in lesser numbers.

[2] *Annuaire statistique de la Ville de Paris,* 1912. Figures are based on the 1911 census. The 170,000 foreign population is made up of 33,000 Belgians, 26,000 Italians, 25,000 Germans, 19,000 Swiss, 18,000 Russians, 11,000 English, 8,000 Americans, 7,000 Austro-Hungarians, and other nationalities in smaller numbers.

[3] Meyer's *Konversationslexikon,* Vol. 20, annual supplement 1910-11. The Vienna figures are unsatisfactory for the reason that the official returns showing the distribution as to habitual language include only the *citizens* of Austria who are living in Vienna rather than the entire population.

police in preserving law and order is correspondingly simplified.

Again, the police problem throughout Europe varies according to national traits and traditions. Though some difference of opinion on the subject exists, there can be little doubt that temperament and historic custom play an important part in determining the task and methods of police bodies. Consider, for example, the policing of crowds. Two hundred thousand men may assemble in Hyde Park, London, to discuss labor grievances without menacing the public order. Like all British crowds they are good-natured, even lethargic. Temperament and habit unite to render such gatherings harmless. A similar assembly in any of the Latin countries or in Austria-Hungary, would need only the spark of some untoward rumor or occurrence to make it dangerous, perhaps destructive. "Our population is too excitable," the police president of Budapest said, in discussing his military plan of organization. "A civilian body or a force officered by civilians would be overwhelmed." A similar remark was made by one of the assistant secretaries of state for Hungary. "In a country where the public has learned to control itself," he said, "no great police force is needed. You Anglo-Saxons have learned the lesson of self-control; our people have not."

In some countries, whether for racial or historic reasons, or both, there is greater respect for law and the established order than in others. In this matter England and Germany are typical. Beyond question the predominant public attitude in these countries is an attitude of instinctive acquiescence to authority, and to this

The Purpose and Function of the Police

extent, at least, the task of the police in maintaining order
is lightened. But even between England and Germany
the differences are so striking as to call for widely divergent police methods. England is frankly individualistic in her point of view. The Englishman wants to
mind his own business, to look to his own safety, to
guard his own rights, to use his own judgment —
in a word, to be let alone. The German point of view,
on the other hand, may fairly be called paternal-
istic. The state must care for its own. So far from re-
senting it, the German seems to require constant direction;
without it he gives the appearance of being unable to take
care of himself. Orderliness in Germany is not born of
individual self-control; it is a social habit enforced by
the arm of authority. The country is placarded from
end to end with *"Verboten"* signs; the things forbidden cover almost every phase of human activity. In
all public conveyances and in stations, on the streets and
in the parks, the citizen is informed by sign and official
warning not only as to actions prohibited but as to actions mandatory. To these symbols of order the law-
abiding German invariably and instinctively submits.
One gets the impression that the Englishman's respect
for law is more basic, more a matter of principle than
that of the German. The respect of the latter runs
rather to correctness in outward form, according to the
prescription of public authority.

The police problem is vitally affected by this distinction. German orderliness is proverbial. The streets
and parks of German cities are spotless. A hundred
thousand people bring their lunches to the *Grunewald*

9

European Police Systems

near Berlin every pleasant Sunday and leave it as clean and clear of rubbish as when they entered. Vandalism is practically unknown. Public disorder of any kind is infrequent. From his childhood the German is drilled to respect outward order and decency. On the other hand, the British individualistic spirit demands a greater freedom from restraint; it is inclined to be impatient of mere rules; it does not readily submit to regulation for the sake of the regulations. As a result the task of the English constable in maintaining order, if less varied, is frequently more difficult than that of his brother officer in Germany.

National traits and characteristics also are responsible for variations in criminality in the different countries of Europe. At least, whether for racial or economic or other reasons, certain crimes are more common in one country than in another. There are more homicides every year in southern than in northern Europe.[1] Enrico Ferri, in his work on the anthropological phases of homicide, classifies the European population under three heads, declaring that homicide is most frequent among the Latins, and least frequent among the Teutons (including the Anglo-Saxons and Scandinavians) while the Slavic population occupies, in this respect, an intermediate position.[2] Unfortunately there are no reliable statistics by which broad divisions of crime may safely be

[1] But the common belief that Italy leads in the proportion of homicides is not undisputed; Enrico Ferri, *L'omicidio nell'antropologia criminale,* Turin, 1895, p. 252, claims that homicide is more frequent in Spain than anywhere else in Europe.
[2] But Ripley, *Races of Europe,* New York, 1910, pp. 522–528, would not attribute the difference to racial causes.

The Purpose and Function of the Police

compared as between one nation and another. Perhaps Augusto Bosco has made the most successful effort in his book on the comparative criminology of European countries.[1] He rates the number of homicides for each one hundred thousand of the population as follows:

Country	Period of time	Number
Italy	1895–1899	12.15
France	1895–1899	3.27
Ireland	1895–1899	2.46
Scotland	1895–1899	1.08
England	1897–1899	1.34

The lack of uniform laws and the varying systems of crime classification have for the most part made extended comparisons impossible. Enough has been adduced, however, to show clearly a wide divergence in degrees of criminality between the various European countries.[2]

[1] *La delinquenza in vari Stati di Europa,* Bosco, Rome, 1903.

[2] Similar variations among different peoples and in different sections are found in the statistics of suicide. Based on the figures of von Mayr in his *Der Selbstmord* (*Allg. statist. Archiv,* 1896, p. 722), Gustav Aschaffenburg (*Crime and Its Repression,* translated by Albrecht, Boston, 1913, p. 35) shows the following comparison of suicides per 1,000,000 inhabitants:

Country	1881–1890
Monaco	301
Denmark	255
Switzerland	227
Germany	209
France	207
Austria	161
Belgium	114
Sweden	107
England and Wales	77
Norway	68
Scotland	55
The Netherlands	55
Italy	49
Roumania	41
Finland	39

(See next page.)

European Police Systems

Peculiarly interesting results are obtained by the intensive study of criminal statistics in particular countries. It appears that in nations whose modern economic development is recent or as yet incomplete the more involved forms of dishonesty increase rapidly from year to year. We therefore expect to find, and do find, that in Germany and Austria, frauds, embezzlements and forgeries are for the time being on the increase. On the other hand, a nation that is advancing very slowly in economic standing, such as Italy, or scarcely at all, such as Spain, displays no increase in these more refined offenses of modern life, while retaining a conspicuously high average in the unpremeditated and savage crimes, such as homicide, rape, assault and battery.

Occasionally, different sections of the same country show striking variations in criminality. In Belgium, the number of illegitimate births varies between 2.6 per cent. in Limburg and 14.6 per cent. in Brabant; [1] in Austria, it varies between 2.6 per cent. in Istria and 44.16 per cent. in Carinthia.[2] In southern Italy, homicide is five

Country	1881–1890
Servia	38
Russia	32
Luxemburg	28
Spain	24
Ireland	23
Bosnia and Herzegovina	6

[1] Bodio, "*Movimento della popolazione,*" *Bulletin de l'institut international de statistique,* Rome, 1897, Vol. X. Quoted from Aschaffenburg, *loc. cit.,* p. 33.

[2] Szalardi, *Der gegenwärtige Stand des Findelwesens in Europa,* 1896. Quoted from Aschaffenburg, *loc. cit.,* p. 34. The astonishing figure for Carinthia is borne out by the consistently high average of illegitimate births throughout Austria. Aschaffenburg is the authority for the following table, based on Bodio's figures (*loc. cit.,* p. 33):

The Purpose and Function of the Police

times as frequent as in northern Italy, and assault three times as frequent, while five robberies occur for every one such crime in the north. The Sicilians show seven times the homicide, four times the brigandage, and four times the obscene crimes committed by an equal number of northern Italians.[1] Murder and manslaughter are fourteen times more frequent in Sardinia than in Lombardy.[2] Similar differences exist between the various States of Germany. The Bavarian Palatinate and the East Prussian Province, for example, show much higher figures for personal assaults than the average for the empire.[3]

Country	Year	Per cent. of illegitimate births
Austria	1894	14.73
Sweden	1894	10.62
Denmark	1894	9.50
Hungary	1894	9.35
Germany	1894	9.26
Belgium	1894	8.99
France	1894	8.94
Scotland	1894	7.29
Norway	1894	7.17
Italy	1894	6.77
Finland	1894	6.39
Roumania	1892	6.06
Switzerland	1894	4.70
England	1894	4.31
Holland	1894	3.12
Ireland	1894	2.73
Russia (excluding Poland)	1894	2.66
Servia	1894	1.07

These percentages are roughly approximate to the figures for the year 1910, as compiled in *The Statesman's Year-Book*, London, 1913, except that Sweden leads with a percentage of 14.25 to Austria's 12.24 per cent.

[1] *Italia barbara contemporanea*, Alfredo Niceforo, Milan and Palermo, 1898. Quoted in *The Old World in the New*, E. A. Ross, New York, 1914, p. 101.

[2] Niceforo, *La delinquenza in Sardegna*, Palermo, 1897. Quoted in Aschaffenburg, *loc. cit.*, p. 38.

[3] Bosco, *loc. cit.*, p. 34.

European Police Systems

Whether we attribute these interesting deviations to racial characteristics,[1] to economic conditions,[2] or to climate,[3] one thing is certain: the police dealing with a community in which homicide is of frequent occurrence will not need to employ the more subtle modes of procedure necessary in a country where homicide is rare, and fraud, embezzlement, mail-order peculation and forgery are the prevailing offenses. Police activity must be adapted to the characteristic crimes.

To summarize, we see, that in spite of the common purpose underlying all police bodies, their problems are often widely different. These differences are due to economic conditions, to the size of a city and the character of its industries, to the relative homogeneity of its population and to national traits and traditions which tend to vary both the volume and the character of crime. Sometimes there are other factors, perhaps equally important, which alter the police problem or which, in specific instances, combine with the factors already mentioned to produce special situations and corresponding tasks.

To this divergence of problem, as well as to the distinct historic evolution through which each of the European nations has come, we must look for an explanation

[1] Ripley, *loc. cit.*, pp. 522–28.
[2] *Criminalité et conditions economiques,* W. A. Bonger, Amsterdam, 1905. *The Relations of Economic Conditions to the Causes of Crime,* Carrol D. Wright, Philadelphia, 1900. *Crime — Its Causes and Remedies,* Cesare Lombroso. Tr. from the French and German editions by H. P. Horton, Boston, 1911, Ch. IX.
[3] *Das Verbrechen in seiner Abhängigkeit von dem jährlichen Temperaturwechsel,* Enrico Ferri (*Zeitschr. f. d. ges. Strafw.* II, p. 13). Aschaffenburg, *loc. cit.,* pp. 13 ff.
Aschaffenburg, *loc. cit.,* p. 54, makes the point that religion may also account for variations in criminal inclination.

The Purpose and Function of the Police

of the differences in power and authority conferred upon the police. In no two countries is the conception of the police in its relation to the public exactly the same. In Great Britain the police are the servants of the community. Their official existence would be impossible if their acts persistently ran counter to the expressed wishes of the people. They depend for their effectiveness upon public sanction. They are civil employees, whose primary duty is the preservation of public security. In the execution of this duty they have no powers not possessed by any other citizens. A policeman has no right superior to that of a private person in making arrests or asking questions or compelling the attendance of witnesses. Further, he must suffer the consequences of any illegal action he may commit, and he cannot divest himself of responsibility by pleading the orders of his superior officer, if those orders happen to be illegal.[1] In the language of Sir James Stephen: "With a few exceptions a policeman is a person paid to perform, as a matter of duty, acts which, if he be so minded, he might have done voluntarily."[2]

[1] In neither a civil action nor a criminal prosecution is it any defense of itself for a constable to allege that he acted under the orders of an officer whose command he was bound, by the regulations of the force, to obey. See *Beckwith vs. Philby*, 6 B. & C., 638.

[2] *A History of Criminal Law*, Vol. I, Ch. XIV. There is but one practical difference between the powers of the police and the powers vested in every British citizen: A police officer may arrest without warrant if he has a reasonable suspicion that a felony has occurred; a private person cannot arrest under these circumstances unless he has certain knowledge that a felony has actually occurred.

The humble position of the English constable has come down through a long course of history and is thoroughly woven into the common law. The following quaint sentence appears in Sir Thomas Smith's *The Commonwealth of England*, edition of 1589: "So that every Englishman is a sergeant to take the thiefe, and

European Police Systems

In sharp contrast is the Continental theory, which, evolved from the necessities of autocratic government, makes of the police force the strong arm of the ruling classes. The Continental policeman is the servant of the Crown or the higher authorities; the people have no share in his duties, nor, indeed, any connection with them. He possesses powers greatly exceeding those of the citizen. Under ordinary circumstances he cannot be prosecuted for illegal action unless permission is obtained from the government,[1] and even then he enjoys the privilege of special laws administered by special courts regulating the relations of public officials to private citizens.[2] Where, in England, the constable may ask no question of those whom he arrests or is about to arrest, criminal procedure on the Continent is based on the inter-

who sheweth negligence therein do not only incurre Evil opinion therefore, but hardly shall escape punishment." (Quoted from *A History of Police in England,* Capt. W. L. Melville Lee, London, 1901, p. 334.)

[1] In Germany, under the recent act of May 5, 1910, the national government has assumed the responsibility determined in paragraph 839 of the Civil Code for deliberate wrong or negligent act which any *imperial* officer may commit against a third person. Hamburg's law on this point is typical of the legislation in the various states. Any one who considers himself injured by a police officer may ask the department whether it will answer for the act of its officer. If this question is answered affirmatively within four weeks, action may be brought against the department. If within this time no answer is made, the question is considered as answered negatively. (*Hamburgisches Gesetz betr. das Verhältnis der Verwaltung zur Rechtspflege vom 23. 4. 1870,* par. 31.)

[2] Thus, in France, if any official from a cabinet minister to a policeman commits acts in excess of his legal authority, as, for example, a police officer wrongfully arresting a private citizen, the rights of the party aggrieved and the mode in which those rights are to be determined, is a question of Administrative Law (*Droit administratif*) — a distinct body of special laws administered by special courts. Dicey, in his *Introduction to the Study of the Law of the Constitution,* 3d edition, London, 1889, Ch. V, has an interesting discussion of this question from an English point of view.

The Purpose and Function of the Police

rogatory system, and the police of Germany, Austria, Italy and France are allowed to resort to what are popularly known as "third degree" methods in their endeavor to wring a confession of guilt from those whom they accuse. "I have asked dozens of educated Germans living in England," says an eminent German jurist, "as to the most characteristic difference between German and English penal procedure. Invariably the answer was: in Germany the accused must prove his innocence; in England his guilt must be proved. This is the impression one gets from our system." [1]

Again, in Germany, where a distinction is made between arrest and detention (*Verhaftung* and *Festnahme*), men may be taken to police stations, questioned and even detained for twenty-four hours, although there is no charge against them and no reasonable ground for suspicion. Moreover, the right of search, restricted by stringent provisions in England and used only in exceptional circumstances under judicial direction, is, in Germany and Austria, much more freely employed, its use resting in many cases solely upon police discretion. [2] Similarly the police in Germany and Austria and to a

[1] Karl Weidlich: *Die Polizei als Grundlage und Organ der Strafrechtspflege in England, Schottland, und Irland,* Berlin, 1908. pp. 106–107. Quotation slightly abridged. Weidlich concludes his paragraph by saying: "Our interrogatory process is subject to great abuse. The police confront accused persons with the utmost severity; they meet real or assumed lies with brutality. Their object is the attainment of a confession. Their most innocent method is an appeal to the defendant's honor; later come threats of detention and even worse methods!" "A wretched spectacle!" he adds.

[2] See Austrian Code of Criminal Procedure (*Strafprozessordnung vom 23. Mai 1873*), §§ 139 ff. Also German Penal Code (*Reichsstrafgesetzbuch*), §§ 123, 124, and 342; Code of Criminal Procedure (*Strafprozessordnung,* February 1, 1877), §§ 102–110; Law of February 12, 1850, §§ 7–9, and 12.

17

somewhat limited extent in France and Italy are given powers to restrict freedom of discussion and the right of public meeting to an extent unheard of in England.[1] In other words, the different ideas as to the powers of the police and their relations to the public arise from different constitutional conceptions. The great safeguards to personal liberty established in England by Magna Charta and the Bill of Rights and sustained by centuries of judicial interpretation are almost entirely lacking on the Continent. While the constitutional struggles of the last hundred years in Germany and Austria have not left police powers entirely unaltered, it is scarcely an exaggeration to say that in spirit and procedure they still represent the Continental absolutism of the 18th century.[2]

We perceive, therefore, a broad distinction between the English and the Continental conception of police. Fundamentally the distinction is based on different ideas as to the extent of police power which a government shall exercise. In Great Britain police organization has been built up around the conception of a constabulary as a prohibitive or repressive power. Until the middle of the nineteenth century, police legislation was looked upon as a body of law prohibiting certain actions regarded as prejudicial to the public welfare. On the Continent, however, the idea early developed that the state, in addition to its prohibitive measures, should resort as well to preventive measures. As Dr. Goodnow points out,[3] the

---

[1] Dicey, *loc. cit.,* contains an interesting comparison of this point between England, Belgium, and France.
[2] Weidlich, *loc. cit.,* Ch. IV.
[3] *Municipal Government,* New York, 1909, Ch. XII.

law was conceived of as a rule of conduct which should not only prohibit actions prejudicial to public welfare, but also prescribe the performance of definite acts which in themselves would make resort to repression unnecessary. Out of this theory grew an extensive supervision of the classes considered dangerous to the community, with a resulting restraint on individual freedom of action. The Continental police were given privileges and powers of control over the population with which the English police were entirely unacquainted. While these powers have, to some extent, been curbed by the liberalism of the nineteenth century, and while, as we shall see, police activity has been greatly limited in modern times, Continental and Anglo-Saxon theories are still widely at variance.

What we have said of British police requires, however, a qualification. While the function of the English constabulary has, it is true, undergone little or no change, and still conforms to the characterization given above, the conception of police power has broadened. With the expansion of British commerce and industry resulting from the Industrial Revolution, new measures became necessary to safeguard the lives and health of the artisan population, and as a result factory legislation and public health laws were enacted. These are essentially police measures of preventive character. Later similar laws were passed on the Continent. An important distinction in the enforcement of these laws at once developed. In the Continental countries the new statutes were left largely to the regular police officials, who, as we have observed, were already engaged in handling other preventive measures. In Great Britain they were given to various national and municipal departments and branches, for the most part specially formed for that purpose. The contrast with the Continent in respect to the function of the regular police bodies has, therefore, been intensified rather than diminished by the progressive legislation of the nineteenth century.

So much for differences of a qualitative nature between British and Continental police — differences, that is, as to the kind of power the policeman possesses. Equally striking is the difference in respect to the scope or extent of police functions — the number of things that the police are charged to look after. Police duties in England are to-day confined roughly to three tasks: first, the maintenance of order; second, the pursuit of criminals; and third, the regulation of traffic. These duties are interrelated; together they form a unified policy whose objective point is public security, and the police are, generally speaking, concerned with nothing else.

In Germany, on the other hand, and to a large extent in Austria and France, police functions far transcend this somewhat restricted scope. In these countries there is hardly a governmental activity that is not more or less directly connected with the police; indeed, in Germany the police force cannot be said to constitute a sharply defined independent authority within the internal administration. Thus in Prussia there are Insurance Police, Mining Police, Water and Dike Police, Field and Forest Police, Cattle-Disease Police, Hunting Police, Fisheries Police, Trade Police, Fire Police, Political Police, Roads Police, Health Police, Building Police and a score of

The Purpose and Function of the Police

others.[1] To be sure many of these divisions represent state functions and are responsible to state officials.[2] But even the municipal police departments are hardly less complex in the variety of their duties. In all the cities of Germany and Austria, and to a large extent in the French cities, the police are engaged in many tasks which in England and Scotland are performed by various branches of the municipal government, if indeed they are performed at all. Of the twelve distinct divisions (*Abteilungen*) into which the Berlin police department is separated, only two, the uniformed force (*Schutzmannschaft*) and the detective force (*Kriminal-Abteilung*), deal with functions which are handled by the police departments of English and Scottish cities. The other divisions are engaged in work which, according to the English standard, does not properly belong to police duty. Thus in Berlin, the fire department, the health department, the prison department, the building department (including the condemnation of land for public purposes) and certain functions of the charity department are all branches of the huge police organization. The police supervise the markets and the sale of provisions; they pass on the quality of food-stuffs; they exercise an oversight of public assemblies and meetings; they abate nuisances; they inspect lodging houses, cafés and

[1] See *Handbuch der Verfassung und Verwaltung,* Hue de Grais, Berlin, 1912, 21st edition, pp. 350 ff., for an interesting discussion of the various forms of police.

[2] *Ibid.,* Par. 219. Some of these divisions are under the jurisdiction of the Prussian Minister of Public Works, some under the Minister of Commerce, others under the Minister of Religion and Instruction *(Kultusminister),* etc. As such their functions are, to a large extent, administrative.

places of amusement; they supervise druggists, veterinaries and the details of various professions; they prepare construction plans for street and river-front improvement; they keep a strict watch on certain classes of banking institutions; they frame regulations for the public conduct of citizens and mete out punishment for violations. A simple list of their functions covers forty-six pages of the official police hand-book.[1] Many of the functions have no counterpart in any governmental function of Great Britain, as, for instance, the compulsory registration of all citizens and strangers (*Meldewesen*),[2] and the minute regulation of various kinds of private business (*Gewerbepolizei*).

These multifarious police functions are not characteristic of Berlin only. They are found in nearly every German city, especially throughout Prussia, although in many of the larger towns, distinct specialties, like the fire and building departments, have been transferred to the jurisdiction of the municipal governments.[3] In Austria and in France, outside of Paris, the Prussian extreme is not followed, but even in these countries the contrast with the simplicity of English police functions is marked. In Paris, aside from the regular patrol, detective and traffic functions, the police department includes a large number of bureaus or branches, such as

---

[1] *Geschäfts und Reviereinteilung der Königl. Polizeiverwaltungen im Landespolizeibezirk Berlin*, Berlin, 1913.

[2] See Chap. IX for a discussion of the purposes of this function.

[3] For example, in Dresden the so-called *Wohlfahrtspolizei*, or welfare police, whose duties relate to health, fire and building functions, etc., were handed over to the municipal government in 1853. In case of conflicting functions, the regular police force has jurisdiction.

The Purpose and Function of the Police

the Health Dispensary, the Medical Inspection of Insane People, the Inspection of Wet Nurses, the Inspection of Private Hospitals, the Tramways and Metropolitan Railway Control, the Bureau of Navigation and Ports, the Architectural Department, the Contagious Disease Department, the Bureau of Public Assistance, and the Inspection of Classified Establishments. While the functions of the police are not so varied in Vienna and Budapest, they are, nevertheless, sufficiently complex. In these cities, as in Prussia, the police assume duties and responsibilities which are alien to the police of British cities.

An insight into the history of Continental police powers, particularly in Germany, is necessary to a full understanding of their broad scope. The term " police," as it was originally employed, denoted all state functions as distinct from ecclesiastical functions. Gradually through the separation of foreign, military and financial affairs the term came to be used, in the seventeenth century, as synonymous with internal administration. It included all the activities of the state which had not been segregated into special administrative branches. The separation of judicial functions was a further and even more advanced step in limiting the powers of the police, so that by the middle of the eighteenth century the scope of police activity had been narrowed roughly to two main lines, the so-called security police (*Sicherheitspolizei*) and the welfare police (*Wohlfahrtspolizei*), the former intended to preserve the individual from dangers threatening his person and property, the latter to further the public welfare by the promotion of interests beneficial to society. Gradually, through legislation and judicial in-

23

terpretation, the term "police" has been generally restricted to the former of these two functions; so that now, after a long process of delimitation, police activity has come to be one of the phases of the internal administration rather than the entire internal administration itself.[1] To this course of development must largely be attributed the broadly marked functions of the police of the Germanic countries. It is scarcely an exaggeration to say that, whereas in England the activities of the police cannot exceed the powers expressly conferred by statute, in Germany, the police have all the functions of government which have not been directly transferred to other branches of the administration.[2]

Of the many functions of the Continental police above enumerated, two, especially in Germany and Austria, stand out in marked contrast with English law and custom and should be particularly emphasized. In the first place, the police have the power to frame rules and ordinances (*Verordnungen* and *Verfügungen*) regulating the conduct of the citizens in respect to all the functions coming within their jurisdiction; that is, the power of supplementary legislation under the general laws of the state, which in England is vested in city or county councils, is, in Germany, given to the police. In the second place, the police have the right, which in England is pos-

[1] The Prussian General Code of 1794 defines the function of the police as the right "to institute the necessary measures to maintain public order, safety and peace, and to remove the dangers threatening the public as a whole or the individual members of it." (*Das Landrecht,* II, 17, Sec. 10.) This definition is still valid in Prussia.

[2] See Hue de Grais, *loc. cit.,* pp. 350 ff. Also *Principles of Prussian Administration,* Herman Gerlach James, New York, 1913, Ch. VII.

The Purpose and Function of the Police

sessed only by the police courts or other courts of inferior criminal jurisdiction, to punish, within certain limits, violations of laws and ordinances; that is, they are allowed to exercise certain judicial functions. These powers are so important and constitute so great a breach between the English and German conceptions of police that a brief discussion of their operation is necessary.

The ordinance-making power of the German police is a right delegated by national or state legislative action, either through general or special provisions. It proceeds on the theory that many laws require elaboration and executive definition by the local authorities. Thus the general sections of the Imperial Penal Code (*Reichsstrafgesetzbuch*) are elaborated by the police officials in scores of local ordinances. The same is true of laws emanating from the various legislative bodies, which in any way require expansion. On this basis each local police authority, with the occasionally required consent and approval of the town council or other communal body, has the right, within certain fixed legal limits, to promulgate and enforce its own regulations for the territory included within its jurisdiction.[1] A regulation

[1] The legal limits of the right to issue police ordinances are fixed for Prussia in the *Polizeiverwaltungsgesetz* of March 11, 1850; for Bavaria, in the Police Penal Code of December 26, 1871 (Arts. 51–57); for Saxony, in the Jurisdiction Law *(Kompetenzgesetz)* of January 28, 1835 (§ 2); for Hamburg in the Revised Law of Administrative Organization *(Gesetz über die Organisation der Verwaltung)* of November 2, 1896 (§ 9). For discussion on this subject see Hue de Grais, *loc. cit.*, pp. 358 ff.; Gustav Roscher, *Grossstadtpolizei,* Hamburg, 1912, pp. 34 ff.; O. Mayer, *Deutsches Verwaltungsrecht,* §§ 20, 22–25; Rosin, *Polizeiverfügungen und Polizeiverordnungen* in Stengel's *Wörterbuch des deutschen Staats und Verwaltungsrechts;* James, *loc. cit.,* Ch. IV.

Other administrative branches than the police often have the right to frame ordinances. Thus in Prussia the various subdivi-

European Police Systems

thus framed cannot conflict with any provision of the original law. It can be overruled by a superior administrative authority on the basis of legality or necessity [1] or by a court on the basis of legality alone.

A knowledge of this ordinance-making right is necessary to one who would understand the vast powers of the German police in regulating the conduct of private citizens. In Prussia, for example, the wide scope of the law of March 11, 1850,[2] gives to local police forces the right to pass ordinances relating to the protection of persons and property, to traffic and markets, to public meetings and strangers, and to an elaborate list of similar matters. Not content with a categorical enumeration, the law concludes, " and all else which must be regulated through the police power in the interest of the communes and their members." [3]   In the same way, section 366, subdivision 10, of the German Penal Code [4] reads: " Any one shall be punished by a fine up to 60 marks or imprisonment up to 14 days who transgresses the police regulations issued for the maintenance of security, convenience, cleanliness and quiet on public roads, streets, places or waterways." These sections, and others like them, have been used as the legal basis for hundreds of police ordinances touch-

sions of the local administration — the ministers, the provincial presidents, the district authorities and the Circle directors — have powers along this line carefully defined by statute.

[1] Thus in Prussia local police ordinances may be overruled by the district president *(Regierungspräsident)* or even by the competent minister. (Law of March 11, 1850, *Preussische Gesetzsammlung,* 1850, § 265. See also the supplementary provisions of the law of July 30, 1883.

[2] See preceding note. This law regulated anew the whole subject of police ordinances.

[3] *Preussische Gesetzsammlung,* 1850, § 265.

[4] *Reichsstrafgesetzbuch.*

The Purpose and Function of the Police

ing every conceivable human activity. On every side and at every turn the German citizen is confronted by newly adopted police regulations. Thus in Berlin, the Police President has recently issued ordinances regulating the color of automobiles, the length of hatpins and the methods of purchasing fish and fowl. He has decreed that a prospective purchaser shall not touch a shad in order to determine whether there is any roe and shall not handle a fowl to verify the market woman's praise of its tenderness. Each such ordinance provides a penalty for violation. Nor is Berlin exceptional in this respect. A glance at any compilation of local police regulations will bring to light similar examples. Thus in Stuttgart, a driver may not snap his whip as he guides his horses in the street; a customer may not fall asleep in a restaurant or a weary man on a park bench; a barber may not keep his official trade card in an inconspicuous place; a cab-driver may not leave his position in front of the railway station during the hours in which the police decree he shall be on duty; a driver may not hold his reins improperly or go through the public streets without having the owner's name in a conspicuous place on his cart or carriage; a delivery boy may not coast on a hand-cart; a passenger may not alight from a train on the side away from the platform or while the train is in motion; children may not slide on a slippery side-walk; a citizen may not be impertinent to a public official on duty nor offer any affront to his dignity.[1] These regulations are not

[1] The dignity that hedges a police official has been made the subject of innumerable laws and ordinances throughout Germany. Thirteen sections of the German Criminal Code deal with the subject of "insult" (*Beleidigung*, §§ 185 ff.). Official dignity and honor

27

European Police Systems

only negative, they are often positive; not only general, but particular and directed against specific parties.[1] Thus a house owner *must* sprinkle his street in hot weather when ordered by the police or a certain striker *must* refrain from picketing when so directed or a given contractor *must* remove building encumbrances on demand.

To grant to administrative bodies like the police broad legislative powers runs counter to the conception of English government. Even the Germans with their political philosophy and their national traits favorable to a paternal regulatory system, occasionally grow restive under the yoke of police rules. The eminent Hue de Grais sees in the intricate network of ordinances an almost unintelligible tangle. " To have a clear view of these multifarious provisions has become next to impossible," he says. " Efforts have been made to get up collections of them, but without permanent success. Only a limitation and a more purposeful application of this important privilege can remedy present conditions." [2] Dr. Karl Weidlich of

are especially protected. Apropos of this matter, Weidlich remarks: "We permit our police to nurse their authority as a sacred thing and thus to develop into a menace, instead of a safeguard to public liberties. A great stir was made to limit the rather infrequent cases of *lèse majesté;* but no one raises a hand to apply corresponding principles to the very much more important matter of 'insults' to policemen or 'resistance to state authority.' Yet this would avoid thousands of needless punishments every year, and would save the state the unprofitable task of training internal foes!" (Weidlich, *loc. cit.,* p. 98.)

[1] A distinction is made between *Polizeiverordnungen,* or general ordinances, and *Polizeiverfügungen,* which have in view a special case or a specific person. Commands as well as prohibitions may come under the latter head and the police are vested with full compulsory and restraining powers.

[2] *Loc. cit.,* p. 360.

The Purpose and Function of the Police

Stuttgart, a judge of the county court (*Amtsgericht*) of Württemberg and an authoritative student of English and German police systems, goes even further. " It is not the true function of the police," he says, " to interfere in the private and business life of the citizen, thus producing annoyance and bitterness. Under our laws, especially under section 366, subdivision 10, of the Penal Code (above quoted) the police are in position to paralyze the fundamental rights of our citizens and the effectiveness of our court decisions, whenever, in their judgment, matters arise involving a danger to public security and quiet. In proof of this we need simply point to the frequency with which the higher court (*Kammergericht*) is compelled to annul police regulations for the violation of which hundreds of persons have already been punished. The excellence of the English police, on the other hand, their non-political functions (*unpolitische Arbeit*), and their respect for personal dignity are the measure of the national spirit of a free people." [1]

Not only have the German police wide legislative powers, but they are also allowed to exercise certain judicial functions. Generally speaking, all misdemeanors or minor infractions (*Uebertretungen*) the penalty for which does not exceed imprisonment for fourteen days or a fine of 60 marks, are punished by the local police.[2]

[1] *Loc. cit.*, p. 98. The quotation is slightly abridged.
[2] The imposition of this maximum penalty is in some of the German states modified by state law. Thus in Prussia, the police officials of a *Bezirk*, or district, can impose a maximum punishment of only three days' imprisonment or 30 marks fine, the larger penalty of fourteen days or 60 marks being limited to superior police authorities. In Stuttgart (Württemberg), the local police can impose punishments of six days' imprisonment or 30 marks fine, or they may hand the case over to the state police authorities of the

European Police Systems

In other words, the functions which in England belong to the police courts and in France to a distinctly judicial branch of the civil service, are in Germany discharged by the regular local police. This power is exercised under a general provision of the German Code of Criminal Procedure [1] supplemented by various state acts.[2] Appeals may be taken from the decisions of the police to the *Amtsgericht,* or lower court, or to the police themselves for a review.[3] An appeal acts as a stay to the execution of the penalty and must be filed within one week of the time that the decree is issued.[4]

This extraordinary power lends to the police of Germany a legal importance difficult to comprehend when looked at from the point of view of English institutions and conceptions. The contrast becomes even more marked when the method by which the police carry out this function is taken into consideration. In the majority

district in which Stuttgart is located, who can impose the fourteen days or 60 marks maximum. In Dresden (Saxony) the local police themselves impose the maximum punishments.

While the legal maximum imprisonment is fourteen days for each offense, it is possible for the police to incarcerate up to twenty-four days on the theory that the prisoner has committed more than one violation. Thus the accused may be charged with three or four different offenses, all of which may have been committed in a single act. The cumulative penalty, however, cannot exceed twenty-four days.

[1] *Strafprozessordnung,* § 453.

[2] In Prussia, the Law of April 23, 1883; in Saxony, the Law of March 8, 1879, and the *Verordnung* of September 15, 1879; in Württemberg, the Law of August 12, 1879, and the Ministerial Decree of September 25, 1879; in Baden, the Law of March 3, 1879, and the Decree of September 7, 1879.

[3] Few appeals are taken to the police because of a general feeling that they are unfair; moreover, in the *Amtsgericht* a hearing can be secured — a thing which the police are not bound to allow, and which, as a matter of fact, they seldom do allow.

[4] *Strafprozessordnung,* § 453.

of cases there is not even a semblance of judicial procedure: no witnesses are called; the accused has no opportunity to explain. The policeman who observes the violation in question files a report with his superior officer; this official determines the penalty, and in due course the defendant (if such he may be called!) is notified of his impending punishment. The penalty is imposed by an official who does not see or hear the accused and who knows nothing of the case except through the unchallenged testimony of the policeman making the charge. Often a week or ten days will elapse before the accused receives notification of the penalty. Sometimes it comes as a complete surprise, punishing him for a violation which he committed unconsciously or the circumstances of which he has forgotten.[1] In Berlin, the notice of punishment is accompanied by a blank post-office order in case the penalty is a fine, so that the accused may be put to no inconvenience in coming personally to police headquarters. If after one week no attention is paid to the notice, the police make a levy on the defendant's property for value to the amount of the fine or the defendant is arrested to serve his alternative sentence.

[1] The lapse of time between the commission of the violation and the notification of punishment is often a boon to members of the criminal floating population, who, perhaps aware that their names have been taken for various misdemeanors, seize the opportunity to disappear. Largely as a result of this clumsy machinery of summary procedure — or rather, the lack of any such machinery properly so-called — every police department in Germany contains thousands of names of men wanted for punishment in connection with various kinds of trespasses and violations. Dr. Weidlich, whose experience as a judge of the *Amtsgericht* in Stuttgart has brought him into intimate touch with the situation, complains bitterly on this score. "The repeated written reports and the business of disposing of these petty things so encumber the police that no time or energy remains for larger matters," he says. (*Loc. cit.*, p. 103.)

European Police Systems

At any time during the week he may appeal to the *Amtsgericht,* or lower court, for a judicial determination of the question. If he wins the state pays the costs, otherwise he pays them himself. Failure to appeal is looked upon as a confirmation of the *prima facie* case established by the policeman's charge. Appeals, however, are costly and troublesome. A poor man cannot afford to run the risk, a busy man cannot take the time. Moreover, an appeal from a judgment of imprisonment, where an arrest has been made, results in the immediate incarceration of the appellant pending the decision of the court — a fact in itself discouraging to one seeking redress.[1]

The system which we have just outlined is in force throughout Prussia. In southern Germany certain modifications obtain. In Württemberg, for example, the theory exists that the defendant has an opportunity to explain before the penalty is imposed. In practice, however, it is assumed that the defendant has made his explanation to the policeman who reports him. Thus, a police officer sees a driver, who, he thinks, is asleep and the driver de-

[1] *Strafprozessordnung,* §§ 112–132. Pending his hearing by the court the appellant is confined in the court prison or *Amtsgerichtgefängnis* as distinguished from the police prison, or *Polizeiarrest,* where the short-term punishments are usually served. Among the floating criminal class the custom prevails of always taking an appeal from police decrees of imprisonment on the theory (altogether too well founded, in fact!) that better treatment and better food are to be had in the court prisons than in the police prisons. In the event that the court upholds the police (and police judgments are seldom overturned), the time thus spent is part of the original sentence, and nothing is lost. The courts, however, have the right to *increase* the punishment if in their judgment the police penalty is too mild, and of late, particularly in Württemberg, they have been using this right to discourage appeals which they think are taken only with the idea of securing the increased comforts of the court prisons.

nies to the policeman that he was sleeping. This is held to be an " explanation." Three or four days later the man is notified that he must pay a fine. " We always take the officer's word as truth," said the chief of the Stuttgart police in discussing the matter with the writer. This absolute reliance on the word of the policeman holds throughout Germany.

With certain modifications, the same system of police punishment which we find in Germany exists in Austria and Hungary.[1] Some of these modifications are rather important. In Austria no opportunity is given for a court review of the police decision. Appeals may be taken to the *Statthalter,* or imperial governor of the province, but they can go no higher nor is there any other method of testing the police judgment.[2] In this respect, therefore, the Austrian system is even less liberal than the Prussian system. On the other hand, whereas in Berlin punishment is imposed by a lieutenant of the uniformed force of the precinct who generally has come from the army and is consequently lacking in legal training or adequate knowledge of the laws of evidence, in Vienna the case is judged and the penalty imposed by a police *Kommissar,* or bureau head, who is in every instance a trained lawyer and a graduate of the university. Moreover, in Austria, before punishment is imposed, the ac-

[1] The right of the police of Austria to fine and imprison is based principally upon the *Kaiserliche Verordnung* of April 20, 1854, although there are many separate statutes that confer similar powers. The maximum punishments are fixed at fourteen days or 200 *Kronen.* Considerable discussion has taken place over the fact that this drastic power of the police is exercised under an imperial decree rather than under general parliamentary legislation.

[2] In Hungary appeals from the police penalty may be taken to the Minister of the Interior.

cused is summoned to police headquarters where he is given the privilege of making a statement, or of calling witnesses in his defense. In these last two respects, therefore, the Austrian system has more of the elements of a judicial determination than the system in vogue in Germany. And yet in Vienna there is some discussion as to the advisability of introducing the Prussian peremptory or " *mandat* " system with the idea of avoiding the inconvenience of being summoned personally to police headquarters.

As may be imagined from the outline just given, the extensive judicial powers in the hands of the police are easily capable of abuse. Indeed, as Weidlich affirms, the police are in a position to nullify fundamental rights and override the decrees of the courts. That their powers are always used beneficially and liberally, as is claimed by German officials, can scarcely be admitted. For example, under the German law, a man suspected of a crime, cannot be detained for more than twenty-four hours by the police without being produced before a magistrate.[1] It is easily possible, however, for the police to imprison a suspect for any period up to fourteen days on the ground that he has violated one or more of their innumerable ordinances. " Wherever we get hold of a man whom we suspect of some crime," said one of the assistant police commissioners in Dresden in talking frankly with the writer on this matter, " we hunt around to find some ordinance which he has violated. Such a thing is not difficult to discover. Perhaps he has no employment card. Perhaps he has been impertinent to an official. What-

---

[1] *Strafprozessordnung,* § 115.

The Purpose and Function of the Police

ever it is, we detain him, and thus have time to work up the case." [1] Such action undoubtedly contributes to the bitter antagonism to the police common among the lower classes of Germany and Austria. " Most men would prefer three weeks' imprisonment from a court to three days from the police," was the significant remark of the chief of the detective division of Stuttgart.

Moreover, when we consider the great number of penalties imposed by the police, it becomes increasingly probable that their judicial powers are abused. In Stuttgart, a quiet, peaceful city of 300,000 population, 40,000 police penalties are imposed each year.[2] At this rate, under the same system, Manchester (England) should have approximately 93,000 police court cases in a year and Liverpool 98,000. As a matter of fact, however, Manchester had in 1911 but 14,000 such cases, while Liverpool had 32,000; [3] and of these cases one-third were for drunkenness, which, under ordinary circumstances, is not punishable in Germany. In other words, there are

[1] One of the commissioners or division chiefs (*Abteilungsvorsteher*) in Berlin told me that another way in which the law is evaded by the police, in case no violation of an ordinance can be urged against the prisoner, is to rush him to the court in a carriage, and have him returned immediately to the police prison upon a requisition approved by the prosecuting attorney, without actually producing him before the magistrate. " I have kept men three days in this fashion," he said, "getting my proof together and finishing my case."

[2] Personally communicated by officials. The fines resulting from police punishments in this city amounted in 1911 to 83,980 marks. This money is turned into the city treasury. Weidlich thinks that German cities would be very loath to lose this revenue, and that for this reason the system will be hard to break down. (*Loc cit.,* p. 103.)

[3] See the annual reports of the chief constables; also *Judicial Statistics of England and Wales,* 1911, (published by the British Home Office) p. 58. Germany has no such statistics as those maintained by the Home Office.

ten times as many punishments for misdemeanors in German cities as in English cities. This comparison is necessarily rough, but it serves to indicate the excessive use of judicial powers by the German police. " Police judgments are showering over us like hail-stones," says Weidlich, himself a loyal subject of the Empire. " A German citizen who has not had at least one such punishment must be looked for with a lantern!"[1]

The combination of legislative and judicial with administrative functions produces an unwieldy and uncontrollable machine. From an English standpoint — indeed, from the standpoint of any democratic government or any liberal political creed — the practice is greatly to be deprecated. Weidlich's word, "monstrous," with which he sums up the entire system, would seem scarcely too strong.[2] But it is important to realize that these added legislative and judicial powers in no way affect the function of the police as an organization for the protection of public safety. Strip off these powers, which often incumber and impede the police in carrying out their simpler duties, and the same problems will be found that, in spite of modifying circumstances, confront the English and French cities alike. Although, as we have seen, many factors vary the character of the problem, the task of the Metropolitan Police Force of London is fundamentally the task of the *Schutzmannschaft* of Berlin, and it is a mistake to assume that, because an official

[1] *Loc. cit.,* p. 102.
[2] *Ibid.* "*Strafgewalt der Polizei gegenüber der Gesamtheit unter dessen Kontrolle sie arbeiten sollte, ist etwas Ungeheuerliches. Kann man sich denn keinen summarischen Prozess ohne Verweigerung der fundamentalsten Rechtsgarantien vorstellen?*"

The Purpose and Function of the Police

belonging to the latter force has other unrelated functions, his ideas and experience have no applicability in London or elsewhere. The German police organization, in spite of its needless extensions, has many points worthy of careful study by the police forces of other lands.

CHAPTER II

THE PLACE OF THE POLICE DEPARTMENT IN THE STATE

European police forces usually under state control.— Municipal control for smaller forces only.— Unique situation of London police force.— London citizens voiceless in the management of their police.— Features and consequences of this control.— Police forces in provincial cities controlled by Watch Committees.— Supervision by the Home Office.— Results of Watch Committee control.— English county police.— State control in Holland and Belgium.— Lack of uniformity in control and organization in Germany.— Municipal control versus state control in Germany.— Uniformity in Austria-Hungary.— Movement toward centralization in Hungary.— Centralized supervision in France.— Lack of thoroughgoing municipal autonomy.— Peculiar situation of Paris.— The National Constabulary of Italy: the *Carabinieri* and the City Guards.— Their common functions.

IN discussing the place of the police department in the state and its relations to other organs of government, it must be borne in mind that municipally controlled police forces exist only in the smaller cities of Europe. In all the capitals and large commercial centers, the police are under the direct control of the state rather than the city. Thus, in London, Berlin, Vienna, Rome, Budapest, Madrid and Lisbon, the head commissioners are appointed by the Crown and are responsible to the Ministry of the Interior or the Home Secretary. In Paris, the head of the police is appointed by the President of the Republic; in Dresden and Munich, by the Kings of Saxony and of Bavaria respectively; in Copenhagen, Stockholm and Christiania, by the Kings of Denmark, Sweden

38

and Norway, respectively. In St. Petersburg, Moscow and Odessa, the prefects of police (*Gradonachalnik*) are appointed directly by the Emperor of Russia; in Constantinople, the Sultan appoints the chief of police upon the nomination of the Minister of the Interior. In the eight largest cities of Austria, the ten largest cities of Hungary,[1] and in all the cities of the Netherlands, the heads of the police are appointed by the Crown; while in Prussia the police departments of the important cities of Frankfort-on-Main, Breslau, Kiel, Cologne, Coblentz, Königsberg and seventeen others are all under royal control. Only in the provincial cities of England and Scotland, and the smaller cities of the Continent, such as Berne, Zurich and Stuttgart, for example, do we find any degree of local self-government in the management of the police forces. Glasgow, with a population of 785,000, is the largest city in Europe with a police department under municipal control.

That the reader may be brought into intimate touch with the machinery of police administration, it is worth while discussing, somewhat in detail, the relations of the departments to the various agencies of government in each of the important countries of Europe where the conditions were studied.

GREAT BRITAIN

London.

The relation of the police force of London to other governmental agencies is unique.[2] In all the other cities

[1] See discussion, p. 80. The legislation effecting this is on its way to adoption.
[2] A careful distinction must be made between the London Metro-

39

European Police Systems

of size and importance in Great Britain, local control, through popularly elected town councils, is the characteristic feature. London alone has a royal police force whose head is appointed by the Crown, and whose policy is determined by a cabinet minister, the Secretary of State for Home Affairs.

The Metropolitan Police Force of London was established by Peel's Act of 1829. It replaced a number of small, separate, local forces of varying degrees of efficiency under whose conflicting jurisdiction the crime conditions of London had steadily grown worse, until remedial measures at last became imperative.[1] With slight

politan police and the police of the City of London. The City of London, occupying an area of one square mile, practically in the center of the Metropolitan district, and maintaining a separate corporate existence under charters and prescriptive rights which date from a very early period, has its own separate police force, regulated by an act of Parliament modeled closely on the first Metropolitan Police Act. This force is under the direct and exclusive control of the Corporation of the City of London, and has no relation with the Metropolitan force or with any other agency outside its own narrow borders. The district in which the Metropolitan police have jurisdiction covers approximately seven hundred square miles, extending over fifteen miles radius from Charing Cross, exclusive of "the City" mentioned above, and including not only the County of London, but parts of five other counties, and an increasing number of municipal boroughs. Wherever in this book the London police are mentioned, the reference is to the Metropolitan police.

[1] For a description of the extent of lawlessness in London in the early part of the nineteenth century, see W. L. Melville Lee, *loc. cit.* Ch. X.

Prior to the organization of the Metropolitan police in 1829, the local government of the populous urban towns which, in the course of centuries of continuous national life had grown up around the ancient City of London, was left in the main to county and parochial authorities invested with the powers largely conferred by the common law, although modified to some extent by various acts of Parliament. Under the strain imposed by the growth of population and modern conditions of urban life, this system broke down and the arrangements for the maintenance of public order and the administration of the criminal law became utterly inadequate.

The Police Department in the State

alterations the force is organized to-day as it was originally constituted in 1829.[1]   The Commissioner is a royal official responsible only to the Home Secretary.[2]   Neither the London County Council, nor any one of the various Metropolitan Borough Councils has anything to do with police matters.   Except in so far as the Home Secretary is a member of Parliament and as such stands for an election at the hands of his own constituents, the element of direct popular control does not enter at all.   Even this slight connection is weakened by the fact that the Home Secretary seldom, if ever, represents a London district, and even if he did, a national election would afford scant opportunity for the consideration of local police issues. To be sure, the Home Secretary is responsible to the Cab-

Prior to 1829, the following *separate* forces policed what is now the Metropolitan district: The City of London had a system of police and watch by night under the control of the municipal authorities. The City of Westminster had a force of eighty constables chosen from persons carrying on trade, and a smaller force of stipendiary police. The Thames Police Office had ninety men for the protection of property and maintenance of order on the River Thames. The Bow Street Office (the old " Bow Street Runners "), under the direction of the Home Secretary, had general charge of the entire Metropolitan district with the exception of the City of London. This force was divided into three classes, the Horse Patrol, the Dismounted Patrol, and the Foot Patrol, and was comprised (in 1821) of 161 men. Finally, there was the system of Nightly Watch, almost without exception a parochial establishment, and notoriously inefficient. (See *Report of the Royal Commission on the Metropolitan Force,* 1908, Vol. I, pp. 9 ff.)

[1] The most important of the special statutes by which the Metropolitan Police is governed are as follows:
Metropolitan Police Act, 1829 (10 Geo. IV c. 44).
Metropolitan Police Act, 1839 (2 & 3 Vict. c. 47).
Metropolitan Police Act, 1856 (19 & 20 Vict. c. 2).
Metropolitan Police Act, 1857 (20 & 21 Vict. c. 64).
Metropolitan Police Receiver's Act, 1861 (24 & 25 Vict. c. 124).
Police Rate Act, 1868 (31 & 32 Vict. c. 67).

[2] The Commissioner is appointed under statutory provision by warrant under the sign manual of the Crown.

inet and through the Cabinet to the country. He has, moreover, to answer in public such questions as members of Parliament may put to him relative to his management of the police. His course of action may also be influenced by newspaper criticism, to which he is constantly exposed. But direct accountability to the London public is lacking. No machinery exists by means of which the police can be popularly controlled, or the preference of the people in respect to them effectively expressed. They cannot be made a local political issue. Except through the pressure of public opinion, the citizens of London are voiceless in the management of their police.

The peculiar status of the Metropolitan Police Force is usually justified by its broad functions. It protects the person of the Sovereign, watches the government dockyards, guards the royal institutions and buildings in London and fulfils other duties of national rather than merely local importance. In answer it is pointed out by those who object to the present arrangement that the local functions of the police are of far greater importance than the national duties which have been incidentally thrust upon them. Moreover, the great bulk of the revenues of the police department is supplied, not by the imperial exchequer, but by local taxes. Why, then, it is asked, should London, alone among the great cities of England, be debarred from the management of her police?

Up to the present time, debate on this question has not attracted any large public interest. The sentiment in favor of popular control of local affairs is, nevertheless, a distinct phase of the rising tide of English democracy,

The Police Department in the State

and suggestions are constantly being made, in an inchoate and indefinite form to be sure, looking to the transfer of the Metropolitan police from the Home Secretary's office to the jurisdiction of some popularly-elected body.[1] It does not appear, however, that the movement to this end has gained force in recent years. Indeed, it is extremely doubtful whether such a change will ever be effected. London is not only the seat of government but the commercial, social and political center of a large empire. It gains a character distinct from that of any other British city by the fact that the Sovereign, the agents of the different colonies and dominions and the diplomatic representatives of foreign governments reside there. In London, too, are located not only the Houses of Parliament and the chief government offices, but the national museums and collections, and the places of entertainment to which British subjects and foreigners from all over the world resort. From the special governmental and cosmopolitan character of London arise delicate questions affecting police administration which may be regarded as beyond the competence of a merely municipal authority to decide. Surely, in view of this situation, it would be too much to expect Parliament voluntarily to surrender to a lesser body the control over the

[1] The suggestion, occasionally made in London and elsewhere, that the Metropolitan force should be placed under the control of the London County Council is obviously based on an incomplete understanding of the situation. The Metropolitan police district is more than five times the size of the County of London. There would be four other county councils and a great number of borough councils to be taken into consideration. Even if a representative agency of control were created, it would be difficult to reconcile the conflicting claims of the various county and borough authorities over whose districts the Metropolitan police have jurisdiction.

43

Metropolitan police which it can now exercise through the Home Secretary.[1]

To the freedom of the Metropolitan police from popular control may be ascribed many of its characteristic features. While Scotland Yard has nothing of the autocratic atmosphere which surrounds the police headquarters of Berlin and Vienna, it does possess a certain air of aloofness and independence quite foreign to the police of the English provincial cities where popular control has long been established. The public is treated courteously, but no information relative to police business is vouchsafed. The Commissioner never gives interviews to newspapers. No police official is ever quoted. Except under extraordinary circumstances, no attempt is ever made to answer a public attack or correct a misstatement in the press. When one of the borough councils within the Metropolitan district asked the Commissioner how many constables were assigned to patrol its streets, the information was curtly refused. The Commissioner assumed all responsibility for the efficient patroling of that district and was answerable for any mistakes that might be made only to the Home Secretary. In other words, the question was one which did not concern the borough council. In the same manner all subpoenas served on the department to compel the production of papers or records are declined on the ground of privilege, a contention invariably sustained by the courts.

Moreover, the Metropolitan police department is finan-

[1] "What would happen if, when suffragettes or unemployed marched on the Houses of Parliament, Parliament could only make representations to a municipal authority?" a Home Office official asked the writer.

The Police Department in the State

cially independent. Its budgetary regulations and estimates are confidential and are withheld not only from
the public, but from Parliament itself, in spite of the fact
that the real head of the police department, the Home
Secretary, holds his position through the suffrance of Parliament. The Metropolitan force is the only police organization in Europe whose contemplated expenditures
are not passed upon by some popularly-elected assembly
or body. In Berlin the police budget for the ensuing year
is considered by the Prussian parliament (*Preussischer
Landtag*); [1] in Vienna by the Austrian parliament; [2] in
Budapest by the Hungarian parliament; in Paris by the
Chamber of Deputies and the Municipal Council. [3] In
these cities no money can be spent unless it has first been
authorized by the legislative assembly after full opportunity has been offered for discussing the proposed expenditure. In London, on the other hand, the police budgetary
estimate is a confidential matter between the department
and the Home Office; the tax is collected through the
Overseers of the Poor under a general act of Parliament
fixing a maximum rate; and all that Parliament ever sees
is a somewhat colorless statement of expenditures at the
end of each fiscal year. [4] To be sure, the presentation of

[1] For an analysis of the annual budget of the Berlin department,
see Appendix III, p. 394.
[2] For an analysis of the annual budget of the Vienna department,
see Appendix IV, p. 396.
[3] For an analysis of the annual budget of the Paris department,
see Appendix II, p. 393.
[4] The Metropolitan police rate is collected through the Overseers
of the Poor, as part of the poor rate. Within the London County
Council area the Borough Councilors are the Overseers. In the
remainder of the Metropolitan police district, Overseers are elected
for each parish, or alternatively, the district council may act as
Overseers upon an order of the Local Government Board.

45 *(See next page)*

European Police Systems

this statement in Parliament is occasionally the signal to the Opposition for severe criticism of the Home Secretary's management of the police department, but as far as the question of budget control is concerned, the money has already been spent and the Opposition is obliged to content itself with futile motions to reduce the Home Secretary's salary.[1]

This arbitrary system of administration is warmly defended by the officials of the Home Office and Scotland Yard. They insist that nothing is to be gained by a parliamentary discussion of proposed expenditures. The Secretary of State for Home Affairs, the Commissioner and his subordinates are far more intimately acquainted with the needs of the police department than are the members of Parliament. Moreover, they argue that the introduction of any system of popular control in the management of police, whether it be in the shape of a Watch Committee or a County Council, would tend to politics and favoritism, which under the present arrangement are entirely eliminated. Not that they condemn the ideals of democracy, but democracy has its practical limitations, and the intricate and complex machinery of a huge gov-

The maximum rate of 11 d. in the £ fixed by act of Parliament, consists of 7 d. from the parishes and 4 d. from moneys appropriated from the exchequer. The contribution of 4 d. in the £ is exclusive of: (a) the exchequer grant in respect of imperial and national services rendered by the police (£100,000 per annum): (b) the reimbursement of the cost of police whose services are lent to government departments (approximately £270,000 per annum); and (c) the exchequer grant towards the police pension fund (£150,000 per annum).

In addition to the maximum rate above referred to, there is power to raise from the parishes an additional rate covering the deficiency of the police pension fund.

[1] For an analysis of the annual expenditures of the Metropolitan police, see Appendix I, p. 389.

46

The Police Department in the State

ernmental system cannot safely be entrusted to the rule of many. Particularly is this true of a police department, where continuity of policy and steadiness of aim are all-essential factors. Under popular control — so it is alleged — these factors vanish; the shifting personnel, the fickle change of opinion, the opportunity for favoritism, and, above all, the untrammeled play of politics make only for demoralization. Therefore, argues the Home Office, we require in our management of the London police a steady hand and an independent authority. You may call it arbitrary, you may call it autocratic, but it is just and efficient. Moreover, although autocratic in external aspect, it is really democratic in essence, but it is democracy with a strong man behind it. Given such a man, sure of himself and knowing his business, democracy will do well to trust him and leave Parliament and public opinion to do the rest.[1]

Whatever the merit of this argument, the good results attained must be admitted. Political considerations play no part in the management of the Metropolitan police. While it is true that the people have no opportunity to express their wishes at the polls on any police question which may arise, it is also true that the policy and discipline of the police cannot be upset as an incidental consequence of the determination of political issues. The police department cannot be made the spoils of any party. Moreover, the very aloofness of the force from popular control closes the doors to petty favoritism and small

[1] See *The Metropolitan Police* (a pamphlet printed by J. P. Bland — The *Times* Office — 1909). The articles in the pamphlet originally appeared in the London *Times,* running from December 24, 1908, to January 15, 1909.

47

politics. Political campaigns come and go; newspaper crusades against the police rise and fall; the personnel of municipal councils shifts a dozen times on ever changing issues; but Scotland Yard remains undisturbed. Even the occasional upheaval of a government and the consequent shift in the Secretaryship of the Home Office does not upset the management of the police. No secretary would ever interfere with the effective operation of the department.

Provincial cities of England and Scotland.

Arrangements in the provincial cities of England and Scotland in respect to police control contrast strikingly with the system which we have just considered. The conditions of crime in the English cities at the beginning of the nineteenth century were similar to those obtaining in London. Such police forces as existed were unorganized and untrained. The Dogberry and Verges type of town watch was all that stood between order and disorder in many an English community. In Portsmouth, twenty-two peace officers pretended to protect a population of 50,000 people, and in Liverpool, where crime was so prevalent that the town was often spoken of as "the black spot on the Mersey," the only police force existing in 1834 was a body of fifty watchmen to keep order among 240,000 inhabitants.[1]

Driven by urgent necessity, Parliament passed the Municipal Corporations Act of 1835,[2] which, with its subsequent amendments, has standardized the system of

[1] W. L. Melville Lee, *loc. cit.,* Ch. XIV.
[2] 5 and 6 William IV c. 76.

The Police Department in the State

urban police administration in England and Wales. As the law now stands,[1] the council of each town maintaining a separate police force is required to appoint from time to time " a sufficient number, not exceeding one-third, of its own body," to serve as a *Watch Committee.* With this committee rests the entire control of the police,[2] subject only to the vote of the council in matters involving expenditures. This comprehensive plan was supplemented by Parliament in 1856 by the passage of the Rural Police Act,[3] which provided for the appointment of Inspectors of Constabulary under the Home Office with authority to visit and inquire into the state and general efficiency of the police in the various towns and counties of England and Wales.[4] It further provided that on certificates from the Home Secretary to the effect that the police force of a locality is efficient in point of numbers and discipline,[5] a sum not exceeding one half part [6] of the total cost of the pay and clothing of the force was to be contributed from the national treasury. Through the operation of this act there was established a complete system of national supervision over

[1] *Municipal Corporations Act of 1882.* 45 and 46 Vict. c. 50, §§ 190–200.

[2] One hundred and twenty-eight cities and boroughs in England and Wales maintain in this manner separate police forces under the control of Watch Committees.

[3] 19 and 20 Vict. c. 69.

[4] Scottish towns and counties were made the subject of practically similar provisions by an act passed in 1857 (20 and 21 Vict. c. 72). In 1885 the inspection was transferred from the Home Office to the Scottish Office, and the certificates of efficiency are now issued by the Secretary for Scotland.

[5] On a third certificate, based on the proper management of a force, a contribution is made by the exchequer to the local police pension fund.

[6] As amended in 1874. The original Act provided for one-fourth.

49

European Police Systems

all the police forces of England and Wales, which, while it in no way robs the cities and counties of the right of local control, stimulates their efforts to maintain an efficient standard and introduces uniformity into their organization and management. To be sure, the Home Office, particularly as far as the towns and cities are concerned, has no positive authority over the police force. It cannot remove an official or compel the adoption of any improvements.[1] It acts only in the capacity of friendly guide. Its sole lever is the national subvention or grant in aid, which may be withheld if the report of the supervising inspector indicates unsatisfactory conditions. A Watch Committee, however, which, through slovenly methods or loose standards, jeopardized the grant of a sum approximately equal to 50 per cent. of its annual police budget, would bring down upon itself the wrath of angry tax-payers. Through the application of this moral force, there are few improvements within reason which the Home Office cannot compel.

In practice, however, the control of the Home Office over the provincial cities has been lightly exercised. The examinations of the inspectors have been exceedingly perfunctory, and while warnings have occasionally been given in cases of marked deficiency, no borough has lost its annual grant within recent years.[2] Indeed, the an-

[1] Note, however, that the by-laws of counties and boroughs touching police regulation, or matters of general good order, not of a sanitary nature, must be submitted to the Home Secretary and may be disallowed by Order in Council within forty days. (*Municipal Corporations Act,* 1882, 45 and 46 Vict. c. 50, par. 23; *Local Government Act,* 1888, par. 16.)

[2] There are two inspectors for England and Wales, one for the so-called "Northern District" and one for the "Southern District." Their reports for the year ending September 29th are annually laid

The Police Department in the State

nual inspection is scarcely regarded as a serious matter by local officials; little or no effort has been made to unify the methods of work, or to introduce a coördinating system in the matter of detecting crime. This timid use of its powers by the Home Office is undoubtedly due in part to its appreciation of the Englishman's passion for local self-government and his distrust of any suggestion of over-centralized control. To an even greater extent it is due to the fact that the only course open to the Home Office in dealing with a refractory police organization is the suspension or withdrawal of the *whole* grant in aid, for which only the absolute inefficiency of a force would be justification. Hitherto the Home Office has had no power to deal with the subvention *in part,* and has thus been unable to adapt the amount to individual cases, or to measure punishments to fit particular deficiencies. The new finance bill, now before Parliament for consideration, incorporates this long-needed reform.[1] With this amendment adopted, England will have a most effective piece of machinery, which, through the combination of local autonomy with a strongly centralized supervision, will prevent the provincial cities from falling much below reasonable standards.

The Watch Committee is the basis of police control in the provincial cities of England and Wales. Elected

before Parliament, and published as a Parliamentary document. There is one inspector for Scotland under the control of the Scottish Office. His reports are also published.

[1] This bill further provides for an increase in the annual subvention or grant-in-aid from the present sum of half the cost of the pay and clothing, and a contribution to the pension fund, to a sum equal to one half the total net cost of the entire police force.

from among the members of the town council as a sub-committee,[1] it has full control of appointments, dismissals, discipline and policy; it makes regulations for the conduct of the members of the force; and has absolute authority in relation to the question of their duties. Only in matters involving expenditure must its decisions be ratified by a vote of the town council.[2] Complete statutory powers being thus vested in the Watch Committee, it follows that the chief constable whom it appoints has only such rights and duties as the Committee may confer upon him. As a result, the functions of the chief constable vary widely in different cities, the office being of greater or less dignity according to the degree of supervision exercised by the Committee. In some towns, punishments for offenses against discipline coming before the Watch Committee in the shape of recommendations of the chief officer are approved as a matter of course, unless the individual appeals. In many others the Watch Committee hears the complaint, decides upon guilt or innocence, and measures the punishment with little or no

[1] Liverpool has a Watch Committee of 16 members; Manchester, 22; the average size of the committee is 11 or 12. The members serve for one year. The committee cannot exceed one-third the number of the Town Council (*Municipal Corp. Act*, 1882, § 190). On the other hand, it is not required to and seldom does maintain the full quota of one-third, as a large committee would be unwieldy. The membership of the Watch Committee is fairly constant, although a change in the political complexion of the council generally involves a change in the chairmanship of the committee, sometimes, indeed, in its policies.

[2] Occasionally the Town Council, although without legal basis, assumes for itself some of the functions of its Watch Committee. In Manchester, for example, and in numerous smaller places, matters relating to discipline, promotion, and even prosecutions, are often discussed in the council meeting. Recently in Cardiff and Swansea, the Town Councils assumed to make appointments in spite of the protests of the Watch Committees and of the Home Office.

The Police Department in the State

reference to the chief officer. In some towns, indeed, the chief constable is little more than a messenger for the Chairman of the Watch Committee, with no room for the play of his own initiative; in others, and perhaps in the majority of towns, he possesses a very real authority, free from direction and interference, even punishing members of the force who carry their grievances to the Watch Committee. The matter is largely one of personality. A chief constable of strong character and independent ideas usually succeeds in dominating his committee; a weaker man under the same circumstances becomes merely a figure-head.

But the life of a chief constable in his relations with a Watch Committee is not always a happy one. Apart from questions of personality, there are often influences to combat, which arise naturally from the popular method by which the committee is brought into being. The personnel of the committee does not always represent the wisest choice. Too often untrained laymen are selected, engaged in the pursuit of various commercial trades, lacking the experience and technical ability to be found in the Standing Joint Committees of the county constabulary, where, as we shall see, half the membership is chosen from justices selected by Quarter Sessions.[1] In too many cases the chief constable is obliged to undergo the humiliation of being overruled in his disciplinary measures through the activity of the culprits or their friends who successfully canvass the Watch Committee.[2] Sometimes members of the committee attempt to keep

[1] Page 62, under "English County Police."
[2] Confidentially communicated by police officials.

European Police Systems

privately in touch with the police situation through members of the force in the inferior ranks, a circumstance prejudicial to discipline and effectiveness.   Moreover, the burden which the English law throws upon the police department in the matter of prosecutions, making the chief constable practically responsible in determining the parties against whom prosecutions shall be brought, furnishes an obvious opportunity for manipulation by individual members of the Watch Committee.[1]   There is scarcely a chief constable in any of the larger cities who will not confess in confidential moments to continued solicitations by representatives of the Committee and Council in favor of saloons and various other interests against which it is the intention of the department to proceed.

[1] A local prosecuting attorney in the American and Continental sense of the term is unknown in England and Wales. Except in cases of the utmost importance, the police themselves prosecute through their own solicitor, retained for that purpose by the chief constable. In offenses punishable with death, and certain other cases of importance, the prosecution is conducted by the Director of Public Prosecutions, a national officer appointed by the Home Secretary. Any private person, under the English law, may institute and carry on criminal proceedings.

In Scotland, on the other hand, as in America and on the Continent, private prosecutions are practically unknown. A crime is regarded as an offense committed against society which society must prosecute through public officials. Thus there is in Scotland a Procurator Fiscal for each county, entirely independent of the police or the municipal government. For serious cases there are four Advocates-Depute, each with jurisdiction in his own circuit under the control of the Lord Advocate. In Germany the public prosecutor *(Staatsanwalt)* is a state official appointed by the Minister of Justice or the Minister of the Interior, and attached to the particular court in which he is to officiate. For literature dealing with this subject, see *The Administration of Justice in Criminal Matters in England and Wales*, G. Glover Alexander, Cambridge, Eng., 1911; *Justice and Police*, Frederic W. Maitland, London, 1885; Stone's *Justices' Manual; Outlines of Criminal Law*, C. S. Kenny, Cambridge, Eng., 1902; *Kriminalpolizei und Staatsanwalt*, Dr. Erich Wulffen.

The Police Department in the State

Furthermore, the Committee has it in its power to hamper the chief constable by refusing him the necessary funds to take up prosecutions which injured parties, through want of means or for other reasons, do not institute.[1] As one of the chief constables who had been retired expressed it to the writer: "It takes a strong man to stand up against the Committee and the Council. My life would have been much happier if I had yielded."

The difficulty of the situation lies in the fact that the power to remove the chief constable rests with the Watch Committee without the necessity of approval by a higher authority. In this respect the Scottish system is preferable. In Glasgow, for example, the chief constable is appointed by the joint action of the Magistrates Committee of the Town Council and the sheriff of the County. He has charge of all matters of discipline relative to members of the force below the rank of inspector,[2] and from his decisions there is no appeal. He is, of course, open to suggestion from the Magistrates Committee, or the Watching and Lighting Committee, which handles the financial measures of his department, or from the Town Council as a whole, but he is not obliged to obey. He can be removed from office only by the joint action of the sheriff and the Magistrates Committee; in case of a disagreement the matter is referred for decision to the Lord Advocate for Scotland.[3] The chief constable thus procures a degree of independence in his work that is lacking in the case of his brother offi-

[1] Many prosecutions which might be brought are left untouched, because the local police authority objects on the ground of expense.
[2] Corresponding to lieutenant in America.
[3] *Glasgow Police Act of 1866,* Sec. 71.

cial in England. The present chief constable in Glasgow stood firm against a resolution passed by the town council demanding the removal of a policeman for an alleged assault upon a citizen. Even in the face of public clamor and an award of damages by a jury to the alleged victim against the policeman, the chief constable refused to comply, as he knew the accusation to be without justice. Such an incident would hardly be possible in an English city.

Susceptible to abuses as it undoubtedly is, from the very nature of its formation, the general character of the Watch Committee has undoubtedly improved during the last quarter century. Twenty-five years ago, the chairman of the Watch Committee in Liverpool was the attorney for large liquor interests of the town, while another prominent member was the physician for most of the prostitutes. Needless to say, the activities of the police in respect to liquor and prostitution were negligible. Ten years later conditions in Manchester were shown to be even worse.[1] In 1899 the investigation of the Royal Excise Commission brought to light the fact that in Wigan the chairman of the Watch Committee was the head of a brewery company, and so powerful were the brewing interests that the chief constable did not dare to apply for a warrant to raid objectionable saloons. In Derby, of the eleven members of the Watch Committee, four were interested in saloons, the chairman of the committee himself holding four licenses. Similar conditions

[1] *Report of J. S. Dugdale, Q.C.*, a Commissioner appointed by the Home Office to investigate complaints as to the relation of the Watch Committee to certain beer houses and brothels. The report is on file in the Home Office.

The Police Department in the State

were discovered in Nottingham, Portsmouth, Hull, Reading, Lincoln, Leeds, Devonport, and other towns and cities.[1] The finding of the Investigating Commission in this matter is significant: " We think that the Chief Constable should hold a more independent position — as in Scotland — and . . . should not be removable without the sanction of the Secretary of State (for Home Affairs)."[2]

This recommendation has never been adopted, but in some towns, at least, the representatives of brewing interests no longer sit upon the Watch Committees. In this respect, therefore, the Watch Committee has improved. Could the position of chief constable be more adequately protected, so that removal would require the sanction of some higher body or official, the Watch Committee form of supervision would represent an efficient piece of machinery for the democratic control of a police force in a city of moderate size. Under its régime, the political use of patronage in the recruiting of the force, particularly in the larger towns, has been successfully curtailed, and this in spite of the fact, discussed in a later chapter, that there are no civil service regulations pertaining to the police in English cities.[3] So, too, in

[1] *Final Report of Her Majesty's Commissioners on the Operation and Administration of the Laws Relating to the Sale of Intoxicating Liquors*, 1899, pp. 158–163.

[2] *Ibid.*, p. 162. This recommendation is contained in the minority report of the commission which was signed by the Archbishop of Canterbury as chairman, and seven members. The majority report made no detailed recommendations in the matter of police organization.

[3] It cannot be denied that in some of the smaller towns personal, political and sectarian prejudices play no little part not only in the recruiting of the force, but in matters relating to discipline and promotion.

the matter of promotions and advancement, political influence is seldom effectual, and it can safely be said that as a rule the police department of an English town is administered without regard to party interests or political issues. Occasionally, of course, party feeling in the Town Council makes itself felt. Thus the efforts of the Watch Committee of one of the largest cities to secure a well-deserved increase of salary for its chief constable were defeated by the brewing interests of the Conservative Party in the Town Council, whose business had been hampered through the effectiveness of the police. There have been other instances where party politics and sectarian prejudice, trade interests and even personal jealousy have strained the relations between the Town Council and the chief constable. But, on the whole, instances of this kind are not frequently encountered.

If the Watch Committee form of police supervision has the defects arising from popular control, it has also the advantages of such control. The provincial cities do not know the more summary methods of Scotland Yard. There is little of the air of secrecy which surrounds the administration of the police in London. The attitude of the administrative officers toward the public is far more friendly, their relations with the newspapers more frank and open. The popular character of the Watch Committee entails a popular administration in which the more autocratic methods of the Home Office would be out of place. To be sure, there is a certain reserve in connection with the relation of the police to the public, even in the provincial cities. Criminal records are not open to inspection, nor are the internal affairs of the depart-

The Police Department in the State

ment, such as the trial and discipline of members of the force, free to public gaze. But in all matters that relate to their external duties, the police departments of the provincial cities are administered with full publicity.

In drawing this contrast between the police organization of London and that of the provincial cities, we cannot escape the conclusion that the more arbitrary methods by which the former is administered are justified by their outcome. It is an undeniable fact that the autocratic management of Scotland Yard produces the more efficient police organization. The failures of the provincial departments, when occurring, are generally traceable directly to their popular control. At first glance, therefore, it would seem that the autocratic type of organization, unhampered by political influences and free from the interference of popular majorities, is a primary requisite of an efficient police. Such an organization can keep order, it can keep secrets, it can maintain a continuous policy. Its efficiency is undisturbed by changes in public opinion or by the rise and fall of political factions. In a city of 7,000,000 people, the ability of such a department to operate without breakdown deprives theoretical objections to this method of control of much or all of their force. Indeed, in a large city whose population is stratified on social, economic, and racial lines, the task of maintaining order is so difficult and complex that strict adherence to the theory of popular control is impossible. In smaller cities and towns, the problem is so much simpler that arbitrary methods are not necessary. That is, a sufficiently good police, under more or less popular control, can be organized to maintain order with

European Police Systems

fair success. But in cities like London the problem is wholly different, and the question to be solved is how far democracy has to be tempered by autocratic methods.

The police problem has, however, wider relationships than are involved in the mere function of keeping order. If the maintenance of order were its only business, a rigid military organization would be well adapted to its solution. But political and economic movements and ideas, as well as social prejudices, cut across and complicate the task. The problem is inseparably connected with many phases of community life and the treatment must take color from opinions and ideals. While the police organization may conserve its efficiency by autocratic methods, it must be so amenable to public will that the people can reach it when changes in social ideals make such a step necessary. On the other hand, the democratic spirit must be made to harmonize with the requirements of effective organization. There must be autocracy enough for efficiency and democracy enough for sympathy and understanding.

How the police are to be made responsive to the public will and yet be kept safe from popular demoralization is obviously a problem of great complexity, affected in different localities by many special influences. One can readily see that with the rising tide of democracy throughout Europe the solution of this problem will be the occasion of many conflicts of opinion in the years to come.

The Police Department in the State

English County Police.

Although not directly within the limits of our subject, the English county police are of so much greater importance than the borough forces that some mention must be made of them. Prior to 1840, the rural districts of England were policed by parochial constables, and the conditions of crime obtaining were similar to those which existed in the larger towns and cities before the Act of 1835. The disastrous consequences of this system in the country districts were portrayed in the exhaustive report of the Royal Commission of 1839, appointed to determine the best means of establishing an efficient constabulary in the counties of England and Wales. As a result of this report, Parliament passed the " Permissive Act " of 1839,[1] which, supplemented by the Rural Police Act of 1856, to which attention has already been called, and other amendatory acts, forms the basis of county policing in England and Wales.

At the present time there are fifty-eight county police forces. With the exception of London and Middlesex, each of which is wholly included in the Metropolitan Police District, a separate force has been organized in every administrative county, including East and West Sussex, East and West Suffolk, the three Ridings of Yorkshire, the three divisions of Lincolnshire, the Isle of Wight, the Isle of Ely and the Soke of Peterborough.[2] Every borough with a population of less than 20,000 is

[1] 2 and 3 Vict. c. 93.
[2] The three Lincolnshire forces, however, are under one chief constable; the Peterborough force is under the chief constable of Northamptonshire, and Cumberland and Westmorland also have a chief constable in common.

debarred from having a separate police force.[1] Many
towns and boroughs with populations exceeding 20,000
have voluntarily given over their police functions to the
counties in which they are located.[2]

The constabulary force of each county is under the
control of a Standing Joint Committee formed of an
equal number of justices appointed by Quarter Sessions
and of county councilors appointed by the County Council. The size of the committee is determined by mutual
consent of the two bodies represented.[3] In carrying on
its work the Committee enjoys an independence denied
to the Watch Committee of a borough. The latter, as
we have seen, is under the control of the Town Council
in all matters relating to expenditure. The Joint Committee of a county, on the other hand, has full authority
in this respect, and the County Council is required to
raise for police purposes such sums as the committee may
deem necessary.[4] This is a matter of especial importance in so far as it relates to the number and pay of a
police force, both of which questions the Standing Joint
Committee can determine, subject only to the approval
of the Home Secretary. The recommendations of a
Watch Committee, on the other hand, especially as regards the strength of the force, are often rejected by an
economical Town Council with a keener eye for tax
rates than for efficient policing.

[1] Act of 1882 (45 and 46 Vict. c. 50), § 215.
[2] Act of 1840 (3 and 4 Vict. c. 88), § 14; Act of 1856 (19 and
20 Vict. c. 69), § 20.
[3] Act of 1888 (51 and 52 Vict. c. 41), § 30.
[4] *Ex parte Somerset County Council,* 58 L. J. Q. B. 513. The
expenses of a county force are paid from the police rate levied with
the county rate. (Act of 1888, § 3.)

The Police Department in the State

Subject to the approval of the Home Secretary, the Standing Joint Committee appoints the chief constable of the county constabulary.[1] In him are vested far wider powers than those enjoyed by the chief constable of a borough force. He appoints the other members of the department and "at his pleasure may dismiss all or any of them" and has "the general disposition and government of all the constables so to be appointed, subject to such lawful orders as he may receive from the Standing Joint Committee."[2] The chief constable of a borough force, on the other hand, has no statutory powers, as all police functions are vested exclusively in the Watch Committee. In this respect, therefore, the county chief constable is free from many of the petty annoyances which often beset the borough chief constable in his relations with his Watch Committee.

As is the case with the borough forces, the county forces are under the supervision of the Home Secretary and the same system of support is in vogue. That is, sums not exceeding one-half the total cost of the pay and clothing of a force are contributed by the national exchequer upon certificates of efficiency issued by the Home Secretary. The weaknesses of this system observed in connection with the borough police are noticeable in the county constabulary. The annual examinations made by the inspectors of the Home Office are more or less perfunctory, and little or no effort has been put forth to

[1] While the Standing Joint Committee cannot appoint a chief constable without the consent of the Home Secretary, such consent is not required in case of a dismissal. The Home Secretary's rules require that on appointment the chief constable shall not be older than forty-five.

[2] Act of 1839 (2 and 3 Vict. c. 93), § 6.

European Police Systems

standardize the methods of work in the various forces.[1] In other respects, however, the control of the Home Office over the county forces is more active than over the borough forces. The Home Secretary is empowered by law to make general regulations as to the government, pay and clothing of the county police.[2] Not only the appointment of a chief constable, but the strength of the force, the division of the county into districts, the number of men in each district, and the allocation of expenditure between the districts and the county are all subject to his approval.[3]

In these three respects, therefore, the county police occupy a unique position: the Standing Joint Committee is independent of the county council in financial matters, the chief constable has statutory rights which free him from the active interference of the Standing Joint Committee, and the Home Secretary has wide powers of supervision. As a result it can be confidently stated that in point of personnel and efficiency the county constabulary are superior to the borough police. Thanks to the guiding control of the Home Office this standard of excellence is generally uniform throughout England and Wales.[4]

---

[1] See discussion of this point, p. 50.

[2] *Act of 1839,* § 3. The rules at present in force were promulgated on April 12, 1886, and may be found in the Statutory Rules and Orders (1894, Vol. 10).

[3] For an interesting *résumé* of the entire subject of the relation between the Home Office and the county police forces, see the article, by H. B. Simpson, on *Police,* in the *Encyclopedia of Local Government Law,* London, 1906–1908, Vol. 5, p. 146.

[4] Ireland, outside of Dublin, is policed by the Royal Irish Constabulary, a semi-military force, instituted in 1787, and responsible to the Chief Secretary for Ireland. It consists of between 13,000 and 14,000 men and is the oldest police force in Great Britain.

 (*See next page*)

The Police Department in the State

HOLLAND AND BELGIUM

The system of police regulation in Dutch towns and cities is a unique arrangement of local autonomy modified by the firm, centralized control of the government. All chief commissioners (*Hoofd-Commissaris*) and commissioners (*Commissaris*) of police departments in the Netherlands are appointed by the Crown upon the recommendation of the Minister of Justice,[1] and are removable only by the same authority. The police officials, however, are, under the law, made responsible to the local burgomasters, who, although appointed by the Minister of Internal Affairs, and therefore representative of the central government, share the administration of the municipality with the popularly elected Town Councils.[2]

The control of the burgomaster over the affairs of the police department is more effectual than is indicated by

Dublin has a special force known as the Dublin Metropolitan Police established in 1836 (6 and 7, William IV c. 29). Like the Royal Irish Constabulary, it is directly responsible to the Chief Secretary for Ireland. It has a total strength of 1,200 men (as of December 31, 1911). Under the terms of the Irish Home Rule bill, just passed, both the Royal Irish Constabulary and the Dublin Metropolitan Police will, at the expiration of six years, be turned over to the control of the proper authorities under the newly established Irish Parliament.

[1] Only four Dutch cities, Amsterdam, Rotterdam, The Hague, and Utrecht, have chief commissioners. In each of these cities there are from two to seven commissioners, responsible to the Chief Commissioner, but appointed and removable by the Minister of Justice. The smaller cities and towns, like Haarlem, Delft, Schiedam, Groningen, etc., have each a single Commissioner.

[2] The burgomasters are appointed for a term of six years. They are generally reappointed to succeed themselves. Occasionally they are transferred or promoted from one city to another. Thus the present Burgomaster at Amsterdam was formerly in the same position at Arnhem.

European Police Systems

the type of organization. The burgomaster cannot indeed remove the commissioner, who, like himself, is a government official; his right to appoint, promote and dismiss the other members of the force, is further limited to the recommendations of the commissioner with whom all initiative rests. But the burgomaster holds the purse-strings. No money can be expended the purpose of which has not first been approved by the local authorities.[1] Even the salary of the commissioner is subject to their control. Moreover, in the practical working out of the relations between the police and the town government, the word of the burgomaster is of final importance. It is he who ultimately determines the policy of the department. Respect for law and authority is nowhere to be found in greater degree than in Holland; and while friction occasionally arises between the burgomaster and the commissioner, the latter recognizes the former as his legally constituted superior.

In Belgium there is more local autonomy than in Holland, and the police departments are to a far greater extent under the direct control of the municipalities. The commissioner of police (*commissaire en chef*) is appointed by the burgomaster,[2] who, in turn, is nominated by the Town Council from among its own membership.[3]

[1] In Amsterdam, for example, the police budgetary estimate for the following year is submitted by the commissioner to the Select Committee, consisting of the burgomaster and four aldermen (*Wethouders*) chosen by the Town Council. After revision it is referred to the Town Council, where it may again be revised before its final approval by majority vote.

[2] This appointment must receive the approval of the central government at Brussels, an approval which is very seldom, if ever, withheld.

[3] The actual appointment of burgomasters is made by the Crown,

66

The Police Department in the State

By a peculiar law the burgomaster himself may be the chief of the police, and as such, is free to exercise the various functions pertaining to that office. Generally, however, those functions are delegated to a commissioner, as in Liége, Ghent and Antwerp, leaving to the burgomaster only general supervisory powers. In Brussels one of the nine commissioners in the department acts as chief or commander under the immediate direction of the burgomaster, who, perhaps, to a greater extent than any other Belgian burgomaster, participates in the details of police management.[1]

The municipal police forces of Belgium are therefore practically autonomous, with only the slightest interference on the part of the central government. The regulations which they issue are, however, subject to the approval of the *Députation permanente* of the Ministry of Justice in Brussels, where their legality is passed upon.

GERMANY

Police administration in the German Empire lies within the jurisdiction of each of the several States. The Imperial Constitution makes no mention of it, nor has there been any general legislation upon the subject. As a result there is no uniform system of administration as in England and France. Each kingdom,

but as a rule the designation is a perfunctory matter. Occasionally, however, the King appoints some one other than the candidate named by the Town Council. Thus the present Burgomaster of Brussels was not the man named by his associates in the Council, and considerable bitterness was aroused by the arbitrary action of the King.

[1] Brussels formerly had a chief of police or head commissioner who took upon himself all the duties now performed by the burgomaster.

dukedom, principality, or free city, regulates the matter in its own way without interference from or supervision by the Imperial government.[1] There has developed, therefore, a singular diversity in the methods of handling the police. In some States they are subject to local municipal control; in others, they constitute a branch of the state government; while in still others, state and municipal supervision intermingle. Thus in the Kingdom of Württemberg all the municipal police forces are locally controlled; in Bavaria and Saxony, only the capital cities, Munich and Dresden, have royal state forces, the police of the other towns and cities being subject to the local authorities; in Prussia the police of all the larger cities are commanded by royal officers under the control of the Minister of the Interior. In this latter class are Frankfort-on-Main, Danzig, Königsberg, Breslau, Magdeburg, Wiesbaden, Coblentz, Cologne, Hanover and fourteen other Prussian cities of lesser importance.[2] It may be said that with two exceptions, Leipzig and Stuttgart,[3] the important cities of Germany are practically debarred from the local management of

[1] The Imperial Constitution reserves to the Empire the power to legislate with respect to the "whole domain of civil and criminal law, including judicial procedure" (Art. IV, § 13). Thus there is a German Criminal Code (*Reichsstrafgesetzbuch*) and uniform court procedure operative in all cities of the Empire.

[2] Potsdam, Stettin, Posen, Zabrze, Kiel, Geestemünde, Bochum, Gelsenkirchen, Cassel, Hanau, Fulda, Essen, Saarbrücken and Aachen. The cost of these police forces is included in the budget of the Minister of the Interior which is annually presented to the Prussian *Landtag* for consideration. With the exception of one-third, which is paid directly by the cities in question, the money is paid from the state exchequer. For discussion, see Hue de Grais, *loc. cit.*, pp. 350 ff.

[3] Leipzig's population is 589,850; Stuttgart has a population of

The Police Department in the State

their police. In Berlin, Dresden, Munich, Hamburg and other important municipalities, the police departments are subject exclusively to state authorities. Thus the Berlin department is under the control of the Prussian Minister of the Interior, and the Police President and all the higher officials are appointed by the Crown. The same condition obtains in Dresden, where the appointments are made by the King of Saxony. In Hamburg the department is subject to the State Senate. Only in the smaller cities and towns is local control permitted, and even in these cases it is so hedged about by state regulations that little is left to the discretion of local authorities.

Particularly is this true in Prussia. Stein's enlightened Municipal Ordinance of 1808, under which, in revised form, Prussian towns and cities are to-day exercising wider powers of self government than any other municipalities in Europe, specifically excepted the police function.[1] " The State reserves the power to es-

286,218. Of the other cities under municipal control, the more important are:

	Population		Population
Nuremberg	333,142	Plauen	121,272
Chemnitz	287,807	Augsburg	102,487
Barmen	169,214	Bromberg	57,696

[1] The Municipal Ordinance of 1808 was revised and to a certain extent curtailed by the Ordinance of March 17, 1831, by the Ordinance of May 3, 1853, and by the General Laws of July 30 and August 1, 1883. Its provisions have generally been incorporated in special municipal laws for the western provinces of Prussia which were subsequently acquired. The towns of the Province of Westphalia are governed under a constitution dating from March 19, 1856; those of the Rhine Province under a constitution of May 15, 1856; those of the Province of Hanover, annexed by Prussia in 1866, under its old constitution of June 24, 1858; Frankfort-on-Main, until 1866 a free city, is governed under a separate constitution of March 26, 1867; the Province of Schleswig-Holstein, annexed in 1864, under a constitution of April 14, 1869.

tablish its own police directions in the municipalities or to transfer the exercise of police functions to the magistracy, which will then exercise the same as agents. In this capacity the magistracies shall be regarded as State authorities." So ran section 166 of the Municipal Ordinance, and in Prussia this provision still remains in force.[1] Under this theory of state responsibility for police action, one of three courses is invariably followed: either the entire police arrangements of a municipality are in the hands of royal officers, as is the case with the twenty-three cities above cited; or the State transfers the police authority to the municipal government, while placing at the head a Crown official; or, finally, it confers the authority personally upon the burgomaster who is for police purposes regarded as a State commissioner.[2] In this last case, the burgomaster often occupies an anomalous position. On the one hand he is the official head of the municipality, chosen by and responsible to the representative assembly; on the other, he is the agent of the State, responsible only to the Minister of the Interior. He thus embodies in his person both democratic and autocratic functions.

In spite of the efforts of those who believe in the ex-

[1] The first liberal draft of the constitution for Prussia (December 5, 1848) drawn up by the National Assembly, included local police functions among the larger powers to be granted to the municipalities, but the constitution as promulgated a year later (January 1, 1850), when the reaction against liberalism had set in, omitted this provision and instead asserted the unconditional right of the Crown to control the police in every department.

[2] The State may also confer police authority upon a member of the municipal executive other than the burgomaster. In that capacity, the official thus chosen, is quite independent of the burgomaster and is answerable for his acts only to State officials.

The Police Department in the State

tension of the principle of municipal home rule and the friction which occasionally develops between the large cities and the government of Prussia on questions of police management,[1] local control of police forces is on the whole unfavorably regarded in Germany. Certainly it has attracted no large degree of popular support. Indeed, as between municipal control and state control there is a distinct trend toward the latter form.

Within recent years, four cities have surrendered municipal police control to the State.[2] It is commonly believed that local police forces, particularly in the large cities and in the thickly populated industrial centers, become too closely identified with local interests, and that a higher degree of efficiency can be secured under state control. Several factors contribute to this conclusion. In the first place, in the German mind, greater authority attaches to a state government, with its royal or semi-royal sanctions, than to a local government of popularly elected burghers. Out of this belief grows an important social distinction. The royal police official of Dresden, responsible to the King of Saxony, looks with condescension upon his brother officer

[1] This discord between the large municipalities and the government of Prussia occasionally assumes a more serious aspect. When, several years ago, a bill came before the Prussian Diet increasing the budgets of the police departments of the larger towns of Prussia, the representatives of Berlin, Breslau, Danzig and Posen vigorously protested and demanded that the entire police administration be transferred to the municipalities, a demand, which, needless to say, was ignored, although the incident created considerable criticism. For a thorough and accurate review of the relations of the central government to the municipalities of Prussia in matters relating to police control, see *Municipal Life and Government in Germany*, William Harbutt Dawson, London, 1914, Chap. II.

[2] St. Johann, 24,000; Kiel, 211,627; Saarbrücken, 105,089, and Malstatt-Burbach, 38,600.

71

in the neighboring city of Leipzig who serves under a burgomaster. Thus it was felt that the assistant commissioner in Munich who accepted the commissionership in Stuttgart had distinctly lowered himself in the social scale, because he went from a state force to a municipal force. For the same reason the state *Gendarme,* patroling a lonely road in Saxony, feels himself superior to the municipal *Schutzmann* of Leipzig or Chemnitz. This distinction attracts to the state forces a police officer of higher social grade. The royal constabulary of Dresden secures a better caliber of man than the Leipzig force, while the ambitious police official would not hesitate to choose Munich in preference to Stuttgart.

Financial considerations also contribute to the superiority of the state-controlled force over the municipal force in Germany. The tax-payer worries the burgomasters and local authorities, particularly in the smaller towns and cities. Under the control of a thrifty town council, largely representing the wealthy tax-paying interests with their deep-seated objections to increases in rates, economy often becomes parsimony, with a resulting down-at-the-heel organization. Economy is not, however, so pressing a matter with the officials of a state-controlled force, for the tax-payers are far removed from the scene of action and the very form and constitution of the state-parliament make budget-paring difficult. With more money to spend, and a freer hand in its spending, the royal state forces are in a position of great advantage.[1]

[1] Thus the royal force of Dresden, a city of 548,000 inhabitants, spent 3,336,629 marks in 1912; while Leipzig, with a population

The Police Department in the State

State control in Germany is further effective for the reason that it unifies the efforts of a police force in its relations with other branches of the state government. In Württemberg, Bavaria, and to some extent in Saxony, there is continual friction between the locally-controlled police organizations on the one hand, and on the other, the state *Gendarmerie*. The latter force is a military constabulary, under the control of the various Ministers of the Interior, employed by each state not only for the protection of the smaller villages and country places, but for the enforcement of certain state and national legislation.[1] The conflict arises from the lack of adequate definition of the rights and powers of the respective forces. In some matters it is difficult even for an expert to determine which force has jurisdiction. In the states mentioned, therefore, divided responsibility is a source of continual confusion and friction. In Prussia,

larger by 40,000, spent only 2,807,761 marks on her police in the same period.

[1] *Gendarmerie* forces are to be found in Germany, France, Italy, Austria, Spain, Holland, and Belgium. In Italy, as we shall see, they are known as *Carabinieri;* in Holland they are called *Marachausses,* in Spain, *Guardia Civil.* The organization was first established in France (Law of January 6 and 30, 1791, supplemented by the Law of 28 Germinal, Year VI). In 1812, it was introduced into Germany and other countries of the Continent. The *gendarmerie* are almost invariably subject to the orders of the civil authorities, although in France and Italy, while forming one of the reserves of the Minister of the Interior, they are directly under the orders of the Minister of War.

Ordinarily the men for this service are recruited from the army. Thus, in Prussia, applicants must have served nine years in the army, and have reached the grade of *Unteroffizier.* The training schools for recruits are among the best police schools on the Continent. Not only do the *Gendarmerie* guard the country places, either mounted or afoot, but they supplement the police work of the smaller towns, where, for lack of money or conveniences, the local authorities are unable to cope with unexpected situations.

European Police Systems

on the other hand, where all police control is centralized, directly or indirectly, in the hands of the Minister of the Interior, friction is minimized. The German, to whom any lack of coördination in the machinery of government is an approach to anarchy, sees in these facts a convincing argument for the necessity of a uniform state control.

Finally, it must be admitted that state control is effective in Germany in eliminating personal interests and party politics, too often found in connection with the local management of municipal forces. In a police force whose president or commissioner is appointed by the Crown upon the recommendation of the Minister of the Interior, whose discipline is subject to the approval of no external body, whose policy is divorced from political principles or movements, whose efficiency is unrelated to the success or failure of any political party, there is neither opportunity nor occasion for the introduction of sinister influences. On the other hand, in a locally controlled police force where the commissioner is responsible to a popularly elected council, where the police policy is determined by majority vote, and where the disciplinary measures of the department are subject to the consideration and approval of the town fathers, personal interests and party politics are apt to make themselves felt. Thus in Stuttgart when the present Police Director assumed control two years ago, he found instances where certain police officers had been dismissed three times by his predecessor for serious offenses only to be subsequently reinstated in each case by the council (*Gemeinderat*). It is small wonder that the force in Stuttgart was demoralized. Even to-day

The Police Department in the State

some of the members of the *Gemeinderat* in that city are not above using their influence and their vote for the benefit of external or incidental interests. In a bitter letter written recently by one of these council members to the Police Director protesting against a small fine which the police had imposed upon him, he concluded by saying: "And this is what I get for supporting you in the *Gemeinderat*." The implication is obvious. In Berlin or Dresden or Munich, where the policy of the police is shaped by the autocratic hand of the state, free from external hindrance or suggestion, we look in vain for conditions of this kind.

State supervision in Germany is of course effective at the expense of popular control. The system is autocratically centralized. Citizens are given no opportunity to express their opinion of the police. The issue is never raised at the polls, nor under the present system could it be raised. As a matter of fact, in the Anglo-Saxon sense of the term, there is no such thing as democratic administration in Germany; in its place is a huge bureaucratic machine. The three-class system of voting, by which the control of municipal policy is practically limited to men of wealth;[1] the maintenance of the old

[1] Under this scheme, which is operative only in Prussia, all voters are grouped into three classes according to their tax-paying strength, each class electing one-third of the candidates to be voted for. Thus in the municipal elections in Essen in 1900, there were three voters in the first class, 401 in the second, and 18,991 in the third; but the three voters of the first class elected one-third of the whole municipal council, while 404 votes out of nearly 20,000 elected two-thirds of it. In 1912, in Berlin, there were 936 voters in the first class, or 0.2 per cent.; 32,096 in the second class, or 8.3 per cent., and 353,704 in the third class, or 91.5 per cent. A recent classification of the electors of 114 Prussian towns showed that 8,600, or 1.3 per cent. fell in the first class; 48,950, or 7 per cent. in the

European Police Systems

political divisions as units of representation despite the
radical change in the complexion of the country; [1] the
conception of the local official as an agent of the state
rather than of the locality that chooses him; the social
superiority and protected position of the official classes;
the rigidity of the press censorship and laws governing
public assemblage,[2] and above all, the firm grip of the
central government upon local affairs — so that in Prussia the choice of burgomasters [3] must be approved by
the Crown, and the higher officers of the police depart-

second; and 629,360, or 91.7 per cent. in the third. In some towns
it happens that a single voter forms the first class by himself, and
thus elects one-third of the membership of the municipal council.
For an interesting discussion of this subject, see Dawson, *loc. cit.*

[1] This change is due to the unprecedented growth of cities during
the last thirty years. Certain towns of over 300,000 inhabitants
are represented in the legislature in the same proportion as country populations of 30,000.

[2] The regulation of the press and the right of assembly are the
subject of Imperial legislation. Under the Press Laws (*Federal Industrial Code of 1869,* and the *Law of May 7, 1874*), a copy of each
paper and periodical, not purely devoted to the interests of the arts
and sciences, must immediately, upon distribution, be delivered to
the police authority of the place of publication; papers may not
publish the news of indictments or other criminal proceedings until
the same have been publicly announced; they are obliged to print
rectifications of facts previously stated; confiscation of publications
without judicial decree can occur if the contents offend the emperor or ruler of a state, urge disobedience to laws, incite acts of
class hatred, etc.

The law of public assembly (*Vereinsgesetz,* April 19, 1908,) provides that all political clubs or societies must file with the police
authorities, within two weeks after formation, copies of their con-
stitutions and lists of their officers; subsequent changes must in
the same way be communicated to the police; public meetings for
the discussion of political subjects must be announced twenty-four
hours before to the police, who may send not more than two representatives; these representatives have the right to declare the meetings dissolved; the proceedings of these meetings must be in the
German language. For an interesting discussion of the Press Law
and the Public Assembly Law, see James, *loc. cit.,* pp. 218 ff., and
Hue de Grais, *loc. cit.,* pp. 380 ff.

[3] In cities with a population exceeding 100,000.

76

The Police Department in the State

ment of a Rhenish city cannot be removed without authority from Berlin — these factors tend to render Germany impregnable against the assaults of democracy. Indeed, the development of liberal principles has received but little encouragement in the last sixty years. The energies of the nation have been totally absorbed in industrial and military development, and the impassioned liberalism of 1848, which gave a momentary promise of a new era in Europe, has been supplanted by the spirit of autocracy.[1] Particularly is this true in Prussia, the most wealthy and progressive State of the Empire. In respect to political thought and the liberty of her institutions, she is far behind the smaller States in the south.

The autocratic spirit of the German government is reflected in the imperviousness of the police to public opinion. The police department is a specialized institution in the details of which the people are held to have no proper interest. Not only are police records withheld from public scrutiny, but in the state-controlled forces no information of any kind relative to administration is ever vouchsafed to the citizens. Indeed, he would be a valiant man who would ask for it. In Berlin no annual report of the department has been issued in twelve years; in Dresden the last report was published in 1897. The so-called annual returns of the royal forces are now forwarded to the respective Ministers of the Interior of the various states and by them jealously guarded. In

[1] See *Reminiscences of Carl Schurz*, New York, 1908; *The Evolution of Modern Germany*, W. H. Dawson, New York, 1908; *The Republican Tradition in Europe*, Fischer, London, 1911.

77

European Police Systems

Berlin the combined newspaper interests are allowed to send but one representative to police headquarters. This particular man has been especially approved by the authorities. Whatever news he is given is written out in a form acceptable to the police, and is printed in the various newspapers exactly as it was sent out, very much as legal notices are published in American or English journals. The same practice obtains in Dresden. When in June, 1913, three plain-clothes men of the Berlin force were arrested on the charge of living on the earnings of the prostitutes whom they were supposed to supervise, the news was given to the public in a dozen lines in an inconspicuous place on the back page of the *Berliner Tageblatt*. Even at that, one of the officials at headquarters, in talking to me of the matter, regretted the publicity which had been given to " a private affair." Occasionally the police are subjected to severe criticism at the hands of the press, the Social-Democratic newspapers leading in the assault, but the general fear in which the police are held, coupled with the curbing effect of the press law, has a restraining influence even on these attacks.

The general attitude of the police toward the public is also indicative of the autocratic spirit of the German government. The unfailing courtesy of the English police is often lacking in the German forces. Arbitrariness too frequently marks the conduct of the latter in their relations with the public. The great powers of the police official, his right to fine and imprison without judicial process, his exemption from prosecution for false arrest, breed an arrogance hardly to be tolerated in dem-

The Police Department in the State

ocratic communities. To be sure, the temper and character of the Teutonic people are attuned to this kind of stern management. They seem even to demand it. If it be true, as has been asserted, that a Berlin *Schutzmann* in Trafalgar Square would provoke a riot in two hours, it is equally true that the peaceful-mannered London "Bobby" would be overwhelmed in Berlin. Back of the sharp contrasts between the English and German police are fundamental differences in race-history and national character.

AUSTRIA-HUNGARY

The absence of state lines and independent jurisdictions in Austria conduces to far greater uniformity in police control than is to be found in Germany. In the eight largest cities,[1] the police presidents or directors are appointed by the Emperor upon the recommendation of the Austrian Minister of the Interior, and to this latter official, exercising control through the *Statthalter,* or governor, of the province in which the city is located,[2]

[1] Vienna, Prague, Lemberg, Trieste, Krakau, Graz, Brünn, and Czernowitz. These cities vary in population from 2,000,000 in the case of Vienna, to 87,000 in the case of Czernowitz. The police of Laibach, the capitol of Carniola, with a population of 41,000, are also under state control, having been handed over by the municipality in 1913. At the present time, Graz and Brünn have both state and municipal control, the uniformed force being under the jurisdiction of the latter, while the former assumes charge of press and public assembly matters, the registration of citizens, the detective bureau, etc. As neither force is under the control of the other, considerable confusion exists, although a passable basis of operation has been established.

[2] For administrative purposes, Austria is divided into seventeen provinces. Each province has a measurable degree of local self-government through its *Landesausschuss,* or council, and the provincial diet. Imperial interests, however, are especially represented by a *Statthalter,* or governor, appointed by the Crown upon the pro-

European Police Systems

the police forces are entirely responsible. In the smaller towns and cities, police control is vested in the local authorities under the famous Municipal Act of 1862.[1] Passed in consequence of the prevailing spirit of unrest and the desire for freedom emanating from Hungary, this act has given the lesser communities of Austria a degree of autonomy in the management of their police affairs such as the small towns of Prussia do not know. Indeed, an eminent Austrian authority has gone so far as to maintain that these lesser communities of Austria possess a larger independent competence than do the communes of any other European state.[2]

In Hungary, the capital, Budapest, is the only city whose police force is under state jurisdiction.[3] All other towns and cities have municipal control.[4] But a

posal of the Minister of the Interior and independent of local control.

[1] *Gemeindegesetzgebung* of March 5, 1862, Art. V. Prior to the passage of this act, police authority was entirely vested in the state.

[2] Dr. Josef Redlich: *Das Wesen der österreichischen Kommunalverfassung,* Leipzig, 1910. See also his recent article in the Journal of the Society of Comparative Legislation — New Series, Vol. VIII, Part I.

Note, however, that even with this large authority vested in the smaller communities, the state maintains through its *Gendarmerie* a fairly firm grip upon matters relating to order and security. (See note on p. 73.) The *Gendarmerie* is controlled by the state officials of the *Bezirke* or units into which the provinces are divided. The system is practically similar to that of France and Prussia. The *Gendarmerie* corps is perhaps the most effective police organization in Austria as regards both patrol and detective work. Certainly it has the confidence of the entire provincial public.

[3] The Police President is appointed by the Emperor in his capacity as King of Hungary, upon the nomination of the Hungarian Minister of the Interior.

[4] Exclusive of Croatia-Slavonia, Hungary is divided into 63 rural counties and 36 urban counties or towns. The latter are practically free cities in which independent self-government has been highly developed. These counties and cities constitute the unit of local government in Hungary.

The Police Department in the State

movement is on foot to place all local forces under the centralized direction of the government. This program has the support of the National Working Party which is in power at the present time,[1] and arrangements are being made to pass through the Hungarian parliament measures which will place under state control the police forces of ten of the largest cities.[2] It is felt that the present system, lacking uniform standards and giving wide opportunity for incompetency and politics, is incapable of coping with the modern criminal. Arrayed against the proposed legislation are the cities whose local autonomy is thus challenged, backed by the Independent Party in the Hungarian parliament which sees in this scheme of centralization a powerful weapon forged by cunning hands for the use of the hated government at Vienna. The project, however, has the support of the authorities at Budapest and will undoubtedly be carried through.

The police forces of all the larger cities of Austria-Hungary, therefore, are under the strict supervision of state authorities.[3] As in Germany, so here, popular control of the police through democratic machinery is

[1] 1914.

[2] These cities include Debreczen (94,000), Pozsony (80,000), Temesvár (75,000), Arad (65,000), Nagyvárad (67,000), Kolozsvár (63,000), Pécs (53,000), and Kassa (47,000). Training classes for the chief police officers of these towns are now being conducted in Budapest in anticipation of the proposed legislation.

[3] The police departments under state control are supported by the national exchequer, although the cities affected make their individual contributions. Thus the municipality of Vienna pays a fixed sum of 1,050,000 *Kronen* a year, while the state contributes the balance. (In 1913 the state share was 16,866,628 *Kronen* voted by the Austrian parliament. The municipality of Budapest pays an annual fixed sum of 800,000 *Kronen*, Hungary contributing the balance, in 1913, 7,670,260 *Kronen*.)

not seriously considered for the reason that in the larger cities, at least, there is no pretense of democracy. A police force is a governmental organ autocratically managed on a semi-military basis, for the purpose of maintaining order. As such it is accepted by the people. In the larger cities there is no popular desire to place the police departments in the hands of municipal authorities where public opinion could make itself more easily felt. The thoughtful people of Vienna and Budapest would regard such a proposal with apprehension.[1] In an excitable population, whose brief experience with limited self-government has been marked by instability and continual inter-racial disorder, the need is felt for the firm control of a centralized police. " A municipally controlled police force in Budapest or Vienna would spell demoralization in six months." This remark of one of the foremost thinkers of Austria, a member of the Austrian parliament, reflects the intelligent opinion of the country.

The administration of the police of Vienna and Budapest does not meet entirely with popular approbation. On the contrary, the arbitrariness of the police in the exercise of their imperial functions has bred a lively animosity particularly among the poorer classes, and a *Wachmann* in Vienna is almost as unpopular as a *Schutzmann* in Berlin. To a large extent, this is due to the fact that the police represent the imperial government and thus the domination of the bureaucracy. The

---

[1] Both Vienna and Budapest are governed by popularly-elected municipal councils, and burgomasters chosen from among the councilmen. The choice of burgomaster must be approved by the Crown.

The Police Department in the State

feeling is a manifestation of the revolt against the rigorous press censorship, the public assembly laws, and other enactments that hedge the liberties of the people.[1] Popular feeling, that is, runs against the political use made of the police rather than against centralized control as such. And it must be admitted that this is a serious objection. More than once the party in power in Budapest has used the police, through its control of the Ministry of the Interior, to dissolve the assemblies and break up the meetings of its opponents. In 1905 the opposition party coming suddenly into power took its revenge by removing the police president who had followed the orders of his superior too faithfully. In the same way, the police are used in both Austria and Hungary to enforce the press law against the opponents and critics of the government. It is because they thus typify the arbitrary use of power that the police are so

[1] The Austrian Press Censorship law is far more harsh than the German Law. The first copies of all newspapers and periodicals must be sent to police headquarters, where they are carefully reviewed for matter offending against morals, religion, or the civil order. If in the judgment of the police objectionable material is discovered, the entire edition is immediately confiscated. Later the courts are called upon to pass upon the action of the police. In the first five months of 1913, there were seventy such confiscations in Vienna alone, the objectionable material consisting, for the most part, of anti-military articles dealing with the Balkan situation. In the same way all placards or signs erected for political purposes, the texts of all plays to be presented, etc., must first be approved by the police. In Hungary there is no police censorship. The Hungarian Press Law (18th- 1848) provides for a deposit of 20,000 *Kronen* by the owners of newspapers publishing political news. From this sum, any fines, levied by the courts for printing improper news, are subtracted.

The Austrian Public Assembly Law is practically similar to the German Law. (See note on p. 76.) In Hungary there is no such law, but an order of the Minister of the Interior of 1868 is enforced by the police with the same effect.

83

cordially feared and disliked in Austria and Hungary. The question does not concern local control against state control — the people are not committed to any particular form of organization — with them the question involves the preservation of their political status against harsh laws and an arbitrary bureaucracy.[1]

FRANCE

With the exception of the three largest cities, Paris, Marseilles, and Lyons, for which special provision has been made, the various municipal police departments of France are under the immediate control of the local authorities. In no country of Europe is there greater uniformity in the management of local affairs, for the Municipal Code of 1884 is the basis of all village, town and city government. The unit of local government is the *commune,* varying in size and population from small villages of a few dozen inhabitants to large cities like Bordeaux.[2] At the head of the commune is the *Maire,* or mayor, elected by the local council.[3] To this official the local police organization is responsible.

[1] That the relations between the police and public in Vienna have greatly improved in the last twenty-five years cannot be denied. This improvement has been largely due to the increasing toleration by the government of liberal ideas. In the early nineties, the government carried on a bitter campaign against the Social Democratic and Universal Suffrage movements, using the powerful weapons of Public Assembly and Press Censorship Laws in an attempt to crush them. In recent years, however, there has been a disposition to deal more amicably with liberal tendencies.

[2] There are 36,229 communes in France: 31,690 have less than 1,500 inhabitants; 18,471 have even less than 500; while only 15 have populations exceeding 100,000.

[3] The *Maire* may be suspended from office for a month by the Prefect of the department, or for three months by the Minister of

The Police Department in the State

The complete autonomy of the English town how-ever is entirely lacking in the French commune. The French government, clinging tenaciously to the principle of centralized administration and fearful of the unre-strained use of the police power by small popularly elected bodies, has interposed many barriers to munic-ipal home rule. The power of the *Maire* over his po-lice department is greatly curtailed. His actions are sub-ject to the rigid scrutiny of the representative of the central government, the Prefect of the department in which his commune is located.[1] While the *Maire* is given the power to appoint, promote, suspend, and dis-miss police officials, none of these actions except suspen-sion is valid without the concurrence of the Prefect.[2] The larger the towns the more stringent become the regu-

the Interior; or he may be removed from office altogether by the President of the Republic.

[1] For administrative purposes, France is divided into 86 depart-ments, each in charge of a *Prefect* appointed and removed by the President of the Republic upon the recommendation of the Min-ister of the Interior. Each department contains a given number of communes. The Prefect and the Sub-Prefects under him have wide and rather undefined functions. As representatives of the execu-tive, they supervise the execution of the laws and maintain a vigor-ous control over all administrative officials of the department, oc-casionally annulling their acts. The Prefect nominates a variety of subordinate officers and exercises an oversight of the communes, some of whose measures become effective only after receiving his assent.

[2] Law of April 5, 1884 (*The French Municipal Code,* Art. 103), The extensive powers of the Prefect in regard to local police mat-ters are indicated in Article 99 of the Municipal Code: "The pow-ers which pertain to the *Maire* . . . are no hindrance to the right of the Prefect to take, for all the communes of his department, or any of them, and in all cases in which they have not been provided by the municipal authorities, all measures relating to the mainte-nance of the public health, safety and tranquillity. The right can-not be exercised by the Prefect . . . until after a demand in due form to the *Maire* proves of no avail."

European Police Systems

lations. The law [1] requires a *commissaire de police,* appointed by a decree of the President of the Republic in all communes having from five to ten thousand inhabitants, and an additional *commissaire* for each ten thousand in excess of that number. These officials, as we shall see later, have functions peculiarly French. The police organization, under the more or less nominal direction of the *Maire,* is practically in their hands.[2] They are the agents of the central authority, of the municipality, and of the prosecuting attorney, with power to make investigations relating to crime, to requisition the *gendarmerie,*[3] to exercise the semi-judicial functions peculiar to their office and to direct the uniformed police in the execution of certain special activities.[4]

Further, the law provides — and it is characteristic of the French passion for uniformity — that the general organization, the salaries and other details of the police departments of towns and cities with more than 40,000 inhabitants shall be regulated by decrees of the President of the Republic,[5] that is, by the central government at Paris operating through the Minister of the Interior.

[1] Law of 28 Pluviose, Year VIII.

[2] There are 781 of these municipal *commissaires de police* in France. Where there are two or more such officials in a single commune, a *commissaire central* is appointed with authority over the others. (Decree of March 22, 1854.) The municipal *commissaires* must not be confused with the special *commissaires* attached to the *Sûreté générale* of the Minister of the Interior. These latter officials, 284 in number, are assigned generally to important railway terminals and seaports, their duties relating principally to international or "roving" criminals.

[3] Decree of May 20, 1903.

[4] Such as vehicular traffic, control of furnished room houses, prostitution, etc.

[5] Law of April 5, 1884, Art. 103.

The Police Department in the State

Exclusive of Lyons, Paris and Marseilles, 34 cities are thus controlled at the present time.

As a final barrier to local autonomy in police matters, the communal councils are obliged by law to grant the appropriations asked for by the police departments. In the case of the smaller communes (under 40,000 inhabitants), the Prefect of the department has authority to inscribe in the budget such necessary sums as the municipal council has failed to vote. In the larger cities, the President of the Republic, with the consent of the Council of State, is empowered to increase the budgets of recalcitrant local councils by such sums as are deemed essential to efficient police organization,[1] and these sums can be collected if necessary by an official impost. By these methods the principle of home rule in police matters is, to a large extent, nullified in France.[2]

It is interesting to note the special provision which has been made for the control of the police in the three largest cities of France: Paris, Marseilles and Lyons. In

---

[1] Law of April 5, 1884, Art. 103.

[2] Through his direct control of the department prefects and his indirect control of the *Maires*, the Minister of the Interior holds the reins of the police power of France in his own hands. The bureau of his office which deals with the matter is called the "*Sûreté générale*," which, in a long course of history, has come to be one of the most powerful and influential divisions of the government. It is this office which issues the police regulations and instructions and exercises a general supervision of the various administrative agents, "thus ensuring" as the official pamphlet expresses it, "that unity of ideas without which no good administration can exist." (*La Police*, published by Paul Dupont, Paris, 1905.) The *Sûreté générale* is itself subdivided into various bureaus, each entrusted with particular functions. To this department are also attached the special *commissaires* and *inspecteurs* for the suppression and investigation of crimes and offenses committed on railroads and for other duties to which they may be assigned. The famous French *Brigade mobile*, of which mention is made on page 288, and the national *gendarmerie* are also attached to the *Sûreté générale*.

the last named city, a number of suburban communes are joined to the large urban commune of Lyons, and the general police district resulting is committed to the control of the Prefect of the Rhône department, rather than to the *Maire* of Lyons.[1] In Marseilles the police force has recently been transferred from the local authorities to the Prefect of the department of Bouches-du-Rhône.[2]

In Paris a unique system of police organization has been in operation for over a century. A special police Prefect, entirely divorced in his functions from the Prefect of the Seine, is appointed by the President of the Republic upon the recommendation of the Minister of the Interior. To this official is committed the responsibility of the police forces of Paris.[3] The *régime exceptionnel,* which has been described as the masterpiece of Napoleon's administrative system, finds its justification not only in the size of the capital city, but in its turbulent traditions. Time and again in the various revolutions

[1] Law of June 9, 1851. The police budget of Greater Lyons forms part of the budget of the Minister of the Interior. Lyons contributes to the national government 30 per cent. of this sum, the balance being paid by the nation. In 1912 the Lyons police budget amounted to 2,337,836 francs, of which 875,065 francs were paid by the municipality.

[2] Law of March 8, 1908. As is the case with Lyons, the police budget of Marseilles is included in the budget of the Minister of the Interior. The municipality of Marseilles contributes to the national exchequer an annual sum of 1,600,000 francs based on an estimated expenditure of 2,880,000 francs, any expenses in excess of this estimate being shared equally by the nation and the city. The Marseilles police budget for 1912 amounted to 3,048,250 francs.

[3] The authority of the Prefect extends over the whole department of the Seine including the communes outside of the City of Paris proper and in addition the communes of St.-Cloud, Sèvres, and Meudon (Decree of 3 Brumaire, year IX). The Prefecture of Police was established by the Law of 28 Pluviose, year VIII, and the Consular decree of 12 Messidor of the same year.

The Police Department in the State

of the last century Paris alone has determined the event, while the political fickleness of her people has become proverbial. As in London, therefore, but for radically different reasons, the police department of Paris has been held under the firm control of the central government.

Subject to the supervision of the Minister of the Interior,[1] the Parisian Prefect of police has absolute authority in the management of the force. His is the most powerful police office in France. In him are centered the police functions not only of the French *Maire* but of the department prefect as well. Moreover, the commanding influence of his position is such that the supervision of the Minister of the Interior is more lightly exercised in his case than in the case of the departmental prefects. He appoints and dismisses all members of his force; he frames and promulgates *arrêtés* and ordinances relating to the protection of life and property, the abatement of nuisances, the supervision of aliens and political suspects, and various matters of national importance. In Paris, as in London, national and local interests are inextricably blended, and those who champion the cause of prefectoral government as against the municipal autonomists base their argument on the necessity, arising out of these conditions, for a perfect understanding and an unbroken harmony between the machines of national and local administration.[2]

In depriving the Parisians of the local supervision of

[1] The control is exercised through the office of the *Sûreté générale*. See note 2, p. 87.
[2] For an able discussion of this point, see *Municipal Government in Continental Europe*, Albert Shaw, New York, 1906.

their police, the French government has maintained a semblance of municipal control which has been of considerable service in softening the harsh outlines of an arbitrary form of administration. Thus it is obligatory upon the Prefect of police to submit his annual budgetary estimates for the ensuing year to the popularly elected Municipal Council, and to consult that body in matters involving the expenditure of money. This would seem hardly more than reasonable in view of the fact that the greater part of the expense of the police is borne by the municipality.[1] Furthermore, the Prefect is required to appear before the Council upon demand to answer such questions as any member may choose to ask him relative to the work of his department, so far as it is connected with finance. To be sure, the power of the Council is limited to the passage of votes of censure. It has no authority to interfere with the policy of the police or their system of organization. It cannot even reduce any item of the budget, but must allow it in sum total. " Need I add that I am already assured of the assent and support of the Minister of the Interior " is the veiled but significant sentence with which the Prefect frequently accompanies his communications to the Municipal Council.[2] At the same time, the Prefect and his superiors in the Ministry of the Interior always attempt

[1] The Paris police budget for 1914 amounted to 46,595,050.60 francs, of which 13,980,744 were paid by the national exchequer, the balance by the city upon vote of the Municipal Council. The amount of the national subsidy is annually determined by a special law passed by the French parliament, generally upon the advice of the Minister of the Interior. For detailed statement of the budget see Appendix II, on page 393.

[2] *Bulletin officiel de la Ville de Paris,* July 13, 1913, etc.

to work in harmony with the municipal authorities, and as far as is practicable to comply with their wishes. The attempt does not always succeed. Of late, a bitter antagonism has marked the relations of the two bodies, so that for three years the Council has refused to vote its share of the police expenditure until forced by the arbitrary action of the Ministry. But the right of the municipal authorities to participate in the activities of the Police Prefect and to be consulted in matters of policy and finance has at least tempered the arbitrariness of the system, and reconciled the majority of the Parisians to a form of administration far more autocratic and severe than that of any other French city.

ITALY

Of the large countries of Europe Italy maintains the greatest uniformity in the control of her police, in this respect outstripping even France. The system is entirely centralized. Local autonomy in police affairs is scarcely more than a name. Indeed, except in minor matters, police authority throughout the kingdom is exercised by national constabulary forces controlled from Rome.[1] Essentially a democratic country, Italy clings to many of the forms of autocracy. The conditions

[1] The local government of Italy has so closely followed the French model, that the resemblance between the two amounts almost to duplication. The kingdom is divided into 69 provinces, corresponding closely to the French departments. At the head of each province is a prefect appointed by the Crown, and directly responsible to the Minister of the Interior. For further details, see *The Governments of Europe,* Frederic Austin Ogg, New York, 1913, pp. 383 ff., and *Governments and Parties in Continental Europe,* A. Lawrence Lowell, Boston, 1896, Vol. I., Ch. III.

surrounding the struggle for a united kingdom are largely responsible for this situation. In view of the menace of foreign interference it was necessary to consolidate the different provinces thoroughly and rapidly, and to destroy, once for all, the effectiveness of local opposition. Italy lacked homogeneity. The country was divided not only by historical circumstance and tradition, but by social, economic, and even racial differences. Southern Italy was, and to a certain extent is to-day, illiterate, disorganized, and suspicious of authority, with an almost total lack of social cohesion. A united Italy involved in the minds of its builders the necessity of a highly centralized and even arbitrary administration.

Out of this situation the police system developed, and such is the force of tradition that, even with the initial conditions modified, but few changes have been made in its organization and control. There are three kinds of police in Italy: the *Carabinieri,* the corps of the City Guards,[1] and the Municipal Police. The first two are military organizations under the direction of the Ministry of the Interior, and the last is made up of the small and relatively unimportant local forces maintained under the authority of the various town councils to enforce local ordinances.

The *Carabinieri* correspond roughly to the French and German *gendarmerie.*[2] There is, however, an important distinction. In France and Germany the *gendarmerie* corps is used to maintain order in the country districts and in the smaller villages and communes which

[1] *Corpo delle Guardie di Città.*
[2] See note I, p. 73.

92

The Police Department in the State

have no adequate police protection. In Italy the *Carabinieri* are employed in cities, towns, and country districts without distinction. Everywhere, throughout the kingdom they represent the authority of the central government. An army of 31,000 men,[1] they are distributed in 3,700 different towns and villages. Rome herself has 900 of them regularly patroling her streets, while an occasion of disorder will bring a thousand more to assist in keeping the peace.

This remarkable corps, in many respects the finest police force in Europe, deserves special attention. Dating from the 16th century as a branch of the army of the Kingdom of Piedmont, it was adapted by Cavour and his followers to the needs of the united country. It is to-day an integral part of the Italian army,[2] equipped and maintained in full military fashion, and dependent, as far as its technical and military organization is concerned, on the Ministry of War.[3] It consists of eleven legions each with a colonel at its head, the whole corps being under the command of a lieutenant-general.[4]

[1] This number includes 720 commissioned officers and about 1800 recruits in the training school.

[2] As a branch of the army the *Carabinieri* corps may be sent to the front in case of war. In fact, a large number of them saw actual fighting in the late war with Tripoli.

[3] The maintenance of the *Carabinieri* is included in the annual budget of the Ministry of War. The Ministry of the Interior, however, contributes to the sum thus raised an amount theoretically designed to cover the cost of the *Carabinieri* as far as their police duties are concerned. The amount contributed by the Ministry of the Interior for the year 1913-1914 approximated 30,500,000 lire.

[4] Every legion has within its jurisdiction several of the civil provinces or departments. As a legion is generally separated into divisions under the control of majors, it generally happens that there is a single division for each province; so that the prefect of a province or his agents, as the representatives of the Minister of the

93

European Police Systems

Service in its ranks is equivalent to service in any other division of the army. Only in the performance of the special police duties to which it has been assigned is it responsible to the Ministry of the Interior. As a matter of fact, the *Carabinieri* are used as the agents of all departments of the government. They conduct judicial investigations, obtain information for the postal and health authorities, make inquiries into the character and standing of civil-service applicants, and perform a great variety of duties of an important and often delicate nature. Supported by the War Department, they are employed by the Ministry of the Interior not only to maintain order, but to act as the agents by which the government is kept in touch with conditions throughout Italy.

Police duty, however, is their important function. Patroling always in pairs, and easily distinguishable by their broad cockade hats, they are to be found in even the smallest villages of Italy. Their ranks are recruited by careful and painstaking selection. Thoroughly trained, always courteous, respected by the people everywhere, they are fairly comparable with the Royal Irish Constabulary among the military police forces of Europe.

The other police force responsible to the Ministry of the Interior is the corps of the City Guards. This organization, established in 1865, was designed to supplement the work of the *Carabinieri*. It was felt that the rigid military organization of the latter body was not adapted to all the requirements of police work in Italy, particularly the work relating to the detection of crime

Interior, deal directly with a major of the *Carabinieri*, and in questions relating to police duty, are his superior officers.

The Police Department in the State

in the larger towns. A new force was therefore created on a more mobile plan and placed exclusively under the jurisdiction of the Ministry of the Interior.[1] At the present time it consists of 10,500 men and officers distributed in 149 of the more important towns and cities of the kingdom.[2] It is organized on a semi-military basis, with a lieutenant-colonel at its head.[3] Theoretically it handles the more subtle phases of police function. It generally assumes charge of the detective work in connection with the more important cases. Practically, it is sometimes difficult to distinguish between its proper functions and those of the *Carabinieri* in the cities in which detachments from both forces are on duty. Thus in Rome one sees both City Guards,[4] and *Carabinieri* engaged in the regular patrol work, to say nothing of the Municipal Police who handle the traffic and enforce the local ordinances. Even in the detection of crime the *Carabinieri* are not without responsibility, and frequently, both in Rome and elsewhere, two independent investigations are made of criminal cases, sometimes with every appearance of rivalry and conflict.[5] As a result, the

---

[1] The entire expense of this body is included in the budget of the Ministry of the Interior.

[2] And two cities in Tripoli.

[3] The force is divided into six groups or divisions, each division, under the direction of a major, having its headquarters in some large city from which the work of the guard in the surrounding towns is controlled. The distinction between the *Carabinieri* and the City Guards as respects organization and discipline is summed up by Italian officials in the words "military" and "militarized" as applied to the two respectively.

[4] The City Guard wears a dark blue loose-fitting uniform with a vizored cap. He lacks the smartness and soldier-like bearing of the *Carabiniere.*

[5] The Camorra scandals in Naples were unearthed by the *Carabinieri* after the City Guards had failed, a fact which has added

relations between the two forces in some of the cities are often far from harmonious.[1]

That they work together with any degree of coöperation is due to the form of control exercised by the Ministry of the Interior. The primary agent of control is the Prefect of the province, directly responsible for police arrangements in his territory. Subordinate to the Prefect, but appointed by the Minister of the Interior, are the officials of the Division of Public Safety,[2] one of whom, generally a *questore*,[3] directs the activities of both the *Carabinieri* and the City Guards for the entire province. Assisting the *questore* either in the city in which he is located or in other towns and cities as his representatives are the *commissari* and *delegati,* who form the lower grades of the service in the Division of Public Safety.[4] Thus there is a *questore* for the province in which Rome is situated,[5] who is responsible for

greatly to the prestige of the former body, and intensified the feeling of rivalry between the two organizations.

[1] Italian students of administrative law have not been slow to recognize that two independent police forces cannot always be made to work harmoniously together, and there has been considerable criticism of the existing system. Indeed, some years ago, a bill was introduced in the Italian Senate proposing the amalgamation of the two bodies. Nothing, however, came of it, and it is doubtful whether any steps will be taken in the near future to correct the anomaly.

[2] *Il Servizio di Pubblica Sicurezza.* See Royal Decree, N. 690, dated August 31, 1907. This division constitutes a branch of the Ministry of the Interior.

[3] In provinces of less than 100,000 population, the police force is under the direction of a *commissario* rather than a *questore.* (See Royal Decree N. 690, Art. 4.) There are twenty-two *questori* in Italy, one for each of the important provinces.

[4] There are altogether in Italy 270 *commissari,* 117 *vice-commissari,* and 1325 *delegati.* The methods by which the men of this service are trained and promoted, we shall study in Chap. V.

[5] Lazio. The *questore* is known by the city in which his headqarters are located. Thus there is a *Questore di Roma,* a *Questore*

The Police Department in the State

the proper policing of the territory. He is indeed the Police Commissioner of Rome and its suburbs, in charge of the *Carabinieri* and City Guards assigned to him. He plans their separate tasks, arranges their patrols, and supervises their activities. In everything which relates to their work, he is their sole director.[1] The police control of his district is centralized in his hands.

In the sixty-nine provinces of Italy similar conditions prevail, the prefect in each case controlling through the *questore* or *commissario,* the given number of *Carabinieri* and City Guards assigned to him. One has only to remember that the prefects are appointed by the Minister of the Interior to realize how firm and uniform is the grip of the government upon the police throughout the kingdom.

A word is due in conclusion to the so-called Municipal Police, who, as we have seen, are organized in various towns and cities of Italy under the authority of the town councils to enforce the local ordinances. Distinctly inferior to the *Carabinieri* and the City Guards, they play a relatively unimportant part in the police problem. They guide traffic in the streets, supervise public markets and slaughter houses, and have generally to do with the police aspects of public health. They are indeed empowered to make arrests for any crime, but they never assume to interfere with the work properly belonging to the *Carabinieri* and the City Guards, by whom they are

di Napoli, a *Questore di Milano,* etc., each in charge of the police arrangements of the *entire province* of which his headquarters city is the capital.

[1] He has nothing to do, of course, with questions of recruiting, training, remuneration, or conditions of service. These matters are handled by the higher officers of the respective forces.

often contemptuously regarded. For reasons of public order, they may be temporarily suppressed by the Minister of the Interior and their functions handed over to the City Guards.[1] There is little uniformity between their various organizations. They are often poorly trained and equipped, and as a rule, poorly paid. Frequent endeavors have been made to consolidate them with the City Guards, but the attempts have been defeated by the municipalities which have clung desperately to this last vestige of local autonomy in police matters.[2] It is improbable, however, that the consolidation proposed will be much longer postponed.

[1] Royal Decree, N. 690, Art. 19.
[2] In 1879 Minister of the Interior Villa actually succeeded in effecting a consolidation, but it did not long hold together. Crispi's attempt in 1889 was equally unsuccessful.

CHAPTER III

WE must now consider the organization or framework of the police departments to discover how their various functions and groups are arranged for systematic cooperation. Here, as in the case of the powers and functions of the police, we must be prepared to encounter wide divergences. The German department is necessarily elaborate, for it is adapted to the many things which it is called upon to do; the English department is relatively simple, as its functions are few and obvious. In order to bring these matters clearly to the attention of the reader, the first section of this chapter will deal with the plan of police organization in London, Berlin, Vienna, Budapest, Paris, Rome, Brussels and Amsterdam, using each of these cities as a standard by means of which the other cities in the same country may be judged; in the second section the characteristic methods and principles previously discovered will be compared.

European Police Systems

I

London.

The Metropolitan Police Force, exclusive of the Commissioner and his administrative staff, consists of 20,529 men: 33 superintendents, 607 inspectors, 2,747 sergeants, and 17,142 constables [1] or patrolmen. This force patrols an area of 447,626 acres or 700 square miles, comprising roughly all the territory within a fifteen-mile radius of Charing Cross, including the whole of Middlesex and London counties and parts of Surrey, Kent, Essex, and Hertfordshire, but excluding the ancient City of London, where, as we have seen,[2] a separate force is maintained by the corporation. This area was arbitrarily created by statute. It has a population (1911)

---

[1] These figures, which are given as of Dec. 31, 1912, include the men assigned to the detective division.

[2] See note 2, p. 39. The City of London covers an area of approximately one square mile, including the heart of the business section of the metropolis. It has a day population of 375,-000 with a night population of only 19,000, while over a million people enter its precincts daily between the hours of 7 A. M. and 7 P. M. Traffic matters and commercial crimes are its chief police problems. Its police force consists of 1100 uniformed men and 80 detectives under the control of a commissioner, an assistant commissioner and a chief superintendent. The commissioner is appointed by the corporation of the City with the approval of the King, the latter step being purely perfunctory, a relic of old struggles between city and Crown.

For police purposes the City is divided into three districts, each in charge of a chief inspector. Each district has two divisions or precincts with a station. The City constables are uniformed like the metropolitan constables, except for a slight variation in the shape of the helmets, and the fact that the former wear red and white striped sleeve bands, while the latter have blue and white. Both the Metropolitan police and the City police have the privilege of making arrests in each other's territories.

[3] The City of London and the Metropolitan police district are together known as "Greater London" and form a recognized area, used in the census and other publications of the Registrar-General, and commonly adopted in the consideration of many of London's problems.

ORGANIZATION OF THE METROPOLITAN FORCE OF LONDON

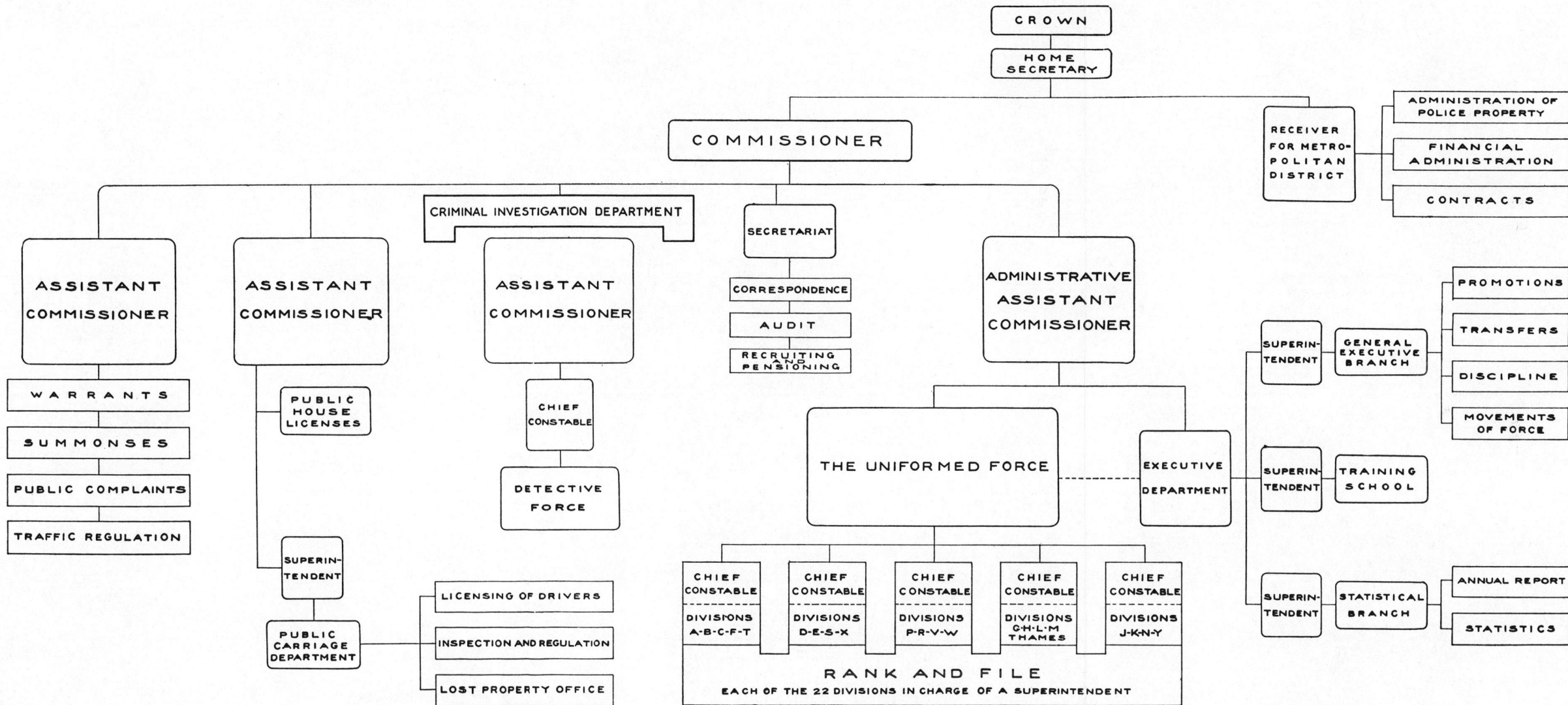

CROWN

HOME SECRETARY

COMMISSIONER

RECEIVER FOR METROPOLITAN DISTRICT
- ADMINISTRATION OF POLICE PROPERTY
- FINANCIAL ADMINISTRATION
- CONTRACTS

ASSISTANT COMMISSIONER
- WARRANTS
- SUMMONSES
- PUBLIC COMPLAINTS
- TRAFFIC REGULATION

ASSISTANT COMMISSIONER
- PUBLIC HOUSE LICENSES
- SUPERINTENDENT
  - PUBLIC CARRIAGE DEPARTMENT
    - LICENSING OF DRIVERS
    - INSPECTION AND REGULATION
    - LOST PROPERTY OFFICE

CRIMINAL INVESTIGATION DEPARTMENT

ASSISTANT COMMISSIONER
- CHIEF CONSTABLE
  - DETECTIVE FORCE

SECRETARIAT
- CORRESPONDENCE
- AUDIT
- RECRUITING AND PENSIONING

ADMINISTRATIVE ASSISTANT COMMISSIONER

THE UNIFORMED FORCE

EXECUTIVE DEPARTMENT

SUPERINTENDENT — GENERAL EXECUTIVE BRANCH
- PROMOTIONS
- TRANSFERS
- DISCIPLINE
- MOVEMENTS OF FORCE

SUPERINTENDENT — TRAINING SCHOOL

SUPERINTENDENT — STATISTICAL BRANCH
- ANNUAL REPORT
- STATISTICS

CHIEF CONSTABLE — DIVISIONS A-B-C-F-T

CHIEF CONSTABLE — DIVISIONS D-E-S-X

CHIEF CONSTABLE — DIVISIONS P-R-V-W

CHIEF CONSTABLE — DIVISIONS G-H-L-M THAMES

CHIEF CONSTABLE — DIVISIONS J-K-N-Y

RANK AND FILE

EACH OF THE 22 DIVISIONS IN CHARGE OF A SUPERINTENDENT

Organization of the Police Department

of 7,233,306. It is not coterminous with any other governmental jurisdiction, exceeding by 582 square miles the territory of the London County Council and by 280 square miles the Central Criminal Court district. This immense territory is divided into twenty-one districts, called "divisions."[1] Each such division has a force of police in charge of a superintendent promoted from the ranks. In addition there are five divisions consisting of the men employed in the dockyards and military stations outside of the Metropolitan district,[2] and another division specially engaged in policing the River Thames. Each of the twenty-one regular divisions is divided into from two to five sub-divisions, in charge of a sub-divisional inspector. A sub-division contains one or more police stations, each under the direction of an inspector or station sergeant.[3] All constables of the Metropolitan force are attached to some station. The district served by each police station is divided into sections in charge of sergeants. Each section is again divided into beats to which constables are assigned from time to time.

This huge organization is under the control of a Commissioner,[4] four assistant commissioners, and six chief

[1] These divisions are lettered from A to Y omitting I, O, Q and U. Each constable wears on his collar and his helmet the letter of the division to which he is attached.

[2] These divisions are located at the dockyards of Woolwich, Portsmouth, Devonport, Chatham, and Pembroke. The force thus engaged consists of 1,200 men. Their services are paid for by the National Government (see note 4, p. 45).

[3] There are, altogether, 198 stations in the Metropolitan district.

[4] Sometimes erroneously referred to as the *Chief* Commissioner. In the provincial cities of England and Scotland the head of the police department generally has the title "Chief Constable." In Liverpool, Cardiff, Newport, and some ten or twelve smaller towns, he is called "Head Constable."

constables,[1] who with a secretarial staff [2] direct operations from the police headquarters at New Scotland Yard.[3] Here, too, are located the headquarters of the Criminal Investigation Department or detective bureau, together with the Public Carriage Office and other lesser divisions of a general nature. An officer called the Receiver for the Metropolitan police district also has his office at New Scotland Yard. Like the Commissioner, he is appointed by the Crown upon the recommendation of the Home Secretary, and is hence independent of the Commissioner. In him is vested the title to all lands, buildings, stores, clothes and other property necessary for the purposes of the police; he purchases sites, builds new stations, enters into contracts, keeps police property in repair, makes up the annual budgetary estimate and is generally responsible, under the authority of the Home Secretary, for the *materiel* of the force and for the administration of its finance. He is in fact the business manager.

Such, in outline, is the organization of the Metropolitan Police Force. Viewed from the standpoint of administration, the Commissioner and the assistant commissioners are engaged on a common task. The enormous

[1] The assistant commissioners are appointed by the Crown upon the recommendation of the Home Office; the chief constables are appointed directly by the Home Office. In making the latter appointments, the recommendation of the Commissioner generally prevails. For further discussion see Chap. V.

[2] This force consists of the Commissioner's secretarial staff of 55 Civil Service clerks whose employment at Scotland Yard is permanent. Constables are not used for this particular service, although they are often detailed to clerical or "inside" duty in the divisions and elsewhere, and undertake the clerical work of the several executive departments of New Scotland Yard.

[3] Popularly known as *Scotland Yard* from the fact that the old headquarters were for years located in Scotland Yard off Whitehall.

Organization of the Police Department

burden of the directive work has made division and specialization necessary, and accordingly, each of the assistant commissioners, under the supervision of the Commissioner, assumes his own particular share of the administrative function. Thus one of the assistants is the head of the Criminal Investigation Department or detective office; another has charge of promotions, discipline and other duties of an executive nature relating to the uniformed force — in fact, he is called the " Administrative Assistant Commissioner"; another handles public carriage problems, and saloon licenses; the fourth has charge of the civil business of the department, the issuance of warrants and summonses, traffic regulations, and the investigation of public complaints. None of the assistant commissioners is assigned to supervise any particular district or territory. Each has, under the immediate direction of the Commissioner, his own specialized functions for the entire Metropolitan district.[1]

Turning our attention to the uniformed force, we find the so-called *division* not only the unit of administration, but the chief factor of the organization. The twenty-one divisions of the Metropolitan police district are ir-

---

[1] In addition to the four assistant commissioners, there is a so-called Executive Department located at Scotland Yard consisting of three branches, the Statistical Branch, the Training School Branch, and the General Executive Branch, each in charge of a Superintendent from the uniformed force. The Statistical Branch compiles the figures shown in the annual report of the department, and in the judicial statistics of the Metropolitan district, published yearly by the Home Office. The General Executive Branch has charge, under the Administrative Assistant Commissioner, of transfers, promotions, movements of force, etc.; it also carries out the instructions of the other assistant commissioners in regard to the issue of process, etc.

103

regularly grouped to form a great circle, thirty miles in diameter, with Charing Cross as its center. The divisions vary in area from three-quarters of a square mile [1] to eighty-three square miles,[2] with an average population of 350,000. The police force of a division numbers from 600 to 1,200 men. Some of the division forces are therefore as large as the entire force maintained in cities like Birmingham, Sheffield, Leeds, or Edinburgh, and the responsibilities of the superintendents may well be compared with those of the chief constables of the provincial towns. As already noted, the superintendent of the division comes from the ranks, rising from grade to grade by gradual promotions. Entering as a constable, he subsequently becomes a sergeant, and later attains successively the positions of inspector, sub-divisional inspector, the chief inspector. As we shall see in a later chapter, these promotions are all discretionary with the Commissioner.[3] It is seldom that a man receives a superintendency unless he has been at least twenty years in service.[4]

The superintendent is responsible for the effective policing of his division. He is the connecting link between Scotland Yard and the divisional organization. All reports to the administrative officials as well as information and orders for the uniformed force pass through his hands. He is answerable for the discipline of his men; he has the power of suspension and may

[1] Division C.
[2] Division S.
[3] Chap. VII, p. 246.
[4] As we have seen, there are 31 superintendents; 21 are assigned to the divisions, one to the Thames branch, and nine to headquarters and the dockyards for special services.

Organization of the Police Department

inflict fines to the amount of two days' pay.[1] He has charge of the detectives assigned to him by the Criminal Investigation Department. The " subdivisions " under him, and the police station districts included in them, are units of his sectional organization whose only relation with the administration of Scotland Yard is through him. In other words, the administrative policy of the Metropolitan force is one of decentralization, each of the twenty-one superintendents controlling his own territory.

This thoroughgoing decentralized organization is modified by the introduction of a factor of control which has been copied in Paris and in other Continental cities. Between the Commissioner and the assistant commissioners on the one hand, and the superintendents of the divisions on the other, there are six chief constables. One of these chief constables is assigned to the Criminal Investigation Department. Each of the other five, however, controls a district consisting of a group of four or five contiguous divisions. In other words, the Metropolitan police territory is divided into five great administrative districts, each containing a group of divisions and each in charge of an officer who does not come from the ranks, but who, as we have seen, is appointed by the Home Office upon the recommendation of the Commissioner.[2] The importance of this arrangement

[1] The question of discipline is dealt with at length in Chap. VII.

[2] The districts are as follows: —

District	Divisions comprising district
No. 1	A, B, C, F, and T.
No. 2	D, E, S, and X.
No. 3	P, R, V, and W.
No. 4	G, H, L, M, and the Thames.
No. 5	J, K, N, and Y.

can scarcely be overestimated. In the district under him, the chief constable is the direct representative of the Commissioner. He must be acquainted with the problems of his district, and the character of his men. He is the Commissioner's eyes and ears. All reports from his superintendents to headquarters pass through his hands; all requests for information relative to occurrences in his district are sent to him. He has charge of the discipline of the men in cases too serious to be dealt with by the superintendents, and exercises a general supervision over all matters connected with the organization and work of the force under him.

It is customary to choose the chief constables either from the army or from the legal profession; *they are never taken from the uniformed force.* It is believed that the man who has entered the force as a constable seldom has the breadth of vision or the point of view essential to the satisfactory performance of the supervisory functions attached to the office.[1] A chief constable occupies a unique position of trust; his relations with the Commissioner are intimate and confidential; his work calls for a high degree of intelligence and judgment. It is felt therefore that better results can be obtained by securing men of thorough training and broad experience in other administrative fields. The chief constable is appointed for an indeterminate period, conditioned only on " good behavior." The retirement of the Commissioner above him has no effect upon his term of office,[2] and except where death or old age nec-

[1] This subject is more fully developed in Chap. V.
[2] As we shall see (Chap. IV), the Commissioner himself is

Organization of the Police Department

essitates new appointments, a change is seldom made.[1]

" Decentralize as far as you can; centralize as far as you must." This is the maxim of Scotland Yard, its program of organization. In carrying out this program, the office of chief constable is the control. Its purpose is to give the Commissioner adequate and trustworthy supervisory machinery. It furnishes the essential element of adhesiveness in the huge decentralized organization of the Metropolitan force. Without that element the organization would fall apart and slip from the grasp of the Commissioner, eventually taking on the form of twenty-one separate departments, or at least, a loose aggregation of divisions over which the Commissioner could exercise at best but a feeble control. For no Commissioner can hope alone to keep in touch with the shifting problems and changing needs of a vast city like London. Even the four assistant commissioners can give him but little help in this respect, for, in a city of London's size, the administrative work of the office is great enough to require the constant attention of four or five men, each performing his own specialized part, with no time for the supervision of any particular district or section. In a smaller city, where the entire administrative function can be handled by the chief constable, the deputies or assistants may well be expected to perform the duty of district supervision. Indeed, in a medium-sized town with but few police divisions or districts, the duty may

seldom changed, there having been but six commissioners in the last eighty-five years.
[1] The office of chief constable was established in 1869, when four were appointed. Until 1886 they were called district superintendents. Although detailed as the Commissioner's representatives in particular districts, their offices are in Scotland Yard.

even be left to the chief constable, who can depend upon the chiefs of his uniformed force. But an aggregation of twenty-one huge districts containing 200 police stations cannot be so administered. Under such circumstances, the office of chief constable in London, filled by trustworthy and experienced men of the Commissioner's own choosing who are detailed as his representatives in their respective districts, is perhaps the most important single feature of the entire Metropolitan organization.

The Provincial Cities of England and Scotland.

The organization of the police departments of the provincial cities of England and Scotland is patterned after that of the Metropolitan system of London. The same plan is followed in dividing the city and the force into "divisions." Each division is presided over by a superintendent promoted from the ranks, and the superintendents are responsible to a commissioner or chief constable. In Liverpool there are seven such divisions, in Manchester five, in Glasgow nine. As in London, the divisions have their subdivisions and substations under the charge of inspectors and sergeants.[1] Each city has its commissioner or chief constable, appointed, as we have seen, by the Watch Committee of the Town Council.[2] The larger cities have one or two assistant chief

---

[1] In Scottish cities the rank of "lieutenant" comes between those of inspector and superintendent, the title "Chief Inspector" being merely an office title. The lieutenant performs practically the same functions as the English chief inspector, namely, acting as the right-hand man and *alter ego* of the superintendent. Occasionally other differences in title are found, as between the various provincial cities. Thus, in Manchester the Assistant Chief Constable is called Chief Superintendent, etc.

[2] See Chap. II, page 51.

Organization of the Police Department

constables, but the supervisory officer known in the Metropolitan force as chief constable, coming between the Commissioner and the uniformed force, has no counterpart in any of the provincial cities. This officer is not needed in a smaller city, for, in the absence of an overwhelming amount of administrative detail, and with but a limited number of divisions under the control of uniformed superintendents, the supervisory functions can easily be handled by the Commissioner and his assistant, or in still smaller towns, by the Commissioner alone.

The structural plan of the police department of the provincial city is therefore extremely simple. The prevailing uniformity is largely due to the London model and to the influence of the Home Office and the Scottish Office, which, through the application of the supervisory powers granted to them by Parliament, have been able, as we have seen,[1] to standardize the provincial police organizations.[2]

Berlin.

Special police provision has been made for Greater Berlin just as it has been made for Greater London. The district over which the Police President presides, called

---

[1] See Chap. II, page 49.
[2] Liverpool has a total police force of 2,148 men of whom 400 are assigned to, and paid by, the Mersey Dock and Harbor Board. Excluding the latter there is one constable to every 426 of the population. Manchester has a force of 1,350, or one to every 536 of the population. Glasgow has a force of 2,020, or one to every 388. Edinburgh, with a force of 624, has one police officer to every 529. The Metropolitan district of London has one officer to every 354 of the population. Comparisons of this kind have little significance, however, as many factors, such as nationality, nature of prevailing industry, etc., alter the conditions in different cities and necessitate a varying amount of police protection.

Landespolizeibezirk, includes not only the city of Berlin proper, but the neighboring suburbs of Charlottenburg, Schöneberg, Neukölln,[1] and Lichtenberg as well.[2] That is, Greater Berlin stretches far beyond the geographical limits of the city. There is an important difference, however, between the *Landespolizeibezirk* of Berlin and the Metropolitan district of London. In the latter, a single police force has jurisdiction throughout the entire territory; in the former, there is a separate police organization under the control of a president for each of the suburbs mentioned above, but the Police President of Berlin is superior to the other presidents. In other words, there are five distinct departments within the area of Greater Berlin, each having jurisdiction in its own territory, but each ultimately subordinate to the Berlin official.[3] The purpose of this peculiar arrangement was undoubtedly to confer upon the Berlin authorities the special powers attaching to a *Landespolizeibezirk,* or state police district, in addition to their powers as local police. The Berlin Police President ranks with a *Regierungspräsident,* or civil head of a district, in his right to enforce the laws relating to detention[4] and domicile.[5] Further, he may assemble the

[1] Formerly Rixdorf.

[2] *Law of June 13, 1900. Collection of Laws 247.*

[3] The jurisdiction of the Berlin police in penal matters and offenses involving the services of the morals police *(Sittenpolizei)* extends to the furthest limits of Greater Berlin (*Laws of June 12, 1889. Collection of Laws 129*).

[4] *Reichsstrafgesetz,* Par. 362. This refers to the right of the police to turn a prisoner over to the local magistrates for further punishment after he has been fined or imprisoned by the police themselves for violations of certain sections of Par. 361 of the Penal Code.

[5] *Law of Freedom of Removal (Freizügigkeit)* of November 1,

ORGANIZATION OF THE POLICE DEPARTMENT OF BERLIN

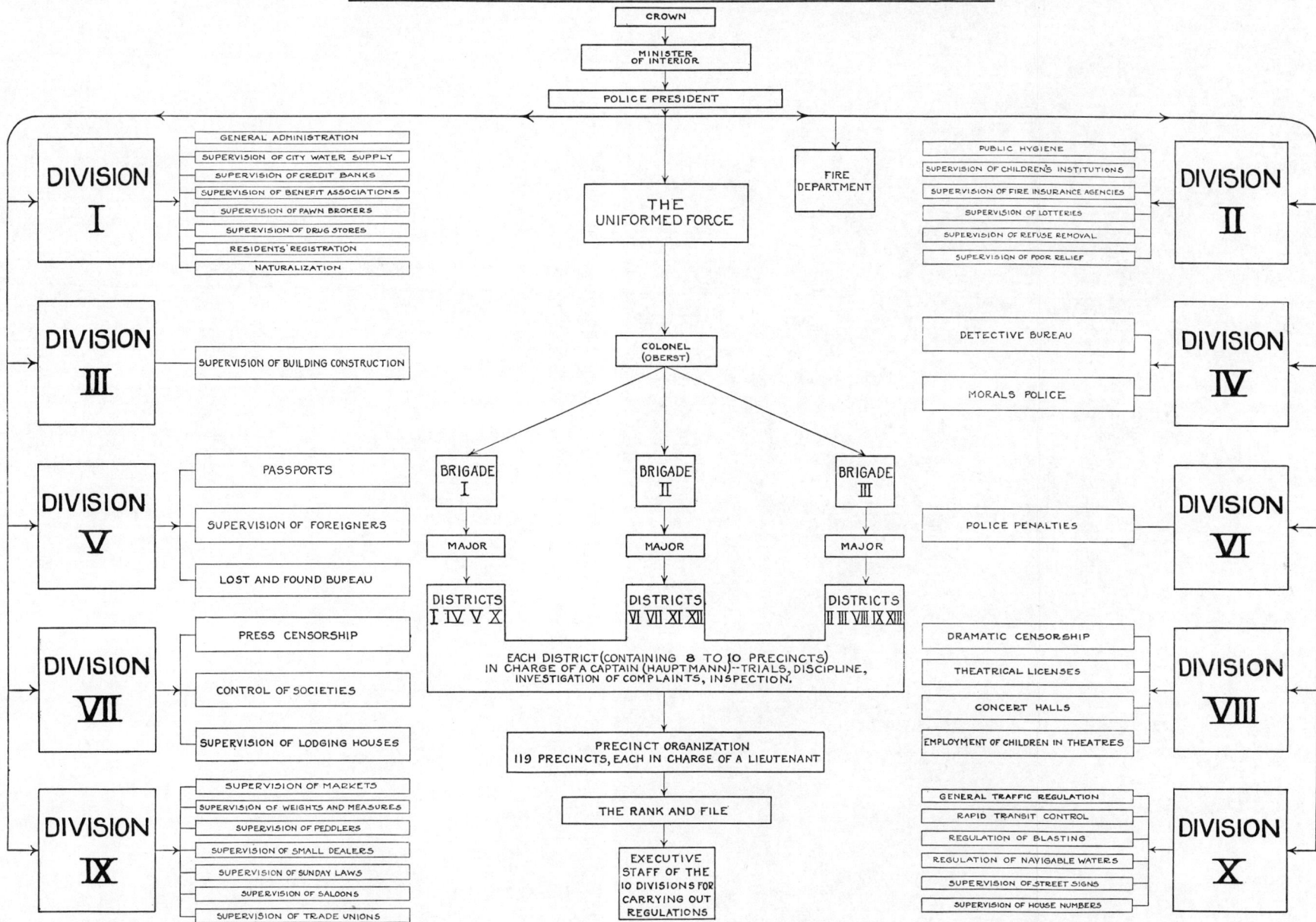

CROWN

MINISTER OF INTERIOR

POLICE PRESIDENT

DIVISION I
- GENERAL ADMINISTRATION
- SUPERVISION OF CITY WATER SUPPLY
- SUPERVISION OF CREDIT BANKS
- SUPERVISION OF BENEFIT ASSOCIATIONS
- SUPERVISION OF PAWN BROKERS
- SUPERVISION OF DRUG STORES
- RESIDENTS' REGISTRATION
- NATURALIZATION

DIVISION III
- SUPERVISION OF BUILDING CONSTRUCTION

DIVISION V
- PASSPORTS
- SUPERVISION OF FOREIGNERS
- LOST AND FOUND BUREAU

DIVISION VII
- PRESS CENSORSHIP
- CONTROL OF SOCIETIES
- SUPERVISION OF LODGING HOUSES

DIVISION IX
- SUPERVISION OF MARKETS
- SUPERVISION OF WEIGHTS AND MEASURES
- SUPERVISION OF PEDDLERS
- SUPERVISION OF SMALL DEALERS
- SUPERVISION OF SUNDAY LAWS
- SUPERVISION OF SALOONS
- SUPERVISION OF TRADE UNIONS

FIRE DEPARTMENT

THE UNIFORMED FORCE

COLONEL (OBERST)

BRIGADE I → MAJOR → DISTRICTS I IV V

BRIGADE II → MAJOR → DISTRICTS VI VII XI XII

BRIGADE III → MAJOR → DISTRICTS II III VIII IX XIII

EACH DISTRICT (CONTAINING 8 TO 10 PRECINCTS) IN CHARGE OF A CAPTAIN (HAUPTMANN)--TRIALS, DISCIPLINE, INVESTIGATION OF COMPLAINTS, INSPECTION.

PRECINCT ORGANIZATION
119 PRECINCTS, EACH IN CHARGE OF A LIEUTENANT

THE RANK AND FILE

EXECUTIVE STAFF OF THE 10 DIVISIONS FOR CARRYING OUT REGULATIONS

DIVISION II
- PUBLIC HYGIENE
- SUPERVISION OF CHILDREN'S INSTITUTIONS
- SUPERVISION OF FIRE INSURANCE AGENCIES
- SUPERVISION OF LOTTERIES
- SUPERVISION OF REFUSE REMOVAL
- SUPERVISION OF POOR RELIEF

DIVISION IV
- DETECTIVE BUREAU
- MORALS POLICE

DIVISION VI
- POLICE PENALTIES

DIVISION VIII
- DRAMATIC CENSORSHIP
- THEATRICAL LICENSES
- CONCERT HALLS
- EMPLOYMENT OF CHILDREN IN THEATRES

DIVISION X
- GENERAL TRAFFIC REGULATION
- RAPID TRANSIT CONTROL
- REGULATION OF BLASTING
- REGULATION OF NAVIGABLE WATERS
- SUPERVISION OF STREET SIGNS
- SUPERVISION OF HOUSE NUMBERS

Organization of the Police Department

entire force of his greater district at any point in any section to quell a riot or handle a strike. He can nullify an ordinance issued by the lesser authorities. As a matter of practice, however, the police presidents of the suburban districts are left practically undisturbed to deal with their own affairs. When we speak of the Berlin police, therefore, reference is made not to the greater district, but to the police organization of the *city* of Berlin,[1] a distinct unit within the wider administrative jurisdiction of the police president.[2]

The police organization of Berlin, like that of all German cities, is shaped to perform the many functions which, as we have seen, are thrust upon that division of the public service.[3] The department is divided into twelve

1867. The liberty to change one's domicile within the state is, historically, a recent right in Prussia. As late as the eighteenth century the state police imposed considerable restrictions. In 1842, however, liberty of abode was formally established by law, and in 1867 the legislature of the North German Confederation passed a general statute covering the whole subject. By this law every citizen has complete right to remain in any place within the country where he is able to provide himself with a living, but exceptions are made in cases of persons who have been punished for offenses, particularly those who have been punished within a year for beggary or vagrancy. Foreigners, however, may be expelled by each of the several states when their presence is deemed dangerous to public safety and order. A foreigner thus expelled has no right of appeal to the administrative courts. Finally, the Penal Code makes it a crime punishable by fine or imprisonment for one liable to military service to leave the federal territory without permission. For an excellent discussion of the operation of this law, see James, *loc. cit.*, Chap. VII.

[1] Greater Berlin has a population of 3,772,962. The city of Berlin has 2,071,257. (1910.)

[2] Thus the uniformed force of Berlin has nothing to do with the force of Charlottenburg or Neukölln, for example, nor may a Berlin officer make an arrest in the other jurisdictions without permission.

[3] The Berlin police department as far as the organization of its uniformed force is concerned, was established in 1848.

European Police Systems

branches (*Abteilungen*), each representing a particular function or group of functions, more or less logically arranged, and each under the control of a director or chief, responsible to the Police President. The branches are as follows:

I.— General administrative oversight of police matters, including buildings, office supplies, uniforms, rates of pay, pensions; supervision of credit banks, benefit associations and pawn brokers; naturalization; oversight of drug stores, doctors' certificates, residents' registration (*Einwohnermeldeamt*); arbitration court for workingmen's insurance; supervision of the city's water supply.

II.— Meat inspection; supervision of veterinaries and stockyards; oversight of children's asylums and matters relating to adoption; fire insurance agencies and lotteries; control of the food supply; supervision of health matters; oversight of snow and refuse removal; destruction of agricultural insect pests; poor relief.

III.— Building department; supervision of all matters relating to the erection of buildings.

IV.— Criminal department (detective branch); morals police; transport of prisoners from state to state.

V.— Passports and banishments; supervision of foreigners; relief to impoverished travelers; funeral permits; lost and found department.

VI.— Supervision of police penalties (*Strafverfügungen*).[1]

VII.— Press censorship; control of societies and

[1] See Chap. I, page 24.

112

Organization of the Police Department

meetings; supervision of guests at hotels and lodging houses. (*Gasthofspolizei.*)[1]

VIII.— Dramatic censorship, control over concerts, moving-picture exhibitions; theatrical licenses and employment offices; concert halls; lectures and recitations; employment of children in theaters.

IX.— General supervision of businesses; supervision of markets and fairs, weights and measures; Sunday laws; trade union matters; return of escaped apprentices; control of inns, saloons and retail dealers in spirituous liquors; trade certificates; supervision of porters, errand boys, truck-men, coopers, scissors grinders, tinkers, plaster of·Paris hawkers; bottled beer dealers; dancing and swimming teachers.

X.— General traffic supervision, street railways, rapid transit, omnibuses and automobiles, roller-skates; naming, closing and lighting of streets; supervision of house numbers, street signs, sign boards, building lines, blasting, monuments, airships, control of navigable waters, sluices, locks, bridges.

XI.— Fire Department.

XII.— Uniformed police force (*Schutzmannschaft*).

All these departments are centralized in the mammoth police headquarters in Alexanderplatz, Berlin,[2] where

---

[1] For the purposes of control over hotels and boarding houses. Berlin is divided into twenty districts with two policemen assigned to each. Their function is to visit twice a day the hotels and boarding houses in their districts, looking for suspicious characters. Their services are particularly valuable in case "alarms" or "informations" have been received from other cities.

[2] Berlin is now trying an experiment in decentralization, called the "*Bezirk-Amt*" plan. It is proposed to divide the city into six administrative districts, giving to each some of the functions which are now exclusively handled from police headquarters. Thus, matters relating to business-control, building and health inspection, etc.,

European Police Systems

the machinery of control is highly concentrated. Each has its own officers and own administrative staff. For the purposes of this study, however, we are especially interested in only two of the branches, namely, the uniformed force (*Schutzmannschaft*) and the detective division (*Kriminal-Abteilung*).[1] The other branches, as we have seen, represent functions not essentially of a police nature, which in Great Britain are for the most part delegated to state and local governments, although some of them have no counterpart in any governmental activity outside of Germany.

The uniformed force of Berlin is therefore a separate division, which, with eleven others, is under the control of the Police President. At the same time, it is the executive arm of all the divisions, carrying out their decrees and policies whenever the services of men in uniform are necessary. Thus the force supervises theaters under the direction of Division VIII, or controls trades and businesses under Division IX. In affairs relating to its own finances, it is subject to the direction of Division I. But in its relation to the Police President it is equal in standing with the other divisions and its chief or colonel (*Oberst*) is responsible to him alone.

would be administered by districts rather than from one central bureau, and the citizens would be saved the necessity of making long trips across the city. The uniformed force, the detective division, the morals police, the fire department, etc., are not affected by this plan, inasmuch as it is believed that these functions cannot be satisfactorily decentralized.

At the present time, only one such administrative district has been established (the inner city — population 215,000). The plan is bitterly opposed by some of the Berlin officials, to whom centralization represents the last word in efficiency.

[1] Discussed in Chap. VIII.

Organization of the Police Department

In respect to its plan of organization, the titles of its officers and the fact that men and officers are recruited from the army, the uniformed force is on a military basis, operating according to military principles and traditions. It may perhaps be more accurately described as the military branch of a civil organization. At the present time (1913), it consists of one colonel (*Oberst*), three majors, nineteen captains (*Hauptleute*), 158 lieutenants, seventeen first sergeants (*Oberwachtmeister*), 452 sergeants (*Wachtmeister*), and 5,724 patrolmen (*Schutzmänner*), a total of 6,374 men. Patrolmen can be promoted to the grade of first sergeant, but no further; the higher officials are recruited from the ranks of army officers.

The city of Berlin is divided into 118 precincts (*Reviere*) each under the supervision of a lieutenant. For the purposes of discipline and control, the precincts are grouped into thirteen districts (*Hauptmannschaften*), each in charge of a captain, and each containing from eight to ten precincts. The districts are in turn grouped into three brigades, each under the control of a major.

The precinct is the unit of administration — the pivotal point of the entire organization. It contains from thirty to a hundred of the uniformed force and serves a district varying from 3,500 inhabitants in the inner precincts to 45,000 in the outskirts. The lieutenant in command is not promoted from the ranks, but is chosen from among officers in the army or from the legal profession after special training.[1] Except in so far as special functions are centralized at headquarters and managed from special bureaus, this officer has entire charge of his

[1] See Chap. V, p. 183.

precinct, and is responsible for the conduct of the men under him. He assigns them to duty and regulates their work. Through the telegraph and telephone he is constantly in touch with headquarters and an " alarm " or an " information " comes to him directly without passing through the hands of his superior administrative officers. His immediate superior is the captain of the district in which his precinct is located. The captain is mainly occupied with discipline and with the investigation of complaints relative to the conduct of the uniformed force. All disciplinary trials are held, in the first instance, before him, and his findings are forwarded through the major of his brigade to the colonel. In addition to these disciplinary duties, the captain has certain inspectional duties relative to conditions in his district, although these matters are generally left to the lieutenants. Under the direction of the major of his brigade the captain shares, also, in the administration of his force.

The functions of the three majors are almost exclusively administrative. They are the adjutants of the colonel. Their duties correspond to those of assistant commissioners in English cities, but with this distinction: the administrative functions of Scotland Yard have been separated and specialized, so that each assistant assumes his proportionate share; in Berlin, the functions are divided by districts, and each major takes entire charge of a particular section.[1]

Finally, at the head of the uniformed division, as its chief administrative officer, is the colonel. He obtains

[1] A comparison of the Berlin majors with the London chief constables is scarcely pertinent, since the former officials have no inspectional functions to perform.

his position by promotion from the rank of lieutenant through the grades of captain and major. Neither in Berlin nor in any other Continental city is a uniformed chief of police ever promoted from the lower ranks. Not only would such a step be regarded as subversive of discipline, but, as in the case of the chief constables in London, it is not believed that the officer who has walked the streets as a patrolman has the education or point of view requisite in a responsible administrative official.

Other German Cities.

With but slight modifications, although on a smaller scale, the method of departmental organization obtaining in Berlin is found in every large German city. Official titles differ, and the grouping of functions into bureaus or branches is never exactly the same, but in broad outline there is a marked similarity between the systems of the various cities. Under the control of a police president or director, each department has a number of branches of which the uniformed force is but one;[1] in each the uniformed division is the executive arm

---

[1] In Dresden there are ten branches; in Hamburg, eight; in Stuttgart, six; in Munich, five; in Leipzig, eight. Hamburg's divisions are typical of the rest. They are as follows: —
  I. General administration, including residents' registration, etc.
  II. Detective branch and morals police.
  III. Business and traffic regulation.
  IV. Political police, including press censorship and control of meetings and societies.
  V. Welfare police, including sickness and accident insurance, missing persons, public safety in theaters, assemblies, etc.
  VI. Health police — hospitals, contagious diseases, ambulances, veterinarians, etc.
  VII. The uniformed force.
  VIII. Harbor police.

European Police Systems

of the other branches, although ranking equally with them in its relation to the police president; in each the uniformed force is organized on a military basis, under the immediate administrative control of a colonel or captain. In other words, throughout the German cities the uniformed force of the police department is, as it is in Berlin, a military branch of a civil organization.[1]

[1] In respect to the method of dividing a city into districts for police purposes, there is but little variation in Germany. The use of the same names in different cities for districts in no way similar or even comparable, occasionally produces the appearance of diversity, but beneath the variable nomenclature the same idea is at work.

Thus, the precinct or unit of administration which in Berlin is called *Revier* is in Dresden called a *Bezirk,* or district, while the Berlin *Bezirk* is the *Revier* in Dresden. In the same way, in Munich and Hamburg, the word *Wache* is used for the precinct. There are thus three words signifying practically the same thing.

In the larger cities there are three classes of districts, the smallest being the precincts. For purposes of supervision, these units are grouped into larger districts, which in turn are assembled into several divisions under the control of superior officers. Thus, as we have seen, Berlin is divided into precincts *(Reviere),* which in turn are grouped into districts *(Bezirke)* and brigades. So, too, Hamburg has its *Wachen,* or small unit areas, three or four of which form a district *(Bezirk),* while two or three districts are grouped into a division. The *Wachen* are in charge of first sergeants *(Oberwachmeister)* ; the districts are controlled by district commissioners; and the divisions are under the captains *(Hauptmänner),* who are recruited from among army officers. In other words, Hamburg intrusts her precincts and districts to the administration of noncommissioned officers coming from the ranks, using the commissioned officers only for the supervision of the largest groups, or divisions; while, in Berlin, none of the administrative work is performed by non-commissioned officers, even the precincts being in charge of those chosen outside of the service.

In the smaller cities of Germany there are generally two groupings rather than three — precincts and districts. Thus, in Dresden there are twenty-five precincts *(Bezirke),* each in charge of a first sergeant (called *"Inspektor"* in Dresden), who comes from the ranks. The precincts are grouped into four districts *(Reviere),* each under a lieutenant or commissioned officer chosen from the army. Practically similar arrangements are to be found in Munich, Leipzig, and Stuttgart.

Organization of the Police Department

Vienna.

In Austria, and especially in Vienna, the relative simplicity of police function produces an organization which is perhaps more nearly comparable with London's system than with Berlin's, although certain interesting characteristics peculiarly Austrian have been developed. The many diverse and often incongruous functions of the Berlin department have no counterpart in the police system of Vienna.[1] The various functions of the Vienna department are grouped into three sections, each under a separate head, with the uniformed force as a distinct division under the immediate control of a colonel or chief (*Zentralinspektor*). In this respect the department approximates the German system. The functions included under the three sections, however, are comparatively simple. The detective department forms one section;[2] another handles passport (*Passamt*) and traffic matters, the lost and found bureau, and residents' registration (*Einwohnermeldeamt*); the third deals with press censorship, the control of public meetings, the morals police and the sanitary department. If three or four of these functions were eliminated, the duties and the organization, if not the spirit, of the Vienna police might well be applicable to an English city.

As in German cities, the uniformed force of Vienna (called *Sicherheitswache*) is a military organization under civil control. More accurately, perhaps, it may be

[1] Many of the functions which in Germany are assigned to the police, are in Austria given to the *Statthalterei*, or Imperial governors of the districts into which, for administrative purposes, Austria is divided. (See note 2, p. 79.)

[2] See Chap. VIII.

described as a civilian body of watchmen, organized, uniformed, and armed on a military model.[1] It differs from the German forces in one striking respect: its higher officers, including its chief (*Zentralinspektor*), are lawyers and university men rather than army men. The preponderance of university graduates in law, occupying the higher positions of the police departments, is one of the striking features of police organization in Austria and Hungary. The uniformed force of Vienna at the present time (1913) consists of 66 commissioned officers, 403 sergeants (called *Inspektors*), and 4,127 *Sicherheitswachmänner,* or policemen, making a total force of 4,596.[2] The same disability which exists in Berlin relative to the promotion of a patrolman to a rank higher than first sergeant holds also in Vienna. Occasionally a policeman is promoted through the grade of sergeant (*Inspektor*) to a commissioned officership of low rank (*Revier* or *Bezirksinspektor*), but he can go no higher. While a few of the commissioned officers are taken from the army, most of them, as we have said, including all of higher rank, are university graduates in law.

For police purposes, Vienna is divided into twenty-one districts[3] (*Bezirke*), each of which has its own organization and quota of officials collectively designated as a

[1] The *Sicherheitswache* of Vienna was established in 1869 by Imperial decree. It took the place of the Military Police Guard (*Militärpolizeiwache*), an organization dating from the year 1776. In the year of its establishment (1869), the *Sicherheitswache* consisted of 15 commissioned officers and 1,352 men.

[2] Vienna's population is 2,031,498 (census of 1910).

[3] The same districts are used which are employed for representative purposes in the City Council, except that one of the larger city districts (*Gemeindebezirke*) is divided to make two police districts.

ORGANIZATION OF THE POLICE DEPARTMENT OF VIENNA

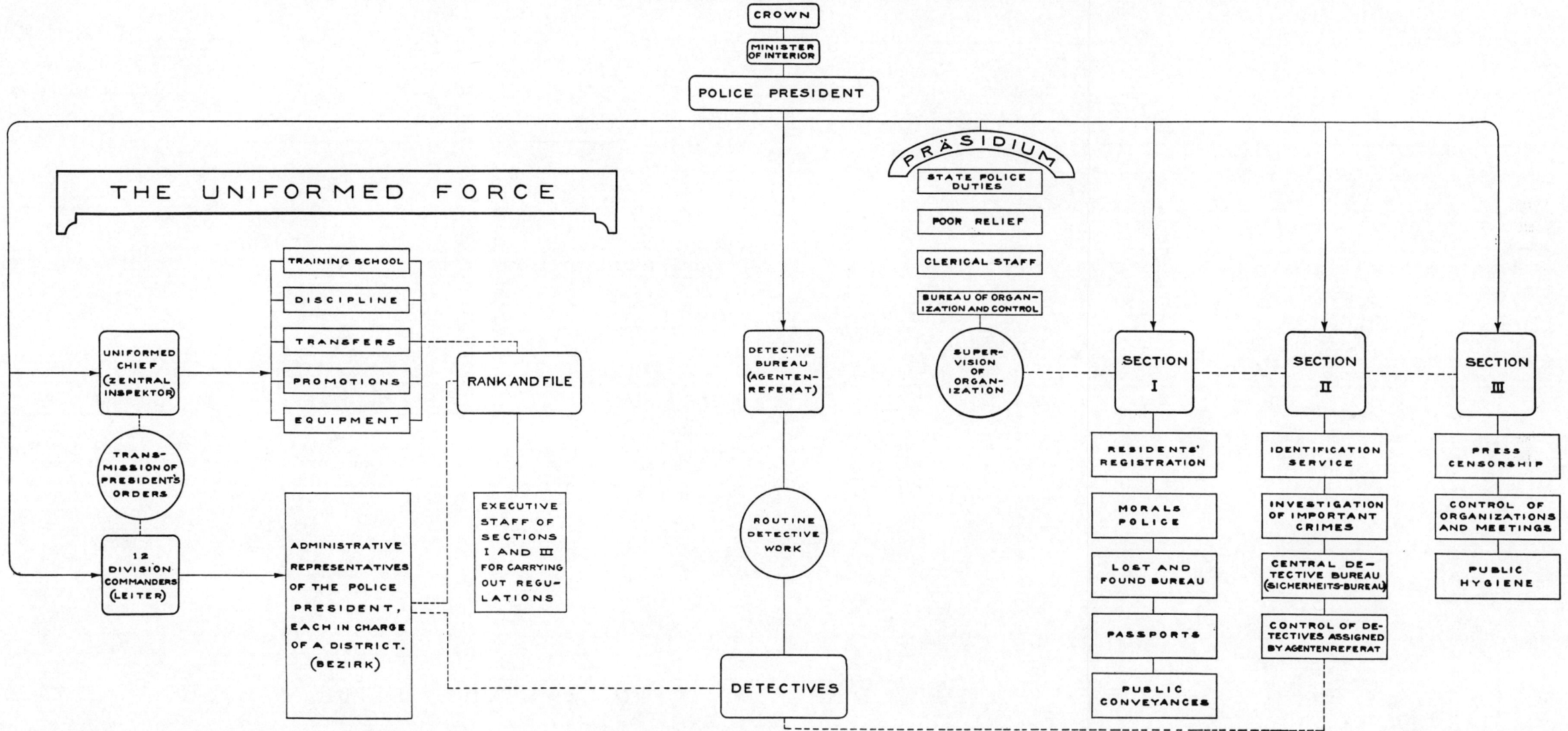

CROWN

MINISTER OF INTERIOR

POLICE PRESIDENT

THE UNIFORMED FORCE

TRAINING SCHOOL

DISCIPLINE

TRANSFERS

PROMOTIONS

EQUIPMENT

UNIFORMED CHIEF (ZENTRAL INSPEKTOR)

TRANSMISSION OF PRESIDENT'S ORDERS

12 DIVISION COMMANDERS (LEITER)

RANK AND FILE

EXECUTIVE STAFF OF SECTIONS I AND III FOR CARRYING OUT REGULATIONS

ADMINISTRATIVE REPRESENTATIVES OF THE POLICE PRESIDENT, EACH IN CHARGE OF A DISTRICT. (BEZIRK)

DETECTIVE BUREAU (AGENTEN-REFERAT)

ROUTINE DETECTIVE WORK

DETECTIVES

PRÄSIDIUM

STATE POLICE DUTIES

POOR RELIEF

CLERICAL STAFF

BUREAU OF ORGANIZATION AND CONTROL

SUPERVISION OF ORGANIZATION

SECTION I

RESIDENTS' REGISTRATION

MORALS POLICE

LOST AND FOUND BUREAU

PASSPORTS

PUBLIC CONVEYANCES

SECTION II

IDENTIFICATION SERVICE

INVESTIGATION OF IMPORTANT CRIMES

CENTRAL DE-TECTIVE BUREAU (SICHERHEITS-BUREAU)

CONTROL OF DE-TECTIVES ASSIGNED BY AGENTENREFERAT

SECTION III

PRESS CENSORSHIP

CONTROL OF ORGANIZATIONS AND MEETINGS

PUBLIC HYGIENE

Organization of the Police Department

Kommissariat. Each district has its own chief station or office, and in addition, from four to fifteen watch-rooms (*Wachzimmer*) which form the centers of control for policemen on duty. That is, each small squad of men under the supervision of a sergeant has a central point from which its movements can be regulated and checked. The units of administration, however, are the districts, with populations varying from 44,000 to 177,-000, and uniformed forces of from 85 to 330 men. The *Kommissariat,* and the district which it represents, is under the control of an official with the title *Polizeirat* or *Regierungsrat,* a title with no equivalent in the English language, but which, for convenience, we shall call " District Commander." The district commander is the administrative representative of the Police President; he is a civil employee in the sense that he is not a member of the uniformed force (*Sicherheitswache*). This characteristic of Vienna's organization stands out in marked contrast, not only with the German system, but, outside of Austria and Hungary, with other Continental cities as well. In Berlin, for example, as in Hamburg or Dresden, the district representative of the Police President, the head of the precinct or division, the official who is responsible for the territory assigned to him as well as for the conduct of his men, is himself a member of the uniformed force even though he may have entered the service, not from the ranks, but in some higher capacity. In Vienna, on the other hand, the district commander has no connection with the uniformed force, and although he may at one time have served as a higher officer in its ranks, he ordinarily enters the department directly from the university as an assistant administrative official (*Konzeptsbeamter*). He and his assistants and clerks who form the *Kommissariat* are the local representatives of the Police President, employing the uniformed force assigned to their district as an executive force to carry out their directions. Each such force in a district has its *Kommando* or captain,[1] who takes his orders, as far as his work and duties are concerned, not from the head of the uniformed force, but from the district commander. The head of the uniformed force (*Zentralinspektor*) deals with matters pertaining to discipline and the material welfare of his men, such as clothing and accoutrements. He also has charge of the police school, and of transfers from one district to another, together with such other functions as concern the force as a whole. With the duties of his men in their respective districts, however, he has nothing whatever to do; being of equal rank with the district commanders, he can issue no orders to them save such as emanate from the Police President.

This arrangement results in the development of a separate administrative staff of civilians for each of the twenty-two police districts into which Vienna is divided. The district commander, as head of the staff, is assisted in his duties by a number of *Konzeptsbeamte,* or deputy administrative officials, all of whom must be university graduates in law. These, with the necessary clerks (*Kanzleibeamte*), make a total administrative force in each of Vienna's districts of from seven to seventeen men,

---

[1] Generally with the title of *Bezirksinspektor*. These men are for the most part selected from those who have entered the service from the army.

Organization of the Police Department

who, while they form no part of the regular uniformed force, are yet responsible for its work in their several territories.[1]

The policy of administrative decentralization above described relieves the heavy burden which the cities of Germany so often lay upon the Police President and his immediate assistants. Indeed, in Vienna, there is but one assistant to the President, a sort of vice-president or deputy commissioner (*Hofrat*), who assumes some of the executive work and takes the President's place in his absence. The remaining administrative functions are exercised by the heads of the three sections, by the *Zentralinspektor* as commander of the uniformed force, and by the twenty-two district commanders. This decentralized administration which is in such marked contrast to the Berlin plan, is coördinated by a device unique in the police departments of Europe — the Bureau of Organization and Control. Under the direct supervision of the Police President, and not included in one of the three sections which we have mentioned, are several smaller bureaus, some of them of a clerical, some of an administrative nature. The Bureau of Organization and Control is one of these smaller departments, created for the purpose of coördinating and adjusting the various parts of the police mechanism. Its object is to eliminate fric-

[1] In addition to the regular police work in their districts, the administrative officials are also local executives in respect to some of the functions coming under the three sections of the police department above noted. The centralization characteristic of Berlin's department in regard to these extra-police duties is foreign to the Vienna organization. In fact, the new "*Bezirk-Amt*" experiment in Berlin (see note 2, p. 113) was copied from Vienna's decentralized method of dealing with the functions which fall outside of the regular scope of police work.

123

European Police Systems

tion, to act as a clearing house for information, and to supervise the investigation of complaints relating to the force. Its director has the right, with the approval of the Police President, to make any changes in the organization or install any forms or devices which he deems necessary. More than any other factor it serves not only to systematize the work of the department and to keep the entire mechanism in smooth running order, but to give the Police President adequate control over the various phases and parts of his organization.

Budapest.

Budapest, in Hungary, has patterned her police organization largely after the Vienna system, although in certain respects she has followed the German model. Thus the uniformed force is a strongly centralized military organization in marked contrast to the decentralized, semi-military system in Vienna.[1] This point deserves particular attention. Budapest is divided into fourteen

[1] Budapest's police department is divided into seven branches of which the uniformed force is one, each branch being responsible directly to the Police President. The branches are as follows:
- I. President's Division, which is the chief executive office.
- II. Administrative Division, which includes many of the unrelated functions which are thrust upon the police department, such as passport matters, character certificates, lost and found bureau, saloon licenses, control of employment agencies and places of amusement, execution of the white slave traffic law, etc. This division also includes the morals police who handle the question of prostitution and street walkers.
- III. The Detective Division, including residents' registration and the assessment of penalties.
- IV. Prison Division.
- V. The Uniformed Force.
- VI. Bureau of Criminal Records.
- VII. Accounting Division.

Organization of the Police Department

Kommissariate, or districts, each in charge of a district commander, who, as in Vienna, is not a member of the uniformed force, but is a civil official of the department and a university graduate in law. The control of the uniformed force assigned to the various districts, however, does not rest with the district commander, as in Vienna, but is vested in the *Inspektor* (lieutenant), who is the district's highest ranking member of the uniformed force, and the direct representative of the chief of the force, the *Oberkommandant.*[1] In other words, under the direction of the President, the *Oberkommandant* controls the uniformed force in all the districts. He is responsible not merely for the discipline and material well-being, but for the entire work of the force, issuing his orders directly to his inspectors in the districts. As a result, the functions of the district commander are more limited than those of his fellow officer in Vienna. He is rather a legal adviser to the district inspector, handling, in addition, matters relating to passports, residents' registration, and penalties imposed by the police (*Strafverfügungen*).[2]

By a curious fiction the district commander is made the superior officer of the *Inspektor,* and as such has the power to countermand the orders issued by the *Oberkommandant.* As a matter of practice, however, the district commander takes but little part in strictly police business, confining his attention to the semi-legal functions which devolve upon his department.

A second point of distinction between the uniformed

[1] The *Oberkommandant* corresponds to Vienna's *Zentralinspektor.*
[2] See Chap. I, p. 124.

forces of Vienna and Budapest lies in the fact that the latter is a strictly military organization, all of whose commissioned officers, from the *Oberkommandant* down to the inspectors or lieutenants, are recruited directly, from the army. The present *Oberkommandant* [1] served twelve years with the Austro-Hungarian troops, reaching the rank of first lieutenant; he entered the police force as an inspector and is now the head of the uniformed division, after twenty-six years of service. Budapest is opposed to the practice of officering the uniformed force with university graduates in law. Not only does she believe in the German military ideal of a police force, but she pushes it beyond anything to be found in Germany. Her uniformed division is simply a military troop of 3,000 men, armed like soldiers, living in barracks under strict military discipline, ready for active service at the call of a bugle. In no other fashion, the authorities of Budapest believe, can their population be adequately controlled. [2]

Paris.

The organization of the police force of Paris is as involved and complicated as Berlin's, embracing many

[1] In addition to the *Oberkommandant* there are two *Oberinspektors* and 14 *Inspektors* among the higher officers. Below them are the non-commissioned officers — the sergeants and corporals — promoted from the ranks. A non-commissioned officer is never promoted to the grade of commissioned officer.

[2] The police of Budapest have jurisdiction in the greater city; that is, the department includes the ten districts (*Bezirke*) of the city, and in addition, three in the suburbs; while the city government of Budapest has jurisdiction only in the ten city districts.

The department consists of 3,000 uniformed men, including 205 mounted men.

ORGANIZATION OF THE POLICE DEPARTMENT OF PARIS

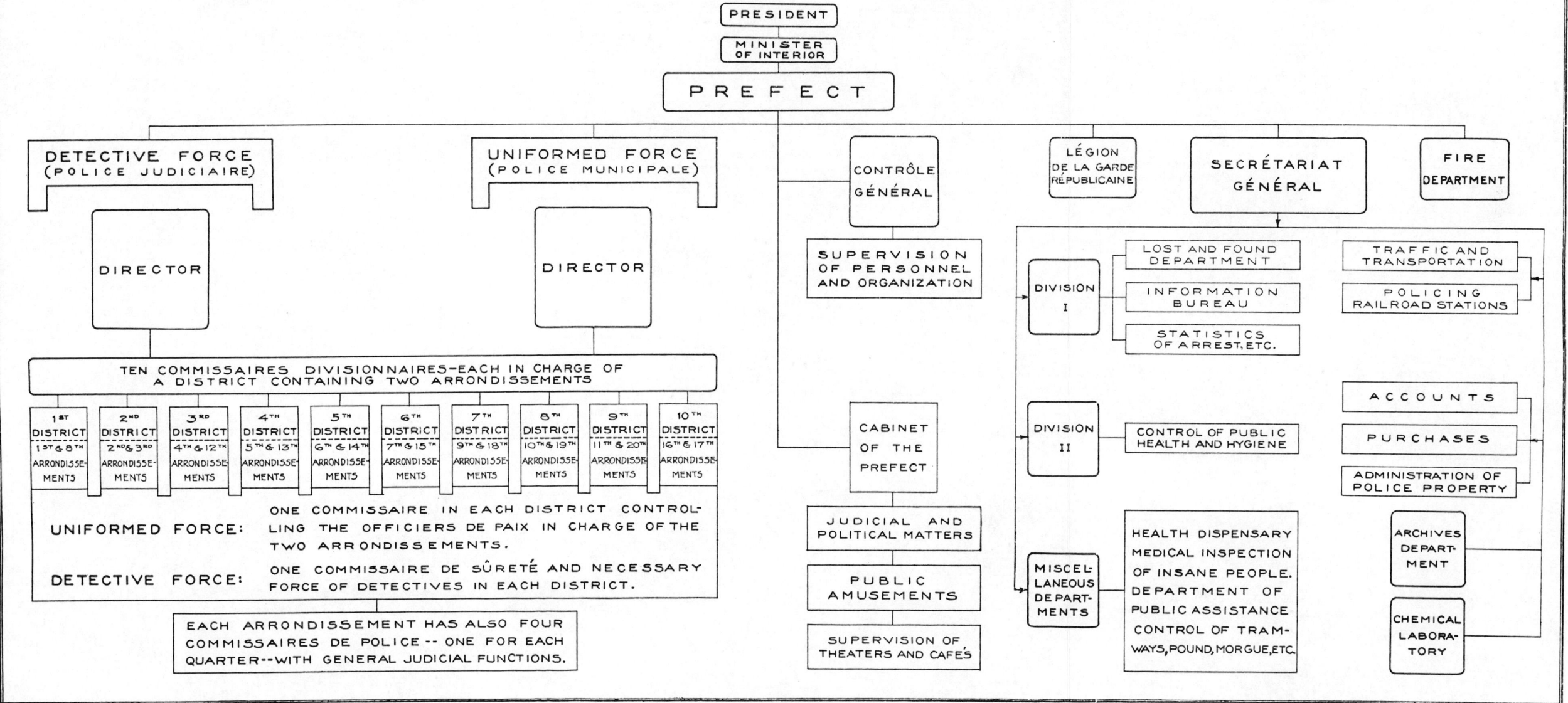

Organization of the Police Department

functions which in England and Austria are handled by municipal and state governments. Matters relating to public health and hygiene, to street railroads, to dangerous substances, to the prevention of fire, to pure food, and to a hundred other subjects are all part of the police function. To execute these many diverse tasks, as we have already noticed in the case of Berlin, a necessarily extensive organization is required; but in respect to the nature of the organization there is considerable difference between the two cities. In Berlin, the functions are grouped, with more or less attention to similarity and relationship, into twelve branches or departments, each under the head of a director or chief, responsible to the Police President. In Paris, on the other hand, a large number of branches, divisions, sections, commissions and committees are grouped irregularly about the Prefect of police, each sustaining to him a more or less direct relationship. The uniformed police (*Police municipale*) constitutes one of these distinct branches or divisions; the detective department (*Direction des recherches*) another; the fire department (*Régiment de sapeurs-pompiers*) still another. The largest single department under the Prefect is the *Secrétariat général,* which, organized by divisions and bureaus, handles the many functions which in England are largely cared for by the state and municipality.[1] In addition

[1] The *Secrétariat général* is organized in four divisions and two departments, each division containing from two to five bureaus which in turn are subdivided into sections. The functions of this branch of the police department cover a wide range of subjects, such as forced sales and liquidations, inquiries regarding old age pensions, visé of passports, registration of peddlers, licensing of messengers, medical examination and registration of nurses, control of day nurseries and lying-in hospitals, destruction of caterpillars,

European Police Systems

to these branches, the so-called *Cabinet du Préfet* has charge of judicial and political matters and questions of general safety and public amusements, together with the oversight of theaters and cafés. There are, in addition, twenty-one smaller bureaus or supervisory divisions (*Services extérieurs*) responsible directly to the Prefect, with functions covering a great variety of subjects, ranging from the inspection of mushrooms to the oversight of street railroads.[1] Finally the *Contrôle général* exercises, under the direction of the Prefect, general administrative supervision over the personnel of the entire force, roughly approximating in function Vienna's bureau of organization and control.

We have spoken of the division of the *Police municipale,* as the uniformed force. As a matter of fact, there are two uniformed forces in Paris under the control of the Prefect. In addition to the *Police municipale,* the " Republican Guard " (*Légion de la Garde Républicaine*) an integral portion of the national gendarmerie, performs many duties which in other European cities are committed to the regular police. Under the direct control of the Prefect, it guards the public buildings and offices, takes charge of the traffic at certain points, as-

beetles and thistles, control of smoke consumers, sirens and whistles, statistics of prices current, surveillance and control of sales in wholesale houses, inspection of foodstuffs, control of traffic and vehicles, building material permits, etc.

[1] Some of the functions of these bureaus are as follows: Medical inspection of aliens, veterinarian supervision, weights and measures, the morgue, the pound, inspection of dangerous establishments, control of automobiles, the medical inspection of the insane, contagious diseases, etc. In addition to these twenty-one bureaus of supervision, there are twelve permanent commissions or committees under the control of the Prefect of police, dealing with matters relating to sanitation, the examination of conductors and motormen on street cars and trams, child-labor, etc.

Organization of the Police Department

sumes responsibility for much of the mounted police work, and handles the crowds in congested quarters and on holiday occasions. It also acts as a reserve force which can be brought at a moment's notice to the relief of the regular police. The French authorities have learned that the handling of an excitable Parisian crowd cannot safely be left exclusively to the regular police force. Therefore, this supplementary guard of approximately 3,000 men, a purely military organization of twelve companies of infantry and four squadrons of cavalry, under the control of a colonel or commandant, is placed at the disposal of the Police Prefect. The striking uniforms and long swords of these guards make them easily distinguishable from the regular police of the city.[1]

Unlike the uniformed police forces of the German cities, which are organized on a military basis, the *Police municipale* — that is, the regular uniformed force of Paris — is a body of civil servants which, with the exception of one or two titles and the fact that some of the men are ex-soldiers, possesses but few military features or characteristics. In this respect, as in other respects which will be pointed out, the organization of the force is very similar to that of the Metropolitan police of London. In fact, in 1854, the force was modeled after the London

[1] The *Garde Républicaine* was organized by the *arrêtés* of July 5, 1848, and February 1, 1849. The force consists (1913) of 83 officers, 792 horsemen, and 2,118 men on foot, 200 of whom are equipped with bicycles. The expenses of this force are entered on the budget of the Ministry of War, amounting (in 1912) to 6,999,-187 francs. The municipality of Paris pays approximately half of this sum.

The Prefect of Police may also have the services of seven sections of the national *gendarmerie* whenever, in his judgment, they are required. (*Arrêté des Consuls du 12 Messidor, Year VIII*, Art. 36.)

pattern. It is under the control of a *directeur,* who, a civil employee himself, is immediately responsible to the Prefect. He is assisted in his duties by a deputy and by ten division inspectors (*commissaires division-naires*) [1] whose functions are similar to those of the chief constables of London, each of them being assigned to one of the ten administrative districts into which Paris is divided. The division inspectors, like the director and his assistant, are civil employees, chosen ordinarily from other grades in the governmental service. In other words, while the German plan is followed in maintaining the uniformed force as a separate branch on an equal footing with the many other branches of the police department, the Parisian force is essentially a body of watchmen commanded by civil employees rather than by army officers as in Germany, and organized with only a slight leaning toward military forms and traditions.

The Paris force consists at the present time of 25 captains (*officiers de paix*), 31 lieutenants (*inspecteurs principaux*), 1,047 sergeants (*brigadiers* and *sous-brigadiers*) and 7,494 patrolmen (*gardiens de la paix*), a total of 8,597 men. [2] The patrolmen are recruited both from the

---

[1] Created by the decree of July 28, 1893, following the London precedent of 1869. Until 1913 there were but four of these officials. The creation of six more is a phase of M. Hennion's new plan for the reorganization of the department.

[2] The department of the Seine, over which the Prefect of police has jurisdiction, has a population of 4,154,042 (census of 1911), or one policeman to every 483 of the population. If the *Garde Républicaine* be counted as part of the police force, as indeed it should be, Paris has one policeman to every 358 of the population. Berlin has one to every 324 people; Vienna, one to every 342; London, one to every 354. As I have already explained, however, (note 2, p. 109) comparisons of this kind must not be pressed, as the necessity for police protection varies with a large number of factors.

Organization of the Police Department

army and from civil life. Promotion to the rank of captain is possible, although, as a matter of practice, the severity of the promotion examinations makes it impossible for a patrolman to reach that grade. The captains are therefore chosen by examination open to other branches of the police and government service.

For police and other governmental purposes Paris is divided into twenty districts, called *arrondissements*.[1] Each *arrondissement* is divided into four quarters (*quartiers*) making eighty in all. The police force is comprised of twenty-five companies, one for each of the twenty *arrondissements*, with the remaining five held in reserve at headquarters, where, unless needed for special emergencies, they are assigned to duty at theaters and the races, and in connection with the supervision of vehicles.[2] At the head of the police of an *arrondissement* is an *officier de paix*, or captain. Each captain has one or two lieutenants (*inspecteurs principaux*) as assistants. In each *arrondissement* there are four police stations, one for every quarter.[3] The police station force is in charge of a *sous-brigadier* or sergeant. One of the four stations of the *arrondissement*, known as *poste central*, is the headquarters of the captain. This latter official, as we have seen, bears a direct responsibility to the division inspector (*commissaire divisionnaire*) of the section in which his *arrondissement* is located. We thus observe

[1] There are thus two *arrondissements* in each of the ten administrative districts.

[2] In addition to the twenty-five companies, there are two brigades, the River Brigade and the Central Markets Brigade.

[3] Nine small supplementary stations have been erected in the larger and more densely populated quarters. If we add the stations of the market brigade and the river brigade, we reach a total number of 91.

European Police Systems

an almost complete similarity in organization between the Parisian force and the Metropolitan force of London; the ten division inspectors corresponding to the chief constables, the *officiers de paix* to the superintendents, the *inspecteurs principaux* to the chief inspectors, and the *brigadiers* to the inspectors. The analogy breaks down in attempting to compare the *directeur* of the *Police municipale* with the Commissioner in London. The former is a subordinate official responsible only for the uniformed force and nothing else, while the London Commissioner is the head of the entire department with jurisdiction over the uniformed force, the detective division, and the other subsidiary bureaus. Nor is it any more accurate to compare the Commissioner with the Prefect of police. In the English sense, the Prefect is much more than a police commissioner; he is a censor of vast authority with jurisdiction over matters which in London would include not only many of the functions of the London County Council and the borough administrative bodies, but a score of other duties which are ordinarily handled by judicial and legislative officials, if, indeed, they are handled at all.

Still another body of officials is subject to the jurisdiction of the Prefect of police. Each of the twenty *arrondissements,* as we have said, is divided into four quarters. Each quarter is in charge of a police commissary (*commissaire de police*) who, although not a member of the uniformed force, bears an intimate relation to it. He has the same administrative and judicial powers as the municipal *commissaires* who, as we saw in the last chapter, are the agents of the central government in the

Organization of the Police Department

larger French communes.   He exercises an authority
which would remind an Englishman now of a justice of
the peace, now of a police court judge, now of a coroner,
now of a sheriff, now of a truant officer, and now of a censor of public morals.[1]   A man of legal education as well
as of experience in police affairs, he is responsible for
what goes on in his quarter.   To this end he receives daily
the reports of the *sous-brigadier* of the quarter's uniformed force in regard to crimes committed, although as
far as the work and duties of the uniformed men are concerned he issues no direct orders, as the *sous-brigadier* is
responsible only to the *officier de paix* of his *arrondissement*. All prisoners arrested in the quarter are immediately arraigned before the commissary who gives them a
preliminary hearing, commits those held for trial to a place
of detention, and makes full report of his cases to the
Prefect.   In a word, the commissary is a judicial officer, combining the duties of a desk-lieutenant or station-
sergeant with those of a police magistrate,[2] and possessing, in addition, a certain local responsibility for
conditions in his district.   In this respect his influence
upon the work of the uniformed police force of his quarter
is very pronounced.[3]

[1] See *Historique de l'institution des commissaires de police, son
origine, leurs prérogatives,* by F. Euvrard, Montpellier, 1911.
[2] It should be understood that the commissary is not a judge in
the true sense, his function in cases of crime or misdemeanor being
merely a preliminary one.
[3] The office of the commissary is a survival from very ancient
times when his lineal antecedent was chosen by the people of each
parish as an arbiter in neighborhood affairs, and a dispenser of
ready justice in cases of petty offense. The present organization
was determined by the Decrees of May 21 and June 27, 1790,
which established a commissary in each of the municipal divisions
of the city, and by the Decree of Messidor 12, Year VIII (1799),

European Police Systems

Rome.

Rome has three police forces: the *Carabinieri* and the City Guards under the direction of the *questore,* and the Municipal Police under the City Council. The functions of the first two are practically identical. They relate specifically to the prevention and detection of crime and include the regular work of patrol and plain-clothes forces. The Municipal Police, confined to traffic matters and the enforcement of local ordinances, have no connection whatever with the *questore* or his department. The two groups are operated independently.

On the *questore,* therefore, rests the responsibility for the policing of Rome. In the performance of his duty, he is allowed the services of 1,730 City Guards [1] and 889

which brought the commissaries under the authority of the Prefect of police. These dispositions were finally confirmed by the Executive Decree of June 1, 1871, establishing the *commissariats* as they are at present constituted.

The commissaries are appointed by the President of the Republic upon the recommendation of the Prefect of police after a competitive examination. Each commissary has his own office situated in his quarter, with a secretary, two or three inspectors and a clerk. In addition to the commissaries of Paris, the jurisdiction of the Police Prefect extends also over the commissaries of the communes of the Department of the Seine and the three communes of Meudon, Sèvres, and Saint-Cloud *(Seine-et-Oise).* In these suburban communes the commissaries have much greater powers than those in Paris.

It will be seen that there is a slight resemblance between the Parisian commissary and the Vienna district commander, and, indeed, it has been claimed that the latter official was patterned after the former. Both have local relations with the uniformed force, although neither is a member of it. The analogy, however, cannot be pushed very far, as the district commander of Vienna has full charge of the uniformed force of his district, while the commissary is a semi-judicial officer whose powers are those of approval only, the control of the uniformed men being vested in the *officier-de-paix* of the *arrondissement.*

[1] Inclusive of ten commissioned officers.

Organization of the Police Department

Carabinieri,[1] a total force of 2,619. These two bodies he is obliged to maintain as separate organizations. Both are assigned to patrol work, both undertake detective work, but they never perform their tasks together.[2] Each is independent of the other, and rivalry rather than coöperation characterizes their activity. They have the same geographical precincts or divisions, but each body has its separate station houses. Such an arrangement would be impracticable were it not for the large force of trained officials (*commissari* and *delegati*) assigned from the Division of Public Security[3] to assist the *questore* in his administration. In charge of the work in each of the precincts, as executive directors, these officials are able not only to minimize friction, but actually to produce effective results. That they are thus successful is creditable to their training and intelligence rather than to any merit in the organization.

The Municipal Police, under the immediate supervision of a Commandant, are responsible to the mayor (*Sindaco*) and the city council (*Consiglio comunale*). More accurately they are responsible to the executive committee of the city council (*Giunta comunale*), appointed to direct the different departments of the city government. The force consists of 750 men including officers. It has its own precincts and station-houses[4] quite distinct from those of the *Carabinieri* and City

[1] Inclusive of fifteen commissioned officers.
[2] The tendency is to allow the City Guards to handle the bulk of the detective work. But the *Carabinieri* generally conduct their own separate investigations independent of the City Guards.
[3] See Chap. II, p. 96. There are over a hundred of these officials in Rome at the present time.
[4] There are twelve precincts in Rome for the Municipal Police.

European Police Systems

Guards. Except for a squad of twenty men in plain clothes permanently assigned to the City Guards to handle cases of begging and street soliciting, the force has no detective functions. Many of its men are on fixed point duty, engaged in traffic regulation. When on patrol they are assigned merely to enforce the local ordinances.

Brussels and Amsterdam.

Largely under French and German influences, Belgium and Holland have devised a composite police organization. The functions of the police are complex and extensive. Thus, in Holland the police have administrative charge of matters relating to the erection of buildings, outdoor advertising, contagious diseases, public amusements, burials, weights and measures. While less complex in Belgium, the functions of the municipal police forces are nevertheless typically Continental, extending to the surveillance of markets and the control of show-windows and other exhibitions.

Perhaps the most characteristic feature of the police departments of both Holland and Belgium is the presence of the French commissary with semi-judicial functions. The commissaries not only sit as committing magistrates, holding for trial or discharging from custody the prisoners arraigned before them, but also serve as assistants to the prosecuting attorneys, helping in the preparation of cases where the crimes are committed in their particular districts.[1]

[1] In Amsterdam, and in one or two of the smaller cities of Holland, the commissaries, in addition to their other duties, are themselves directly in charge of the uniformed men in their particular districts, while in The Hague, and in some of the Belgian

Organization of the Police Department

Brussels is to a large extent typical of other Belgian cities. As we have seen,[1] the burgomaster is himself the chief of police, with power to delegate such authority as he chooses to one of the various police commissaries. Although a commissary-in-chief has been thus designated to act as head of the department, the burgomaster himself exercises all the more important powers, including those of appointment and dismissal.[2] The police force of Brussels is relatively small and unimportant, for the reason that no advantage is taken of the opportunity to organize a single department for the greater city. " Greater Brussels " is made up of ten towns and cities with a total population of 660,000.[3] Instead of a single police force for the entire area, each town has its own separate force responsible to its own burgomaster, and operating under its own rules. A policeman of one

cities, an attempt has been made to limit the activities of the commissary by placing the district control of the uniformed men in the hands of the regular officers of the force.

[1] Chap. II, p. 67.

[2] For police purposes Brussels is divided into seven sections, each in charge of a commissary; the sections are subdivided into *quartiers* as in Paris At headquarters there is a large central office squad of 150 men *(division centrale)*, under the direct control of the commissary-in-chief, which handles all the general police duties such as the control of cabs, theaters, etc., as distinguished from the regular work of the police of the *quartiers*. Each of the seven section commissaries is responsible directly to the burgomaster for the condition of his district and the conduct of his men.

The Brussels police force consists of 1 commissary-in-chief, 8 commissaries, 60 sub-commissaries, 20 *agents spéciaux principaux* (captains), 83 *agents spéciaux* (lieutenants), 98 *agents inspecteurs*, and *brigadiers* (sergeants), and 547 *agents de voirie* (patrolmen).

[3] The towns and population are as follows (as of June 1, 1912);

Brussels	176,947	Etterbeek	33,227
Schaerbeek	85,399	Ixelles	76,405
St. Gosse-ten-Nood	32,474	Koekelberg	12,663
St. Gilles	66,592	Laeken	35,714
Anderlecht	64,425	Molenbeek-St.-Jean	73,247

town cannot effect an arrest in another town without special permission. While the inevitable friction arising from this condition is to some extent alleviated by the work of the national *Sûreté générale,* which coördinates the detective departments of all the cities of Belgium, and by other national supervisory agencies,[1] the net result of the arrangement is confusion and ineffectiveness. Under a metropolitan system such as London has devised, which would include all the communes or boroughs of Greater Brussels, the city would be at once more efficiently and less expensively policed.

Amsterdam's police department is fairly typical of the municipal forces of Holland.[2] Responsible to the Chief Commissioner are six commissioners or *Commissarissen* possessing the usual semi-judicial powers, but each responsible for the uniformed men in his own division.[3] The relation of the commissaries to the chief commissioner is worthy of particular notice. These officials are appointed by the Crown upon the recommendation of the Minister of Justice.[4] They are removable only by the

[1] As, for example, the *Députation permanente.* See Chap. II, p. 67.

[2] Amsterdam, with a population of 580,960 (January 1, 1912), has one police officer to every 410 of her population; Brussels has one to every 211; Rotterdam, one to every 440.

[3] Amsterdam is thus divided into six divisions. Each of the six has two or three subdivisions *(Afdeelingen),* which in turn have from two to four precinct districts *(Posthuizen),* the whole system representing a modification by French ideas of the German plan of organization. Altogether, Amsterdam has a force of 1,416 men (as of April, 1913), consisting of 59 *inspecteurs* (lieutenants) of various grades, 89 brigadiers or sergeants, and 1,282 agents or patrolmen. The patrolmen cannot rise above the rank of sergeant; the *inspecteurs* are recruited from the so-called middle class, and have generally received what is equivalent to a high-school education.

[4] Chap. II, p. 65.

Organization of the Police Department

same authority. Although he is ultimately responsible for the force, the burgomaster may not dismiss his commissioner, nor may the commissioner dismiss any of his deputies. In case of trouble or disagreement between the commissioner and a deputy, all the commissioner can do is to complain to the burgomaster; all the burgomaster can do is to remonstrate with the recalcitrant official or complain to the Minister of Justice. As may be imagined, this system has resulted in endless friction. The deputies, each in charge of his own district, have developed a spirit of great independence, at times, indeed, almost overriding the commissioner. Although the Dutch sense of respect due to rank and title generally ameliorates the situation before it becomes acute, a strong and tactful hand is continually required, and complaint is often made that a deputy in charge of a district is a law unto himself. Some years ago, the feeling between the commissioner and his deputies became so bitter in two or three of the Dutch cities, that the Minister of Justice issued a proclamation warning the deputies that, except in so far as they were assistants to the prosecuting attorney, they were subordinate to their commissioners. In Rotterdam, thanks to the tact of a very able commissioner, no difficulty has arisen. Unfortunately for Amsterdam, however, the police department of that city has in the past been rent with dissension, due entirely to the inability of the commissioner to discipline his deputies and the equal inability of the burgomaster to deal with any of these officials.[1]

[1] Since this was written the police commissioner of Rotterdam has been called to the same position in Amsterdam.

European Police Systems

The foregoing account exhibits two main types of police organization, readily distinguishable from one another — the English and the Continental. The English type is characterized by its simplicity, for it comprises merely a uniformed force and a detective division. The Continental type is complex and intricate, adapted to the variety of functions which the Continental states have committed to their police departments. The English organization is built up around the work of the men in uniform; in the Continental organization the uniformed force is but one of a number of branches, each bearing an equal relationship to the head.

Of the two types, the English possesses the advantages that go with simplicity. It is framed for a single purpose — to carry out one line of work. Compact, responsive, and easily controlled, it performs its functions silently and with a minimum of friction.

To an outsider, the Continental type of organization appears less successful. The centralization of miscellaneous functions in one department does not seem conducive to efficiency. The duties of the various divisions of Berlin's huge organization, for example, are too heterogeneous to be assembled under one head. It is scarcely credible that one man is equipped intelligently to supervise such widely divergent matters as meat, children's asylums and fire insurance agencies, as the head of Division II of the Berlin organization is called upon to do, or that another official should have under his immediate control credit banks, naturalization affairs, and the city's water supply, as is the case with the chief of Division I. Even the German genius for detail can scarcely overcome the inherent objections to such arrangements and the constant complaints of delay and red tape and ponderous processes, which come not only from citizens of Berlin, but from headquarters officials as well, seem more or less justified. I was told that important letters are sometimes three or four days in reaching the proper officials, while being referred from one bureau or department to another. A headquarters official who spoke very frankly to me of this matter phrased his opinion as follows: " We are over-centralized. We have too many different things to do. There is too much rubbing of elbows. We get our feet caught in our own processes." Moreover, there seems to be a lack of co-ordination and coöperation between the branches in Berlin, because each man serves his own bureau without regard either to the work or the aims of the bureaus next door. The detective division pays scant attention to the uniformed force. The uniformed force works in ignorance of what is being done along preventive lines, for example, in any other branch. It is difficult to find a *Kommissar* who is familiar with anything in the department outside of his own specialty, and the objections of some of the under-officials with whom I talked were loud and bitter on this score. " How do I know what my neighbor is doing? They keep me with my nose on my own narrow work." This was the remark of the chief of an important sub-division.

If it were possible to sum up in a word one's impression of the Berlin department, it would be " over-organization." There are bureaus and sub-bureaus, specialties and sub-specialties, with an interminable line of reports and documents proceeding through official channels to the president's office. Every official method is carefully prescribed; every action, even to the smallest detail, is hedged about with minute rules and regulations. Police business is reduced to a methodical and, as far as possible, automatic routine, the rigidity of which is accentuated by the laborious formalities of official courtesy and the stiff respect paid to rank and position. It almost seems as if the German genius for organization had exhausted itself in perfecting a piece of machinery from which the human element has been completely eliminated, leaving no room for individual initiative or imagination. This, at least, is the constant complaint that one hears from the younger officers in the service, and from those citizens whose business brings them into touch with its bureaus; and certainly, as one surveys the entire organization of the Berlin department, the impression becomes firmly fixed that it is a huge, ponderous machine, impeded by its own mechanical intricacy and clogged with work. If it were not for the superb training of many of its higher officers, I very much doubt whether the machine could be made to run at all. Certainly it could not be made to run outside of Germany.

Hardly less unwieldy is the police organization of Paris, which, as we have seen, is composed of a series of branches, divisions, and sections centered irregularly about the office of the Prefect. More loosely put together than the organization in Berlin, it suffers from a lack of proper coördination. Its many diverse functions are grouped with little regard for cohesiveness or common action, while the whole inarticulated plan is rendered even less coherent by a clumsy attempt at centralization of control, which has succeeded only in crowding together the various agencies of administration. The cumbersomeness of this huge organization has not escaped criticism even in Paris. The performances of the Bonnot gang, which terrorized Paris for weeks during the year 1912, aroused a storm of hostile but pertinent comment. In a speech delivered at the time in the Municipal Council, and subsequently approved by the Police Prefect, one of the members, M. Massard, expressed in cogent fashion the strong opinion that prevailed.

" One is often struck," he said, " by the lack of coherency which appears to exist among the admirable parts of this vast system, and it seems evident that the various active sections of the police prefecture would render greater service if certain modifications could be effected. . . . It often happens that several departments of the police prefecture, even several sections of one department, are called upon to deal with an evil doer, and the efforts of the men, thus divided up, hinder rather than help. . . . It would prove ignorance of the French character not to conclude that the police endeavor to give satisfaction to the department to which they personally belong, without caring at all for the objects pursued in other branches of the same administration, thus hindering the final results of a project which their coöperation might aid." [1]

[1] This speech, which was one of many made in criticism of the police department, was printed in the official municipal journal, *Bulletin municipal officiel de la Ville de Paris.* The section which

European Police Systems

It was undoubtedly this growing feeling of distrust of the police department and its whole plan of organization that led to the retirement of M. Lépine as Prefect in 1913. At least, this is the belief in official circles. Certainly, M. Lépine's successor, M. Hennion, started the immediate and thorough-going reorganization now under way. In a letter to the Municipal Council, dated July 4, 1913, M. Hennion outlined the steps which he proposed to take in coördinating and readjusting the various branches of his department:

> " From the moment of my arrival, I have had only too many opportunities to notice the lack of cohesion existing in my office. . . . Our first duty is to ventilate (*décongestionner*) the central organization, which is far too much crowded, so that we may restore to the police corps that activity and freedom of movement which are so desirable. To effect this we must decentralize." [1]

The Police Prefect then proceeds to outline a plan of organization shifting the control of the many functions intrusted to the department from headquarters to a number of districts or divisions, with the idea of eliminating the bureaucratic method of supervision.[2] He ad-

I have quoted was repeated with approval in a letter addressed by the present Police Prefect, M. Hennion, to the Municipal Council and printed in the *Bulletin officiel* of July 13, 1913.

[1] This communication is printed in the *Bulletin officiel* of July 13, 1913.

[2] M. Hennion's plan of reorganization involves the creation of ten districts, or divisions, each containing two *arrondissements*. Each division will be under the supervision of a commissary, although the present system of *quartier-commissariats* dealing with law proceedings and other judicial matters will not be disturbed, nor will the *officiers de la paix* be withdrawn from the *arrondisse-*

mits, however, that his plan is only a step preliminary to others which must be carefully thought out and introduced. The Paris department, therefore, is in a stage of transition, with all the confusion accompanying such a change. How far M. Hennion will pursue his reorganization plans is not yet known; but the Paris force has had a rude awakening, and under vigorous leadership, is making a brave attempt not only to coordinate its many departments, but to cut loose from the unwieldy concentration both in function and administration, such as handicaps the organization in Berlin.

Of the large Continental cities, Vienna has the simplest type of police organization, approximating the English form more closely than the Continental. Austria vests the control of public health and kindred matters in her municipal governments, and the machinery of her police departments is not clogged by unrelated or at least only indirectly related functions. The Vienna department, therefore, has a great advantage over the departments of Berlin and Paris, an advantage which becomes apparent when one sees the struggles of the Berlin office to handle intelligently its own tremendous powers. Furthermore, Vienna, like London, has developed along lines of decentralization. Instead of centering all authority at headquarters, where the guiding strings are apt to become interwoven and tangled, and where a few men are

---

ments. To each of the ten divisions will be assigned a definite number of plain-clothes men, with the object of giving to all the quarters of Paris detectives who will be thoroughly acquainted with their prescribed localities. The Prefect's plan also involves the organization of a central archives department, which will bring together the many separated filing systems of the different branches.

called upon to decide a great number of unrelated questions, Vienna has transferred a large part of the administrative responsibility to the districts and the district officials, using the headquarters only as a center for ultimate control. In this way the intense concentration and consequent confusion which characterize the police organizations of Berlin and Paris have been avoided, and the Police President and his immediate assistants, freed from the petty details of their work, have had time and opportunity to formulate broad plans for the intelligent development of the force. In matters relating to the education of policemen, in their equipment and in the thoroughness of their general work, Vienna is ahead of any other city on the Continent. Undoubtedly one of the causes contributing to this superiority is the form of organization which relieves the executives from the entire administrative responsibility.

It is to England, however, that we must turn for the simplest, and perhaps, in the last analysis, the most effective type of police organization — a decentralized organization constructed around a single function. The ease with which administrative operations are handled at New Scotland Yard, the smooth articulation of the different parts of the Metropolitan police machinery must be explained by something more than the proverbial British genius for government. The machinery has been constructed in a workmanlike manner to perform a single task. It has not been allowed to complicate itself by undertaking other functions more or less unrelated. The English have perceived clearly that the task of maintaining law and order is itself onerous enough, and they

Organization of the Police Department

have refused to allow the police department to be used as a depository for such miscellaneous functions as could not easily be fitted into other branches of the government. One or two minor exceptions exist to this general policy. For example, the police forces of England are called upon to license chimney sweeps,[1] and the Police Commissioner of the Metropolitan district must license shoeblacks and messengers within the County of London.[2] But, except for a few insignificant instances of this kind, the efficiency of the police as a force for the maintenance of order is not hampered by the addition of extraneous duties.

It would, of course, be an exaggeration to assert that the English type of organization is flawless. We have already noticed the serious disadvantages growing out of the dependence of the chief constable upon the Watch Committee in some of the provincial cities, and even the Metropolitan force is not free from fault in the framework of its organization. The utter lack of control by the Commissioner over the acts and functions of his business manager, the Receiver, is a source of weakness which has led in the past, as it will inevitably lead in the future, to friction and irritation. The work of the two offices is too inextricably related to admit of each being independent of the other, and under the circumstances there appears to be no reason, except the force of tradition, why the Receiver should not be made responsible to the Commissioner rather than to the Home Secretary.

But even with its faults, the English police organiza-

[1] *Chimney Sweepers Act of 1875*, § 6.
[2] *Metropolitan Streets Act of 1867*, §§ 19-20.

147

tion is a better piece of machinery than the police organization of the Continent. It is a curious fact, therefore, that as far as the discharge of fundamental police duty is concerned, no essential superiority can be claimed for the English department. Indeed, with all the divergences in type not only between the English and Continental organizations, but between the police organizations of European cities everywhere, it cannot be denied that law and order are, on the whole, uniformly well preserved. As far as external appearances go, Berlin and London are equally well policed. Indeed, as between the German and English cities generally, the advantage in this respect may perhaps fairly be claimed by the former. Obviously, therefore, other factors than the type of organization must bear vitally upon the police problem. National habits and characteristics and a score of other influences alter the task of the police in maintaining order. A peaceful, law-abiding population presents to the police a comparatively simple problem which even faulty administrative machinery may not seriously complicate. Or again, grave defects in the type of police organization may be balanced by the superior personnel of the force. Indeed, intelligent commissioners and well-trained subordinates, obtaining and holding office on proper conditions, and carefully selected patrolmen, appear to be of even greater consequence than any particular variety or type of administrative machinery. Certainly in searching for the factors which make for efficiency in police work we are bound to look beyond the merely mechanical arrangement of a department.

CHAPTER IV

THE COMMISSIONER

European police administration a distinct profession.— Army officers not generally desired.— Jurists preferred on the Continent.— Examples.— System of promotion in Germany.— The Austrian *Rangsklasse* system.— The Italian system.— The Dutch system.— English provincial chief constables promoted from the ranks.— Examples.— London's commissioners.— Indefinite tenure of office of the European commissioner.— Dismissal of inefficient or dishonest men.— Examples.— Long term of office of average commissioner. — Exceptions.— London's experience.— System on the whole excellent.— Commissioners' salaries.

HAVING outlined the functions and plan of organization of the European police departments, we must now turn our attention to the men who administer them. First of all, we must consider the official at the head of the system — his training and experience, his tenure of office, his emoluments and his relations to other officials. We shall then be able to form a general estimate not only of the standards which Europe applies in the selection of her police executives, but of the scope which she allows them in the development of their ideas and policies.

The selection of a police commissioner is naturally a matter of great importance. The success or failure of an entire police policy is largely dependent upon the head of the force. He must be a man of strength combined with tact, of keen intelligence and incorruptible integrity. Indeed, in this last respect he must be beyond suspicion. He must be able to handle his men with an iron hand, without impairing their confidence in his absolute fairness and justice. He must be firm in his relations with the public without arousing antagonism. A man who combines these various capacities is not easily found, and the European authorities are correspondingly painstaking and cautious in their search and selection. In some cities, indeed, the task of finding the right man begins two or three years before there is any intention of retiring the immediate incumbent. Sir Edward Henry was brought from India in 1901 and made an Assistant Commissioner of the Metropolitan force in London, with the deliberate intention of testing his fitness for the commissionership. Two years later he succeeded Sir Edward Bradford, the latter official stepping out voluntarily after an honorable service of thirteen years. In Vienna, at the present time, two men, one in the police department and the other in a related branch of the government service, are known to be in training for the police presidency.

Generally speaking, European police administration is a distinct profession. It is seldom that a man is chosen from an unrelated line of activity to fill a commissionership. The popular idea that European police departments are in charge of men taken directly from the ranks of army officers is without foundation. Only in the larger cities of Holland and in two or three instances in England [1] has this practice been followed, and in

[1] This does not apply to the English county forces, which are generally commanded by ex-army officers.

The Commissioner

these cases, as we shall see, the experiment has not always been a happy one. It is true that on the Continent the man who is in immediate command of the uniformed force of a police department is often an ex-army officer; but the head of the whole police department—the president, the commissioner, the director, the prefect, whatever his title — is more apt to be a jurist trained in government work than a soldier, although, under the compulsory system of enlistment which exists in most Continental countries, he has probably seen some military service. In the minds of the European authorities, military experience is not the *sine qua non* of police management; of itself it does not constitute a sufficient guarantee of effectiveness or intelligence in supervising the complex and extensive affairs of a police department.[1] So, too, a man who has made a record as an efficient engineer, or who has established a reputation as a physician or health expert, is not necessarily equipped for the task. A police head must be specially trained for his work. Ordinarily the man whom the Continental authorities select as commissioner has served his apprenticeship either as an assistant in the same department, or as a commissioner in a less important city, or as an official in another governmental branch. Karl Ritter von Brzesowsky, the President of the police force of Vienna, was for twenty-eight years an officer in the

[1] This statement appears not to hold for Russia and Portugal. I am informed by the consular officers of St. Petersburg and Moscow that the Chief of Police *(Gradonachalnik)* is invariably an officer of high standing in the army, generally with the rank of Major-General. Similarly, the American Consul at Lisbon informs me that the *commandante* of police is always selected from among the higher officers of the regular army, the present incumbent having been a colonel in the artillery.

same department before he was promoted to his present position. Similarly, the Police President of Budapest served twenty-three years before promotion to the post he now occupies. On the other hand, M. Hennion, the present Prefect of police in Paris, was Director of the *Sûreté générale* in the office of the Minister of the Interior, a department which controls the *gendarmerie,* the *Brigade mobile,* the local *commissariats* and other national police bodies and functions; while Dr. Bittinger, Police Director of Stuttgart, was called from an assistant-commissioner-ship in Munich. Dr. Domenico Castaldi, the recently appointed Commissioner of police in Rome,[1] held similar positions in Ancona and Naples before he was called to his present post. Previously he had served not only as an assistant in the police departments of several Italian cities, but as an official of the division of Public Security in the office of the Minister of the Interior. He is a university graduate, a doctor of jurisprudence, and one of the most cultivated men in the public service of Italy.

Ordinarily, in Germany, but with the notable exception of Berlin, the police presidents are promoted from among the lesser officers of the force.[2] Dr. Gustav Ro-

[1] His title is *Questore di Roma*.
[2] This is not always the case. The police commissioner of Munich (Van der Heydte) was appointed from a kindred branch of the government service; Dr. Robert Heindl, assistant commissioner *(Polizeirat)* in Dresden, was called from a similar position in Munich. In Prussia, where the police commissioners of all the important cities, such as Frankfort-on-Main, Coblentz, Cologne, Königsberg, Breslau, etc., are appointed by the Crown upon recommendation of the Minister of the Interior (see Chap. II, page 68) officials for these positions are often selected from the district *(Bezirk)* or Circle *(Kreis)* authorities in the employ of the Prussian government.

The Commissioner

scher, Police President of Hamburg, was chief of the detective division for seven years prior to his appointment, having previously served as an assistant prosecuting attorney. Dr. Paul Koettig, Police President of Dresden, served twenty-one years in the department as a higher official, being promoted to his present position, like Dr. Roscher, in Hamburg, from the directorship of the detective bureau, although he originally entered the force as a lieutenant (*Assessor*). In Berlin the custom has existed of choosing an official from some other branch of the governmental service, as, for example, from the civil force in charge of one of the provinces of Prussia. Thus, President von Jagow, the present incumbent, was promoted, four years ago, from the position of assistant in the office of the *Oberpräsident* of the province of Brandenburg. His predecessor in the presidency had been the chief civil officer of a *Kreis,* or section of a province.[1] Like most of the higher official class in Germany, President von Jagow is a university graduate in law, who, after passing the necessary qualifying examinations, chose government work as a career. In fact, in nearly all the large cities not only of Germany, but of Austria-Hungary and Italy as well, the administrative police heads are jurists of university training,[2] who enter the government service in a minor capacity, sometimes as assistant officers in a police depart-

[1] Von Stubenrauch.
[2] It must be remembered that the graduates in law of Continental universities have had a far broader training than is usually associated in other countries with the word "lawyer." They are thoroughly drilled in public law as distinguished from private law. Indeed, political economy and administrative law may be said to form the basis of their legal education.

ment, sometimes as under-secretaries or deputies in a state or provincial department, and are thereafter promoted step by step up the official ladder. It may be safely affirmed that in these countries no police head is ever appointed who has not had some previous experience in governmental work. The fact that the larger police departments are for the most part state institutions constituting an integral part of the great web of officialdom which centers about the state ministries makes a promotion scheme of this kind easily possible. In this scheme the commissionership of a police force is by no means the termination. The president of Berlin's force is almost certain, sooner or later, to become the *Oberpräsident* of a province, or at least a *Regierungspräsident* in a district.[1] The same thing is true in Munich, where a police commissionership is looked upon as a stepping stone to more desirable positions under the government. In Hamburg and Dresden, conditions are more static, and a police head whose services are appreciated is apt to find himself permanently retained. In Stuttgart, on the other hand, an undesirable police commissioner was recently promoted in a somewhat forceful fashion to a higher position in the state service, where his peculiar habits of mind would be less objectionable.

It has remained for Austria and Hungary, however, to evolve the most thoroughgoing system of official promotion in Europe. The entire civil service for the higher governmental officers is divided into eleven classes, called

[1] President von Jagow's immediate predecessor died in office. The two prior incumbents (von Windheim, 1895-1903, and von Borries, 1903-1908) were both promoted to higher positions in the government.

The Commissioner

Rangsklasse. The Prime Minister alone represents the first class; in the second class are the ministers of the cabinet; in the third, the assistant ministers. The fourth class is represented by police presidents, the chief justice of the court of appeals, the directors of finance of the various provinces of Austria, and other dignitaries. In each of the remaining classes are a large number of officials of various titles, who fill the numerous positions in the different departments of the national civil service. The eleventh rank-class is occupied by the *Praktikants.*[1] They are the beginners, serving their apprenticeship in the higher grades of governmental service — all of them graduates in law fresh from the university. They may be assigned to any one of a large number of departments, to the secretary of state's office or to one of the other ministries, to the police department, the prosecuting attorney's office, the customs or revenue service, or one of the branches of the provincial government. They may even be shifted from one department to another as they develop peculiar fitness for a particular line of work. Many of them hold the degree of doctor of law, having passed a higher examination than that required for entrance into the state service.[2] In fact,

[1] Clerks (*Kanzleibeamte*) are also admitted into the rank-class system, recruited from those who, after twelve years' service in the army, pass the qualifying examination. They enter in the eleventh rank-class as *Kanzlisten,* but are limited in promotion to the eighth rank-class with the grade of *Hilfsämterdirektor.* So, also, physicians in the police service cannot rise above the seventh rank-class and the title *Polizeichefarzt.*

[2] Legal training, as a necessary prerequisite to entrance into the higher positions of the governmental service, was established in Austria by the decree of the Minister of the Interior, December 20, 1887; in Hungary by the Law of 1883, I. Torvenyczikk, § III, although in both countries there were prior statutes or decrees.

fully forty per cent. of the higher officials of Vienna's
police department have the title " doctor " thus obtained.

Around this system of ranks or classes has been built
up an elaborate scheme of promotion. Step by step, as
their abilities and experience warrant, the men are promoted from one class to another. Thus, as we have seen,
the division commanders of the police department of Vienna are all university men, most of them belonging to
the seventh rank. So, too, the *Bezirksinspektors,* or
lieutenants, in the uniformed force have been graduated
from the university with a degree in law. The fact that
the Police President of Vienna has been in the department
thirty-five years is, in view of this system, no astonishing
matter. It means that thirty-five years ago he entered the
department as a *Praktikant* fresh from the university, and
that step by step he has risen from the eleventh class to
the fourth. It further means that his successor and the
man who will follow his successor as president are even
now in training in one of the various classes.

In no other country in Europe except Hungary and
Italy is there anything approaching this elaborate system
of training and promotion. In several of the States of
Germany, particularly in Bavaria and Württemberg, and
to some extent in Saxony, an attempt has been made to
approximate it, and in all the other States there are more
or less prescribed ranks or classes among the govern-

The Austrian state examinations which the applicants are required
to pass involve four years' residence in a university and a mastery
of the following subjects: History of Law, Civil and Criminal
Law, Political Science and Economy, and International Law. In
Hungary applicants must possess a lawyer's diploma or a doctor's
degree in political science or law, or a certificate of four years'
residence in a law university of Hungary.

mental office holders; but they are used largely for the purpose of defining official precedence rather than for the sake of training and promoting according to regular modes of procedure.

The Italian system is in many ways unique. As we have seen, the police forces throughout the kingdom are administered by representatives of the Division of Public Security, one of the branches of the Ministry of the Interior. Service in this department is looked upon as a profession. Entrance is determined by a competitive examination, preference being given to university graduates. A course of study at the police college [1] introduces the candidates to the details of their new work, and with the title *delegate* they are assigned to the police force of some town or city. Later, as their abilities warrant, they are promoted to the rank of *commissario,* and finally, to that of *questore,* in charge of a provincial force. Continually transferred to places of greater importance, their rise in the service is based on merit and achievement alone. When, therefore, the authorities seek a new head for the police force of an important city, they have only to choose from a group of trained specialists with years of practical experience in police problems behind them. To the Italian it is a matter of course that the present *questore* of Rome has spent his life in police work, serving in various capacities and in many cities.

In marked distinction to the system of training and promotion generally prevailing in other countries on the

[1] *Scuola di Polizia Scientifica.* For details of the course, see Chap. V, p. 192.

Continent, Holland has tried the doubtful experiment of taking officers directly from the army to fill the commissionerships in her larger cities.[1] That is, instead of following the natural line of promotion and selecting one of the assistant commissioners of a department, who, entering the force with the rank of lieutenant,[2] has been promoted after years of training and service, Holland generally chooses an army officer. As may be expected, the army officer knows nothing of police business. He comes with a point of view entirely different from that of the force. His military training makes it difficult for him to conceive of his work as fundamentally a civil problem; in his relations with the citizens he is inclined to be blunt and tactless. He is not nearly so well equipped for his task as some of his assistants, who, coming from the same social class as the Commissioner and as well educated as he, resent their subordination to an untrained man. Needless to say, the experiment has proved a failure in Holland. One has only to examine the police organization of Amsterdam and talk with some of the subordinate officials to realize its defects. The continual friction between the Commissioner and his deputies, the lack of a well-conceived policy, the antagonism of the uniformed force to the head of the department, are all evidences of ineffective control. To be sure, this condition is partly due, as we have seen, to a faulty plan of organization which allows the Commissioner no adequate means of disciplining his assistants; to a much greater extent, however, it is due to the attempted appli-

---

[1] This is not true at The Hague, where a deputy commissioner from Amsterdam was appointed to the commissionership.
[2] Called *inspecteurs* in Amsterdam and Rotterdam.

The Commissioner

cation of military ideas and a military training to a problem that is essentially one of civil administration.

In Great Britain there is no fixed system by which police executives may be trained and developed. Each city and county is free to adopt its own standards and select its own men. As a result, police executives are sometimes taken from the departments of other towns, or they are promoted from among the assistants in the same force, or, occasionally, they are drawn from the army or the Royal Irish Constabulary. In contrast with the Continental officials there are few among them who have received a legal degree. Most of them are men who have made police work a distinct profession, entering the service as ordinary constables and rising from the ranks. Of the 128 borough police forces in England and Wales, the chief constables of all but fourteen have come from the ranks, promoted gradually on the basis of merit, and often called from one city to another.[1] In this respect, therefore, English and Continental practice differ widely. In Germany, Austria, France, and Italy, it would be impossible for a man who has served as a patrolman ever to become the chief of his force in his own or in any other city. The prevailing class distinctions and social lines forbid. Indeed, the idea appears never to have been considered on the Continent, and questions on this score elicit stares of amazement. It is only in democratic England that such a practice could prevail. Even in England there are

[1] Quite the reverse is true of the heads of the *county* forces of England and Wales. Only eleven out of fifty-eight have come from the ranks. Of the remaining forty-seven, thirty-seven are ex-army officers.

those who doubt its advisability, not on the grounds of
social distinction, to be sure, but because they hesitate to
place their police forces in the hands of men of limited
education and point of view. " Once a constable always
a constable," is the remark that one occasionally hears —
which is another way of stating the argument that a man
whose preliminary education and advantages were such
that he could secure nothing better than a position as a
patrolman, is not equipped to handle large questions in a
large way, or deal administratively with the intricate
business of a complex department. " We would greatly
prefer an Oxford or Cambridge graduate thoroughly
drilled in police work," said the Chairman of the Watch
Committee of a large English city in discussing the matter with me.

But there is another side to the question. The men
who join the police forces as constables and subsequently
are promoted to the top are frequently men of good education, who have entered upon their work with the deliberate intention of making it a life career. Better
equipped officials it would be difficult to obtain. They
have served their apprenticeships in the smaller forces
of less important towns; they have risen gradually
from one position of responsibility to another; they are
thoroughly acquainted with their tasks. Indeed, this
is the point of view generally accepted in England
and Scotland. The present Chief Constables of Liverpool, Manchester, Bristol, Leeds, Edinburgh, Nottingham and Bradford, not to mention a score of other important municipalities, have thus come from the ranks.
Similarly, the chief constables of smaller towns and

The Commissioner

cities are often recruited from the inferior officers of larger departments. Former superintendents, inspectors and even sergeants of the Metropolitan force of London are at present the Chief Constables of Cardiff, Lincoln, Brighton, Highwycombe, and Barnstable; while Chester, Bolton, and Wigan have recruited their Chief Constables from the Liverpool force. All of these men at one time served in the ranks.

Police administrators in England and Scotland are occasionally taken from the Royal Irish Constabulary. The present Chief Constables of Birmingham, Glasgow, Newcastle-on-Tyne, Hull and the City of London, not to mention a number of others who have recently retired, served long apprenticeships with this force, entering as district inspectors after competitive examination. College graduates from Oxford and Cambridge, army officers who have served their term, representatives of prominent families, all attracted by the possibilities of policing as a profession worthy of intelligence and ability, enlist as commissioned officers in its service.[1] In fact, the demand for district inspectorships is greater than the supply, and the waiting lists are always full.[2]

[1] Applicants for appointment as commissioned officers must be unmarried and between the ages of 21 and 26. An officer in the army or navy having five years' service may be admitted up to the age of 28. (See *Regulations under which Gentlemen are admitted as Cadets to the Royal Irish Constabulary,* issued by the Inspector General from Dublin Castle, September 1, 1910.)

[2] District inspectors in the " R. I. C.," as it is familiarly known, are recruited in part from the ranks and in part from outsiders who pass the competitive entrance examinations. These examinations, which are conducted by the Civil Service Commissioners, cover many subjects, including the following: Arithmetic, English Composition, Geography, British History, Latin or French, Elementary Principles of Law, Law of Evidence.

The successful candidates receive their appointments as " Cadets,"

European Police Systems

The case of Mr. Leonard Dunning is a typical illustration of the way the system works. An Oxford graduate, he entered the Royal Irish Constabulary as a district inspector. After twelve years of efficient service, he was appointed Assistant Head Constable in Liverpool, a position which he occupied for nine years. At the end of that time he was made Head Constable, seven years later he received an appointment as His Majesty's Inspector of Constabulary for the Southern District of England under the supervision of the Home Office, a position which he now occupies. "A trained policeman," one of his colleagues called him. So, too, the experience of Sir William Nott-Bower, C.V.O., Commissioner of the City of London Police, is illustrative not only of this system of training, but of the opportunity for advancement which it presents. Formerly a captain in the English army, he joined the Royal Irish Constabulary as a district inspector. After a few years' service in that capacity he was called to the City of Leeds as Chief Constable; from Leeds he went to Liverpool, where he served as Head Constable for twenty years; he was then called to the commissionership in the City of London, the position that he now holds.

In this manner, it would be possible to furnish illustration after illustration. The point is this: no English city of size or importance would think of selecting a man as chief constable who had not already demonstrated his ability in police work, either in connection with a municipal force, or as an officer of the Royal Irish Constabulary

and for from six months to a year are thoroughly drilled in law, military tactics and practical police duty. They are appointed to district inspectorships as vacancies occur.

The Commissioner

or other similar organization. The Chief Constable of Edinburgh served with the Northampton County Police; the Chief Constable of Manchester held the same position in Oldham and Canterbury for terms of seven and five years respectively before he was called to his present post. When the authorities of the Town of Preston wanted a chief constable, they did what is often if not generally done by an English community seeking a trained public official: they advertised in the newspapers.[1] Of the seventy candidates who applied they selected a man who, at that time, was Superintendent of Police in the small town of Devizes, having previously served in the ranks at Swindon. Their choice was justified by the fact that this same man was later selected by the Watch Committee of Liverpool as Assistant Head Constable out of forty or fifty candidates who presented themselves as the result of an advertisement. In the same way when the Watch Committee of Liverpool wanted to secure the services of a second assistant head constable, they chose out of the eighty applicants a graduate of Cambridge, who at that time was serving his fifth year as a district inspector in the Royal Irish Constabulary. J. V. Stevenson, Chief Constable of Glasgow, and C. H. Rafter, Chief Constable of Birmingham, served as officers in the Royal Irish Constabulary for seventeen and twelve years respectively before they were called to larger duties. Leonard Dunning's title could well be applied to them also: they too are " trained policemen."

[1] This is not at all unusual in Great Britain. Many different kinds of vacancies are filled in this manner. Thus, universities advertise for professors, hospitals for doctors, etc. There is no obligation to appoint from the list of applicants. It is hardly more than a method of notifying the public of a vacancy.

European Police Systems

It is safe to say that the majority of the police executives in the provincial towns and cities, and in the counties as well, are obtained in this fashion. The result is, that except in cases of promotion, it is seldom that the official is a resident of the city which chooses him. He may hail from anywhere between John O'Groat's and Land's End. There is no catering to home talent. Indeed, residence in the same town is, if anything, a handicap to availability. " He had too many local connections," was the terse explanation given to the writer in a typical English city when he asked why a certain man of prominence and ability had not been appointed chief constable. In brief, the English provincial city inevitably selects as its police executive the man whom it deems best fitted, without regard to birth, residence, or any other incidental factor.

The police commissionership of the London Metropolitan district involves the handling of such important problems and responsibilities that it deserves separate consideration. The Commissioner is the head of the largest uniformed police force in the world, with jurisdiction over the largest municipal police area. His is a post of honor and distinction, requiring the highest ability and statesmanship. Outside of the Cabinet itself, there are few more important offices in the entire kingdom, for the influence of the Commissioner and of the organization under him makes itself felt in every city and town. The selection of the right man is therefore a matter of grave concern to the Home Office. Six commissioners have commanded the Metropolitan force since its institution in 1829. The first, Sir Richard

The Commissioner

Mayne, whose energy and capacity placed the force on a working basis and established it in the confidence of the people, was a graduate of Dublin and Cambridge and an attorney of distinction.[1] His successor, Sir Edmund Henderson, had been trained as a soldier, although he came to the commissionership from the head of the Prison Department of the Home Office. General Charles Warren, the next incumbent, was a well known officer of Engineers, whose talent for administration had been proved in Bechuanaland and elsewhere and who relinquished the governorship of the Red Sea Littoral to take up the commissionership in London. His successor, Mr. James Monro, had been an assistant commissioner prior to his appointment, although his original experience was obtained in the Indian Civil Service. Sir Edward Bradford, who followed him, was an army officer who had also served with distinction in India. Sir Edward Henry is the present incumbent. His previous training is perhaps typical of the kind of man that the Home Office seeks as a Commissioner. In 1873, he entered the Indian Civil Service as an Assistant Magistrate. In 1888, he was placed in charge of the District of Bahar, where an ingenious tribe of criminals called *Doms* gave him opportunity for the exercise of his special abilities. In 1891, he was appointed Inspector General of Police in Bengal, and later was made Commissioner for the entire southern district of India. During the South African War, he

[1] From 1829 to 1850 the force was administered by a double-headed commission, Col. Sir Charles Rowan, a soldier of distinction, who had already gained some experience with the Royal Irish Constabulary, serving with Sir Richard Mayne. Colonel Rowan resigned in 1850. In 1856, the Department was organized under a single commissionership with a number of deputies or assistants.

organized the civil police of Johannesburg and Pretoria. Appointed Assistant Commissioner of the Metropolitan police of London in 1901, he was placed in charge of the Criminal Investigation Department of Scotland Yard. In this position, he established the finger print method which he had brought with him from India. Upon the resignation of his predecessor in 1903, he was appointed Commissioner. With von Brzesowsky of Vienna, and Roscher of Hamburg, he represents the best equipped type of police official in Europe.

It is noteworthy that of the Commissioners of the Metropolitan force, one had been an attorney, two had been in the civil service of India and had afterward accepted appointments as assistant commissioners at Scotland Yard, while the remaining three were trained in the army, although they had occupied various civil positions under the government. Military experience has never been regarded as a necessary qualification in England. In fact, of recent years there has been a growing conviction, both in the Home Office and in Scotland Yard, that far better results can be secured with a civilian head, preferably a man who has had some previous governmental experience either in connection with police organization, or perhaps, in one of the ministerial or colonial offices. In his interesting memoirs, recently published in England, Sir Robert Anderson, for thirteen years Assistant Commissioner of the Metropolitan force, expresses the following opinion:

"Sir Charles Warren's appointment to the head of the force was a risky experiment: The police cannot

The Commissioner

tolerate military discipline, and this was their first experience of a military chief commissioner. For it is no disparagement of Sir Edmund Henderson (General Warren's predecessor) to say that he was more of a civilian than a soldier; and moreover, he came to Scotland Yard from Whitehall, where he had been at the head of the Prison Department. The effect was precisely what might have been anticipated. I speak with knowledge such as few others possessed, and I can say with definiteness that there was a dangerous want of sympathy between the Commissioner and the rank and file." [1]

It is interesting to note that General Warren's term of office lasted but two years. His career emphasized the conviction that the handling of a large police force is not a military problem, nor is the military model too closely to be followed, either in organization or discipline. Mr. James Monro, who succeeded General Warren in office, expressed the matter as follows:

" The police are not the representatives of an arbitrary and despotic power, directed against the rights or obtrusively interfering with the pleasures of law-abiding citizens: they are simply a disciplined body of men, specially engaged in protecting ' masses,' as well as ' classes,' from any infringement of their rights on the part of those who are not law-abiding." [2]

[1] *The Lighter Side of My Official Life,* Sir Robert Anderson, K.C.B., p. 127, London, 1910.
[2] Quoted in W. L. Melville Lee, *loc. cit.,* London, 1901, p. 332.

This is the emphasis which one finds continually expressed in regard to the Metropolitan Police Force and its leadership.

It follows naturally that when men are as carefully trained and selected for commissionerships as they are ordinarily in Europe the length of their term of office should in no way be limited or defined. Hence the European police commissionership is indefinite in tenure. There is not a single city of size or importance in England or on the Continent, the head of whose police force is appointed for a definite period. In fact, the idea of fixing in advance the term of a police commissioner, of establishing by some arbitrary rule the time when his administration shall come to an end, seems never to have occurred to European authorities. They appoint their commissioners as a board of directors selects a general manager or other official, not for a definitely established term, but on the basis of satisfactory work. That is, it is assumed that a commissioner will hold office so long as he can give efficient service, or, at least, until his conduct proves unsatisfactory to his superiors. The fact that the European police department is ordinarily responsible to the state rather than to the local government facilitates this arrangement, although the principle holds even in those cities which maintain a municipal control over their police. Periodic changes may indeed be made in the personnel of the Watch Committees of English provincial cities or in the administrative boards (*Magistrat*) of the smaller German municipalities, but there is no corresponding change in the police head. Such action would be totally repugnant to the European idea of efficiency.

The Commissioner

" Why introduce a new man to the position? What is wrong with the present incumbent? Our commissioners have too much valuable experience which has accumulated in years of effective administration. We cannot afford to change." This remark of a prominent civil official in a large German town is illustrative of the European spirit.

Indefiniteness of tenure in no wise jeopardizes the ability of European governments to rid themselves of inefficient or dishonest commissioners. The Home Secretary of England can at any time remove the head of the Metropolitan force, just as the respective Ministers of the Interior in Austria and Prussia can discharge the Police Presidents of Vienna and Berlin, or the Watch Committees of any of the English or Scottish provincial cities can dispense with the services of their Chief Constables.[1] That is, there is nothing in the law or in the agreements between governments and police commissioners to prevent summary action when necessary. Occasionally indeed, such action is taken, as, for example, when the Watch Committee of Carlisle removed its Chief Constable on the charge of accepting free rides from a taxicab company,[2] or when the Assistant Commissioner of Kiel, Germany, was not only discharged, but sentenced to prison for a term of years for dishonesty involving thousands of marks,[3] or when the Police President of Cologne was forcibly retired, ostensibly for abusing the

[1] In Germany, Austria, France, and other Continental countries, as we shall see in Chapter VII, royal officials and those occupying the higher state ranks· are tried before special courts of discipline, which, under ordinary circumstances, present their findings of fact to the Minister of the Interior for action.

[2] In 1912.

[3] In 1911.

rights of a Russian prisoner, but in reality because his administration was tainted with graft and dishonesty.[1] Examples of this kind, however, are strikingly exceptional, and they are noted only to show that the power of summary discharge exists and can, when necessary, be invoked. As a matter of fact, it is only in rare instances that police commissioners have for any reason whatever been removed from office. Such a thing has never occurred in Vienna, Berlin or London, although, as we shall see, in the latter city there have been three resignations more or less forced by the Home Secretary. Indeed, so seldom have actual removals taken place, that in several of the German cities the police authorities, when questioned on this matter by the writer, were obliged to consult their law books to find out how such action could be taken. Ordinarily, unsatisfactory officials are allowed to resign, or they are retired on a pension, or, on the Continent, they are transferred to some other branch of the government service. But instances of unsatisfactory commissioners are difficult to discover, so careful and painstaking is their selection, and so great is the desire of the state and municipal authorities to secure and to retain as long as possible the services of thoroughly trained men.

As a consequence, a term of office extending over many years is the rule rather than the exception. In the 85 years in which the Metropolitan Police Force of London has been in existence there have been, as we have seen, but six commissioners; that is, Sir Edward Henry, the present incumbent, is the sixth in line since 1829, which makes an average of a little over fourteen years apiece.

[1] In 1914.

The Commissioner

Taking into consideration the fact that two of the commissioners served but two years each, the usual average is greatly increased.[1]

London's experience is in no way peculiar. Chief Constable Stevenson of Glasgow has been in office twelve years; Robert Peacock has served Manchester in a similar capacity for sixteen years; C. H. Rafter has been thirteen years Chief Constable at Birmingham; Leonard Dunning, as we have seen, was seven years Head Constable at Liverpool after nine years' service as Assistant Head Constable. Louis Lépine, the former Prefect of Paris, who resigned in 1913, had served continuously since 1899, besides a term of four years in the same position between the years 1893 and 1897. The police president of Dresden has held his office for nine years, Hamburg's president for fourteen years, Vienna's president for seven years, Amsterdam's commissioner, eleven years, Copenhagen's commissioner, twenty-six years. Dr. von Jagow is the tenth police president of Berlin since 1848, an average of nearly seven years for each incumbent. Three of his predecessors died in office; three were promoted to higher positions in the government service; the remaining four were honorably retired.[2]

[1] The terms ran as follows:

Sir Richard Mayne, K.C.B.	1829–1868
Col. Sir Edmund Henderson, K.C.B.	1869–1886
General Sir Charles Warren, G.C.M.G.	1886–1888
Mr. James Monro, C.B.	1888–1890
Col Sir Edward Bradford, Bart., G.C.B.	1890–1903
Sir Edward Henry, G.C.V.O., K.C.B., C.S.I.	1903–

[2] The names of the ten commissioners and their terms of service are as follows:

von Hinckeldey	1848–1856
von Zedlitz-Neukirch	1856–1861
von Bermuth	1862–1867

171

European Police Systems

To this general rule there are a few exceptions to which, on account of certain weaknesses which they illustrate, it is necessary to call special attention. It occasionally, though rarely, happens that a police commissioner is sacrificed in the clash of political or other interests. In Budapest, in 1905, Police President Selley was summarily removed by a political party just come into power on the ground that he had been instrumental under the direction of the opposing party in dissolving many assemblies and meetings. So too in Dresden, some nine years ago, a police president who had served effectively for ten years was compelled to resign, following a sharp difference of opinion with the Minister of the Interior in a matter involving a royal scandal.[1] Paris, the city of shifting sentiment and fickle tradition, has had perhaps the unhappiest experience of all. Until M. Lépine's administration added an element of stability to the office, there was a long period of constant change. Forty-nine Prefects have held the position since 1800, the year of its estab-

von Wurmb	1867–1872
von Madai	1872–1885
von Richthofen	1885–1895
von Windheim	1895–1903
von Borries	1903–1908
von Stubenrauch	1908–1909
von Jagow	1909–

[1] In a number of the store windows of Dresden appeared pictures of the schoolmaster with whom the Crown Princess of Saxony had eloped. The police president, Le Maistre, was ordered by the Minister of the Interior to seize the pictures. He declined to do so on the ground that there was no law forbidding their exhibition. After his resignation, his successor confiscated the pictures in question. It is interesting to note, however, that the High Court of Saxony subsequently held with Le Maistre that there was no law forbidding the exhibition of the pictures, but the resignation of the police president having already gone into effect, was allowed to stand.

The Commissioner

lishment,[1] an average of two years and four months to each incumbent. From the formation of the Third Republic in 1870, to 1893, when M. Lépine first took up the responsibility, there were thirteen different Prefects in office, an average of one year and nine months to each man, one official following another in rapid succession after a short and occasionally inglorious career.[2] The kaleidoscopic change of ministries, the constant quarrels between the prefecture and the Interior department, the frequent outbursts of public criticism and mob violence combined to make the post the most precarious in the governmental service.

Even the Metropolitan force of London, with its stable traditions and relatively long tenure of office of the commissioner, has not been without its sudden and inexplicable shifts in program and personnel. Ordinarily the support which the Home Office has given the Commissioner has been cordial and sustained, but to this policy

---

[1] Year VIII. See note 3, p. 88.

[2] The names of the prefects from 1870 to the present time together with their terms of service are as follows:

Comte de Kératry	1870
Edouard Adam	1870
Ernest Cresson	1870–1871
Albert Choppin	1871
Général Valentin	1871–1873
Léon Renault	1873–1876
Félix Voisin	1876–1877
Albert Gigot	1877–1879
Louis Andrieux	1879–1881
Ernest Camecasse	1881–1885
Arthur Gragnon	1885–1887
Léon Bourgeois	1887–1888
Henri Lozé	1888–1893
Louis Lépine	1893–1897
Charles Blanc	1897–1899
Louis Lépine	1899–1913
M. C. Hennion	1913–

European Police Systems

there have been exceptions at once glaring and regrettable. For example, on February 8th, 1886, a mob collecting in Trafalgar Square made its way to Hyde Park, breaking windows and looting shops en route. The disturbance caused a storm of newspaper criticism levied at the police for their stupidity in handling the situation. In the heat of the excitement, the Home Secretary,[1] who had just come into office, publicly censured the Police Commissioner, Sir Edmund Henderson, and in spite of his seventeen years of honorable and effective service he was allowed to resign.[2] His successor, Sir Charles Warren, was, as we have seen, a military officer of imperious temper, selected because he was regarded as preëminently fitted to handle the outbreaks of mob violence which had terrorized London in the spring of 1886. His term in office was a period of constant friction. Hampered by his training, disliked by his subordinates, and unsupported, as he rightly or wrongly believed, by the Home Office, he resigned after two years.[3] His successor, James Monro, fared little better. Sir Robert Anderson, who served as his principal assistant, presents the case as follows: " His

[1] Hugh Childers, in the Conservative Government of 1886.

[2] Captain Lee, in his book, *A History of Police in England,* is inclined to excuse the action of the Home Secretary, referring to Sir Edmund Henderson's resignation as "perhaps inevitable under the circumstances." "During his tenure of office," he says, "the peace had been so well maintained, and the police mechanism had worked so smoothly that his experience had taught him to underestimate the dangers that lurk below the surface in all large crowds, and to over-estimate the preparedness of the men under his command to deal with any possible outbreak" (pp. 385–386). But see Sir Robert Anderson, *loc. cit.,* pp. 123 ff. "Mr. Childers' tenure of the Home Office was happily brief," he says, referring to the attempt of the Home Secretary "to make a scapegoat" of the Commissioner.

[3] "He could no longer brook the nagging Home Office ways of that period," says Sir Robert Anderson, *loc cit.,* p. 129.

The Commissioner

predecessor had been driven out by the Home Office and he soon yielded to the same influence . . . Godfrey Lushington's intervention and influence as Under-Secretary (of the Home Office) were generally provocative and his manner irritating. To show how grotesquely Mr. Monro was misjudged at Whitehall, I may mention that when he summoned the police heads to a private conference on the Police Pension Bill, he was suspected of a design to foment sedition and an appeal was made to me confidentially to watch the proceedings."[1] Much, perhaps, might be said in defense of the Home Office officials. Certainly they were anxious to remain on amicable terms with the Commissioner and made an honest endeavor to support his policies. However, difficulties soon arose which required tact and good humor on both sides to compose. A period of friction ensued, and like his predecessor, Mr. Munro resigned in two years.

It is a noteworthy fact that of the five commissioners whose connection with the Metropolitan force has terminated, one died in office, one was retired for old age, while three have resigned after difficulties with the Home Secretary. It must be remembered, however, that all three resignations referred to occurred in the four years between 1886 and 1890; for the first fifty-seven years of its history, and during the twenty-four years just past,

---

[1] *Loc. cit.,* pp. 130–131. This, it must be remembered, is the testimony of a man who did not himself succeed in maintaining very friendly relations with the officials with whom he had to deal, either at the Home Office or at Scotland Yard. There is probably no English civil servant whose memory is more respected and even revered than Sir Godfrey Lushington, and it is safe to say that the responsibility for the friction which notoriously distinguished the Metropolitan police administration during the rule of General Warren and Mr. Monro did not rest wholly on one side.

175

European Police Systems

the relations of the Metropolitan force with the Home Office were marked by the utmost cordiality, the latter department supporting the police through many difficulties and in more than one crisis.[1]

These various incidents in the history of the European forces have been mentioned merely to show that even with a method as excellent as that which Europe employs to choose and support her police commissioners, there must inevitably be a few failures. No device is absolutely perfect; no machinery runs without occasional breakdown. The failures noted, however, have in Europe been surprisingly few — one must search the records to find them — and even when occurring, they have left no permanent mark to prejudice the quality or efficiency of the force. If there is any one factor which contributes predominantly to the popular respect with

---

[1] For example, in 1855, under the régime of Sir Richard Mayne, Lord Robert Grosvenor attempted to pass through Parliament a Sunday Observance Bill for the Metropolitan district. The bill was met with strenuous objection, and popular feeling ran high. Public sentiment was expressed in the following doggerel which was current at the time:

> "Sublime decree, by which our souls to save —
> No Sunday tankards foam, no barbers shave,
> And chins unmown, and throats unslaked display
> His Lordship's reverence for the Sabbath day."

Ultimately, a series of riots broke out which culminated in a grave clash with the police. So sharply were the police criticized on this occasion for their alleged brutality and misconduct, that a committee of three was appointed by the Government to hold an investigation. During its progress every attempt was made by his enemies to discredit Sir Richard Mayne, the Commissioner, and many charges were laid against him. However, he came through the investigation unscathed, and for thirteen years more maintained his command of the force, rounding out a distinguished career of 39 years of service. For an interesting account of this and other incidents relating to the history of the force, see W. L. Melville Lee, *loc. cit.*

The Commissioner

which the European police are regarded, it is the personality of the Commissioner, whose character alone is a guarantee of the integrity and efficiency of the force which he commands. In her appreciation of this fact, Europe has come close to the heart of the police problem. To obtain the right men she has made the position one of great honor. The police commissionership of a European city is a career of prominence and dignity attracting the best talent that the university or the government service can produce. Of the six commissioners of the Metropolitan force, five have been knighted in addition to receiving other honors and decorations. The Police President of Vienna has been made a baron and his titles received in Austria and from other countries fill ten lines of type in the police hand-book. Similar honors have been conferred upon the Police President of Berlin and to a lesser extent, perhaps, upon the police heads of other German cities.

Not only in honors but also in substantial remuneration does Europe show her appreciation of an effective police commissioner. As will be seen from the table on the opposite page, a police head is invariably retired with a pension after satisfactory service. If he is called from the department of one city to another, he draws a pension from the city he leaves, dependent ordinarily upon his tenure of office there.[1] In many cities he is provided with an official residence. His salary is, for Europe, always a large one, in every case greatly exceeding the rate which is paid most of the higher governmental officials.[2]

[1] Thus the present Commissioner of the City of London, having previously been Head Constable in both Leeds and Liverpool, receives a pension for the time served in both cities.

[2] In the next table will be noticed the sharp contrast in sal-

ANNUAL SALARIES OF EUROPEAN POLICE COMMISSIONERS.

City	Annual Salary of Commissioner.	Equivalent in American Money.	Additional Perquisites.
London:			
Metropolitan Police...	£ 2,500	$12,165	$500 horse allowance. Pension on retirement.
City of London...	£ 1,250	$ 6,072	Pension on retirement.
Liverpool ...	£ 1,000 to £ 1,500	$ 4,866 to $ 7,290	Pension on retirement.
Manchester ...	£ 1,250	$ 6,072	Pension on retirement.
Birmingham ...	£ 1,100	$ 5,353	Pension on retirement.
Edinburgh ...	£ 900	$ 4,379	Pension on retirement.
Glasgow ...	£ 1,000	$ 4,867	Pension on retirement.
Berlin ...	M. 13,000	$ 3,098	Pension on retirement. $715 special allowance. Official residence. $670 carriage allowance.
Hamburg ...	M. 16,000	$ 3,808	Pension on retirement.
Dresden ...	M. 9,300 to M. 10,500	$ 2,213 to $ 2,499	Pension on retirement.
Stuttgart ...	M. 9,000 to M. 12,000	$ 2,142 to $ 2,856	Pension on retirement.

City	Annual Salary of Commissioner.	Equivalent in Amer. Money.	Additional Perquisites.
Vienna	Kr. 14,000	$ 2,842	Pension on retirement. $1,218 special allowance.
Budapest	Kr. 12,000	$ 2,436	$974 horse allowance. $487 special allowance. Official residence. Pension on retirement.
Paris	Fr. 40,000	$ 7,720	Pension on retirement. Rent allowance. $2,779 carriage allowance.
Marseilles	Fr. 8,000	$ 1,544	$386 local allowance. Burial and disinterment fees, about $193. Official residence. Pension on retirement.
Lyons	Fr. 8,000	$ 1,544	Rent allowance. Pension on retirement.
Copenhagen	Kr. 6,000	$ 1,620	$135 entertainment allowance. Pension on retirement.
Christiania	Kr. 6,800	$ 1,822	Proceeds from articles found and unclaimed, about $161. Pension on retirement.
Stockholm	Kr. 9,000 to Kr. 10,000	$ 2,412 to $ 2,680	Pension on retirement.
Rome	Lire 7,000	$ 1,351	Pension on retirement.
Madrid	Ps. 20,000	$ 3,600	Pension on retirement. Entertainment expenses, $1,800. Rent allowance, $900.
Amsterdam	Fl. 5,500	$ 2,211	$402 house allowance. Pension on retirement.
Rotterdam	Fl. 5,000	$ 2,010	Pension on retirement. Official residence.

179

With such an income he lives in dignity and comfort, secure in the thought that his position is established and that when he wishes to retire, he can do so on a substantial pension. Demanding much of her police administrators, Europe gives much in return.[1]

aries as between one city and another. To a certain extent, this must be interpreted in the light of the marked variations in the cost of living between the different countries of Europe. Thus the cost of living, on the whole, is greater in Holland than in Germany; Vienna is a more expensive city to live in than Berlin; the rate of living in Budapest is generally higher than in Paris. It must of course be borne in mind in interpreting these figures that the cost of living in the United States is greatly in excess of that in European countries.

[1] For a tabulation of the qualifications and modes of appointment of European police commissioners, see Appendix VIII.

CHAPTER V

London.— The provincial cities.— Continental aversion to promotion from the ranks.— Berlin's method of training.— Methods in
Germany.— In Amsterdam and Rotterdam.— Austrian method most
thoroughgoing.— The result in Vienna.— The practice in Italy.—
The Scientific Police School of Rome.— Advantages and disadvantages of recruiting officers from outside the department.— The
Vienna District Commander and the London Superintendent.— A
compromise between the two extremes desirable.

WE have now to consider the assistant commissioners
and their deputies, the men who in rank come between
the head of the force and the officials promoted from the
grade of patrolman. Who are they? What kind of
training do they receive? What are their relations to
the Commissioner?

In respect to the superior officers, there is considerable divergence between England and the Continent.
In London, the ultimate promotion of the constable of
the ranks to the grade of superintendent, leaves only the
assistant commissioners, four in number, and the chief
constables, six in number, between the Commissioner and
the uniformed force. The chief constables, as we have
seen,[1] have supervisory functions, each having charge of

[1] For discussion of the functions of chief constables and assistant commissioners, see Chap. III.

181

a certain district embracing a group of divisions.[1] The assistant commissioners share with the Commissioner the responsibilities of administration. The latter are appointed by the Crown upon recommendation of the Home Office; the former are appointed directly by the Home Secretary, presumably with the advice and consent of the Commissioner. Of the four assistant commissioners serving at the present time [2] in London, three were trained as lawyers, while one was an army officer; one has held his office for thirty years, one for twelve years and two for eleven years each. One served as chief constable for fourteen years before he was promoted to the grade of assistant commissioner; another was assistant commissioner of the City of London police for twelve years prior to his appointment to the Metropolitan force. Two have been knighted by the Crown for their services. Of the six chief constables, four are ex-army officers, each with the rank of major. The fact that the chief constable in the course of his supervisory duties is brought directly into contact with the uniformed force of his district has made it appear advisable in the minds of the London authorities to choose for this office men of disciplinary training. Army experience, however, as in the case of the Commissioner, is not the *sine qua non* of qualification. Two of the six chief constables are university men, chosen because of peculiar fitness.

The provincial cities of England and Scotland follow London's ideas in regard to promotion. Superior officers up to the grade of superintendent are recruited from the

[1] As we have seen, one of the chief constables serves as deputy to the assistant commissioner in charge of the detective bureau.
[2] 1913. Some retirements have taken place since this was written.

Assistant Commissioners and Their Deputies

uniformed force, a circumstance which leaves but one or two administrative officials in each department under the rank of Commissioner to be appointed from outside sources. As I have already shown in the previous chapter these officials are taken from smaller forces in less important towns or they are recruited from the Royal Irish Constabulary.

On the Continent, as we have observed, officials under the rank of Commissioner are uniformly introduced into the department from outside sources. The Continental aversion to extensive promotion from the lower classes makes it necessary to appoint to the higher places in the police department men who hitherto have had no connection with it. Although this policy may have its root in a social prejudice, it has nevertheless a certain rational basis. It is founded on the belief that the superior officers of a department should possess a degree of education and culture which the men who enter the force as patrolmen usually lack. A perspective and point of view other than those of the rank and file are deemed essential to an officer whose function touches important and complicated social and political activities. On this theory, therefore, practically all the police officials of the Continent above the grade of first sergeant are appointed, not by promotion from the ranks, but from outside sources.[1]

Berlin furnishes an excellent example of this practice. The patrolmen of the force are recruited from the army and may be advanced as far as the grade of first sergeant (*Oberwachtmeister*). The next rank is that of

[1] This question is discussed more at length in Chap. VII.

183

the lieutenants who have charge of the precincts. Instead of being promoted from the grade of first sergeant, they are chosen from outside the department. They come directly from the army, where they have been commissioned officers, or from the university where they have studied law, or, in a few cases from miscellaneous professions. If not active army officers they must be officers in the Reserve.[1] Before receiving permanent appointments as lieutenants in the police force, they are obliged to undergo a training lasting eighteen months, during which period they receive no salary and wear no uniform. According to the requirements, they must possess " excellent manners and be in a position to give evidence of a broad general education, which proof will be regarded as given by producing a certificate of examination from a *Gymnasium* or other institution of learning of equal standing." [2] Candidates must be able to give satisfactory references, must be over 24 and under 30 years of age, must have a minimum height of five feet, seven inches, must successfully pass a physical examination, and must prove to the authorities that they have private incomes of 1,800 marks per annum to cover the period of training. When finally appointed, they receive a salary of from 3,000 to 4,500 marks per annum with an allowance of 800 marks for house-rent and additional fees (*Zulage*) amounting to 300 marks.

The eighteen months' training period is spent in prac-

---

[1] Or they must be retired officers with a prospect of appointment in the civil service, or they must have obtained at least the rank of sergeant major of the Reserve. See *Bestimmungen über die Annahme von Anwärtern für den Exekutiv-Polizeidienst in Berlin.* Form 977.

[2] *Ibid.*

tical work in various sections of the police department, where the candidates are obliged to become thoroughly familiar with business and routine. Thus, the first three months are spent in a precinct station, or perhaps in two or three different stations, where the applicants work under the direction of the superior officers. Of the next twelve months, five are spent in the detective bureau, two in the bureau that supervises business establishments (*Abteilung* IX), three in the division which supervises health matters (*Abteilung* II), one in the traffic division (*Abteilung* X), and one in the bureau that has clerical charge of the police penalties (*Strafverfügungen*). The last three months of the training period, like the first three, are spent in precinct stations. During all this time, the lieutenant gets from four to six hours a week in direct instruction in the shape of lectures given by higher officials on police organization and practical detective work. At the end of the eighteen months the candidate is obliged to pass a written examination which covers the subject matter of his entire course both as to lectures and practical work. If successful, he is given the rank of temporary lieutenant at a small salary[1] and is permanently appointed with full title when a vacancy occurs. The appointment is made by the Minister of the Interior upon the recommendation of the Police President.

It is noteworthy that the lieutenant's training does not cease with his appointment. From time to time lectures are given at headquarters on subjects connected with police work, which the lieutenants and even the captains and majors are obliged to attend. These

[1] 1,500 marks per annum.

lectures, given by surgeons, chemists, lawyers and other experts in various lines, cover many phases of police activity. In this way, the officials are kept in active touch with the developments of their profession; every superior officer becomes a trained police expert, well acquainted with all phases of his work.[1]

The uniformed force of Berlin constitutes but a single division out of twelve. At the head of the other divisions and in their principal subdivisions are officials who in rank generally surpass the officials of the uniformed force. They are dignified with the titles *Regierungsrat* and *Polizeirat;* some, indeed, particularly those who are the first assistants of the Police President, have the title *Oberregierungsrat.* These men do not come from the army as is the case with most of the uniformed lieutenants. They are university graduates in law who have entered the governmental service as a profession and have been advanced through various grades either in the police department or in another branch of the state employ. Some of them have thus been brought into the department from county or provincial service or from one of the numerous ministerial offices. ·Probably, too, they will ultimately be promoted from the police department

---

[1] If capable, the lieutenant may be promoted to the rank of captain *(Hauptmann)* in charge of a district; from this grade he may be advanced to that of major, and if fortunate in this, he may eventually become the head of the entire uniformed force under the control of the police president. It is probable that he could never become police president; at least, no member of the uniformed force has ever had such a promotion. The police president, as we have seen, is generally taken from the Prussian civil governmental service where he has had charge of a county or has been an assistant in a province. These men, as we shall see, represent a still higher step in the Prussian bureaucracy and are all university graduates in law.

Assistant Commissioners and Their Deputies

to higher offices in the state. In Dresden, where the
same system is in force, as indeed it is in force throughout Germany, the writer talked with four officials holding the rank of *Regierungsassessor,* which corresponds
roughly to that of deputy assistant commissioner, who
expected soon to be promoted to other branches of the
state service, one entering the Royal Insurance Office,
and three going to take charge of county governments in
Saxony. Similarly in Munich, and in every other German city where the police force is part of the state
service, the higher officers, the officers who may be termed
assistant commissioners, the men who are connected with
the administration of the department, are all university
graduates in law, trained specialists who have made government work their profession. The police department
is but one of many offices to which they may be assigned;
indeed, it is but one rung in a long ladder of promotion.
Administrative service of every kind in Germany has
become a profession for which men must qualify by
thorough training and an examination which varies according as the candidates intend to pursue a strictly administrative, a judicial or a semi-judicial career. Members of this service are representatives of the upper class
of German society and constitute what is known as the
governmental bureaucracy.

With more or less variation, Germany's system is to be
found in almost every city on the Continent, particularly
in the cities whose police departments are under the control of the state. Some years ago in Amsterdam, the
inspecteurs, who correspond to Berlin's lieutenants and
represent the first rank above the grade of sergeant, were

customarily promoted from the lower orders of the uniformed force. Indeed, this was the practice in a number of Dutch cities. It has almost without exception been abandoned. " The police authorities were unable to get the kind of men they wanted," the Head Commissioner of Amsterdam told me. " *Inspecteurs* were ignorant and sometimes dishonest; they lacked stability." To-day, in Amsterdam, Rotterdam, and in all the other Dutch cities, *inspecteurs* are recruited from outside sources. They come from the middle class of Dutch society and must have received what is equivalent to a good high-school education. Entering the police department between the ages of 22 and 26,[1] they must be intelligent and well-bred, physically healthy and of good character, and the references which they are obliged to present from all former employers running back to their school days must be satisfactory in every respect. Before being admitted to the training class, they are required to pass a written and oral examination in Dutch, French, German and English, which languages they must speak and write fluently. In addition, they are examined in the geography and history of Holland. They are then admitted as probationary *inspecteurs* and are assigned to practical work in the different parts of the police organization, a course of training similar to Berlin's. In Amsterdam, the training lasts for a year; in Rotterdam, for six months.

In addition to these features Rotterdam's system includes a regular school course consisting of lectures and

---

[1] This is true of Amsterdam; in Rotterdam applicants must be between the ages of 20 and 30.

Assistant Commissioners and Their Deputies

recitations which the candidates are obliged to attend. At the end of the training period, they must pass an examination covering such subjects as police organization, the penal code, the laws of evidence and the laws relating to citizenship, associations, weights and measures and many other regulations. Moreover, they must have become fairly proficient in the working of the Morse code of telegraphy. These various subjects involve not only careful attention to their daily work, but a large amount of evening study. If successful in passing the examination, they are appointed to vacancies as they occur.[1] All the higher officials in the department with the exception of the commissioners in the largest cities, who, as we have seen, are taken directly from the army, are promoted from the men who enter the police service in the manner just described.

This elaborate training of those brought in from outside sources to fill the higher places in the police department is characteristic of many other cities on the Continent. It exists in Brussels, Copenhagen, and even in Paris, although the leveling effect of French democracy has to a certain extent curtailed the development of the system.[2] In Christiania, Norway, and in other northern cities, the Commissioner, the inspectors, the chief of detectives and the lieutenants must all be university graduates in law.

[1] In Amsterdam, there are two classes of *inspecteurs,* in Rotterdam, three classes. After a period of training, a man enters the lowest class. He may be promoted from time to time after passing other qualifying examinations.

[2] Examinations for the higher ranks are practically open to all, both within and without the uniformed force. The severity of the examinations, however, serves to eliminate the unfit.

European Police Systems

Austria and Italy, however, have developed the most thoroughgoing method for the training of their superior police officers. In Vienna the operation of the *Rangsklasse* system makes it necessary for every official above the grade of non-commissioned officer to be a university graduate in law. Fresh from the university where he has perhaps spent five years and obtained his doctorate in law,[1] the candidate takes the severe examinations for entrance into the government service. If successful he may be assigned to any one of a number of public departments. If he comes to the police department he enters as a *Praktikant* in the eleventh rank-class. Here his course of training lasts five years, the first of which is served without pay.[2] During this long period he receives class-room instruction four months in the year (9 A. M. to 2 P. M.), and the rest of his time is spent in practical work in the various bureaus. He is drilled in police laws and ordinances, in the organization and administration of the different branches of the department, in criminal methods and procedure. It is the intention of the authorities to develop a fully trained police expert who will devote his life to his specialty as a profession.

The result is that the heads of the precincts of Vienna and their lieutenants, the heads of the detective bureau, and the chiefs of all the specialized detective squads at headquarters, in fact, all persons of importance in the

---

[1] A student enters the university at the age of 18 or 19 from a *Gymnasium* or other similar institution of learning. A four years' course is required before the candidate is eligible to try the governmental examinations. To become a doctor of laws requires at least five years and sometimes a longer period.

[2] His salary begins at 1,000 *Kronen* ($200) per annum.

Assistant Commissioners and Their Deputies

department from the Police President to the *Praktikant* are university trained men. A citizen who makes a complaint at his precinct station, who calls on the chief of the Lost and Found Bureau at headquarters, or who comes to see any other department head, will probably transact his business with a college graduate, who must be addressed with the title "Doctor." Service in these upper ranks of the police department offers a career of dignity and distinction. It attracts the best talent. It is eagerly sought after as an honorable profession in which promotion is practically unlimited. Its conspicuous representatives are often decorated by the Crown for effective service, or by visiting rulers from foreign countries, and more than one official at headquarters and even in the divisions is able to write after his name the coveted "*Ritt.*" Throughout all the cities of Austria and even in Hungary this system is in force; and while comparisons are difficult to draw it is scarcely too much to say that in point of culture and education the higher police officers of cities like Vienna and Budapest are generally superior to those to be found elsewhere in Europe.

Hardly less thorough and effective, however, is the method which Italy has adopted to train the administrators of her police forces. The Italian system is unique in that it comprehends a national constabulary, equipped and officered on military lines, but directed, so far as its police functions are concerned, by a corps of trained civilians — the members of the Division of Public Security. The representatives of this staff — there are over 1700 of them in Italy in different grades of the service — are taken from the legal profession, which they

European Police Systems

must have followed for at least two years. Their average age is twenty-seven. Many of them have received university degrees in law or in sociology. Chosen on the basis of a competitive examination, they at once enter upon the four months' course of the Scientific Police School of Rome,[1] presided over by the renowned Dr. Ottolenghi.[2] Maintained by the Ministry of the Interior, this school combines the training course of police executives with the national identification service of Italy. Here are located the criminal files, the record photographs and finger prints by which the Italian police everywhere keep track of the criminal population. This service is under the control of the well-known Dr. Gasti.[3] Here, too, is the chemical and physical laboratory used by the police of Rome in their investigations. In the vicinity is the jail or remand prison,[4] in which are confined the prisoners awaiting trial or sentence. In other words, a wealth of material for school purposes is near at hand and the aim is to give the students an intimate knowledge of practical police work. The course consists of lectures, recitations, and demonstrations. Adapted to the developments of Italian criminal procedure it is designed to teach the candidates how to cross-examine a prisoner and how by the use of simple psychological factors to break down the defense of a suspect. It includes instruction in dactyloscopy, record-keeping, photography and the penal law, together with a series of remarkable

[1] *Scuola di Polizia Scientifica.*
[2] Formerly Professor of Criminology of the University of Sienna.
[3] For a description of this system, see Chap. IX, p. 329.
[4] *Carceri giudiziarie.*

Assistant Commissioners and Their Deputies

lectures by Dr. Ottolenghi and Dr. Gasti on the motives and methods of criminals. How far-reaching has been the influence of this latter course may be gathered from the fact that not a few of the school's graduates have contributed materially to the sociological literature of Italy in a series of scientific and highly interesting monographs.

Examinations conclude the four months' course.[1] If successful, the candidates enter the division of public security as *delegati,* and are assigned to active service in some town or city of Italy. Ultimately, as we have seen, they may be promoted to the rank of *commissario* and later to that of *questore;* in the latter capacity they have sole charge of the police forces of a province.[2]

The Continental practice of introducing new but well-trained material from outside sources to take practically all the superior positions in the police departments has this undoubted advantage: it procures a better grade of official than is the case where the higher positions are filled by promotion from the ranks. The Continental officers, particularly in Austria and in many of the cities of Germany, bring to their work a vision and a training which English officers often lack. One gets the impres-

[1] The Scientific Police School of Rome has been in existence twelve years. The course for *delegati* is given once a year. In 1914, this course contained 77 pupils; in 1913, 105 pupils. In the same school is also given, twice a year, a four months' course for twenty-five selected City Guards, who are instructed in the *portrait parlé* system and other phases of practical detective work.

[2] Every year twelve of the most promising *commissari* are selected by the Ministry of the Interior to attend an advanced course in applied criminology given by the University of Rome under the direction of the celebrated Dr. Niceforo. The course is attended by magistrates, prison employees and other governmental servants. It includes instruction in judicial statistics, identification, the principles of evidence and practical criminology.

sion that more real intelligence is devoted to police work on the Continent than in Great Britain, and certainly the contrast between the university-trained district commander of Vienna, for example, and the London superintendent who has risen from the ranks bears out the impression. Where the former is quick, keen, farsighted and resourceful, the latter is slow, somewhat unadaptable, ploddingly faithful, working with little imagination. This description is roughly impressionistic — there are sharp variations on both sides — but it serves to bring out the general distinction. The distinction cannot be laid to national or racial characteristics; at least such characteristics play but a small part in the results. It is due to divergent principles in training and selection and to different social environments.

The Vienna official enters the police department fresh from the university. Starting with a trained mind, he is given every facility for acquiring a practical grasp of his work; he is promoted from one responsible post to another as his abilities warrant. He belongs to a superior social order. The life, the thought, the habits of mind of the lower grades of the uniformed force are unknown to him. His acquaintances and friends are university men like himself. He moves in a world of practical scholarship. After years of responsible work he is made head of a *Bezirk* or division — a position of honor and distinction in the community, which carries with it a remuneration ample for Vienna, an official residence, and of course the ultimate right to a pension.[1] He can reason-

[1] The salary of the district commander approximates 7,000 *Kronen* ($1,421) per annum, besides certain small extras. His resi-

ably anticipate further promotion to still higher positions in the department.

The London superintendent, on the other hand, comes unlettered and untrained from the country districts of England. Entering the force as a constable he rises slowly by gradual promotions. The quickest, shrewdest minds in the department are absorbed in the detective bureau; his own promotion in the uniformed ranks follows more as the reward of faithfulness than of brilliancy or adaptability. Indeed, of these latter qualities he has none. He is a big, slow-moving, rugged type, working deliberately and carefully. His point of view is largely that of the uniformed ranks. He would probably lack the initiative and imagination to make an efficient commissioner or to carry on unaided a big administrative project. In education, training and potential ability he is distinctly inferior to his brother officer in Vienna.[1]

But recruiting the superior officers of a police department from outside sources rather than by promotion from the ranks has certain disadvantages. In the first place, this method, by limiting the possibility of promotion, dulls

dence is furnished free. The London superintendent gets £340 to £450 ($1,654 to $2,146) per annum besides various extras of a somewhat liberal character, but has no official residence allowed him.

[1] But see the testimony of the Commissioner of the Metropolitan police, Sir Edward Henry, before the Royal Commission in 1907. "There is a great advantage," he said, "in having a man (as superintendent) who has been right through the mill. If twenty or thirty men come through and become superintendents, it must be because they are exceptional men and have strong qualities. They have seen police work in all its phases and they know how a constable in the street ought to behave. . . . If I were a dictator I would not be prepared from my actual knowledge at the present moment to change the system." (*Report of the Royal Commission,* Vol. II, p. 15.)

the spirit and perhaps the effectiveness of the rank and file of the uniformed force. The Continental policeman may become a sergeant, but he can seldom go higher.[1] His position is fixed. Merit and ability may bring him the gratitude of his superiors but increases in rank and income are denied him. Save for the fear of discipline there are few compelling inducements to efficient work. His actions tend to become perfunctory and his attitude listless. He is a cog in a machine, without the incentives which spur the English constable to faithful effort. He is not dissatisfied, because with his social environment he does not expect promotion, but he does not grow in ability as the English policeman grows. As we shall see in a later chapter, the rank and file of English police forces are in spirit and intelligence generally superior to the Continental rank and file. Undoubtedly one of the contributing factors in this situation is the incentive to faithful and painstaking work which the possibility of extensive promotion holds out to the English police.

In the second place, the introduction of new material from outside sources to fill the higher positions in the force produces an organization that is socially stratified, and in some departments results in a certain lack of unity and sympathetic coöperation in the performance of official business. The point of view, the habits of thought, and even the grievances of the lower ranks are utterly unknown to many Continental officials. On the other hand, the attitude and perspective of the officials are not understood or are misunderstood by the rank and file. Each group lives its own life, touching the life of the

[1] See Chap. VII, under heading " Promotion."

other only in official relationship. Outside of the Italian *Carabinieri,* a distinctly military organization, welded together by an iron discipline, one looks in vain on the Continent for the splendid *esprit-de-corps* which permeates the entire Metropolitan Police Force of London.[1] The social cleavage in the Continental department is too sharp and well-defined to admit of any such feeling. Three distinct classes of society are represented in the Berlin force and no bridge can span the gulfs that separate them. Under such circumstances, it is idle to expect the same kind of conscious unity, departmental pride, or even coöperation which one finds in an organization socially more composite.

It is difficult to arrive at any settled opinion as a result of this comparison of English and Continental methods. In this, as in other matters, local conditions and national administrative ideals must be taken into the reckoning. One cannot overlook the advantages of introducing into the department well-trained officials of a higher grade of efficiency than can usually be obtained by promotion from the ranks. On the other hand, the results of this practice, if consistently carried out, are not entirely wholesome. A compromise between the extremes of the two systems might prove the best solution. Certainly for the sake of efficiency the uniformed men should be allowed to advance further than the grade of sergeant. On the other hand, it is possible that much might be accomplished even in London if the superin-

[1] As we have seen, there are only eleven positions on the Metropolitan Force which are not filled by promotion from the lower ranks: the commissionership, four assistant commissionerships, and six chief constableships.

tendents and perhaps the chief inspectors, the men who command the large divisions, were recruited from those whose education has been more extensive and who would enter the force as trained administrators after a special schooling in police work. This suggestion, however, is debatable. The London superintendent suits London. He is honest and reliable, he does his work slowly but well. The sole question is whether men of broader training and larger imagination would not do the work better.

Perhaps the most that can be said in the form of a general proposition is that every police department ought always to be able to introduce outsiders into the higher positions when more effective men can be secured in this manner than by promotion. A department obligated by law or rigid custom to choose its officials from its own ranks is apt to become mechanical in carrying out its routine work and unadaptable in meeting new problems. Where there is no possibility of outside competition, where no fresh imagination can ever revitalize the task, the department suffers from perfunctory service. The right to correct this condition by the infusion of new blood in high administrative positions should never be denied a police organization.

CHAPTER VI

THE UNIFORMED FORCE

Continental policemen taken from the army.— English policemen taken from private life.— The country districts the source of London's recruits.— Methods of recruiting in London.— In the provincial cities.— The army under-officer the basis of the Continental department.— Kind of men obtained.— Older than the English policemen. — Police training school in Vienna.— In Berlin.— In Paris.— In London.— Variations in Great Britain and on the Continent.— Courses generally too brief.— Lack of adequate equipment.— Instruction too narrow.— Army *versus* private life as source of recruits. —Objections to army men.— Berlin *Schutzmann versus* London constable.

WE must now turn our attention to the men who constitute the rank and file of the uniformed force, and upon whom the burden of police work falls — the patrolmen.[1] We must note the sources from which they are obtained, their training and equipment, their opportunities for promotion, their pay, and their pension systems. Finally we must observe the patrolmen at work, their life and habits, and the methods by which they are supervised and controlled.

At the outset, we are again confronted by a contrast between Great Britain and the Continent. The Continental policemen almost without exception are taken

---

[1] These men have varying titles in different cities. They are called " Constables " in London and throughout England generally; " *Agents* " in Holland; " *Schutzmänner* " in Berlin; " *Sicherheitswachmänner* " in Vienna; and " *Gardiens de la paix* " in Paris.

European Police Systems

directly from the army, where they have served as soldiers in the ranks. The English constables, chosen from private life, come for the most part from the country districts, and have only in rare instances served in the army. This fundamental distinction finds its basis in the separate points of view from which, as we have already noticed, England and the Continent conceive the object and purpose of a police force. In England, the police are civil employees whose primary duty is the preservation of public security; on the Continent, on the other hand, and particularly in Germany and Austria, the police force is the right arm of the ruling classes, responsible to the Crown or the higher authorities rather than to the people. The police problem on the Continent is chiefly a military problem, whereas in England and Scotland, it is a problem of civil administration. The Continental authorities, therefore, in their search for well equipped policemen, naturally look to the army, while it is just as natural for the English to avoid military training in a policeman and to turn for recruits to the more peaceful trades and callings.

Taking London as typical of English habits and ideas in this respect, we find the majority of her 17,000 patrolmen recruited from the agricultural districts of the counties of England and Scotland. Only a small proportion of the men — approximately twenty per cent.— come from London itself. There are two reasons for this. In the first place, London in common with other cities and towns of Great Britain does not care to have on her force policemen with local ties and connections. Probably one-fourth of the municipalities of England refuse

200

The Uniformed Force

to permit men to join the constabulary who for any length of time have lived in their cities,[1] and while London does not carry the matter to this extreme, her authorities regard a long established residence in the Metropolitan district as a disqualification. In the second place, the police officials of London entertain serious doubts as to the serviceability of city bred men in the force. " They know too much," said the head of the police training school,[2] in discussing this matter with the writer, " too much that is detrimental to good discipline. You have to knock so much out of their heads before you can begin their training." The London " Bobby " is, therefore, recruited for the most part from the country districts. Miners, chauffeurs, plumbers, and clerks are taken, but farmers are preferred. " We like to take them right from the plow," Sir Edward Henry told the writer. " They are slow but steady; you can mold them into any shape you please."

In the absence of accurate statistics, it is a safe assumption that sixty per cent. of London's constables have been country born and bred.[3] Probably the most prolific sources of supply for recruits are the counties in the west and south-west of England, although men are often chosen from as far north as Scotland. Recruiting agents are constantly traveling from place to place in the country districts of England and even in Scotland and Wales, looking for available men. They go about their business

[1] Personally communicated.
[2] Supt. A. W. Gooding.
[3] Personally communicated by officials. Some of them, of course, come from the provincial cities. Occasionally they are taken from other police forces, but only under exceptional circumstances.

very much as an army recruiting squad handles its work, by means of newspaper advertisements and bill posters setting forth the attractiveness of service in the Metropolitan force.[1] News of their coming is heralded in advance, and applicants are advised that they may present themselves for examination at a given time and place. The candidates must conform to certain physical requirements as to age, height and general condition, they must be able to read, write, and have a fair knowledge of spelling, and must pass a very rudimentary and informal examination in arithmetic. If able to conform to these simple tests, they are tentatively accepted by the recruiting agents,[2] provided their testimonials are satisfactory, and are sent to the police training school in London, of which we shall speak later. In case of need, their expenses to London are advanced.

In making these preliminary tests the greatest care is taken to weed out the unfit. The testimonials above re-

[1] The newspaper advertisement is the usual method of attracting recruits in the provincial cities. An example of the form used follows:

"Liverpool City Police. Wanted: Young men of good character, 21 to 25 years of age; height over 5 ft. 9½ in.; commence at 27s. a week. Good prospects for intelligent men. Ample facilities for recreation.— Apply, giving age, height, and occupation, to Head Constable, Liverpool."

A typical bill poster reads in part as follows:

METROPOLITAN POLICE
RECRUITS WANTED.

There are vacancies for several hundred young men of good health, character and education.— Good prospects of promotion — permanent employment and pension for life after 25 years' service — free medical attendance provided during sickness with continuance of pay — annual holidays.

[2] The recruiting party consists of a Superintendent, who is the head of the recruiting department of Scotland Yard, two assistants, and one medical man.

The Uniformed Force

ferred to are regarded as of prime importance. Not only is the candidate required to furnish the names and addresses of two responsible people who have known him for more than five years, together with the names of the persons by whom he has been employed during the preceding six months, but the statements from these parties in regard to the character and standing of the applicant are carefully obtained, and are verified in every case by the local police officials of the community in which the candidate lives. These local officials are asked to subscribe to the following form:

" I certify that I have seen the persons named by the Candidate as reference and employer, that they have given the answers shown against the questions, and that they are persons whose recommendations are deserving of the confidence of the Commissioner of Police. I have also enquired in the neighborhood, and I am unable to learn anything to the prejudice of the Candidate, and I believe his connections and associates to be respectable. It is not known that the Candidate has ever served in any Police Force, or that he has had any employment other than that stated." [1]

It is estimated that from $2\frac{1}{2}\%$ to 5% of the applicants, otherwise acceptable, are dropped as a result of these independent inquiries.[2] It is not necessary that the candidate should have a criminal record to effect his rejection. Any flaw in his character or any uncertainty as to his general standing in the community is sufficient.

[1] Metropolitan Police. Form No. 20a.
[2] Personally communicated.

European Police Systems

Cases are on record where men have been refused because they came of families whose reputation was unsavory. " We cannot afford to take chances; we must be sure of our men," was the significant remark of the Superintendent of the London Training School.

The practice of recruiting from country districts is not peculiar to London alone. It obtains in every important municipal police force of Great Britain. " Give us the hardy northern farmers," said the Head Constable of Liverpool. " They are the easiest to train and make the best officers." This same preference was expressed in Glasgow, Edinburgh, Manchester and Birmingham. Indeed, competition to secure the best of the able-bodied farmers for the city police forces sometimes engenders a feeling approaching resentment between the municipalities. " They might stay in their own territory," complained one of the superintendents of the Glasgow force, referring to the recruiting squad of the Metropolitan police. " They take the best of Scotland because they are in a position to offer superior inducements. It's striking below the belt for them to come up here."

The provincial cities are as painstaking as London in weeding out the unfit candidates. In every instance, the applicant's references are verified by the independent scrutiny of the local police.[1] In Liverpool, satisfactory

[1] The forms used are practically the same for all the provincial cities. For example, a typical letter from a Chief Constable to the head of another police body is as follows:

" SIR: I should be obliged if you will kindly have enquiry made as to the character of —— —— who applies for appointment to this Force, and inform me at your earliest convenience whether his statement is correct, and, in your opinion, his antecedents are such as to qualify him for appointment as Constable." (Liverpool City Police, Form No. 13.)

The Uniformed Force

recommendations are required from the candidate's employer or employers for the previous ten years; in Glasgow, for the previous five years; in Manchester, separate character references are required, which, together with the employer's references, must cover the previous ten years; in the City of London the references must include the whole scope of the applicant's life, beginning with his school days. As with the Metropolitan force, great emphasis is laid on the standing and reliability of the men who endorse the candidates. So careful are the recruiting authorities in this respect, that in Glasgow I was told that certificates of clergymen are generally not considered with favor. "They are too kind-hearted, too apt to overlook flaws," said the superintendent, "or perhaps they are unaware that the flaws exist!"

In marked contrast with the English point of view is the practice prevailing on the Continent. There, policemen come directly from the army where ordinarily they must have reached a certain grade or rank. Thus, throughout Germany, Austria and Hungary, the recruit must be an *Unteroffizier,* a grade approximately corresponding to the English rank of corporal.[1] The length of army service required varies in different cities. Berlin demands a minimum of nine years; Hamburg and Dresden, six years;[2] Stuttgart, five years; Budapest, three

---

[1] The grades of the rank and file of the German army are as follows:

> Gemeiner (Private)
> Gefreiter
> Unteroffizier
> Sergeant
> Vize-Feldwebel

[2] "We prefer a longer service in the army if we can secure it,"

years. Vienna does not specifically prescribe army service as a necessary qualification, but preference is by law [1]
given to the *Unteroffizier,* and it is seldom that recruits
are taken from any other class. Formerly Dresden required twelve years' service in the army, and even now
the regulations call for nine years,[2] although the difficulty of obtaining the necessary number of men under
this rule has led to the temporary substitution of six
years. On the other hand, Berlin formerly required six
years' army service; later the period was changed to
seven years; and in 1907, the present nine year term was
made obligatory. These changes were brought about
through the instrumentality of the Prussian War Office
which felt that the army was being deprived of the services of too many of its younger and more valuable non-
commissioned officers, through its inability to compete
with the police force in the matter of salaries.[3]

was the remark of the Police President of Hamburg in discussing
this matter with me.

[1] Law of April 19, 1872. *R. G. Bl.* No. 60.

[2] *Dienstvorschriften für das uniformierte Stadtgendarmeriekorps
der Königlichen Polizeidirektion zu Dresden.* § 29.

[3] As we shall see, the Berlin *Schutzmann* receives 1,400 M. per
annum; the army *Unteroffizier,* in addition to his maintenance, receives 8.40 M. every ten days, or approximately 306 M. per annum,
together with certain small and comparatively insignificant extras
—" *Zulage.*"

The *Unteroffizier* in the German army is encouraged to serve a
longer rather than a shorter period by the operation of the law
relating to civil papers, or " *Zivilversorgungsschein.*" (Imperial
Law, May 31, 1906 — *Reichsgesetzblatt* 593. See also *Bundesrats-
beschluss* of June 20, 1907.) According to this law, the positions
of the lower officials and clerks in the state and imperial service
are reserved exclusively for soldiers who have served twelve years
in the army; that is, at the end of such a period, a soldier is entitled to a position as postman, clerk, etc., in one of the government
branches.

If, however, the soldier leaves the army at the end of nine years
and enters a police department, he must serve there for six years

The Uniformed Force

In Amsterdam and Rotterdam, there is no specific requirement of army service for policemen, but preference is always given to army men, and it is estimated that eighty per cent. of the police force have had previous military training.[1] The same condition is true in Brussels, Paris, and throughout the French cities generally. Army training is not specifically demanded, but candidates for the police force are required to have served their prescribed term under the compulsory enlistment laws,[2] and preference is given to the men who have reached the grade of *sous-officier*. Occasionally it happens that a civilian is appointed to the Paris force. In that case, however, he is placed on a year's probation, while the man who has served in the army is at once permanently appointed.[3]

more, fifteen years altogether, before he is entitled to his *Zivilversorgungsschein*. The effect of this law is to keep many men in the army who otherwise would leave for more desirable situations.

[1] Personally communicated by the police officials of Rotterdam.

[2] Compulsory enlistment laws are common throughout the Continent. Every man in Germany must serve two years in the army, although there is an exception — the *Einjährigen* system — by which men of higher school education are allowed to serve for one year provided they pay their own expenses. According to the new French enlistment law, the term of conscription is raised from two years to three years. The new German war measures do not involve the lengthening of the compulsory term of enlistment, but provide for more regiments. In Germany, if a man serves longer than his prescribed two years, he is appointed automatically to the grade of *Unteroffizier*.

[3] In this chapter I have purposely avoided reference to the national police of Italy, that is, to the *Carabinieri*, inasmuch as it cannot be considered as a municipal force. It cannot be said that their recruits are chosen from the army, for the corps constitutes part of the army. A well-qualified Italian may serve his required military term with the *Carabinieri* or with some other corps, except that if he joins the *Carabinieri*, he must serve three years rather than two. The City Guards, on the other hand, are chosen from those who have fulfilled their two years' army requirement. Enlistment in this corps is for five years.

European Police Systems

The army under-officer, therefore, forms the basis of the police forces on the Continent. In every case his army record must have been satisfactory before he is accepted. To that end his history is carefully scrutinized. In Vienna he must present certificates of character covering the period from the time of his tenth birthday. Breaches of army discipline which have resulted in punishment or demotion are regarded as sufficient cause for rejection. In Berlin candidates are obliged to file sworn statements showing the amounts of their debts, including the payment of alimony. For the most part, also, the under-officers applying for appointment on a police force are subjected to a medical examination, and in some cities, to a preliminary though rather elementary test of intelligence. " Non-suitable candidates will at once be sent back to their regiments without refunding of fees or traveling expenses " is the rather ominous declaration of the Berlin entrance requirements,[1] in referring to this point. As a matter of practice, however, throughout Germany and Austria it is generally assumed that a man who has reached the grade of non-commissioned officer in the army is intelligent enough to become a policeman, and while mental examinations, both written and oral, are occasionally given before permanent appointment, they generally follow the prescribed period of training of which we shall speak later in this chapter. In Paris and other French cities, *sous-officiers* in the army must pass satisfactorily in arithmetic, reading and writing before they can enter the

---

[1] *Einstellungsbestimmungen. A. V. Bl. Nr. 19 vom 13. September, 1912. § 4.*

The Uniformed Force

police training schools. As a matter of fact, non-commissioned officers in European armies are all passably well educated, that is, they have had the regular common school education. Indeed, in Germany, the non-commissioned officers in the army are obliged to attend school classes during the winter months where they receive instruction in writing and spelling as well as in arithmetic and geography, with the idea of refreshing their early training. To a lesser extent, perhaps, this is true of the armies in other European countries, so that the non-commissioned officer who applies for admission to a police force is by no means an uneducated man. Indeed, in respect to his school advantages, he probably compares favorably with the constable of London or any of the English provincial cities, while in his military training, he is, of course, greatly superior to the English policeman.

The requirement of army service as a necessary prerequisite to admission into the police ranks has the effect, as will be seen from the table on the next page, of increasing the age at which men enter the force. In London, constables are not admitted who exceed the age of 27; Liverpool and Glasgow will not admit constables over 25; Manchester fixes the maximum at 28. Across the Channel the maximum age limit is greatly increased. Berlin and Vienna, and in fact most of the cities of Germany, Austria, Holland, and Belgium, take policemen up to the age of 35. With a required army service of nine years, as is the case in Berlin, it would be practically impossible to fix an age limit lower than this. A man who enters the German army at the age of twenty,

AGE, HEIGHT AND ARMY SERVICE REQUIREMENTS FOR POLICEMEN OF EUROPEAN CITIES.

City.	Age.	Minimum Height.	Army Service Required.
London:			
Metropolitan Force.	20–27	5 ft. 9 in. ⎫	None.
City of London	20–27	6 ft. ⎬	None.
Liverpool	21–25	5 ft. 9½ in.	None.
Glasgow	25 max.	5 ft. 9½ in.	None.
Manchester	28 max.	5 ft. 10 in.	None.
Amsterdam	23–35	5 ft. 7 in.	Must have satisfied compulsory enlistment laws.
Rotterdam	23–35	5 ft. 9 in.	Must have satisfied compulsory enlistment laws.
Berlin	35 max.	5 ft. 5 in.	Nine years in army, with rank of *Unteroffizier.*
Dresden	25–35	5 ft. 7 in.	Six years in army, with rank of *Unteroffizier.*
Hamburg	25–35	5 ft. 5½ in.	Six years in army, with rank of *Unteroffizier.*
Stuttgart	24–35	5 ft. 5½ in.	Five years in army, with rank of *Unteroffizier.*
Vienna	24–35	5 ft. 2¼ in.	Former *Unteroffizier* in army preferred.
Budapest	25 max.		Three years in army, with rank of *Unteroffizier.*
Paris	21–30	5 ft. 7 in.	Must have served prescribed term under compulsory enlistment law. Preference to *Sous-officier.*
Brussels	23–35	5 ft. 7 in.	Must have served prescribed term under compulsory enlistment law.

210

The Uniformed Force

wishing to take advantage of the civil rights accruing from full service,[1] will be thirty-two before he can apply for admission to a police force; or waiving his civil rights, he will be twenty-nine before the Berlin force can receive him. As a matter of fact, the average age of entrance into the police service of Berlin is 31,[2] whereas in London it is 23. Accordingly, the police force of Berlin is manned by older and correspondingly less active men. It is a noteworthy fact that the young, fresh, keen, vigorous look of the London " Bobby " is almost totally lacking in the Berlin *Schutzmann,* who, although he may snap his heels together and salute with more precision than his fellow officer in London, has a heavy, inactive appearance. The Berlin authorities do not hesitate to admit that their men are rather too old for the kind of service required. Without in any way disavowing their belief that the army furnishes the best training for police-men — a principle with which they are thoroughly imbued — they are frank to state that nine years is too long for a required term of service, and that the former requirement of six years is preferable. One or two of them even express qualified indignation that in the clash between the interests of the army and the police, the police should be made to suffer.

Let us now examine the methods by which the new men are trained for their work. Police training schools for recruits have long been established institutions in European municipalities. The first one — in Paris — was founded in 1883. At the present time there is no

[1] See note 3, p. 206, relating to the *Zivilversorgungsschein* provisions.
[2] Personally communicated.

city of size or importance in Europe that does not provide some kind of school training for its police recruits. Some of the schools are elaborate organizations with separately constructed buildings and complete equipment; others are scarcely more than names to cover a desultory and rudimentary instruction. On the whole, the schools of the Continental cities are better equipped and the courses more complete than those operated in connection with the English police. Ordinarily the required school term of the Continental course covers a longer period than the English school term. London's course lasts for eight weeks; Liverpool's, for eight weeks; Glasgow has a term of "two months more or less," a period which frankly varies with the need for new men; Manchester's school term averages from two to three months, although the term is in part dependent upon the adaptability of the candidate; the term of the Paris school is four months; Berlin's, five weeks; Dresden's, six weeks; Hamburg's covers two periods of six weeks each, separated by practical service on the street for a term of six weeks; Vienna's school term extends over an entire year, although during part of this period the men are on active duty in uniform; the Budapest school lasts for four months. The *Carabinieri* and City Guards of Italy have six months' training. Some of the schools require the entire time of the recruit during the period above mentioned; in others, theoretical training goes hand in hand with practical duty on the street.

The scope of the police training school and its methods of operation vary sharply from city to city, even in the same country. The difference between the training

The Uniformed Force

schools of Hamburg and Berlin is almost as striking as the difference between those of London and Berlin. In order that we may see in what this difference consists and arrive at a common basis for discussion, brief attention is called to the courses of instruction in the schools of Vienna, Berlin, Paris, and London.

Vienna's school for recruits is by far the most elaborate and the best equipped in Europe.[1] Utilizing the old university buildings for the purpose, the police authorities have fitted up class rooms and dormitories, with such accessories as a museum, a library and a gymnasium. The school has 350 pupils, and the course, as we have said, lasts for one year. During this period the recruits are obliged to live in the dormitories and to take their meals in the school dining-room. They are divided into classes of twenty-five, called *Kameradschaften*. Each class has its leader or teacher, generally a non-commissioned officer of the police force. The class is the working unit of the organization. By classes, the recruits eat and sleep; by classes they are taught to swim and row, to shoot and fence, to use the Morse telegraph and the appliances for first aid to the injured; by classes, too, they attend fires and riots, where the work of the regular police is carefully studied. Occasionally they are themselves called upon to assist when some public celebration or parade, or a riot or disturbance, creates a dif-

[1] In making this statement, I have not taken into consideration the training school of the *Carabinieri* in Rome. This institution is a military school rather than a police school, and as such cannot be compared with the institutions in Vienna, London, Berlin and Paris. In so far as size, buildings, and general equipment are concerned, it is immeasurably superior to any of the police schools of Europe.

ficult situation. In this respect the school recruits con-stitute a reserve force for the regular organization.

For the first eight weeks of their stay in the .police school, the recruits are drilled in the practical duties of patrol. This work is supplemented by occasional lectures on rudimentary legal matters delivered by the higher police officers before groups of classes. During this period, their school hours run from 8 to 11 A. M., and from 2.30 to 5.30 P. M., the lectures and recitations following each other in close succession. At the mid-day recess, the recruits are sent into various sections of the city with maps to learn the location of buildings and monuments, the routes of street cars and busses, and the general geography of Vienna. In the evening, they practise gymnasium exercises and fencing. At the end of eight weeks, they receive their uniforms and begin their work on the street in the company of experienced policemen. From now on, the school exercises consume only the mornings, the afternoons being devoted to patrol work. After three months, the recruits are allowed to patrol alone. During the last six months of his probation period, each man is assigned to a model precinct located in the heart of the city where he assumes his regular hours of police work, his entire class being on duty with him at the same time. His theoretical training, how-ever, is not neglected during this period. In addition to his instruction in practical police duty, he must become thoroughly familiar with the operations of the Austrian criminal code and the code of criminal procedure; he must have a working knowledge of the elaborate legal provisions relating to the various functions of the police;

The Uniformed Force

he must be able to read and write fluently in the German tongue, and is occasionally instructed in foreign languages; he is taught the mystery of bombs and explosives; he must understand poisons and their antidotes; he is instructed in bullet-marks, blood spots, knife wounds, and methods of identification; he must be an expert telegrapher, and have a practical knowledge of first-aid appliances. He attends illustrated lectures on traffic conditions and the control of crowds; he is taught by object lessons to read the numbers and license signs on swiftly moving vehicles; finally, he is thoroughly drilled in the conduct and bearing befitting a policeman of Vienna. Much of his work is done with the aid of an elaborate series of police textbooks prepared for the uses of the school. At the end of the year's term, he must pass written examinations in the subjects which he has studied; if successful, he is promoted to the regular force and assigned to a precinct.

His life during his year's probation is not at all unpleasant. He is paid seventy cents a day,[1] the meals which he obtains at a nominal price in the school restaurant constituting his only expense.[2] He is graduated in splendid physical condition, and with a thorough grasp not only of the practical and theoretical aspects of police work, but of the intricacies of Austrian criminal law and procedure. His education, however, does not stop when he leaves the police school. His whole official life is one long period of instruction. Every precinct house has its schoolroom, and at least once a week the

[1] 3 *Kronen, 68 heller.*
[2] His breakfast costs four cents; dinner, twelve cents; supper, ten cents.

patrolmen [1] are obliged to meet in classes, regardless of their length of service or experience. In these classes matters relating to new ordinances and decrees and to recently promulgated traffic regulations are thoroughly discussed, and lectures are given on new methods of detecting criminals. Similarly, new phases of police duty, mistakes in patrol work or in report writing, are taken up for discussion and elucidation. The schoolrooms are very attractively equipped with desks, blackboards and maps, and the whole life in the precinct centers around this unique institution. From the standpoint of training, there is no police force in Europe which can excel the *Sicherheitswache* of Vienna. Indeed, the only police department which even approximates it in this respect is Budapest's, where the Vienna model has been more or less closely followed.[2]

In comparison with Vienna's method of training her recruits, the Berlin school seems inadequate. Not only does the term last but five weeks, but there is no regular school building, nor indeed any centralized or coördinated system of training. Berlin's faith in the intelligence and serviceability of army under-officers is in no way better illustrated than by the casual manner in which she prepares them for active police work. Of the five

---

[1] *Sicherheitswachmänner.*

[2] Budapest, however, as we have seen, has reduced the period of school work to four months. Recruits are not given their uniforms or allowed to do any practical work on the street until they have satisfactorily passed the written examinations which are held at the end of this period. They are then assigned in groups of two or three to the control of a sergeant, and with him they begin their practical work. After two months of this supervision they receive a permanent appointment, provided, of course, their conduct has been satisfactory.

The Uniformed Force

weeks during which the school lasts, the first nine days are spent by the recruits at Police Headquarters, where they listen to lectures on such topics as the principles of discipline, the necessity for secrecy, the duties and rights of officers, and the use of automatic pistols. During the remaining four weeks of the term, the recruits are assigned to a precinct where they are instructed by higher police officers in a great variety of subjects, mainly theoretical, and by the station sergeants in practical duty and routine. Their theoretical training includes a drill in some of the more important provisions of the German criminal code and code of criminal procedure. It relates also to the functions of the police in connection with buildings and repairs, health matters, pawn shops, societies and meetings, newspapers, public amusements, traffic, post and beat duty. For two hours each day during this period of four weeks, the probationer is assigned to patrol duty on the street in company with an older officer. His uniform and full pay as a *Schutzmann* are given him when he first enters the school. At the end of the five weeks' term, without examination or test, written or otherwise, he is assigned to a precinct for regular duty, and while his actual probationary period does not expire for six months, he is to all intents and purposes a full-fledged patrolman. There are no continuation instruction classes such as we have seen in Vienna.

The Paris recruit begins his regular work as a policeman from the first day he enters the force. While his instruction in the training school extends over a period of four months, he goes but once in three days, from eight to eleven o'clock in the morning, the rest of his time being occupied with his regular duties on the street. The school, which occupies three or four rooms at head-quarters, aims merely to assist the new policeman in working out the practical difficulties with which he finds himself confronted. As in Berlin, the fact that a recruit has been a *sous-officier* in the army is considered a suffi-cient guarantee of worth and effectiveness. The school is not used as it is in Vienna and London as a means of elim-inating the unfit. The inspector in charge of the Paris school refused to admit that there might be *sous-officiers* totally unfitted by temperament to become policemen. In-stead of dropping a recruit who appears stupid or dull in his classes, the authorities at Paris retain him for a longer period at the school. Adapted only to immedi-ately practical ends, and organized so as not to interfere with the regular work of the recruits, the course of the Paris school is plain and simple. The gymnastics and broadsword work, the drill in the technique of identifica-tion, and in the rudiments of law and medicine, which play so prominent a part in the Vienna school, do not figure in the Paris course. The work consists of a course on the proper method of writing reports, together with lec-tures on the subject of emergencies, arrests, fires, and the general behavior of policemen.[1] No examination con-cludes the course. The school is not expected to aid in the selection of effective policemen; rather it is organ-ized to initiate into their work the men who have already been chosen. Furthermore, there is no continuation in-

[1] M. Hennion, the new Police Prefect of Paris, has recently introduced the cinematograph as an aid to instruction, following the lead of Vienna.

The Uniformed Force

struction given in the *arrondissements* to which the men are assigned.

London's school is necessarily adapted to the peculiar conditions surrounding the recruiting of her police force. Her recruits, taken from the country districts, are raw, untrained and awkward; they have nothing of the military carriage which distinguishes the recruit in the Continental cities. If assigned immediately to active street work in uniform concurrently with their school duties, as is the case in Paris, they would make a sorry showing. The authorities, therefore, do not even provide them with a uniform until their school term has been completed. For the first two weeks of their eight weeks' course their instruction consists principally of physical exercise according to the Swedish system, and formation drill, a discipline which appears to liven them both mentally and physically. This drill is continued periodically during the entire eight weeks. The third week begins their instruction in practical police work, the details of beat and point duty, the necessary action to be taken in case of accident or emergency. At the end of each lecture, a specific case of disturbance by accident is described concerning which each recruit must draw up a report. This course of instruction is continued through the fourth week together with lectures on ordinances, regulations, and the criminal laws, the latter course lasting through the following week. In the sixth week, the recruit is taught to observe identification plates on swiftly moving vehicles, his legal instruction is continued, and he is given a thorough drill in the art of presenting his evidence and testifying in court. During the final two weeks, he is reviewed in all the subjects that have been brought before him, and is given a course of short talks on some of the necessary attributes of English constables, such as truthfulness, civility, and courtesy. Hand in hand with this instruction during the six weeks goes a drill in reading, writing, grammar, spelling, composition, and the use of maps. Throughout the course, a careful record is kept of each man's work, and while no written examination is required, recruits who at any time show themselves unfit or unadaptable are immediately dropped. In cases where a recruit shows signs of promise but has not fully satisfied the school authorities as to the quality of his work, he is assigned to a division on trial, where, as we shall see, he receives further instruction. It is estimated that 20 per cent. of the graduates of the school are sent out under this condition. Of this number, approximately 1 per cent. are subsequently dropped.

London has perhaps the best planned police school building in Europe —" Peel House "— erected in 1907, with eating and sleeping accommodations for 210 men, each of whom has his separate room or cubicle. With a billiard room, a library, a rifle range, and a gymnasium, it represents a well considered attempt to provide the recruit with every possible advantage. Food is served at club rates, costing each man approximately $1.87 a week; but the allowance which is made to the recruit of $3.75 a week is ample to cover this and other expenses.

Like Vienna, London has devised a system of continuation work, which, however, instead of dealing with police duty, is confined to instruction in reading, writing, spelling and arithmetic. Unless he has had exceptional edu-

The Uniformed Force

cational advantages, every patrolman who leaves the London training school is obliged to attend the night school or the continuation classes maintained by the London County Council. Six hours a week for six months he must give to his work, under the instruction of the city's regular teachers. Periodically during this term the teacher reports to the Superintendent of the division the progress of the patrolman in his studies. If a satisfactory showing is not made, the man is recommended by the Superintendent for dismissal.[1]

In this way it would be possible to consider the police training schools in the smaller cities of Great Britain and the Continent. For the most part, however, they are variations of one of the forms which we have just described. Amsterdam requires a written examination at the end of a two months' course, but continues the instruction for ten months longer, the recruits dividing their time between patrol work and school work. At the end of the ten months' period they must pass another written examination, and only then do they become full-fledged patrolmen. Rotterdam's system is practically the same. Dresden's six weeks' course is modeled after Berlin's. On the theory that a recruit will comprehend his theoretical instruction more rapidly and completely if he has been engaged in actual practical service, Hamburg has developed a system of two periods of training,

---

[1] At the end of three months the division Superintendent files a report with the Commissioner on the aptitude and general efficiency of every new man assigned to him from the training school. (Form No. 267.) The report comments on the man's degree of success in his continuation studies, his progress in police knowledge, his manner and deportment, etc. Unpromising men are allowed to resign.

European Police Systems

separated by an equal period of uninterrupted patrol
work. Stuttgart requires three full months of schooling
relieved by occasional patrol work. The training schools
of the provincial cities of England and Scotland are
neither so well equipped nor so systematically maintained
as the Continental schools. In Liverpool and Manchester, the facilities and courses are fairly satisfactory;
indeed, in Liverpool they are very good, including an
excellent system of continuation instruction in police duty
for a period of ten months after the recruit leaves the
school. In Glasgow, on the other hand, the instruction
in police duty is exceedingly limited, sometimes lasting
but two weeks " in the case of very bright men." Most
of the work consists of physical drill. " I lecture to
them half an hour a day on police duties," said the Inspector in charge of the school, although he admitted in
the same breath that he had had no opportunity during
the previous two months to give them even the half hour.
" But they pick it up fast enough," he continued, " from
the older constables with whom they are assigned to
patrol." This haphazard system of training is plainly
evidenced in the rank and file, who, frequently coming
from the Gaelic Highlands, are often unacquainted both
with the geography of Glasgow, and the essentials of
criminal law. Indeed, in a few cases, they appear to have
little knowledge of the English language, accustomed
as many of them are to the use of the Gaelic tongue. Of
the large police forces which I had the opportunity of
observing in Great Britain and on the Continent, I have
no hesitation in saying that Glasgow's is the poorest both
in training and equipment.

The Uniformed Force

On the whole, however, the police training schools of European cities are effective institutions. At least, they tend to equip men to handle the practical aspects of police work. The brevity of the courses offered by some of them is, however, open to criticism. It is impossible to believe that the great amount of technical information which a Berlin *Schutzmann* is supposed to possess, over and above a knowledge of his routine work, can really be gained in five weeks. The same remark applies to all the German cities. The immense responsibilities which are given to the German police, the wide sweep of authority which they enjoy in the regulation of the everyday life of the citizen, would seem to make doubly necessary a thorough and complete training. Obviously this necessity is not so great in England or Scotland, where the functions of the police are comparatively limited — certainly there would be no need in Great Britain for a course extending over an entire year, as is the case in Vienna — but even in England there is reason enough for providing well-trained, well-drilled men. The work of a policeman is everywhere of the most arduous nature, demanding not only integrity and capacity, but a cool judgment and a sense of proportion. The individual officer upon the spur of the moment must exercise a levelheaded discretion in matters of difficulty, acting promptly and decisively, with but little time for reflection. The Royal Commission appointed to investigate the Metropolitan force expressed itself on this point as follows:

" When one reads in the Instruction Book the discipline to which members of the force have to conform, one cannot help realizing that it either presupposes in recruits or creates in Constables a condition of mental and physical strength and health of a degree greater than that possessed by average workers in this country." [1]

In view of his responsibilities, it is of prime importance that the policeman's training should be deliberate and thorough. Even the splendid equipment of the school cannot overcome the superficiality of London's method of instruction. The London "Bobby" who enters the force after his eight weeks' training is a rough and untried specimen. A month more at the school, or two months more, with practical duty on the street in the company of an older officer, would greatly improve him. This, the officials of Scotland Yard willingly concede. Indeed, it is a point to which much attention has been given and it is possible that within a year or two the period of training will be further lengthened.[2]

In this respect, the police school of Vienna is really the model. The thorough drill which her recruits receive during their year's course, the painstaking manner in which the training is shaped to meet not only the practical needs of policemen on the street, but the demands of a community for intelligent public servants, is in marked contrast to the attitude not only of English and Scottish cities, but those of Germany and France as well.[3]

[1] *Report of the Royal Commission,* Vol. I, p. 56.
[2] The course was recently lengthened (October, 1913) from six weeks to eight weeks.
[3] The haste and superficiality which characterize the methods of training in many English and Scottish cities at the present time

The Uniformed Force

Another objection to be urged against many European training schools is their inadequate equipment and their lack of building accommodations. Only in London, Vienna and Budapest can arrangements be called satisfactory. In many other cities the training school is confined to two or three dingy rooms at police headquarters, as is the case in Paris, or, as in Berlin, it has no quarters at all, but is scattered throughout the precincts wherever available space can be found. London and Vienna have shown that the best results are obtained in a particular building or group of buildings — a police college, if you like — where, with ample accommodations and a fair degree of comfort, the recruits meet daily by classes and groups. Indeed, "Peel House" in London might well be imitated by every city in Europe.

Aside from the defects above pointed out, the general character of the instruction in many European police schools is open to criticism. The training is too often limited to a bare rehearsal of laws and ordinances and a statement of their interpretation in terms of police action, supplemented by physical drill. Instruction of this kind tends to turn out a machine rather than a man. It develops a narrow-visioned official who does not appreciate properly either his position or his duties. The

are attributable to a large extent to the operation of the "One-day-rest-in-seven Bill," which went into effect on April 1, 1913. *The Police (Weekly Rest-day) Act 1910, 10 Edw. VII and 1 Geo. V c. 13.* This law, which provides that every police officer shall have one day's rest in seven, necessitated a large augmentation of the police forces of England and Scotland, with the result that in many cases men had to be hastily recruited and trained to meet the emergency. With the police forces adjusted to this new measure a greater degree of thoroughness and care is hoped for in the training methods.

human element, the place of the policeman as a social factor, the relation of the police department to social problems, the interpretation of crime in terms of its causes, are matters which, except in Vienna, and to a slight extent in the English cities, are seldom touched upon. To be sure, the police of many of the Continental cities, particularly in Germany, have health functions, poor-relief functions and other duties more or less related to the larger social problems; but these matters are for the most part segregated into specialized departments with which, except on rare occasions, the uniformed men in the street have nothing whatever to do.

The failure of the European cities to give the policeman on beat a larger place in dealing with their social problems, to use him in connection with the preventive and remedial efforts of other organizations, public and private, to resort to him as a source of information concerning conditions which ultimately produce crime, is due to the necessarily subordinate position which the policeman occupies in the organization of the whole department, to his lack of extensive mental equipment and to the novelty of the conception itself. The hurried manner in which the recruit in so many European cities is trained to handle the merely practical aspects of his work is to some extent also a factor. As I say, Vienna and some of the English cities have made a beginning — a faint beginning, perhaps — in a new line of teaching by placing some emphasis upon the human relationships of the ordinary policeman and his connection with the complex problem of poverty and crime. The Liverpool Police Instructions contain the following paragraph: "Anything which helps the very poor and so relieves them from the temptation to crime, and anything which helps to take the children of the criminal classes away from evil surroundings and companions, and, while there is yet time, implants in them instincts of honesty and virtue, is true police work; and a policeman should throw himself heart and soul into such work just as readily as he does into the ordinary work of preventing and detecting crime."[1] I believe that the next developments in the police training schools will be along this line — giving the uniformed men a new point of view, acquainting them with the modern ideas of society concerning the criminal, and the larger social problems in which he plays an ominous part.

The distinction between the police forces of Great Britain and those of the Continent, so far as the source of their recruits is concerned, has already been pointed out. The former select their men from private life, the latter from the army. This distinction furnishes the

---

[1] See *Liverpool Police Instructions*, p. 9. In this connection the efforts of the Police-Aided Clothing Association of Liverpool are typical of the work that is being done. This association is a private organization, maintained by outside funds, formed to furnish clothes to "all insufficiently clothed children who come under the notice of the police, irrespective of any questions as to why their clothing is insufficient, or whether their parents are drunkards or bad characters, able or unable to buy clothing."

The Police Standing Order No. 13 reads as follows: "If a police constable sees or has his attention called by others to a child who seems to him to be insufficiently clad, he will question him or her, being careful to do so kindly so as not to let the child think it has got into trouble; he must find out where the child lives, and, if it lives on his beat, tell his Sergeant of the case on his next visit. The Sergeant will then accompany the constable to the home and will assist him in inquiring into the circumstances of the child. If they think the child should be clothed, the constable will, at the first convenient time, fill in Form A." This form is thereupon sent by the Head Constable to the offices of the Association.

key to a number of peculiarities both in organization and personnel to which attention should be called.

The idea that an army training produces the best police officer is based, as we have seen, upon the military conception of the police commonly held in Continental countries. This conception runs through the entire organization of the departments and shows itself in many outward forms. It finds expression, for example, in police orders and service books. The Berlin regulations begin as follows: " Members of the police force are under military discipline, and must mold their conduct while on duty in accordance with military forms. . . . The feeling of military subordination must always be expressed in the bearing of the individual toward his superior." [1] Then follows a series of rules describing with minute care the method and occasions of saluting the Emperor and members of the Royal Household, together with cabinet ministers and other dignitaries. Throughout the regulations emphasis is laid upon the necessity of maintaining " a military posture." In Dresden the emphasis is perhaps even more pronounced. The proper bearing of the patrolman toward his superiors is prescribed in extravagant detail — how and when he must salute them, his proper attitude in passing through a doorway, his proper posture on a bicycle and the manner in which he shall accompany his fellow officers on the street. " When a subordinate is in the company of a superior," reads the regulation, " he is to walk on the left side. If the superior is in the company

[1] *Allgemeine Dienstvorschrift für die Königliche Schutzmannschaft in Berlin,* par. 4.

The Uniformed Force

of several subordinates, the subordinate who is older in service or in rank must be on the left, the other on the right side of the superior." [1] Or again: "The speech of the police must be short, definite and clear, and should not be accompanied by explanatory gestures, or motions of hand or body. The hair of the head and the beard are to be trimmed in accordance with military instructions." [2]

In London and in the English provincial cities we look in vain for such details. The word "military" is not mentioned in the official instruction book of the Metropolitan Police except where a reference is made to army deserters. The same is true of the instruction books of the provincial cities. Indeed, the police forces of England are not military forces in any sense of the word. Englishmen have no sympathy with the view that the preservation of the King's peace is a military problem to be entrusted to military hands.

But the English objection to a force composed of ex-soldiers and commanded by ex-army officers has more than a sentimental basis. From a practical standpoint all the important advantages lie with the civilian police.

---

[1] *Dienstvorschriften*, par. 75.

[2] *Ibid.*, par. 68. In this connection it is interesting to note the respect and reverence with which army men are treated by the police. Any interference with an army officer by a policeman is a serious matter, not lightly to be undertaken. The Berlin police regulations on this point read as follows: "If an army officer should forget himself and his position to the extent of committing a crime, and if there is danger of jeopardizing the public peace and order by delaying in the matter, then, and then only, have the police the right to interfere directly, and if necessary, make an arrest. . . . But the responsibility which the police incur in direct interference with army officers is a grave one. . . . The uniform of His Majesty the King must not be compromised." *Allgemeine Dienstvorschrift*, par. 28.

European Police Systems

An army does its work through groups of its units —
divisions, brigades, regiments and companies — in all of
which the private is little more than a cog. Initiative
and imagination not only have no place in his career, but,
for the sake of discipline, their exhibition is discouraged.
The work of a police force, however, depends upon the
capacity of the individual policeman. On his beat or at
his post he must do his duty alone, usually dealing with
emergencies by his own unaided action. However difficult or novel the circumstances which confront him, he
must decide instantly on his own responsibility whether
or not they call for his interference. Only occasionally
is there an opportunity for concerted action in connection with his brother officers. For the most part he
must depend upon his own resourcefulness and originality, characteristics which an army training leaves un-
developed. Certainly, in hard-headed common sense, in
ability to meet situations and handle perplexing and
unanticipated problems, the ordinary English constable
is far superior to the Continental *Schutzmann* or *gardien
de la paix*. Initiative and imagination have been too
largely drilled out of the German policeman by the rigid
discipline of his army life, leaving him with an excellent
physical carriage and a certain military smartness, but
otherwise not so well adapted as the English constable to
meet the perplexing responsibilities which he individually
is called upon to handle.

Army training for the policeman has another result
that goes to the heart of the distinction between English
and Continental police systems. With the rank and file
of a police force recruited from non-commissioned of-

The Uniformed Force

ficers who have spent from six to twelve years in the army, a certain degree of indifference to the general public tends to develop. The German policeman is apt to lose sight of his function as a protector and guide, and to treat the citizens as he was accustomed to treat the awkward squads of raw recruits whom it was his duty to knock into shape during his career as an *Unteroffizier* in the army. Although the official orders make frequent reference to the necessity for courtesy and kindness in dealing with the public,[1] the German police, particularly in the larger cities, are at times unsympathetic, even harsh. Traffic is handled in Berlin by dint of much shouting and some verbal abuse. A citizen who inadvertently, perhaps, disobeys a rule of the road is apt to be made the object of an impassioned denunciation audible for half a block. A German policeman on patrol is armed as if for war. At night a Berlin *Schutzmann,* in addition to his heavy short-sword, carries an automatic pistol strapped outside his coat, while the Dresden patrolmen carry swords, pistols, and brass knuckles. Nor are these weapons merely ornamental. I have my-

[1] Thus the Berlin service regulations speak of the "accommodating, fraternal" attitude required in the relations of the police to the public. (*Allgemeine Dienstvorschrift,* par. 4.) The Dresden regulations provide as follows: "Officers of the local police force must maintain a polite and accommodating attitude towards the public, yet they must be serious and sedate, and avoid, on principle, any annoyance of the public by pettiness, unnecessary severity or interference in affairs which do not touch the service. They must in all matters be certain of the fact that they are intended to be the protectors of the public against violators of the law, or against disturbers of the public peace and order. Yet they must not aim to improve their efficiency by making many complaints regarding transgressions, but rather by warning the public as much as possible against perpetrating such transgressions and keeping them from such acts." (*Dienstvorschriften,* par. 66.)

self seen a poor wretch bleeding from saber cuts brought into a Berlin police station for a misdemeanor. At the so-called " Battle of Moabit," a strike riot in Berlin in 1911, four English newspaper men standing in an automobile watching the proceedings were cut down by the police, who, apparently losing their heads, slashed right and left, sabering even the members of their own force who had been detailed to the scene in plain clothes. Similar incidents have occurred in other German cities. In view of their occasional behavior in public, the continual charges of brutality levied against the police all over Germany, of beatings and abuse received in police stations behind closed doors, can scarcely be without some foundation. Certainly the policeman in Germany, and to some extent in Austria, is the object of marked dislike on the part of the lower classes.

It cannot be claimed, of course, that the attitude of the German police toward the public is attributable solely to their military training, although that factor undoubtedly plays a prominent part in their conduct. German society is organized throughout on severe class lines. The policeman deals for the most part with his social inferiors, and the accepted code of general behavior does not require any particular degree of diplomacy or finesse on his part. If military service were universal in England and London's police officers had all served from six to nine years in the army, it is scarcely conceivable that they would be inconsiderate or even undiplomatic in their treatment of the English public, for the reason that English society, even with its class distinctions, is comparatively democratic. Manifestations of severity or contempt on the

The Uniformed Force

part of one social class toward another are not readily tolerated. The instruction book of the Metropolitan police aptly covers the point: " The first requisite of discipline," it says, " is obedience to superiors, the second is consideration for inferiors." [1] Or again: " Every member of the force must look on himself as a servant and guardian of the general public and treat all law-abiding citizens, irrespective of their social position, with unfailing patience and courtesy." [2] The same note is struck in the report of the Royal Commission previously referred to. " It is extremely important," it says, " especially in dealing with a people in which the sentiment

[1] *Metropolitan Police Instruction Book,* Chap. III, par. 1. Similarly the Liverpool Instruction Book emphasizes the same point: " The first duty of a member of a disciplined force such as this is to show proper respect for and to give unquestioning obedience to the commands of his superiors; and the second is to give considerate treatment to his subordinates; the punishment for failing in the latter is not less but greater than that for failing in the first." *Liverpool City Police Instructions,* p. 10.

[2] *Ibid.,* Chap. I, Par. 11. Recruits at the Police School are thoroughly inoculated with this spirit. I watched a class at Peel House that was being drilled in the methods of presenting a case of arrest to the Inspector at the station house, the instructor of the class acting for the time being as the Inspector. The following dialogue ensued:

Recruit: "At 2:40 this afternoon, sir, I was on duty, in Oxford Street, when I heard loud cries of ' Stop, thief '! I saw this man running toward me, closely followed by the prosecutor. I stopped him until the prosecutor came up. He said (here the recruit referred to his official pocket-book): ' This man has stolen a gent's gold wristlet watch from my shop; I wish to charge him.' The prisoner then said (again referring to his pocket-book), ' This is monstrous; I really must protest.' I then took him into custody and brought him here, sir."

Instructor (suddenly): "Suppose he had been a well-dressed man and had said, ' You are a fool, constable. I am Lord So-and-so, and I shall report you to the Commissioner for this stupid insolence.' "

Recruit: "I should still have brought him to the station, sir."

Instructor: "Certainly; all men are equal before the law in England, regardless of rank or social position. Don't forget that."

233

European Police Systems

of liberty is so ingrained and intolerance of authority so marked as is the case in this country, that executive powers should be used in as wise and as gentle a manner as is consistent with the maintenance of public order."[1] This point of view is reflected in the very weapons which the London "Bobby" carries. Instead of a sword and pistol, supplemented by a black-jack and brass knuckles, he has a light wooden truncheon, incapable of inflicting serious damage.

It is this distinction which stands out most prominently in any comparison of English and German police. The London "Bobby" from the time he enters the force is persistently drilled to treat the public with courtesy and patience. The police instruction book speaks of it most emphatically. "Above all, remember always to keep your temper," it says. "A policeman in a passion is not only ridiculous but useless."[2] Or again: "By the employment of tact and conciliatory methods the public ordinarily can be induced to comply with directions and thus the necessity of employing force may be obviated."[3] The calm, patient, undisturbed attitude of the London constable, sometimes under circumstances of the most irritating and provoking nature, has become proverbial. I saw a large squad of them standing unmoved and apparently unobservant, when well-aimed stones were being hurled at them by a group of strikers. When

[1] *Report of the Royal Commission,* Vol. I, p. 51.
[2] *Metropolitan Police Instruction Book,* Chap. IV, par. 4.
[3] *Ibid.,* Chap. I, par. 12. The instruction book contains much good advice to policemen. For example: "All sorts of questions are addressed to a policeman, and you must answer them civilly and to the best of your ability, and should not be put out by silly or impudent enquiries or remarks." Chap. IV, par. 3.

The Uniformed Force

ordered to charge they did so, calmly and deliberately. Scorning to use their truncheons, they rolled up their rubber ponchos and with these weapons beat back their assailants. The disorder was effectually quelled and nobody was hurt. A similar situation in Berlin would have meant bloodshed and perhaps loss of life. I have seen London " Bobbies " handle with the greatest good nature and gentleness crowds of violently disposed suffragettes. " Now, lady," I heard one of them say, as he picked his battered helmet from the ground, " I don't want to make you any trouble, but if you do that again I shall be obliged to take you into custody." Had the dignity of a Berlin *Schutzmann* been thus ruffled, I hesitate to think what might have happened to the assailant. " I am seventeen years on the force," a London " Bobby " told me, " and never once have drawn my club." This remark reflects the prevailing spirit of the force.

To this general attitude there are unfortunately occasional exceptions. In a force of 20,000 men human feelings are at times bound to make their appearance. In January and February, 1913, a number of constables were discharged from the force and three were given prison sentences for " clubbing " and other brutalities. Occasionally one hears complaints of unnecessary roughness and discourtesy and even violence, some of which are probably well based. On the whole, however, the force enjoys a splendidly deserved reputation for courtesy, patience, and consideration in its dealings with the public. Indeed, a London " Bobby " is more or less a favorite with the people. He is liked, respected, and generally admired. I once saw a crowd of working-men

235

European Police Systems

roughly handling a chauffeur whose machine had narrowly escaped knocking down a constable on point duty. "If 'e 'd 'it you, we 'd ha' killed 'im," they told the "Bobby" when he went to the man's rescue. This public attitude of support, which seems to amount almost to affection, is the product of many years of unstrained relationship between police and people. It is due to the fact that the public generally is in full accord not only with the methods of their constables, but with the laws which the constables are called upon to enforce. With unpopular methods or with laws which lack the support of the community, no such friendly relations can exist. It is this fact which chiefly accounts for the cordiality with which the police of Great Britain, as distinguished from the police of the Continent, are generally regarded.

CHAPTER VII

THE UNIFORMED FORCE (*continued*)

Salaries.— General inadequacy of pay.— Extra allowances.— Provisions for care of police.— Promotions.— Pensions.— Hours of duty.— Discipline.— Absolute power of Commissioner in enforcing discipline.— Exceptions.— Methods of controlling force.— The centralized supervision of the Paris *Contrôle général.*— Objections to this method in London and Berlin.— Vienna's Bureau of Organization and Control.— Annual divisional examinations in Budapest.— Berlin's "Beat Control Book."— Variations in Amsterdam, Hamburg, and London.— Periodic change of London's beats.— Berlin's records of employees.— Mechanical equipment in Berlin headquarters.— Presence of supervising inspectors in London police courts.— Daily reports of London's divisions.

IN connection with the uniformed force, questions relating to salaries, promotions, pensions, hours of duty, discipline and the general systems of report and control remain to be considered in this chapter. For the sake of clearness and convenience, these various topics will be discussed under appropriate headings.

Salaries.

The salary schedule of European policemen appears in the table on the next page. The average maximum wage is $464.61 per annum. The average minimum wage is $326.01 per annum. These figures do not include certain small extras which are often given the police, such as boot, coal and rent allowances, and it should be remembered that the men receiving these sal-

European Police Systems

ANNUAL SALARIES OF PATROLMEN IN THE PRINCI-
PAL CITIES OF EUROPE

City	Minimum	Maximum
London:		
Metropolitan Force	$336.96	$436.80
City of London	355.68	549.12
Liverpool	336.96	449.28
Manchester	336.96	449.28
Glasgow	313.04	436.80
Berlin	333.20	499.80
Hamburg	464.10	666.40
Dresden	404.60	499.80
Stuttgart	380.80	571.20
Paris	405.30	482.50
Vienna	283.18	503.44
Budapest	203.00	203.00
Amsterdam	292.60	344.85
Rotterdam	282.15	344.85
Brussels	347.40	434.25
Rome (Municipal Police)	231.60	231.60
Madrid	180.00	225.00
Barcelona	180.00	225.00
Lisbon	180.00	270.00
Berne	425.00	618.00
Zurich	386.00	637.60
Christiania	348.00	536.00
Bergen	351.00	432.00
Copenhagen	348.00	509.00
Stockholm	402.00	616.40
Average	326.01	464.61

The Uniformed Force

aries are not required to furnish their own uniforms and equipment. Throughout Europe uniforms are provided either directly by the departments, or in the shape of specified annual allowances which the men are not permitted to exceed. Other details of their equipment are furnished directly by the departments.[1]

In estimating the apparent inadequacy of these wages, there are several factors which must be considered. In the first place, each policeman, at the completion of a fixed period of definite service, is assured of a pension which in part at least will relieve the anxieties of his declining years.[2] In the second place, it must be remem-

---

[1] In most European cities, the uniforms are provided by the department's tailors. In fact, the tailoring branch of a police force is often a very elaborate establishment and the budget item is correspondingly large. In London, the annual cost to the department for clothes and equipment averages $575,000, approximately $25.00 for each man. In Liverpool, the cost amounts to $65,000; in Amsterdam, $47,000; in Paris, $360,000. The uniforms range all the way from the extreme simplicity of the English constable's costume to the elaborate military regalia used in some of the Continental cities. The poorest uniforms of any of the police departments which I visited I saw in Glasgow, where, as I have already remarked, the whole force presented a down-at-the-heel appearance; the most elaborate uniforms were seen in Hamburg. Generally speaking, the uniforms of the Continental police are cut on a strict military pattern, while the English uniforms are for the most part loose-fitting garments, not suggestive of the military.

The equipment of the European police follows along similar lines. In London, a constable carries no firearms of any description, his only weapon being, as we have seen, a light truncheon. On the Continent, the policemen invariably carry swords and pistols. Generally the former weapons are short and serviceable. In some countries, particularly in Austria and Hungary, very heavy cavalry swords are carried, implements which frequently impede the movements of the police in regulating traffic, etc. In addition to these weapons, the Continental police often carry "blackjacks" and brass knuckles. In Amsterdam the police carry around their waists ropes fitted with hooks to rescue unfortunates who have fallen into the canals.

[2] The matter of pensions is discussed in a later section of this chapter.

bered that the cost of living in European cities, particularly on the Continent, is comparatively moderate, in no way approaching that of the cities of the New World. A salary that would be totally inadequate in New York, San Francisco or Rio Janeiro, would not necessarily be so in London, Berlin, or Madrid. Not only is the cost of living lower in Europe, but the standard of living is lower. The stratified organization of European society involving the fixed position of those classes which contribute the recruits to the police departments, produces a type, which, because opportunities for great advancement are closed, is contented with far less in the way of comfort and convenience than would be the case in a less rigid social order, where all may compete more or less freely for great prizes.

The low salaries of the European police are further offset by the painstaking provision which is made by the departments to enable their men to live economically and with a fair degree of comfort. In London, approximately 4,500 unmarried men are housed in regular police barracks, called section houses, of which there are twenty-eight. These houses are equipped with such conveniences as billiard and lounging rooms, libraries, locker rooms and baths. Each man has his separate cubicle or sleeping apartment, neatly and often attractively arranged with a writing table, a clothes press and other appropriate furniture. Breakfasts and teas he prepares for himself in the section house kitchen; dinners are served on the club plan. Each section house has its " canteen," where bread, biscuits, and other food stuffs, together with ale, beer and stout, can be had ap-

The Uniformed Force

proximately at cost. The expenses of the house, including the cleaning, are averaged weekly among the men and amount approximately to $1.75 for each individual. Married constables are generally given a lodging allowance of from 36 to 62 cents a week, according to the district in which they live. In the City of London proper, the corporation owns 52 tenements which are reserved for the use of married policemen and which rent for from $1.37 to $2.37 a week. For its unmarried constables, the city maintains six section houses with accommodations similar to those in the Metropolitan district. Liverpool has no such system for housing her police. Twenty years ago, a large section house was maintained for 300 unmarried constables. It was abandoned, however, as a consequence of many complaints concerning gambling and the misuse of the canteen. In Glasgow, 130 married policemen and their families live in houses owned by the corporation, the rent in each case being a moderate one, graded according to location. In addition, there are two rather inferior barracks, housing altogether approximately 175 men, where each has his own room for which he pays 43 cents a week. Dinners are served on the club plan, as in London. No canteens are allowed.

Berlin, Paris and Hamburg are without police barracks and the policemen live in their own homes. Many of the Continental cities give weekly or monthly allowances to members of their police forces to cover the cost of rent. Berlin, indeed, spends over $1,000,000 a year on this item alone, the individual allowances varying from rank to rank. In Vienna, each division has its own barracks for single men where the constables are housed in immaculate dormitories containing from three to seven beds, rather than in rooms or cubicles. The lodging is free. The barracks are well equipped with lounging rooms and lavatory facilities, and each has its own canteen. As in London, the men obtain their breakfasts and teas themselves, and dinners are served in the barracks on the club plan at a cost of 13 cents (64 *heller*). Policemen are not allowed to marry until they have been three years in the service, and after marriage they are given an allowance of $40.00 (200 *Kronen*) annually for house rent. Budapest has six excellently equipped barracks, where the men are housed on the dormitory system at a very small cost. In Dresden, the precinct stations are attractively fitted up to serve as barracks, with baths,[1] lounging rooms, and other conveniences. Indeed, a Dresden police station with its lawns and flowers looks more like a private residence than an official building.

Policemen throughout Europe are entitled also to free medical service. In many cities this privilege includes their families, and in some instances the other advantages to which they are entitled are worth taking into account. Thus, in Rotterdam, a policeman's children in bad health may be sent to the seashore, or his wife may enter a sanitarium, at the expense of the city.

But even with the efforts which are made in many cities to furnish the policemen with living conveniences at moderate cost, it cannot be denied that the salaries paid them are, in many instances, too low. In Rome, for

[1] As an example of the German passion for system, each precinct station in Dresden has its "shower-bath registry book" to control the bathing of the men.

The Uniformed Force

example, $230 a year is not a living wage for a man with a family. The same remark is applicable to other cities. The recent police demonstration in London over the question of salaries and the recurring attempts to "unionize" the force find substantial basis in a real need. The willingness of the police in many English and Continental cities to accept tips from the public is ascribable in part at least to the fact that they are underpaid. Even the rugged London constable is not free from the habit. Indeed, it is seldom that one finds a "Bobby" who will not gratefully receive a small recompense for a favor. I have seen one of them, upon the receipt of a sixpence, run half a block to call a cab.

This condition, of course, is not entirely due to low wages. It is due as much to social custom. In a country like Austria, where one must tip the street-car conductor and the shop-keeper, the sales-girl and the bank-clerk, where many hands are outstretched for a bit of silver, it is not surprising that the police should expect their proportionate share.[1] But a niggardly policy such as is practised in many cities puts too great a strain upon the ability of the average policeman to withstand the temptation from which, more than most governmental employees, he should be specially shielded. Sooner or later, European cities will have to face this situation. Hamburg and Stockholm have led the way with some substantial increases. London, Glasgow and the English

---

[1] Occasionally the greed for tips ripens into something worse. The American consular officers of some of the smaller cities in Spain inform me that the dishonesty of their police forces is notorious and is due to nothing less than the inability of the policeman to live upon the salary which he receives.

cities generally, together with Paris, Berlin and all the other Continental municipalities, cannot long afford to lag behind.

An interesting point in connection with the matter of salaries is the fact that police departments often charge private individuals and companies for the wages of men specially detailed. This system obtains in many of the Continental cities, and especially in London and the provincial cities of England. It is based on the theory that every person in the community is entitled to an equal share of police protection; if an individual wishes an excessive share he can have it only if he pays for it. Thus, the police of London are often detailed to weddings, receptions and other social functions, or to railroad-stations and theaters, and the parties benefited are charged for the service, the charge consisting of the salary of the men on duty for the time of the detail and in addition the proportionate overhead cost of maintenance and supervision. Similarly the owner of extensive property may have a constable or constables in his grounds during the night if he is willing to pay.[1] Certain manufacturers have policemen in uniform at their gates twenty-four hours out of the day. At Ascot and Derby, the great racing events are all policed by the London Metropolitan police and are paid for, not by the department, but by the proprietors of the race tracks. During the fiscal year ended March 31, 1912, the Metropolitan Police Force received roughly $83,000 from

[1] Private "patrols" operated by private companies as an extra precaution against criminals are not allowed on the public streets of London, although there is no objection to maintaining watchmen or guards on one's own property.

The Uniformed Force

business corporations and individuals for what might be called " extra-police " work. Similarly in Liverpool, 400 men are continuously assigned for duty to the Mersey Dock and Harbor Board, and their salaries, the cost of their clothes, and their proportion of supervision charges, amounting to $225,000 per annum, are paid by the Board to the police department.

Promotions.

We have seen that promotion from the grade of policeman to higher grades in the department, is possible in Europe only to a limited extent. In Berlin, Stuttgart, Budapest, Amsterdam, Rotterdam and many other cities, the patrolman may not rise above the grade of first sergeant. In Vienna, he may occasionally become a commissioned officer of low rank, but such promotions are exceptional. In Dresden and Hamburg, he may never become a commissioned officer, although he appears frequently to perform the functions of one.[1] In Paris, while there is no regulation to prevent promotion to the rank of captain (*officier de paix*), the severity of the qualifying examinations serves as an intentional check, and few patrolmen ever reach even the grade of lieutenant. Only in England are the restrictions to promotion removed, and even here definite limits are sometimes imposed, as, for example, in London where no constable is allowed to rise above the rank of superintendent.

In nearly all European departments these promo-

[1] In Dresden and Hamburg patrolmen may rise to the rank of *Inspektor* and *Distriktkommissar* respectively. The former title corresponds to Berlin's first sergeant (*Oberwachtmeister*); the latter is more than a first sergeant, and less than a lieutenant.

tions from rank to rank, wherever allowed, follow as a result of qualifying examinations and sometimes of a prescribed course of school work. This, however, is not always the case. Even in so progressive a department as Dresden's there were, until recently, no courses or examinations of any description, and the promotions were made by the Minister of the Interior of Saxony upon the recommendation of the Police President. The general English system of promotion is by examination; the Continental system ordinarily involves a special school course given by the police authorities.

London's methods in this matter are sufficiently characteristic of the English system to warrant separate consideration. A candidate for promotion to the rank of sergeant in London must have served at least five years as a constable,[1] and must receive from the Commissioner, before he tries his examination, a certificate of fitness issued upon the recommendation of his division superintendent. The Commissioner has the absolute right to bar a man from trying an examination when he believes him unfit on the ground of character, temperament, general efficiency, or for any other reason. Ordinarily, however, the Commissioner intervenes only when a man's record of punishments [2] is such as to raise doubts as to his general steadiness or sobriety.

The candidate attends no regular school or class. Whatever knowledge he acquires he must pick up for himself from his officers or from the "general orders book" and police manuals. There are two sets of exam-

[1] The average length of service of a constable before promotion to the grade of sergeant is eight years, three months.
[2] Called "Defaulter Sheet" in London.

The Uniformed Force

inations which he must try — one given by the Civil Service Commission to test his general educational capacities, and the other, a very searching one, by the officials of the police department in police duty. The latter examination is regarded as of far greater importance; it is both oral and written, the oral examination being given by a board of three superintendents and a chief constable. The civil service examination is not a statutory obligation. Officially the Civil Service Commission has nothing whatever to do with London's police force as regards either entrance or promotion. Its examinations are given only upon the invitation of the Police Commissioner and are not binding upon him in any way. Its services are employed merely to assist the police department in weeding out men whose lack of education makes them unfit for promotion. In special cases, men are promoted who cannot pass the civil service examination, although under such circumstances, it is generally customary to secure the formal approval of the Home Office. Thus a thoroughly equipped policeman, with a good record, who gives promise of making an excellent officer and passes his examinations in police duty with no difficulty is occasionally promoted regardless of his inability to satisfy the Civil Service Commission. The entire system rests upon the judgment of the Commissioner. It is assumed — and the assumption is well based — that favoritism and politics will play no part in the result, because it is greatly to the advantage of the department, and of the Commissioner as head of the department, that the best men obtainable should be secured as officers. Who, therefore, has any greater interest in securing the best men than the Commissioner himself?

With the examination passed, promotion does not necessarily follow in the order of marks received. Here again the matter rests entirely in the discretion of the Commissioner. Marks alone count for little; police serviceability is the all-important factor. Lists are made up of those who have passed the examinations, the names being arranged in order of merit as determined by the Commissioner, his assistants and the superintendents who have had relations with the men. The Commissioner is not obliged by statute or otherwise to promote men whom he does not regard as fitted for the new tasks. Indeed, it sometimes happens that men who have satisfactorily passed their examinations never receive a promotion. This is true not only in London, but in every provincial city of England and Scotland, although for the most part undesirable candidates are not allowed to take the examinations in the first place. The Head Constable of Liverpool expressed himself to the writer on this point as follows: " Examination for promotion is important, but it is the least important standard. The personal equation must always be the final determining factor." [1] The officials of the Home Office spoke in similar vein. " An examination cannot test a man's

---

[1] The system in provincial cities is very similar to that of London. In Liverpool, a candidate for the grade of sergeant must have served seven years as a constable before he is allowed to try his examination, which is a written one, and includes police duty, arithmetic, and writing from dictation. Promotion from sergeant to inspector is also by written examination, in police duty, arithmetic, geography, and "general intelligence," the last named designed to bring out not only the general efficiency of the candidate but his ability to express himself in English.

The Uniformed Force

ability or fitness for promotion," said one of them.
" He may neglect his duties and cram on fine points that
look and sound well, so that in the examination he appears to far better advantage than the man who has in
him the makings of a better officer." Perhaps the most
emphatic testimony on this point came from Manchester.
For some years they tried the system of promoting men
in the order in which they passed their examinations.
Eventually they gave it up. " It did n't work," the Chief
Superintendent told me. " We were n't getting in our
best men as officers. We came to the conclusion that an
examination is only one test out of many of a man's
efficiency."

With more or less variation, the process of examination which I have outlined above and the method of
selecting the candidates which follows from it are repeated for promotion as between all ranks, that is, in
London, from sergeant to station sergeant, from station
sergeant to inspector, from inspector to subdivisional inspector, from subdivisional inspector to chief inspector.
No separate examination is necessary, however, for promotion from chief inspector to superintendent.[1] That
such a system of promotion is successful in bringing to

[1] In his testimony before the Royal Commission, Sir Edward
Henry, the Commissioner of the Metropolitan Police, gave the
following average periods of total service in the force before promotion from one rank to another:

	Years	Months
Constable to Sergeant	8	3
Sergeant to Station Sergeant	14	7
Station Sergeant to Inspector	15	11
Inspector to Subdivisional Inspector	18	5
Subdivisional Inspector to Chief Inspector	20	5

(*Report of the Royal Commission*, Vol. II, p. 5.)

the front the best men available, that it is carried through without favoritism or political considerations, that in its fairness and justice it has the confidence of the uniformed force, is a splendid commentary, not only on the integrity of the Commissioner and his administrative assistants, but on the stability and sound traditions of the entire department.

In marked distinction to the English method, promotion to the rank of sergeant (*Wachtmeister*) in Berlin involves a prescribed course of study, with lectures, recitations and other features of a regularly organized school. Indeed the *Wachtmeister* school is one of the important activities of every well organized police department in Germany and Austria. According to the German theory, a course of private study by an individual with the idea of passing an examination is not sufficient in itself to equip a policeman for his new duties as a sergeant. He must enter a school and be thoroughly drilled by competent police instructors. In Berlin,[1] therefore, the first step is to select from the ranks of the patrolmen the most promising material. These selections are made by the captains of the districts upon the basis of record, aptitude, and intelligence, and approximately thirty men are chosen at a time. In charge of the higher commissioned officers of the department, both from the uniformed and detective forces, the course is repeated twice a year, for two hours a day, a total of 120 hours. It includes instruction in reading, writing, geography, arithmetic, and history, together with a thorough drill in German police theory and duty. In this

[1] The course in Berlin was first established in 1895.

The Uniformed Force

last respect it covers the laws relating to construction of buildings, hospital regulations, homeless children, the supervision of business and the many general functions in which the Berlin police interest themselves. It also includes instruction in some of the advanced sections of the penal code and the code of criminal procedure, and in matters relating to the prevention and detection of crime, such as the various methods of identification, the *Meldewesen* and *Steckbrief* systems,[1] and other similar aids.[2] At the end of the course the candidates are obliged to pass a series of examinations, both written and oral. If successful, they become "trial" *Wachtmeisters,* and are promoted to vacancies in the order of the marks which they have received.

In Vienna, the term of the promotion school lasts an entire year, occupying two hours a day for three days a week, and the course is even more elaborately organized than in Berlin. Candidates are required not only to understand the intimate details of Austrian criminal law and police duty, but also to have an expert knowledge of telegraphy and to be intimately acquainted with many of the technical arts and sciences which are associated with the policeman's profession. In addition to this, instruction is given in geography, history, reading and writing.[3] As is true of the Vienna training school for recruits, so too the Vienna promotion school is the best

[1] See Chap. IX, p. 350.
[2] For a complete syllabus of the course, see *Lehrplan für die Vorbereitungsschule der Polizei-Wachtmeister-Aspiranten,* a leaflet issued by the police department.
[3] An outline of the course is given in the police instruction book, *Organisation und Instruktion der Wiener k. k. Sicherheitswache,* pp. 69 ff.

European Police Systems

of its kind in Europe. The man who becomes a police sergeant in Vienna is a thoroughly trained officer, with a broad knowledge of police duty and the basis of a good education.[1] To a greater or less extent this statement is true of every city on the Continent.[2]

Pensions.

Almost without exception the police of Europe are entitled to a pension upon retirement, or at least a money premium or superannuation allowance. For the county and borough forces of England and Wales, including the Metropolitan system, pensions are governed by a general act of Parliament.[3] Under that act a police officer is entitled to a pension for life when he has completed twenty-five years of approved service, or if, after completing fifteen years of service, he becomes incapacitated, or at any time if he becomes incapacitated

[1] Space is lacking in which to describe fully other schools of promotion. In Amsterdam, the candidates for promotion are chosen to try the qualifying examinations on the basis of seniority. Only a passing mark is required and the men are appointed to vacancies as they occur, in the order of seniority. Rotterdam, on the other hand, has a promotion school to which men are appointed on the basis both of capability and seniority. Stuttgart holds its *Wachtmeister* school in the evening, so as not to interfere with the regular work of the men. In Dresden, there is a new *Wachtmeister school,* which began its work in 1914, and which extends over a period of eight and a half months. It is divided into two parts: the first, of four hours a week, includes theoretical instruction; the second part has to do with practical instruction and lasts from 8 to 12 and from 3 to 6 o'clock for the last three weeks of the course. The course concludes with a written examination.

[2] In the general absence of any machinery of promotion above the rank of sergeant, there is, of course, no necessity to repeat the system of instruction with other grades.

[3] The Police Act of 1890, supplemented by the Act of 1906. Pensions of the police of the City of London are similar to those of other English police bodies and are based on the police superannuation act of 1889 and 1894.

The Uniformed Force

as a result of an injury received in the execution of his duty. Elaborate scales, on a minimum and maximum basis, have been worked out under the authority of the law. At the end of twenty-five years' service, a policeman may ordinarily retire with a pension of 31-50ths of his pay. If he elects to continue for another year or more, he receives a maximum pension of two-thirds of his pay. The pensions based on injury have their own rates and scales.[1]

In Paris, practically similar arrangements are in force. A policeman is entitled to a pension at the end of twenty-five years' service, which includes, however, his service in the army. The pension amounts to the average yearly salary for the previous three years, although at any time after fifteen years of service he is entitled to a pension which is estimated at the rate of one-fiftieth part of the average salary of the previous three years for each year of approved service.

In Amsterdam, pensions are granted to police officials who have served thirty consecutive years and have reached the age of sixty-five, or who at the time of retirement are seventy years old, or who become incapacitated for duty. Ordinarily, the pension is one-half the amount of the salary at the time of retirement. In case an official is retired who has served less than thirty years, the pension is one-half of his salary at the time of his retirement, minus one-fiftieth thereof for each full year less than thirty that he has served.

---

[1] For a complete statement of the working of the pension act in England, see the article on "Police" in the *Encyclopedia of Local Government Law*. The article is written by H. B. Simpson, Principal Clerk in the Home Office.

European Police Systems

In Berlin and in German and Austrian cities generally, owing to the fact that the police departments are usually controlled by the government rather than by the municipalities, the police pension system has no separate existence, but is part of the general system for the pensioning of all government employees. In Berlin, sergeants and policemen, at the end of eighteen years of service with the police force, are entitled each to a premium of 1,000 M. in addition to their regular pension under the Civil Pension Act. The pension is given only in cases of actual unfitness for duty, so that a policeman serves until he becomes incapacitated instead of being retired at the end of a stated period.[1] As we have already seen,[2] however, fifteen years' service in the army and police force combined entitles a policeman to his civil papers (*Zivilversorgungsschein*) by which he has the preferred right of employment in the governmental service; and most of the policemen of Germany, availing themselves of this privilege, enter some other branch of the government where so active a life is not demanded.

In Vienna, after ten years of service, a policeman is entitled to a pension amounting to forty per cent. of his salary.[3] To this sum two per cent. is added for each

[1] Bearing in mind the fact that in Prussian cities, except in the case of officers who have reached the age of 65 years, pensions are given only in cases of unfitness for service, the pension amounts after ten years of service to $20/60$ths of the salary, the length of service including the time served by the police officer in the army. For each additional year up to the thirtieth year of service, $1/60$th of the salary is added, and thereafter $1/120$th per year is added up to a total of $45/60$ths. Final decision is in the hands of the Minister of Finance. For a description of the various classes of the Civil Pension Act, see Hue de Grais, *loc. cit.*, par. 74.

[2] See note 3, p. 206.

[3] Law of April 20, 1873.

The Uniformed Force

additional year of service, so that after forty years the full salary is due in the form of a pension. Ordinarily, however, the full salary as a pension is allowed after thirty-five years' service. In case of bodily injury received in the execution of his duties, ten years are added to a policeman's service record in calculating the amount of his pension.

Hours of Duty for Policemen.

Nearly every European city has developed its own system in regard to the hours of duty of its police force. In English cities, the police work a total of eight hours a day and no more. In London, for example, the night duty of the patrol beats is from 10 P. M. to 6 A. M.; day duty is divided into two reliefs. The men of the first relief perform their duty between the hours of 6 A. M. and 10 A. M., and 2 P. M. and 6 P. M., while the second relief is on duty from 10 A. M. to 2 P. M. and from 6 P. M. to 10 P. M.[1] In addition to this regular duty there is " point " duty (largely for the control of traffic), also divided into two reliefs, the first relief being on duty from 9 A. M. to 1 P. M. and from 5 P. M. to 9 P. M., and the second relief from 1 P. M. to 5 P. M., and from 9 P. M. to 1 A. M. In addition, there are men on " reserve patrol duty " for crowded sections, covering the principal highways and difficult traffic points. Their hours are from 10 A. M. to 7 P. M., with one hour off for lunch. There is also an

[1] This statement holds true for the inner divisions only: that is, for the divisions where business and population are most thickly centered. In the outer divisions the hours of duty are eight hours straight.

European Police Systems

" evening patrol " to augment the regular beats, from 7 P. M. to 3 A. M.

In Liverpool and other of the provincial cities of England, the " beat duty " consists of three shifts of eight hours each, from 6 A. M. to 2 P. M., from 2 P. M. to 10 P. M. and from 10 P. M. to 6 A. M., the last shift containing twice as many men as the first two shifts combined. In addition to this there is fixed point duty and evening patrol, similar to London's system. Throughout England, under the operation of the new law,[1] every patrolman has one day's rest in seven.

Berlin has experimented with many systems, and has finally adopted an alternating form under which her policemen are on duty for twenty-four hours and free for the succeeding twenty-four hours. A policeman in Berlin goes on duty at 1 P. M., and between that time and 11 P. M. he alternates between street duty and reserve duty at the station, in two and a half hour periods. From 11 P. M. to 8 A. M., the alternating periods are three hours long, the reserves at the station being allowed to sleep. At 8 A. M., the day's service with its two and a half hour periods again begins. At 1 P. M. he is relieved for 24 hours. For example, a patrolman goes on duty at 1 P. M. and is assigned to the reserve at the station house. At 3.30 he goes to his beat; at 6 o'clock he is again on reserve; at 8.30 he goes on the street; at 11 P. M. he is on reserve and is allowed to sleep until 2 A. M., when he once more goes on street duty, returning at 5 A. M. He sleeps until 8 A. M., then resumes his patrol duty until 10.30 A. M. Between 10.30 and 1

[1] Act of 1910. 10 Edw. VII & 1 Geo. V. c. 13.

The Uniformed Force

P. M. he is on reserve at the station. He is then relieved for twenty-four hours, having had six hours' sleep at the station, or three hours if he had the first tour of night duty on the street.

The systems of Vienna, Budapest, and Hamburg are similar to that of Berlin: twenty-four hours' duty is followed by twenty-four hours' free time. In Vienna and Budapest, however, there is no distinction between day and night duty in terms of two-and-a-half and three-hour periods as in Berlin, the alternating periods being uniformly three hours each. In Dresden and Hamburg, the alternating periods are two hours each. Paris has its own peculiar system. The force of each *arrondissement* is divided into three parts, known by the letters A, B and C, each relaying the others in accordance with the following table:

Hours on duty	First day	Second day	Third day
Midnight to 6 o'clock...................	A	B	C
6 o'clock to noon......................	B	C	A
Noon to 6 o'clock......................	C	A	B
6 o'clock to midnight..................	A	B	C

Under this system a policeman is on duty twelve hours every third day and six hours on other days, an average of eight hours a day. Reserve duty is performed by regular reserve men stationed at headquarters, who have their own hours and are used for this particular kind of duty only.

European Police Systems

Discipline.

In discussing the methods by which discipline is enforced in the European police departments, we must first call attention to one or two general principles. Almost invariably the right to discipline members of the police force, particularly of the rank and file, rests in the last analysis with the Commissioner, although to this there are exceptions. The usual attitude of a European city toward its Police Commissioner is one of trust. When, after careful selection, it chooses a man to head its police force, it endows him with ample powers and expects him to use them wisely. Only in a few of the provincial cities of England, in the Dutch cities, and in the smaller municipalities of Germany, is there any disposition to tie the hands of the Commissioner, or to prevent his exercising free and almost unrestricted control over the men who constitute the uniformed force. Seldom is there an attempt to surround him with any system of checks and balances, or to erect barriers against the possible abuse of his powers. Thus, in London, the Commissioner is the final and absolute authority on all matters of discipline, and while occasional endeavors are made to secure from the Home Secretary a reversal of the Commissioner's decisions, such attempts have invariably proved fruitless. The Commissioner may levy fines, make reductions in rank or in rate of pay, or dismiss uniformed members of his force, and no court, tribunal or other external body, has power to review his action. This is true in nearly every large city of Europe. To be sure, in Berlin and in other German

The Uniformed Force

cities where the police department is controlled by the central government, and where its members are part of a vast and intricate official system, the higher officers and even the representatives of the uniformed force who have received life appointments must, before they can be removed, be tried before a special court [1] of which we shall speak later; but as a matter of practice the police president experiences little difficulty in ridding his department of inefficient men.

We have seen that in the Dutch cities and in some of the smaller cities of England and Germany there is a disposition on the part of the authorities to hamper the action of their police commissioners in matters of discipline. We have also seen [2] how the restrictions which the Watch Committees of some of the English towns throw around their chief constables have often led to unhappy consequences. The fact that the chief constable is often overruled in his attempted disciplinary measures and the opportunity offered an accused policeman to solicit sympathy and support among the individual members of the Committee have resulted in inharmonious conditions, and occasionally in badly disorganized departments. Indeed, where the Watch Committee has assumed to pass in the first instance on all disciplinary cases, as in Manchester, situations bordering on demoralization have more than once developed.

In Amsterdam, Rotterdam, Stuttgart, Leipzig, Ulm, and in other cities where the municipal authorities have asserted their right of interference, similar conditions

[1] *Disciplinargerichtshof.* See p. 262.
[2] See Chap. II, page 53.

have arisen. In Stuttgart, for example, the Commissioner's disciplinary power is limited to transfer, demotion, or fines not exceeding fifteen marks. Fines from fifteen marks to one month's salary can be levied only with the consent of the Burgomaster. Dismissal is impossible except with the concurrence of the town council (*Gemeinderat*). As a result the force has at various times been badly disorganized and the relations between the council and the Commissioner (*Polizeidirektor*) are often strained. There are cases on record in Stuttgart, as has already been pointed out, where an officer has been dismissed by the Commissioner three times, only to be reinstated in each instance by the town council. In speaking to me of this matter, the Commissioner gave three reasons why he is so often overruled: the failure of the town council to understand the case, politics, and " soft-heartedness." " They do not appreciate," he said, " the effect of their actions on the discipline of the force." Stuttgart's disastrous experience is, however, exceptional. In most of the cities of Europe, certainly in the larger capitals and centers of trade, the Commissioner possesses adequate authority to discipline the men of the rank and file as he deems best.[1]

As may be expected, the machinery by which disci-

[1] In Amsterdam, Rotterdam and the Dutch cities generally, and in many of the smaller towns on the Continent where the police department is under the control of the municipality, policemen can only be removed by the burgomaster, although lesser punishments are ordinarily imposed by the commissioner. In Rotterdam, all members of the police force, except the Head Commissioner and his assistants, who, as we have seen, are designated by the Crown, are appointed by the burgomaster for one year only, a survival of an ancient city ordinance. Legally, the burgomaster could at any time appoint an entirely new police force. Advantage, however, has never been taken of this situation.

The Uniformed Force

pline is enforced in the different police departments varies widely. In London, punishments are meted out by the superintendents of the divisions, by the chief constables, and by a Disciplinary Board, consisting of the Administrative Assistant Commissioner, a chief constable and a superintendent. The cases which come before the superintendent involve minor derelictions committed by constables, punishable with a maximum of two days' pay. The chief constables handle the more serious cases relating to constables and sergeants punishable with fines amounting to not more than four days' pay. The assistant commissioner handles cases relating to higher officers or involving severe penalties, while the Disciplinary Board, which is called at the direction of the assistant commissioner, sits practically as a court-martial to consider cases punishable with dismissal or reduction in rank or pay. There is an appeal from a punishment imposed by a superintendent to a chief constable; from the chief constable to a Disciplinary Board; and from the Board to the Commissioner, from whose decisions there is no appeal. An appeal is only allowed, however, if the accused has made his whole case and called all his witnesses at the original hearing, and it must be lodged at the time the punishment is imposed. The higher authority may reject or allow the appeal or may vary the original decision either by increasing or reducing the punishment.[1] A fine cannot exceed seven days' pay. On the other hand, reductions in rates of pay are often made. A strict record is kept of all penalties imposed on any police officer. If a man has

[1] See *Metropolitan Police Instruction Book*, Chap. III, par. 6.

no offense recorded against him for ten years, and if his service has been meritorious, the Commissioner may allow entries on his defaulter's sheet more than ten years old to be canceled.[1]

In the provincial cities of England, the Watch Committees have full authority to discipline the officers and the men of the police force.[2] The right of the chief constables, therefore, depends altogether upon the powers delegated to them by the Watch Committees. Some chief constables are given large powers in the way of discipline, and their acts are ratified without question. Others are compelled to seek from the Watch Committees authority for every act, a necessity detrimental not only to good discipline but to the general *morale* of the force.

In Berlin, all disciplinary cases are investigated in the first instance by the *Hauptmann* or head of the division, who makes a report to his major. Matters involving only a reprimand are handled directly by the three majors; more serious delinquencies are punished by the head of the uniformed force (*Oberst*) or by the Police President. From the decision of the Police President there is no appeal. The punishments include reprimand, fine, imprisonment, not exceeding eight days, transfer and dismissal. In case a policeman has received a life appointment, which is ordinarily given him after he has served creditably for seven years in the department, he may not be removed except after a trial before the *Disciplinargerichtshof,* a state court composed of a president

[1] *Ibid.,* Chap. III, par. 5.
[2] See Chap. II, page 51.

The Uniformed Force

and five associates which sits to determine the guilt or innocence of royal officials. This holds not only for Berlin but also for other Prussian cities whose police forces are royal forces controlled by the central government. All officials, whether in the police department or not, whose tenure of office is for life, have the right to be tried before this court for offenses involving dismissal. If found guilty they are dismissed by the Prussian Minister of the Interior, to whom an appeal may be taken from the finding of the court.[1] The wishes of a police president, however, readily find support.

Vienna's system embodies certain modifications of the foregoing plan. There is no administrative court for the trial of officials, as in Berlin. Cases involving demotion or dismissal are heard, as in London, before a disciplinary court, appointed by the Police President. The personnel of the court changes with each case; it consists ordinarily of four commissioned officers of varying ranks, one of whom, the chairman, is not allowed to vote. Only the Police President has the right to demote or dismiss and he may accept or reject the finding and recommendation of the disciplinary board. However, an appeal is allowed from the action of the Police President to the *Statthalter*, or royal governor of the province of Lower Austria, the officer under whose general supervision, as we have seen, the entire management of the police department falls.[2] Appeals must be filed within fourteen days.[3] As a matter of fact, few appeals are

[1] Prussian Disciplinary Law of July 21, 1852. (*Gesetzsammlung*, 465.)
[2] See Chap. II, p. 79.
[3] Imperial Order of March 10, 1860. (*R. G. Bl.* 15.)

ever taken, and it is a characteristic circumstance that the judgments of the Police President have not been reversed within the memory of headquarters officials.[1] Minor derelictions are punished by the *Zentralinspektor,* or head of the uniformed force, the punishments consisting of reprimands, which may or may not be published in the orders of the day, and the imposition of extra tours of duty. Fines are not included in the list of penalties in Vienna.[2]

There is one fact in connection with the question of discipline which holds for all police departments throughout Europe: trials of charges against police officials involving the possibility of punishment are invariably held *in camera.* They are regarded as private affairs between the commissioners and the defendants, domestic difficulties to be settled behind closed doors. " It is a matter of internal economy and does not concern the public; there is no more reason for making such a matter public than for holding an army court-martial in public." This was the remark of one of the officials of Scotland Yard. A Glasgow superintendent was even more frank. " We could not afford to wash our dirty linen in public," he said. " A man on charges receives the fairest kind of treatment anyway and publicity would do him no good. It would have the disadvantage of creating the suspicion that everything on the inside of the police department is rotten. Many people will judge an institution by one or two exceptional instances."

Not only is there no publicity in regard to police trials,

---

[1] Personally communicated.
[2] For discussion, see *Organisation und Instruktion der Wiener k. k. Sicherheitswache,* pp. 44–45.

The Uniformed Force

but a policeman on charges is never allowed to appear with an attorney; indeed my question on this score seemed incomprehensible to most of the police authorities both in England and on the Continent. "What would be the object of his having an attorney?" they invariably asked. "It is a matter of discipline, not a breach of law." Throughout Europe a commissioner need only satisfy himself as to the guilt or innocence of the accused. The methods by which his opinion is reached are largely his own concern. Once announced, his opinion is seldom challenged, nor is there any disposition to question his justice, disinterestedness, or competency.

Method of Control.

It is impossible, in the space allowed, to describe the great variety of methods by which the European police authorities control the activities of their uniformed forces. Instead, therefore, of attempting a catalogue of the systems, we shall note a few of the more interesting phases of control in particular cities. In adopting this course, it is not implied that the systems described are characteristic only of the cities mentioned.

Generally speaking, there are two methods by which police administrators may control the work of their uniformed forces: through regular supervision by divisional or precinct officers and through the direct oversight of a centralized headquarters staff. These two methods are not mutually exclusive. As a matter of practice, the second, when employed at all, is used only to supplement the first. In France, Belgium, and Holland, the police departments generally adopt the second method. That is, each department is equipped with a bureau or staff — sometimes popularly known as a " shoo-fly squad "— whose purpose is to control from headquarters, by a system of espionage, the uniformed men assigned to the various divisions. The police officers of this bureau, detailed to duty in plain clothes, watch for and report to the disciplinary authorities any police delinquency that they observe. In Paris, the bureau, known as the *Contrôle général,* constitutes a very important part of the police organization. Established in 1854,[1] it has for years been the principal method of testing the effectiveness not only of the uniformed force but of all branches of the department. Of late, owing to the resentment which its activity always has awakened in the rank and file, less emphasis has been placed upon secret surveillance and the force of the bureau, reduced to thirty inspectors, has been used rather to investigate complaints and to search out the weak points of the organization. Even with its modified functions, however, it is still the main instrument by which the Prefect keeps in touch with his department.

In the same form, and with the same functions, this bureau is an essential part of the police organizations of Brussels, Rotterdam, Amsterdam, and other cities in the Low Countries. In Germany, Austria and England, however, it is looked upon with great disfavor. While plain clothes men are occasionally assigned to observe some suspected weakness in organization or personnel,

[1] Decree of September 17, 1854, modified by the Law of July 29, 1881.

The Uniformed Force

the systematic employment of a regular squad to watch the activities of fellow officers is, in these countries, universally condemned. "We want no spies on our force," said one of the assistant commissioners at Scotland Yard. Similar sentiments were expressed by officials in Berlin and Vienna.

In Austria and Hungary considerable attention is paid to the question of "constructive control," by which is meant the constant striving for improvement in organization and method. As we have seen, the Vienna department has a so-called bureau of organization and control, established to adjust the relationships of the various branches and subdivisions, to eliminate friction and to make any changes or install any devices deemed necessary. This bureau, really a bureau of scrutiny inside the department, is headed by a practical expert whose long experience in police business is a guarantee against useless innovation. His duty involves the continual study of other police departments both in Austria and in foreign countries in the search for better methods and more effective systems. Budapest has no such bureau, but once a year an exhaustive examination is made of each of the precincts or divisions (*Kommissariate*) by a carefully selected headquarters committee. The examination includes a study of functions and practices, and especially of the relations of the precinct force, in point of numbers and service, to the changing needs of the neighborhood. The complaints and suggestions of the local officers are carefully considered, and improvements follow immediately upon the recommendations of the committee.

European Police Systems

In supervising the work of her uniformed force, Berlin adopts the expedient of maintaining a " Beat Control Book " for each of the beats into which a section is divided. The book is carried by the patrolman and is passed from one succeeding relief to another. In it the patrolman enters with an indelible pencil the *time* of any particular event, as for example, when he steps into a yard to try a door, or when he leaves the beat at the call of another officer. In this book, too, the sergeant or lieutenant on his rounds, writes his initials and the hour. There is thus maintained a continuous history of the patrol.[1] Amsterdam has modified this system by having a book for each man rather than for each beat which, viséed and initialed by the sergeants and other supervising officers, and turned in to headquarters at the end of the day's work, furnishes a control both of the sergeant and of the patrolman. In Hamburg, too, each patrolman has a book in which he jots down the streets which he traverses on his beat, together with the hour. The sergeant on his rounds initials the entries.

Each London constable has an " official pocket book " in which he writes the history of any important occurrence coming within his notice on his point or beat, such as the remarks of a prisoner arrested, a warning given to a street-walker, a summons served on a reckless driver, the names and addresses of witnesses. These notes, initialed by the sergeant, are subsequently copied into the

[1] Berlin has also a series of " Post instruction books " in which the duties pertaining to each fixed post in the city are minutely described. There is one such book for each precinct; an officer assigned to a new post has only to turn to the book to find an exhaustive enumeration of his duties. Berlin has no fixed posts at night.

The Uniformed Force

" Occurrence Book " at the station house by the station officer. The pocket book is used by the constable to refresh his recollection in cases of subsequent procedure, judicial or otherwise, and is often produced before the magistrates in the police courts.

The beat of a London constable is changed regularly every month; there are no permanent assignments either for patrol or point duty. A man is seldom transferred out of his division, but he is shifted periodically from beat to beat and from point to point, progressing from one part of his division to another and constantly coming under the supervision of new sergeants and inspectors. During one month, his beat may be in a residential district; the next, in a business section; the following month may find him on fixed point duty or handling traffic at a crowded corner. Under this system of monthly transfers, it takes him two or three years to work from one end of his division to the other. The professed object of this arrangement is to develop the constable, to acquaint him intimately with the various phases of police duty. Incidentally, the London authorities believe that this arrangement eliminates evil influences. " It prevents a constable from getting too thick with any particular people," the Superintendent of a large division told me. " I believe that the system makes it quite impossible that there should be any systematized form of blackmail," said Sir Edward Henry in his testimony before the Royal Commission, in referring to the steps taken by the department to guard the police against the efforts of street-walkers to purchase protection.[1]

[1] *Report of the Royal Commission,* Vol. II, p. 10.

European Police Systems

Berlin aims to keep in touch with the life and record of each of her officers. To that end, a file or "book" is maintained at headquarters for each employee of the department which gives all the personal details of his service — his age, height, military record, date of marriage, names of his parents-in-law, names and dates of birth of his children, residence, punishments, commendations, transfers, ratings, promotions, and salary. In this book, too, are kept all letters of complaint, anonymous or otherwise, which have formed the basis of any disciplinary action in relation to the officer in question, together with papers and records of every description relating to him or to his work. Some of these "books" contain a thousand pages. There is thus at hand a detailed history of each officer from the time he enters the department.

Berlin also aims to maintain continuous contact between police headquarters and the station houses. The headquarters building and the 118 precinct stations are bound together by a telegraph system which works on the principle of a stock exchange "ticker." A single operator flashes to all the precincts at once, or to any group desired, the news of crimes committed, descriptions of stolen property, general alarms, or other information of police interest. Appearing on the tape in the station houses it is read and discussed by the entire uniformed force.[1] The various departments of the huge headquarters building are connected by swiftly moving mail-chutes (*Rohrpost*), operated on the principle of department-store cash carriers. Papers, telegrams and despatches fly

[1] Most of the Continental departments have their own telegraph systems and a study of the Morse code constitutes an important phase of the work of the training school.

The Uniformed Force

from one bureau to another and back again in a few seconds. In its mechanical equipment the Berlin organization is greatly superior to the other organizations both in England and on the Continent.

As a matter of fact, every department has its own points of excellence. For example, the attitude and bearing of police officials in presenting their cases in court is a matter to which London gives close attention. The constables must present their testimony concisely and unfalteringly, they must answer questions courteously, and above all, they must adhere to the facts. To control this important phase of police work, therefore, an Inspector is assigned to every police court in London and to every other criminal court where constables are called as witnesses. He is a factor of great importance. Armed with a list of the cases on the calendar, he knows the witnesses to be called and the testimony to be given in each. He reports daily to the division Superintendent on the conduct of the constables on the witness stand and the character of evidence submitted. Furthermore, he controls the amount of time which the constables spend in court. Each constable appearing as a witness carries with him a " court card " which, when the testimony is completed, is initialed by the Inspector and stamped with the hour. Returning to the station house for assignment to further duty, the constable presents the card to his superior officer who is thus in a position to know of the time spent on the case.

Each of the European departments has its own system of daily reports by which the administrative officials at headquarters are kept in touch with the work of the force

in the various divisions. These systems vary greatly
from city to city. In some departments they are exceedingly perfunctory, maintained merely for the sake of
having reports, but seldom utilized. In other cities, in
fact, in most cities, they furnish the basis of all control;
by them the efficiency of a division is accurately determined. London has perhaps developed the most complete
system of reporting, and in discussing this important
topic, I shall confine myself briefly to her plan. Three
reports are received daily at New Scotland Yard from
the head of each of the twenty-two divisions. The first
is called the " Report of Occurrences," popularly known
as the " Morning Report." Based on information forwarded from the subdivisions, it contains a list of all important and unusual occurrences during the preceding
twenty-four hours. A murder, a burglary, a riot, a fire
— events above the ordinary and the trivial — are all
listed in this sheet; so that on the Commissioner's desk
each morning is an accurate statement of the city's health
in terms of police activity.

This report is supplemented by the " Morning Report
of Crime," which, compiled in the same manner, contains
a complete record of indictable offenses occurring in the
divisions during the preceding twenty-four hours, together with a statement of officers engaged and action
taken. Less comprehensive in scope than the first report,
it is more elaborate in detail. It is forwarded first to the
chief constable in whose district the division is located
and by him, after examination, to the assistant commissioner in charge of the detective bureau (Criminal Investigation Department). Both the chief constable

The Uniformed Force

and assistant commissioner make notes on the report, suggesting further inquiry, commending an officer, ordering a reward or a rebuke. These orders, whatever they are, are entered on a form and sent for execution to the superintendent of the division concerned, while the report itself is forwarded to the Statistical Branch for filing.

The third report is called the " Morning State " sheet. Compiled by the superintendent of the division and forwarded daily to the Administrative Assistant Commissioner, it contains a statement of the general condition of the force in matters relating to numbers, health, and discipline.

Around these three main reports, centers the control of New Scotland Yard over the work of the divisions. Of course they are supplemented by special reports on the more important subjects of which they briefly make mention. The Commissioner or one of his assistants has only to enter a note after any item in the reports to obtain a complete statement from the officers concerned. But the three daily reports furnish the framework of operation, the basis of administrative control. In the happy figure of a Scotland Yard official, they are the Commissioner's " reins."

CHAPTER VIII

THE DETECTIVE FORCE

Two main types of detective organization in Europe.— The centralized plan and the decentralized plan.— Centralization develops specialized detectives.— Decentralization develops general detectives. — Decentralized system in London.— Centralized system in Berlin. — Vienna's organization a compromise.— Paris changing from centralization to decentralization.— Advantages and disadvantages of the two plans.— Selection and training of detectives in different European cities.— Superiority of the English detectives over the German.— Reasons for superiority.— Equal success of German detectives.— Legal advantages of German detectives over English detectives.— Superior office facilities of detective bureaus in Germany.

IN the preceding chapters we have discussed the organization of the uniformed forces, their methods of work and the systems by which they are controlled. We shall now consider another branch of the police organization, common to all departments both in England and on the Continent — a branch as essential to the preservation of public security as the uniformed division itself. I refer, of course, to the detective bureau which I shall discuss in this chapter under three heads:

    I.   The plan and structure of the various types of organization.

    II.   The selection and training of the detectives.

    III.   The character of the detective force.

The Detective Force

I

In analyzing the structure of the detective department, it is first necessary to distinguish between two main types of organization found in European cities. For want of better names, they may be designated respectively as the centralized plan and the decentralized plan. Under the former the activities of the detective force are controlled from headquarters and the detectives are assigned to the performance of specialized duties; that is, centralization in control involves a specialization in task. Under the latter plan, each division or district has its own permanent detective force operating exclusively in the territory to which it is assigned. The centralized system makes of the detective branch a distinct group of technical officials working independently of the uniformed force and having but little connection with its organization. The decentralized system utilizes the district lines of the uniformed force and to a certain extent its method of control, and tends to develop in these districts detectives for general work rather than specialists for particular tasks. Roughly speaking, the centralized system is the Continental system, while the decentralized plan represents the English method of operation, although this classification is, of course, as we shall see, subject to modification.

London.

The London form of detective organization is typical for England and Scotland. Indeed, in respect to the " Criminal Investigation Department," as the detective

275

bureau is usually called in English cities, London has served as a model which the other municipalities have been at pains to follow.

The detective bureau of London is in charge of an Assistant Commissioner, with offices at New Scotland Yard. The bulk of the detective work, however, is done by divisional detectives — squads of men permanently attached to each of the twenty-two divisions into which the Metropolitan district is separated. Within the divisions, men are assigned to particular station houses. Each squad or group confines itself to the area of the division and precinct to which it is assigned, handling all crimes occurring therein of whatever description. The detectives in a station house are in charge of a detective sergeant or inspector; the detective work of a division is controlled by a " divisional " detective inspector, who is primarily responsible to the uniformed superintendent of the division, on the theory that the superintendent must be fully acquainted with the work of his district in all its branches. In a truer sense, however, the divisional inspectors are under the direct control of Scotland Yard where the whole work of the detective department is centered in the hands of the Assistant Commissioner.

The control of the uniformed superintendent over the detectives of his division is almost exclusively confined to matters of discipline. He seldom interferes with their actual work, for the reason that his experience has been entirely with the uniformed force. He reads the reports that pass from the divisional detective inspector to headquarters, in order to keep in touch with occurrences in his division, but his approval of the reports is largely a mat-

ORGANIZATION OF THE DETECTIVE BRANCH OF THE METROPOLITAN FORCE OF LONDON

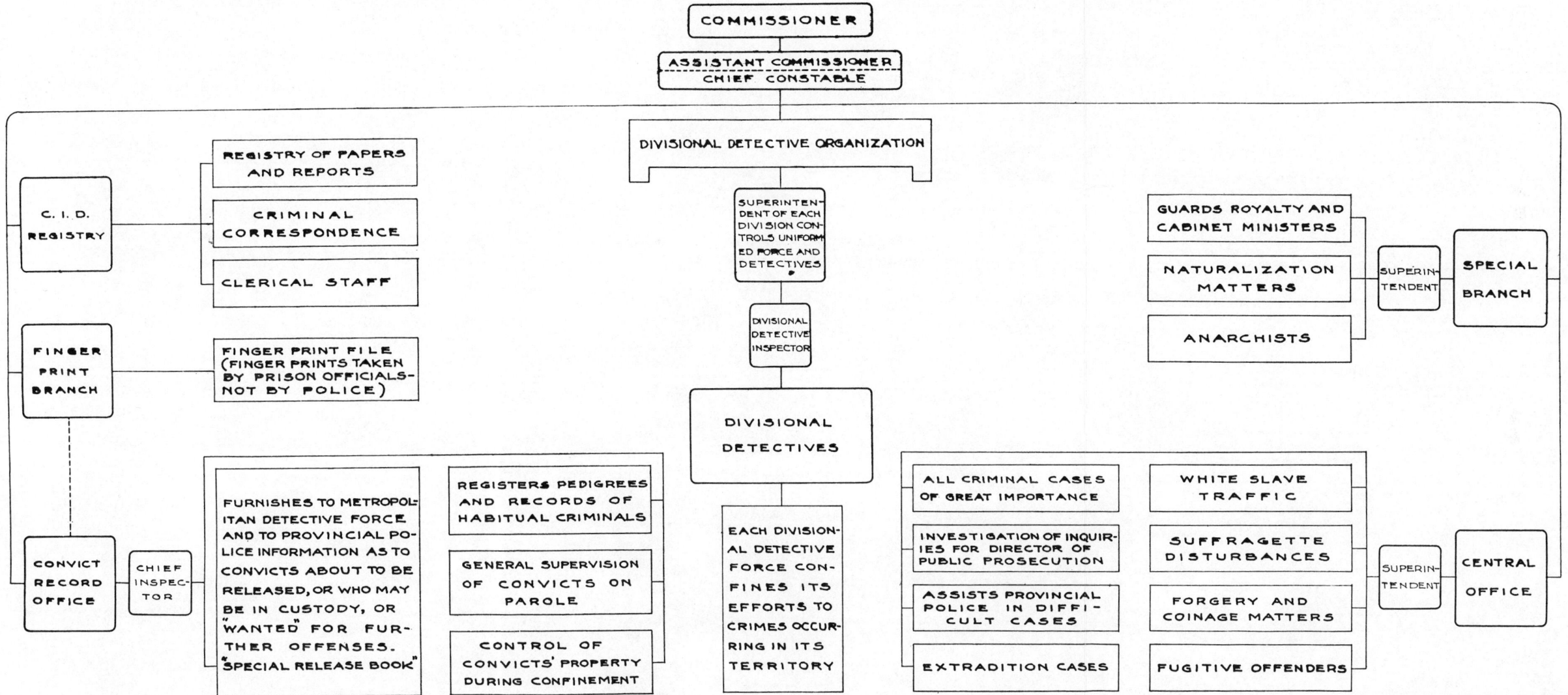

COMMISSIONER

ASSISTANT COMMISSIONER
CHIEF CONSTABLE

DIVISIONAL DETECTIVE ORGANIZATION

C. I. D. REGISTRY

REGISTRY OF PAPERS AND REPORTS

CRIMINAL CORRESPONDENCE

CLERICAL STAFF

FINGER PRINT BRANCH

FINGER PRINT FILE (FINGER PRINTS TAKEN BY PRISON OFFICIALS— NOT BY POLICE)

SUPERINTENDENT OF EACH DIVISION CONTROLS UNIFORMED FORCE AND DETECTIVES

DIVISIONAL DETECTIVE INSPECTOR

DIVISIONAL DETECTIVES

GUARDS ROYALTY AND CABINET MINISTERS

NATURALIZATION MATTERS

ANARCHISTS

SUPERINTENDENT

SPECIAL BRANCH

CONVICT RECORD OFFICE

CHIEF INSPECTOR

FURNISHES TO METROPOLITAN DETECTIVE FORCE AND TO PROVINCIAL POLICE INFORMATION AS TO CONVICTS ABOUT TO BE RELEASED, OR WHO MAY BE IN CUSTODY, OR "WANTED" FOR FURTHER OFFENSES. "SPECIAL RELEASE BOOK"

REGISTERS PEDIGREES AND RECORDS OF HABITUAL CRIMINALS

GENERAL SUPERVISION OF CONVICTS ON PAROLE

CONTROL OF CONVICTS' PROPERTY DURING CONFINEMENT

EACH DIVISIONAL DETECTIVE FORCE CONFINES ITS EFFORTS TO CRIMES OCCURRING IN ITS TERRITORY

ALL CRIMINAL CASES OF GREAT IMPORTANCE

INVESTIGATION OF INQUIRIES FOR DIRECTOR OF PUBLIC PROSECUTION

ASSISTS PROVINCIAL POLICE IN DIFFICULT CASES

EXTRADITION CASES

WHITE SLAVE TRAFFIC

SUFFRAGETTE DISTURBANCES

FORGERY AND COINAGE MATTERS

FUGITIVE OFFENDERS

SUPERINTENDENT

CENTRAL OFFICE

The Detective Force

ter of form. Nevertheless, there is some feeling at Scotland Yard that the detective force should be entirely divorced from the uniformed force, and a project has even been discussed according to which London would be divided into four criminal districts each in charge of a chief constable with full control of the detectives of his territory, thus completing the absolute separation of the detective and uniformed forces.[1] As yet this plan is unofficial. Indeed, lacking the support of the present Commissioner, who believes firmly in a close relationship between the two branches of the service, the project may never materialize.

The detective bureau at Scotland Yard consists of a Central Office Squad and four branches, namely: The Special Branch,[2] the Criminal Registry, the Convict Supervision Office, and the Finger Print Branch. The Central Office Squad,[3] under the control of a superintendent, has functions at once peculiar and important. Not only does it aid the Assistant Commissioner in his supervision of the detective work in the twenty-one divisions, acting in an expert and advisory capacity, but it

[1] This plan has been adopted in Dresden, where the city has been divided into four detective districts in no way corresponding to the geographical divisions used by the uniformed force. At the head of each district is a detective officer responsible directly to headquarters.

[2] The " special " squad handles secret service matters relating to the protection of royalty, cabinet ministers, etc. It further has charge of anarchistic disturbances, naturalization frauds, suffragette riots, etc. The Criminal Registry files all papers, reports and correspondence relating to crimes; its work is entirely of a clerical nature. Of the Convict Supervision Office and the Finger Print Branch we shall speak in a later chapter.

[3] The Central Office Squad consists of one superintendent, four chief inspectors, ten detective inspectors, nineteen detective sergeants, and fourteen detective constables.

277

European Police Systems

also assumes direct charge of grave and complicated cases occurring in any of the divisions, or cases which relate not to any one division but to the entire Metropolitan district, even extending its work to the provinces if necessity demands. Thus any one of the provincial cities can obtain on short notice the services of a member or members of this squad for the detection of local crimes of a specially serious nature.[1] Moreover, the squad is engaged in such cases of an international character, as involve extradition, " white-slave " matters and fugitive offenders.

Unlike the headquarters forces of the Continental department, this Central Office Squad of Scotland Yard is not divided into groups of specialists — men trained for the detection of a particular crime. The fact that all local crimes are handled in the divisions makes any such intensified specialization unnecessary. There is not enough of any one variety of crime to demand the entire attention of these headquarters men. Nevertheless, a certain sort of specialization comes about almost spontaneously in the Central Office Squad. The detectives are encouraged to make themselves proficient along certain given lines, and crimes like forgery or counterfeiting, for example, are generally handled by the same men. Occasionally, too, those who have proved themselves adapted to the work are sent out on a roving commission to look for pickpockets, although this matter is generally left to

[1] Home Office Circular of April 20, 1906, addressed to Chief Constables of English cities. In this respect the services of the squad are similar to those of the *Brigade mobile* of France. (See p. 288.) In both countries it is the intention of the government to give the smaller cities the advantages of the highly skilled detectives of the capital city.

The Detective Force

the division detectives. But in the sense of maintaining fixed groups of men to handle specific classes of crime there is no specialization in the Central Office Squad. Similarly there are no definitely specialized groups among the division detectives, although men are often picked for their tasks on the basis of ability or aptitude. Indeed, under a decentralized plan of organization, definite specialization is impossible, as a small group of detectives assigned to a district or precinct must deal with all classes of crimes from serious felonies to minor misdemeanors. It is this decentralization with its consequent lack of specialization which sharply distinguishes the English detective organization from the system prevailing on the Continent.

Berlin.

Prior to 1876, Berlin's form of detective organization was somewhat similar to London's at present. A policy of limited decentralization was in force. The city was divided into six criminal districts, each in charge of a detective officer and a squad of men who handled all cases of crime occurring within its limits. In 1876, however, began the process of specialization and centralization. "The criminals specialized, so we had to," the head of the detective force told the writer. At first two or three trained groups were assigned to headquarters to deal with prevalent crimes. From this modest beginning specialization and centralization were gradually developed until, at the present time, there is hardly a serious crime covered by the penal code which does not have its corresponding squad of detectives at headquarters. This intense centralization is in part, at least, a reflection of a national characteristic. The Germans, particularly the Prussians, believe in centralization. To them it spells strength and efficiency. Their industrial organizations are built around this principle; the government of their entire state is based upon it. That the detective bureau should be so constructed is a circumstance which can occasion no surprise. There are now at the Berlin headquarters thirty-one specialized squads, each, under the control of a trained officer (*Kriminalkommissar*), dealing with a specific crime or group of crimes. The thirty-one squads are as follows:

1.— Church thefts, counterfeiting, safebreaking.

2.— Thefts on squares, in streets, staircases, hallways, cemeteries and gardens, including thefts of leadpipe, zinc and other metals.

3.— Thefts of luggage and packages in railroad stations, including thefts committed against foreign travelers.

4.— Thefts in large stores, storage rooms, offices, institutions, hospitals, etc.

5.— Burglaries in jewelry and watchmaking stores; thefts in museums.

6.— Larcenies in flats or tenements; receivers of stolen goods, " fences."

7.— Thefts in disorderly flats, in bathing places, and from children.

8.— Thefts of packages from delivery wagons and tricycles.

9.— 10.— Thefts in saloons, and burglaries in flats.

ORGANIZATION OF THE DETECTIVE BUREAU OF BERLIN

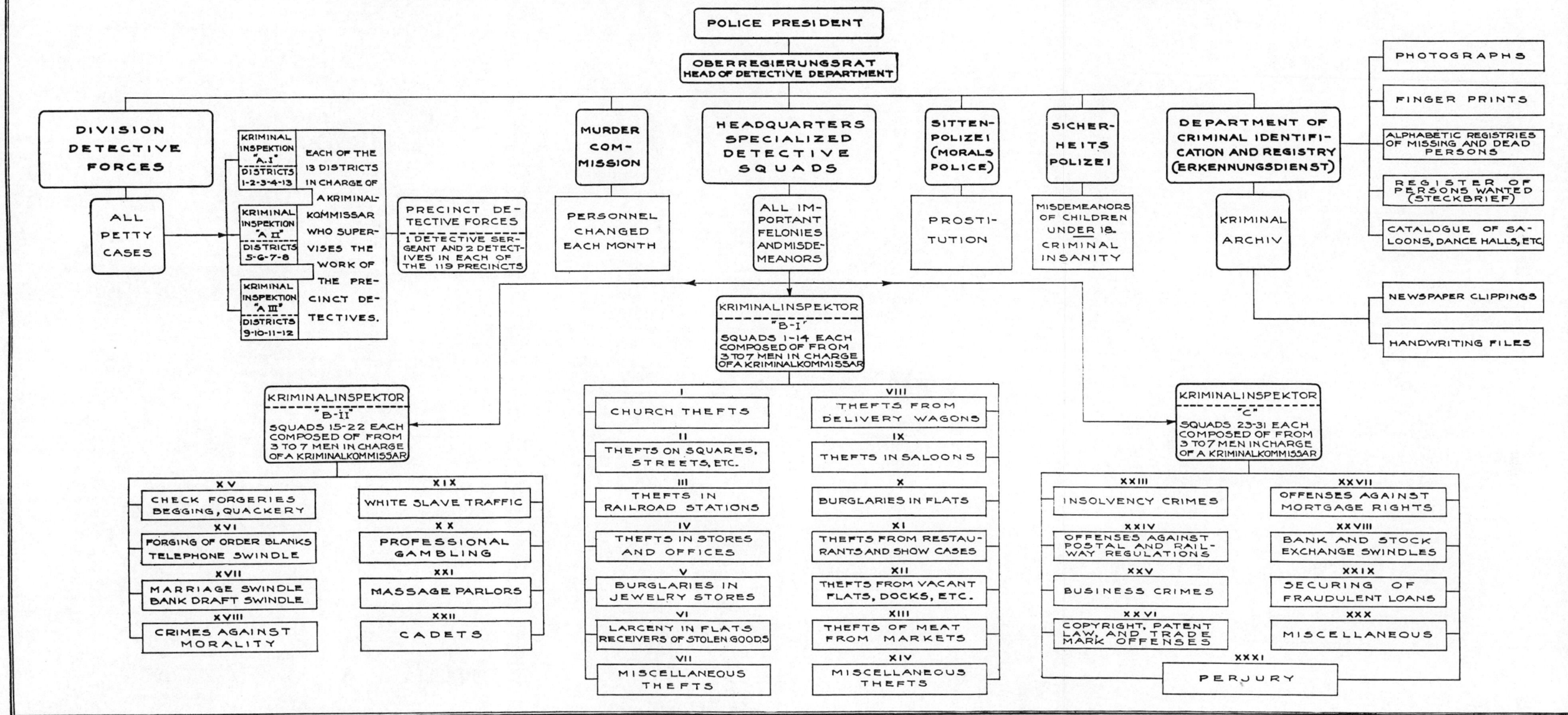

POLICE PRESIDENT

OBERREGIERUNGSRAT
HEAD OF DETECTIVE DEPARTMENT

DIVISION DETECTIVE FORCES

KRIMINAL INSPEKTION "A I" DISTRICTS 1-2-3-4-13

KRIMINAL INSPEKTION "A II" DISTRICTS 5-6-7-8

KRIMINAL INSPEKTION "A III" DISTRICTS 9-10-11-12

EACH OF THE 13 DISTRICTS IN CHARGE OF A KRIMINAL-KOMMISSAR WHO SUPERVISES THE WORK OF THE PRECINCT DETECTIVES.

ALL PETTY CASES

PRECINCT DETECTIVE FORCES
1 DETECTIVE SERGEANT AND 2 DETECTIVES IN EACH OF THE 119 PRECINCTS

MURDER COMMISSION

PERSONNEL CHANGED EACH MONTH

HEADQUARTERS SPECIALIZED DETECTIVE SQUADS

ALL IMPORTANT FELONIES AND MISDEMEANORS

SITTENPOLIZEI (MORALS POLICE)

PROSTITUTION

SICHERHEITSPOLIZEI

MISDEMEANORS OF CHILDREN UNDER 18. CRIMINAL INSANITY

DEPARTMENT OF CRIMINAL IDENTIFICATION AND REGISTRY (ERKENNUNGSDIENST)

KRIMINAL ARCHIV

PHOTOGRAPHS

FINGER PRINTS

ALPHABETIC REGISTRIES OF MISSING AND DEAD PERSONS

REGISTER OF PERSONS WANTED (STECKBRIEF)

CATALOGUE OF SALOONS, DANCE HALLS, ETC

NEWSPAPER CLIPPINGS

HANDWRITING FILES

KRIMINALINSPEKTOR "B-I"
SQUADS 1-14 EACH COMPOSED OF FROM 3 TO 7 MEN IN CHARGE OF A KRIMINALKOMMISSAR

KRIMINALINSPEKTOR "B-II"
SQUADS 15-22 EACH COMPOSED OF FROM 3 TO 7 MEN IN CHARGE OF A KRIMINALKOMMISSAR

XV CHECK FORGERIES BEGGING, QUACKERY

XVI FORGING OF ORDER BLANKS TELEPHONE SWINDLE

XVII MARRIAGE SWINDLE BANK DRAFT SWINDLE

XVIII CRIMES AGAINST MORALITY

XIX WHITE SLAVE TRAFFIC

XX PROFESSIONAL GAMBLING

XXI MASSAGE PARLORS

XXII CADETS

I CHURCH THEFTS

II THEFTS ON SQUARES, STREETS, ETC.

III THEFTS IN RAILROAD STATIONS

IV THEFTS IN STORES AND OFFICES

V BURGLARIES IN JEWELRY STORES

VI LARCENY IN FLATS RECEIVERS OF STOLEN GOODS

VII MISCELLANEOUS THEFTS

VIII THEFTS FROM DELIVERY WAGONS

IX THEFTS IN SALOONS

X BURGLARIES IN FLATS

XI THEFTS FROM RESTAURANTS AND SHOW CASES

XII THEFTS FROM VACANT FLATS, DOCKS, ETC.

XIII THEFTS OF MEAT FROM MARKETS

XIV MISCELLANEOUS THEFTS

KRIMINALINSPEKTOR "C"
SQUADS 23-31 EACH COMPOSED OF FROM 3 TO 7 MEN IN CHARGE OF A KRIMINALKOMMISSAR

XXIII INSOLVENCY CRIMES

XXIV OFFENSES AGAINST POSTAL AND RAILWAY REGULATIONS

XXV BUSINESS CRIMES

XXVI COPYRIGHT, PATENT LAW, AND TRADE MARK OFFENSES

XXVII OFFENSES AGAINST MORTGAGE RIGHTS

XXVIII BANK AND STOCK EXCHANGE SWINDLES

XXIX SECURING OF FRAUDULENT LOANS

XXX MISCELLANEOUS

XXXI PERJURY

The Detective Force

11.— Thefts of overcoats, umbrellas and canes from restaurants, reading rooms and institutions; thefts from show-cases and hand wagons.

12.— Thefts on boats and from untenanted flats; in boat-houses, stables and sheds; thefts on docks.

13.— Thefts of meat from markets.

14.— Miscellaneous thefts, including ladies' handbags.

15.— Swindling, forging of checks, safe deposit books, diplomas, titles and decorations; fraudulent begging; " Spanish treasury " swindle; quackery.

16.— Forging of order blanks and rent contracts; telephone swindle.

17.— Marriage and matchmaking swindles; bank draft swindles (*Wechselfallen*).

18.— Abortion and crimes against morality.

19.— Pederasty; perversion; white slave traffic.

20.— Bookmaking, professional gambling, etc.

21.— Massage parlors, newspaper advertising for immoral purposes.

22.— Cadets.

23.— Crimes and offenses against the regulations concerning insolvency and bankruptcy.

24.— Usury, offenses against postal and railway administration.

25.— Business crimes, including violation of limited liability acts, lottery acts, etc.

26.— Copyright, patent law and trade-mark offenses.

27.— Offenses against mortgage rights.

28.— Bank and stock exchange swindles, fraudulent procuring of advertisements from real estate agents.

29.— The securing of fraudulent loans.

30.— Miscellaneous.

31.— Perjury.

In addition to these squads there are murder commissions, each composed of seven or eight men, chosen every month to handle any murder cases which may occur during that period. No commission is allowed to handle more than one murder at a time. If there are two murders in a month a second commission is immediately appointed.[1] Finally, under the detective bureau there are special squads of plain clothes men to supervise prostitution (*Sittenpolizei*),[2] and a force (*Sicherheitspolizei*) which handles cases of misdemeanors committed by children under eighteen years of age, criminal insanity, etc. These two groups are separately organized under special officers and are responsible directly to the head of the detective bureau.[3]

[1] A murder commission consists of three or four officers of the detective force, a police surgeon and a photographer, assisted by the detectives assigned to the squads of the *Kriminalkommissars*, who are members of the commission. The object of changing the personnel of the commission every month is to develop as many clever men as possible so that the work may not be exclusively handled by one or two experienced detectives whose deaths or resignations would cripple the force before other men could be trained. During the month of service the members of the commission must be available day and night. This commission operates for Greater Berlin, that is, for the *five* police jurisdictions under the control of the Police President (see Chap. III, p. 109).

[2] For a discussion of the organization and methods of the *Sittenpolizei*, see *Prostitution in Europe*, Abraham Flexner, New York, 1914, (p. 147, pp. 270–273, 281–282, 341–342), published in this same series.

[3] There are various other groups of police engaged in work of a detective or semi-detective nature, such as the *Gasthofspolizei* (see p. 113), for example. These groups, however, are responsible not to the detective bureau but to other branches of the police department. (See discussion in Chap. III.)

The Detective Force

Each of these thirty-one regular squads above enumerated is in charge of a *Kriminalkommissar,*[1] who has under him a number of detectives varying from three to seven. The squads are grouped into three divisions.[2] Each division is in charge of a *Kriminalinspektor* who represents a higher rank of detective official. The *Inspektors* are responsible to an *Oberregierungsrat,* corresponding to an assistant commissioner, who has under his supervision the entire detective organization.

Thus all important felonies and misdemeanors are handled directly from headquarters, and the administration in its actual working is highly concentrated. Petty cases are cared for in the precincts (*Reviere*), that is, each of the 119 precincts includes in its force two detectives and a detective sergeant, responsible in the first instance to the uniformed head of the precinct.[3] For minor cases,[4] there is thus a well developed plan of de-

[1] Three of the squads are in charge of detective sergeants, that is, of *non-commissioned* detective officers. As we shall see, the *Kriminalkommissars* are *commissioned* officers who are brought into the department from private life and not by promotion from the ranks.

[2] Squads 1–14 inclusive constitute the first division; 15–22 the second division, 22–31 the third divison. They are popularly referred to at headquarters as "B. I.," "B. II." and "C," respectively.

[3] The work of these men is supervised, however, by thirteen *Kriminalkommissars* at headquarters, one for each of the thirteen districts (*Hauptmannschaften*) into which Berlin is divided (see Chap. III), so that each *Kommissar* has from eight to eleven precincts under his control. As is the case with the headquarters force, the *Kommissars* are in turn responsible to *Inspektors,* of whom there are three, controlling three separate groups. These groups are popularly known as "A I," "A II," and "A III."

[4] The precinct detectives also handle manslaughter and arson cases on the theory that such crimes are committed by persons in the locality. If, for example, the crime of arson should become widespread, there would undoubtedly be a special squad formed at headquarters to handle it.

283

European Police Systems

centralization, similar to the arrangement which London uses for all crimes.[1]

Vienna.

The detective organization of Vienna is representative of the unreconciled clash between theories of centralization and decentralization. Each of the twenty-two police divisions (*Kommissariate*) has its own small detective squad which handles not only the petty misdemeanors, as in Berlin, but many of the more important cases, such as burglaries and assaults. At first glance, therefore, the system appears similar to London's. Theoretically, the only crimes which the Vienna division detectives may not handle are forgery, counterfeiting, usury and matters involving international criminals. But Vienna is unable wholly to escape from the Continental belief in centralization, and like Berlin, has a highly specialized central office force. All larger matters, such as felonious assaults and serious defalcations are handled by headquarters detectives, though not exclusively. Such is the arrangement of the work that there are generally two sets of detectives working on all important cases, one from the division in which the crime occurs and the other from headquarters. There are thus two independent examinations of every serious crime, con-

[1] Berlin's centralized plan of detective organization, with a large number of specialized squads at headquarters, has been followed in most of the German cities. In Dresden and Hamburg, criminal districts have been established, and more latitude is allowed the district detectives. All serious crimes, however, are handled directly by headquarters men as in Berlin. In curious contrast to the German cities in this respect are the Dutch cities, in which crimes are handled almost exclusively by the divisons.

ducted without coöperation, sometimes with actual friction.

The headquarters staff in reality consists of two staffs: one (called the *Agentenreferat*) assumes charge of the discipline, assignments, transfers, and material well-being of the entire detective force. It also handles many important cases directly, such as burglaries, thefts and assaults, often duplicating the work of the division men. The other branch, the *Sicherheitsbureau,* which, as a matter of organization has no relation to the *Agentenreferat,* acts in the capacity of expert adviser to the whole detective organization. The *Sicherheitsbureau* is made up of twelve branches or departments, each in charge of a highly trained detective officer, and each specializing in a particular variety of crime.[1]   To these bureaus detectives are assigned by the *Agentenreferat* as their services are needed.   As a matter of fact, this expert *Sicherheitsbureau* is the heart of the entire detective organization.   It has the right to assume exclusive jurisdiction of cases which are of leading importance.   For example, if a burglary is committed in one of the divisions, it is im-

[1] The twelve squads (*Referent*) of the *Sicherheitsbureau* are as follows:
- I.— Usury; title and decoration swindles; offenses committed on the Bourse; supervision of pawnbrokers' shops.
- II.— International swindles.
- III.— Business swindles; check frauds; forgeries, etc.
- IV.— Fraudulent beggars; sharpers; gamblers; thefts of goods in transit.
- V.— Burglary, including " fences."
- VI.— Burglary, including bicycle thieves.
- VII.— Sneak thieves.
- VIII.— Pickpockets; extortion; blackmail; incest.
- IX.— Counterfeiting; mail frauds.
- X.— Missing persons and suicides.
- XI.— Fortune tellers.
- XII.— Administrative, including editing of official reports.

European Police Systems

mediately taken up by the detectives of the division as well as by the detectives of the *Agentenreferat* and two independent inquiries may be started. Either or both of these inquiries may receive the expert assistance of the *Sicherheitsbureau*. If the case is of sufficient importance the *Sicherheitsbureau* assumes exclusive control and conducts the investigation in its own fashion with detectives who must be assigned by the *Agentenreferat*. Thus the *Sicherheitsbureau* is the controlling factor in every situation which may arise.

Paris.

The detective organization of Paris is at present in a state of transition. Until the year 1913 it probably represented centralization of function and concentration of administration to a greater degree than any other organization in Europe. The new administration of Police Prefect Hennion, however, has largely modified this condition, as will be seen from the opposite chart, and the old organization is rapidly being made over.

The aim of the reform is decentralization, " to ventilate the entire organization," as the Police Prefect has expressed it.[1] Instead of centralizing the functions at headquarters, the London model has been followed and the detective work has been given to the ten districts into

[1] The details of this plan of organization were outlined by the Prefect of Police, M. Hennion, in a communication dated July 4, 1913, addressed to the Paris Municipal Council and printed in the *Bulletin municipal officiel*. The Prefect's plan involved other features than are noted here; for example, the formation of two flying brigades to visit suburban towns lying within the police periphery, and the establishment of a central archives department for statistical purposes.

ORGANIZATION OF THE DETECTIVE BUREAU OF PARIS

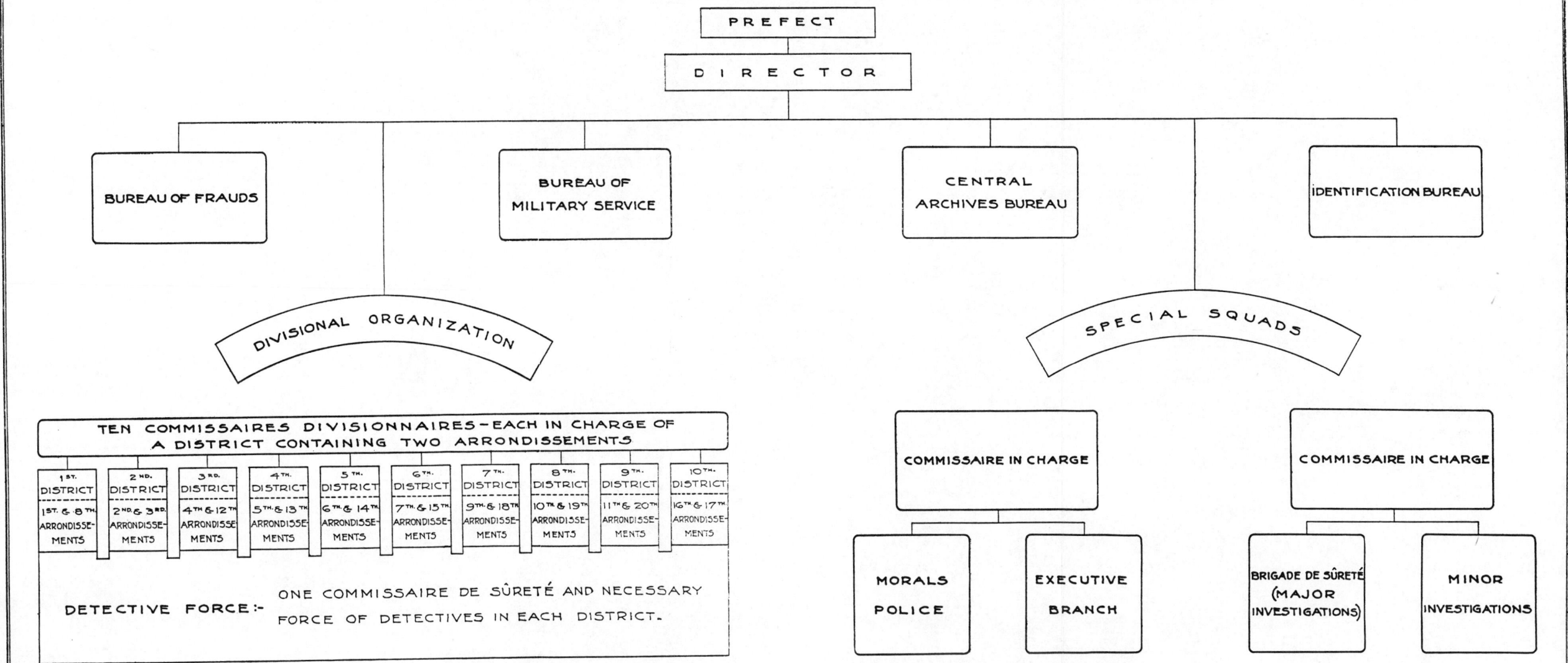

PREFECT

DIRECTOR

BUREAU OF FRAUDS

BUREAU OF MILITARY SERVICE

CENTRAL ARCHIVES BUREAU

IDENTIFICATION BUREAU

DIVISIONAL ORGANIZATION

SPECIAL SQUADS

TEN COMMISSAIRES DIVISIONNAIRES — EACH IN CHARGE OF A DISTRICT CONTAINING TWO ARRONDISSEMENTS

1ST. DISTRICT	2ND. DISTRICT	3RD. DISTRICT	4TH. DISTRICT	5TH. DISTRICT	6TH. DISTRICT	7TH. DISTRICT	8TH. DISTRICT	9TH. DISTRICT	10TH. DISTRICT
1ST. & 8TH. ARRONDISSEMENTS	2ND. & 3RD. ARRONDISSEMENTS	4TH. & 12TH. ARRONDISSEMENTS	5TH. & 13TH. ARRONDISSEMENTS	6TH. & 14TH. ARRONDISSEMENTS	7TH. & 15TH. ARRONDISSEMENTS	9TH. & 18TH. ARRONDISSEMENTS	10TH. & 19TH. ARRONDISSEMENTS	11TH. & 20TH. ARRONDISSEMENTS	16TH. & 17TH. ARRONDISSEMENTS

DETECTIVE FORCE:- ONE COMMISSAIRE DE SÛRETÉ AND NECESSARY FORCE OF DETECTIVES IN EACH DISTRICT.

COMMISSAIRE IN CHARGE

MORALS POLICE

EXECUTIVE BRANCH

COMMISSAIRE IN CHARGE

BRIGADE DE SÛRETÉ (MAJOR INVESTIGATIONS)

MINOR INVESTIGATIONS

The Detective Force

which Paris, for police purposes, is divided.[1] As was
pointed out in a previous chapter,[2] each of these districts
is in charge of a *commissaire divisionnaire,* responsible
both for the uniformed forces and the detective forces
assigned to him. The detectives in a district are immediately under the control of a *commissaire* subordinate to
the *commissaire divisionnaire.* This decentralized plan
is in marked contrast to the system in force in Paris up
until 1913. Instead of having 665 detectives operating
from headquarters, approximately fifty detectives in each
of the ten divisions now handle the crimes occurring
within their own territories.

This plan, however, does not entirely eliminate the
headquarters staff. Approximately 265 men are assigned
to the main office to deal both with the more important
crimes which call for prolonged investigations and with
the international phases of detective work. In other
words, on a somewhat enlarged scale, this headquarters
squad has practically the same functions as the Central
Squad at Scotland Yard.

The headquarters force in Paris is organized into a
number of divisions or bureaus. For example, one bureau
composed of thirty-seven inspectors and special agents
devotes its time to questions of commercial fraud. The
Brigade des moeurs has exclusive charge of the regulation
of prostitution. The *Brigade de sûreté,* divided into a
number of departments or sections, takes charge of the
more important specialized cases which are handled by
headquarters rather than by the districts.[3] The Identifi-

---

[1] Each of these districts is made up of two *arrondissements.*
[2] Chap. III, p. 130.
[3] The principal subdivisions of the *Brigade de sûreté* are the

287

cation Bureau, until recently under the control of the celebrated M. Bertillon,[1] has charge of the anthropometric and finger-print records. The judicial *commissaires,* both for the suburbs and the regular *arrondissements,* are also placed under the control of the director of the detective bureau, and the whole department, both in the districts and at headquarters, forms a distinct branch of police activity, officially known as the *Police judiciaire.*[2]

Thus of the four great capitals of Europe, Berlin alone

Brigade criminelle, the *Centre,* and the *Voie publique.* The first of these, which in turn is divided into three sections, handles such matters as murder, theft, swindling, etc. The *Centre,* where all novices begin their work, handles the minor matters. The *Voie publique* supervises questionable resorts and "shadows" persons of suspicious reputation.

[1] Died February 13, 1914.

[2] Although not strictly within the limits of our subject, mention must be made of the famous *Brigade mobile* of France, the national detective organization, created in 1907 and placed under the control of the Minister of the Interior. This special detective department coördinates the various measures for the prevention of crime and the detection of criminals. Under this plan, France is divided into fifteen criminal districts, the office of the *Brigade mobile* in Paris acting as a clearing house for criminal information throughout the country. Thus, the names, measurements and photographs of all persons arrested in France are sent to the Paris bureau for identification and comparison. The bureau works in conjunction with all local police forces. It has a staff of 39 officers and 160 detectives who are distributed through the fifteen districts as their services are needed. Each district is under the control of a special officer (*commissaire divisionnaire*). If a local police force is unable to cope with some baffling crime, the *Brigade mobile* immediately comes to the rescue with its detectives. It further issues a weekly bulletin (*Bulletin hebdomadaire de police criminelle*) of persons wanted for crime, containing pictures or descriptions, or methods of operation Since its creation in 1907, the *Brigade* has effected 18,320 arrests, 2,575 being for serious crimes.

This department should not be confused with the local Identification Bureau of Paris, above noted. The two organizations work in close coöperation. By special arrangement finger-print and anthropometric records for all criminals are filed in the Identification Bureau, together with the photographs of local criminals; the *Brigade mobile* has the photographs of criminals from outside of Paris, relying on the Identification Bureau for other information.

The Detective Force

maintains a policy of extreme centralization in the organization of its detective bureau. Vienna, while in a measure favorable to centralization, has hit upon a compromise which involves a duplicate investigation of crimes, one by the precinct and one by headquarters. Paris, from a policy of rigid concentration, is swinging rapidly toward decentralization, with a form of organization which will perhaps ultimately approximate the organization of Scotland Yard. The detective force of London is arranged throughout on a decentralized basis.

Both centralization and decentralization as forms of organization for a detective force have merits and defects. As has been suggested, centralization almost without exception involves specialization. When detectives operate from headquarters they group themselves instinctively, if not officially, to handle particular crimes or varieties of crime; whereas detectives assigned exclusively to a district or precinct, necessarily few in number, are forced to cope with all crimes of whatever nature occurring in their territory, and hence have little opportunity for specialization.

A detective working from headquarters, handling all cases of a given crime for an entire city, has a great advantage over the precinct detective, in developing acuteness and proficiency, by reason of his wider experience. He comes to know the professional criminals in his line, their characteristics, haunts, and methods of operation. His entire attention and energy are directed toward one activity. He is in position to study and follow up without distraction the particular crimes that fall within his province. In Berlin the chief of each of the special-

289

ized squads at headquarters keeps a minute and detailed index of all complaints and offenses coming within his jurisdiction,[1] and cases are never classified as " dead." They are always alive, always fresh in the minds of the detectives. There are cases on file to-day that are four or five years old. " We never give up. We never forget," said the head of the detective bureau.

On the other hand, the supporters of decentralization argue that many crimes are local in character, requiring a special and detailed knowledge of neighborhoods and their people. Certain classes of criminals tend to operate in restricted localities rather than over an entire city, and a precinct detective who has studied local conditions thoroughly and is intimately acquainted with the people is far more likely to succeed in his work than a headquarters man who can have at best but a superficial knowledge of particular neighborhoods. Moreover, not only does specialization produce a narrow type of official fitted for little else than his own given task, but the whole plan results in inefficiency and waste of time by reason of the fact that no given crime, indeed no group of related crimes, is prevalent enough to keep a squad continuously busy. Consequently idle periods of long duration are unavoidable. In Berlin it is admitted that market thefts and burglaries are not frequent enough to demand the continuous attention of a specialized group, and even a pickpocket squad has leisure periods. On the other hand, the sup-

---

[1] The index, on the card catalogue plan, consists of three parts: (1) Criminals known but not caught (Alphabetical list); (2) criminals seen, but not known, classified by height and age; (3) cases where there is no knowledge of offenders, chronologically arranged, giving description and details.

The Detective Force

porters of centralization argue that a decentralized system often results in a lack of coöperation between the various divisional detective groups, each division or district being so anxious to effect an arrest and make a record that it fails to furnish other divisions with information which they ought to have. This is a criticism justly lodged against London's form of organization; in the rivalries that exist between the various divisions it happens occasionally that a criminal makes good his escape.

On the other side of the question is the argument that centralization tends to divorce the preventive functions of the police from their detective functions to the detriment of both. That is, it draws so sharp a line between the uniformed and the plain-clothes forces of a department that thoroughgoing coöperation between the two groups is impossible. As a result, the uniformed man is inclined to regard himself free from further duty as soon as the detective steps into the case. Indeed, because he feels that the credit for the entire case will be claimed by the detective, he is at pains to give him no assistance whatever. This jealousy between the two branches of the service is not so marked under a decentralized control which throws representatives of both groups into a precinct or division where under the management of a single officer the line of distinction is less sharply defined and coöperation is more effectively enforced.

The champions of centralization and decentralization respectively are waging their battles in the police departments throughout Europe. In Vienna, the subject has perhaps been most heatedly debated, with a resulting compromise giving complete victory to neither party.

European Police Systems

The brilliant and talented head of the *Sicherheitsbureau,* whose work is known throughout Europe, is one of the stanchest supporters of centralization. " Give me thirty specialized squads," he told the writer, " operating here at headquarters, and I will handle all the crimes in Vienna. The precinct (*Bezirk*) men have too much to do, too many different kinds of crime to take care of, with the result that important cases are treated as if they were trivial, or their significance is unnoticed and they are left unsolved." On the other hand, the Police President of Vienna, as well as the head of the *Agentenreferat,* men of recognized ability and standing, take the opposite ground. In an official document about to be issued by the department setting forth the details of organization for the benefit of members of the force occurs this significant paragraph, expressive of the opinion of the police administration: " A direct official treatment of all crimes by headquarters, in spite of its obvious advantages, would carry many shortcomings in its train, and would be felt by the public as an oppressive measure. . . . Due appreciation must be given to the advantages, up to a certain point, of decentralization." [1]

The controversy does not admit of a single or simple solution. Rigid adherence to either system universally would be impracticable, as the problem to be faced is a shifting problem modified by local conditions. It is therefore impossible to lay down any specific rule to fit all cases, or to draw any hard and fast lines. Too great

[1] This document or pamphlet is being published by the Bureau of Organization and Control (see Chap. III, p. 123). Through the courtesy of *Regierungsrat* Porm, to whom I am indebted for many kindnesses, I was allowed to see the advance sheets in manuscript form.

The Detective Force

a degree of centralization produces a clumsy, unmanageable machine and thus defeats its own purpose; on the other hand, decentralization in excess is scattering and ineffective. There are, however, one or two factors which may aid in determining which of the two general types of organization is in the main better adapted for a given city. Of these the first is the size of the city. Berlin's strongly centralized system may suffice for that city for the reason that its police area covers only twenty-four square miles, a comparatively limited district. London's police district covers seven hundred square miles. To attempt to centralize at Scotland Yard the activities of the number of detectives necessary to cover this immense territory would be quite impracticable. Confusion with a consequent loss of efficiency would inevitably result. Such an arrangement would preclude any intimate knowledge of particular neighborhoods on the part of plain-clothes men. In other words, a territorial distribution of detectives is practically unavoidable in a police department that covers a large area. This is the lesson that Paris has learned; this is what M. Hennion, the Police Prefect, meant when he spoke of the necessity of *ventilating* his detective organization.[1]

Again, the type of detective organization best adapted to a city depends to a large extent upon the volume and variety of crime to be handled. The detective force of a quiet, orderly city like Stuttgart or Munich, for example, in which the number of serious crimes is comparatively limited, may well be centralized at headquarters, for the reason that there is not enough work to keep

[1] *Bulletin municipal officiel* of July 13, 1913.

precinct men busy, and no immediate advantage is to be gained from specializing in particular neighborhoods. In a city like Paris, however, where crimes against the person and against property are proportionately much more numerous and more varied, requiring local vigilance and local knowledge, territorial distribution of detectives is apt to prove far more effective. In the same way it may be argued that where a particular crime is common, as assassination is in Palermo, or blackmail in Naples, specialized groups of detectives can cope with the situation with greater success. Even then, local conditions have to be considered. If an intimate knowledge of particular neighborhoods were essential to success, a decentralized organization might even, under these circumstances, prove more effective. In this connection the relative homogeneity of a population is a factor of great importance. A city population, made up of various nationalities, each with its own particular characteristics, as far as prevailing crimes and methods of committing crimes are concerned, may easily make necessary a series of special groups to handle the situation. In a district in which Italians, Russians, Sicilians and Poles, for example, constitute the bulk of the population, it is self-evident that the problem of crime cannot so readily be dealt with by a single squad of general detectives as it can be by three or four small groups of men, trained in the customs and habits of the particular nationalities represented. This is a condition, however, met with only occasionally in European cities. Their populations, as we have seen,[1] are for the most part surprisingly homogeneous.

[1] Chap. I, p. 6.

The Detective Force

Finally, the type of detective organization best adapted to a given city depends in large measure upon the quality and experience of the detectives themselves. Inexperienced or untrained men, or men in regard to whose integrity there is even a shadow of doubt, ordinarily require a greater degree of centralized control than thoroughly tested and reliable officials. Decentralized supervision can succeed only where the men in charge of the various units are trustworthy and efficient. Otherwise a form of organization which will bring the activities of the detective force more closely under the supervision of headquarters is necessary. " Never attempt to decentralize until you are sure of your men," they told me at Scotland Yard — a precept well founded in experience. On this principle, therefore, a detective organization in a given city might well be altered from time to time as the personnel of the detective force improves. Beginning with a rigid headquarters control and an organization strongly centralized, it could work toward decentralization slowly by the gradual adoption of local areas of activity, shifting the supervision from headquarters to the districts as rapidly as they are formed, and gradually increasing the number of the districts by decreasing their size. How far this process should go must depend upon local conditions, as must also the precise number of specialized squads to be maintained at headquarters. It is possible that the size of the city or some other factor, such as a peculiarity in population, might favor an intermediary form of control between headquarters and the districts, such as has been adopted for Dresden and Hamburg and has been suggested for London; that is, three or four criminal areas or divisions which would each include a number of districts. But no hard and fast rule can be laid down. Subject to the general principles above stated, local conditions and local problems must ultimately determine the question.

II

Selection of Detectives.

Throughout Europe generally, detectives are promoted from the uniformed force. To this there are a few exceptions. In Berlin, the police regulations make it possible for fifty per cent. of the detectives to be taken from civil life. As a matter of practice, however, the proportion is one to twenty. The prejudice against men who have not served the nine-year term in the army prescribed for those who enter the police force is difficult to overcome. The head of the detective training school in Berlin expressed the general opinion when he said, in speaking of detectives coming from private life, " They are not drilled the way the *Schutzmann* is; they have no discipline; they do not know how to stand or salute "— a comment which raises the query as to the true function and purpose of a detective.[1]

In Paris, the great majority of detectives at the pres-

---

[1] In addition to the regular detectives, there are in Berlin approximately one hundred men and women employed by the police as "stool pigeons" for private detective work. They are paid three marks a day and their expenses, but have no official standing and are not allowed to make arrests. Popularly known as police spies, they are cordially hated by the public. There are also a varying number of political detectives or spies employed by the police, whose purpose is to find out the secrets of the different political societies. Perhaps one reason for the hatred with which the German police are generally regarded is the fear of these secret officials.

The Detective Force

ent time have come not from the uniformed force but directly from the army, where they have served as under-officers. It is possible for men entering the police force to choose whether they will go into the uniformed force or the detective ranks. Coming from the army where they have served their compulsory enlistments, they naturally divide themselves into two groups, those who spring from the working classes and those who come from the business and professional classes — the French middle class. The latter group represents a higher grade of education and ultimately finds its way into the detective service, for the reason that keener intelligence is there demanded. The former group enters the uniformed force. In Vienna, while a few of the detectives are chosen from the uniformed force, most of them come from the state *Gendarmerie,* where they have already had some experience in detective work in the country districts. Men who desire to be promoted from the uniformed force must have served three years in that force and have shown special aptitude. A few detectives, perhaps fifty in all, are taken from private life because of some special qualification in the way of languages or technical education. In Budapest, approximately forty per cent. of the detective force is chosen from outside the department. Army officers, sheriffs of small towns, town clerks, and others possessing equal fitness, represent the kind of men selected. In some of the smaller German cities it is possible to find three or four detectives who, because of their ability to speak a foreign language, or for some other particular qualification, are taken into the detective force from outside the department.

European Police Systems

In London and throughout the English cities generally, detectives are chosen invariably from the uniformed force.[1]

Training of Detectives.

With detectives ordinarily chosen from the uniformed force, some course of training or apprenticeship is obviously necessary to fit them for their new tasks. The European cities have adopted various systems. In London, promotion from the uniformed force to the detective force is by examination. A constable must have served at least twelve months as a patrolman before he is eligible; thereafter he may be selected to take the examination by his superior officers on the basis of aptitude, intelligence and appearance. Ordinarily the men who are chosen to try the examination have already shown their ability in plain-clothes work; they have been selected for special duty by their superior officers to handle such special problems as begging, street betting, and prostitution, which are committed to the uniformed force rather than to the detective division. In London, a distinction is made between detectives and plain-clothes men. The latter are merely patrolmen who are assigned from time to time to clear the streets of special nuisances.

[1] In Liverpool, and in one or two of the English cities, clerical assistants in the detective bureau — that is, the men who have charge of the finger-prints and the criminal registers and histories — are taken not from the uniformed force, but from outside the department, inasmuch as it is believed that the necessarily higher grade of intelligence demanded for this kind of work can be more readily obtained from that source. These men, of whom there are ten in Liverpool, hold regular police titles and draw the corresponding salaries. It is an interesting fact that the present Head Constable was promoted by gradual steps through this clerical force.

The Detective Force

The examination which the constable takes for promotion to the rank of a detective is both written and oral, and is given by a police board composed of a chief constable and two chief inspectors. It consists of reading, writing, composition and arithmetic as well as questions on practical police duty and procedure. It involves on the part of the applicant a fairly thorough knowledge of detective work and of the criminal law,[1] and while there is no special school course, the candidate must necessarily have given to the subject a considerable amount of private study. In this work he has the assistance of the " General Orders Book," which contains much practical information; he also observes the work of detectives in his own precinct, and profits by his association with experienced officers.[2]

[1] The examination questions for previous years are issued in pamphlet form by the Metropolitan police as a guide to candidates. Some of the questions asked are as follows:

1 — In cases of burglary and housebreaking, what are the principal points to which an officer should direct his attention, and what precautions should he take?

2 — To establish a charge of receiving stolen property against an accused person what evidence is necessary?

3 — What are the principal publications issued by the police to assist in the investigation of crime? Describe each of them and say how they should be utilized.

[2] Promotion from the rank of detective to that of detective sergeant is also by examination. The ranks in the London detective force are as follows:

> Detective or " patrol."
> Third-Class Sergeant.
> Second-Class Sergeant.
> First-Class Sergeant.
> Detective Inspector.
> Divisional Detective Inspector.
> Chief Inspector.
> Superintendent.

There is no examination for promotion from the rank of third-class sergeant to that of second-class sergeant, nor from second-

Practically similar arrangements for training detectives are to be found in the provincial cities of England and Scotland; promotion to the grade of detective follows as a result of an examination for which men are selected on the basis of special qualifications after a prescribed period in the uniformed ranks.

Berlin's method is quite different. After one year's service as a *Schutzmann,* a man is entitled to apply for entrance to the detective force. As a matter of practice, however, he must have served in the uniformed force five or six years. If his application is granted, and this is determined by the recommendation of the head of his precinct and the need for additional men, he is assigned, on a year's probation, to the small detective force which, as we have seen, is attached to each precinct. Here he studies the files and systems used by the detectives and accompanies the older and more experienced men in their practical work. There is no regular school course and no examination. Permanent appointment at the end of the year depends upon the recommendation of his superior officer. The detective who comes from civil life must go through the same course of training, except that at the end of the year he must attend the beginning school

class sergeant to first-class sergeant, the advancements being made on the basis of recommendations. Promotions from first-class sergeant to the grade of detective inspector follow as a result of a civil service examination designed to test the applicant's educational qualifications, and a medical examination. As is the case with promotion in the uniformed ranks, the Civil Service Commission gives its examination on the invitation of the Commissioner and not as a result of statutory obligation. It is very seldom that a man is promoted to the grade of detective inspector under sixteen years of service. There are no further examinations for promotion to the higher ranks, advancement depending on past record and ability.

The Detective Force

of the uniformed men which we have described in a previous chapter.

Promotion to the rank of detective sergeant (*Kriminalwachtmeister*), which is as high as a man can go in this branch of the service, follows as the result of a course of study at the regular *Wachtmeister* school, which is the same school provided for those members of the uniformed force who would become uniformed sergeants.[1]

We have already seen that each of the thirty-one specialized squads at headquarters is supervised by a detective official known as a *Kriminalkommissar,* and that the minor work which is cared for in the precincts is also under the direction of officers of the same rank. The fact that there is no promotion in Berlin above the grade of detective sergeant makes it necessary to introduce, as in the case of the uniformed force, special officers from outside the department. Unlike the uniformed lieutenant, who, as we have seen, is ordinarily chosen from the ranks of army officers, the *Kriminalkommissar* is often a university man.[2] For detective officers a general education is preferred to military training. At the same time the candidate must have fulfilled the requirements which the general conscription law makes necessary for every able-bodied citizen of Germany. Like the uniformed lieutenant, the *Kommissar* must be of good health, must be endorsed as to character by respectable parties and must give proof of an annual private income of at least 1,800

[1] Occasionally police sergeants are promoted to the rank of detective sergeants, in which case a special course is given in order that they may brush up on the work which they had in the regular *Wachtmeister* school.

[2] Approximately 45 per cent. of the *Kommissars* are university graduates in law.

301

marks for the period of two years, commencing with the date of service. As in the case of the uniformed lieutenant, too, the period of training lasts eighteen months, during which time the candidate serves without pay. The training consists of practical work in the shape of assignments to different sections of the police department,[1] together with courses of lectures on police organization and police theory which approximate from four to six hours a week. At the end of the eighteen months' course, the candidate is obliged to take a written examination. If successful he is appointed as vacancies occur. It is a noteworthy fact that his education as a detective officer does not cease with his appointment. As is the case with the uniformed lieutenant, the *Kommissar* is obliged to attend frequent lectures which are given at headquarters by experts in various lines — surgeons, chemists, criminologists, and higher police officials. The lectures deal with subjects relating to some branch of detective work or theory.

In Vienna, inasmuch as most of the detectives are taken from the state *gendarmerie,* and have already had considerable experience in detective work, the school period, which lasts from six to seven months, is not allowed to interrupt the regular duties of the men. They are assigned to detective tasks, ordinarily in a minor

---

[1] The assignments are as follows:

Three months in a precinct.

Three months in the detective bureau with an experienced *Kriminalkommissar* engaged in precinct work.

One month in Division IX of the police department (supervision of businesses, etc.).

Two months in a precinct.

Nine months in the detective bureau with the various specialized squads and in the criminal identification registries, etc.

The Detective Force

capacity, but are allowed an hour or two a day to attend the lectures and recitations of the school. The men are drilled in the theory and methods of detective work and criminal identification. They are also given a certain amount of instruction in geography, history and composition. Promotion to the rank of detective sergeant may follow ordinarily after ten years of service as a detective. In this case, too, the men are obliged to attend a school whose term extends over an entire year, three days a week, two hours each day. Before admission to this school, the men are obliged to try an examination for qualification, the candidates being chosen for the examination on the basis of merit and aptitude. The school course, which is elaborate, includes lectures and recitations in such subjects as geography, ethnology, history and composition, together with a drill in Austrian criminal law and the theory and practice of criminal police work. The lectures are held at headquarters in class rooms well fitted up and equipped;[1] indeed, the promotion school is the best of its kind which the writer saw anywhere. Vienna thus carries the education of her detectives, as she carries that of her police, further than any other city in Europe.

In Paris, as we have seen, the detectives are taken directly from the army after passing qualifying examinations of a rudimentary nature. At first they are assigned to the simplest kind of detective work in that branch of

[1] Ordinarily there is no promotion above the rank of detective sergeant. As we have seen in a previous chapter, all the higher officials of the department, both in the uniformed force and the detective force, enter under what is called the rank-class system, and may be called upon to perform any kind of police work.

the *Service de la sûreté* which is known as the *Centre*. Later they are attached to one of the other branches of the service. Lectures are given on detective work, but no great importance is attached to them. No detective, however, may be appointed to the *Brigade criminelle,* that is, to the section of the headquarters force which handles the more serious crimes, unless he has passed an examination after a course of study at the Identification Bureau. This study consists of a practical exposition of the workings of the Bertillon system, together with lectures on the organization of the Prefecture, the elements of the penal code and the general administration of justice in France. The lectures do not cover any fixed term; indeed, they are given perfunctorily and irregularly, and the whole method of training, in comparison with Vienna's system, appears meager and inadequate.

III

The Character of the Detective Force.

As a result of our review of the methods of training detectives in the four large capitals of Europe, it is easy to summarize the situation by classifying London's system as " good," Berlin's, " fair," Vienna's, " excellent," and that of Paris as " meager." But local conditions as well as national characteristics make it impossible to judge of the merits of the respective systems or to estimate the efficiency of the different forces so summarily. London may reasonably claim that, looked at from the standpoint of results, from the standpoint of the ability and success of her officials in apprehending crim-

The Detective Force

inals, her record compares favorably with Vienna's, in spite of the fact that Vienna's system of training detectives is more elaborate than her own. Such a claim may or may not be true. Unfortunately there is no statistical basis by means of which exact comparisons can be made. The diversity of laws, customs and criminal problems make such comparisons useless and misleading. The best that we can do in attempting to estimate the results of the training and the effectiveness of the forces is to point to certain outstanding characteristics of a general nature by means of which the detective bureaus may roughly be distinguished.

To an outsider, conscious of no prejudices, endeavoring to judge men and systems impartially, the striking difference between English and German detectives lies in the originality and initiative of the former. We have seen that the English constables are brought from the country districts at an age which in most cities cannot exceed twenty-five years. Coming to live in the city for the first time, they are modest and frankly ignorant. Their easy susceptibility to impressions is used to advantage by their instructors during their training period and by their officers in the divisions. Discipline, patience, courtesy are the lessons driven home. Big, slow-moving, honest, steady men, they develop rapidly into reliable officers. They are young enough and their minds are open enough to acquire through contact with their work and with their fellow-officers a certain ease and resourcefulness in meeting new and unexpected situations. The *esprit de corps* which exists in the force awakens a pride in achievement; the possibility of promotion spurs ambition. They

European Police Systems

see high up in the department men who started like themselves, gaining promotion not through influence but through effective work. The competition is fair, there are no favorites, and the best man wins. Under this stimulus, they begin their careers. After due trial and careful elimination, those showing the keenest and quickest minds are chosen for the detective force. The neophyte detective is perhaps 27 or 28 years old. He is developing a certain shrewdness and longheadedness in his work because these qualities are essential to promotion. He realizes that it pays to succeed; he grows with each case. In time there is developed the typical Scotland Yard detective, cool, keen, patient, resourceful.

To this kind of training and to this result the German detective offers a marked contrast. In Berlin, for example, as will be remembered, a candidate for admission to the police force must have served at least nine years in the army. During this period he is subject to the rigid discipline of military life from which independence and initiative are excluded. Indeed, whatever initiative he has is drilled out of him. He is converted into a well-fitting cog of a perfect machine. When he enters the police force he is thirty years old, although in Berlin he may be thirty-five. For five or six years he serves in the uniformed ranks, patroling streets, regulating traffic and handling crowds. There is no opportunity, as in London, for plain-clothes work to test his ability or train him for his new tasks. He is thirty-seven or forty years of age before he is taken into the detective division, where he is called upon, all unprepared, to display a high degree of originality and initiative. Once appointed, he

306

The Detective Force

finds few opportunities for promotion. True, he may become a detective sergeant, but that is as high as he is allowed to aspire. In that position, he is fixed for the rest of his official life. There are no prizes for success as in England in the way of constant promotion to spur his ambition. He is of the lower social order and he cannot climb higher. True to his army training and to the limitations of his outlook, the detective leads a life of perfunctory routine, doing his work ploddingly, often grudgingly, seldom brilliantly. " Out of a thousand of them there are only fifteen or twenty that are good for anything." This was the remark — exaggerated, perhaps,— of a high official of the Berlin detective force, whose position lends some authority to his words.

It would not be fair to imply — indeed, the statement would be far from true — that all German detectives work without imagination or initiative. There are many individual cases in which the representatives of the Berlin bureau are fairly comparable with those from Scotland Yard. The most that can be said is that Scotland Yard as a whole shows a far higher degree of resourcefulness and common sense in its work than the Berlin detective force — a fact easily explicable, as we have seen, on the basis of training and social environment.

In view of these facts, the question naturally arises as to the reason for the success of German detectives. Why should their activities result in the apprehension of criminals to a degree which is perhaps comparable with the work of Scotland Yard? For surely the lack of a statistical basis of comparison does not justify us in assuming that the German detective is strikingly less suc-

307

cessful than his brother officer in London. Indeed, from what can be gleaned from the Berlin statistics and from a knowledge of crime conditions in German cities, it can be confidently stated that such is not the case. Criminals are apprehended as readily in Berlin as in London. In the light of the inadequate and even misshapen training of the German detective, why should this anomaly exist?

The answer is easy to discover. The German laws, as we have already seen, confer upon the police forces extraordinary powers with which the English police are totally unacquainted. The constitutional safeguards by which the freedom of the individual is protected in England, the theory that a man's house is his castle and may not ruthlessly be entered, the principle that no person shall be obliged to give evidence against himself, the whole conception of liberty as implied in the use of the writ of *habeas corpus* — in short, the bulwarks which English tradition and the common law have erected against official tyranny and abuse are unknown to the German people. The German police, therefore, simply by the use of their legal powers can discover evidence and extort facts which in England can be obtained only by devious and often laborious means. Said Sir William Harcourt: "You must not be surprised if the English police are sometimes foiled, baffled, and defeated by wits they cannot match. It is the price England pays for a system which she justly prefers." [1]   Where the work of the London detective demands resourcefulness and ingenuity as well as time and

[1] Quoted from Sir Howard Vincent's testimony before the Royal Commission, *Report of the Royal Commission*, Vol. II, p. 1088.

The Detective Force

patience, the German officials employ methods far more direct. The mere use of their inquisitorial powers alone frequently obviates the necessity of real detective work. Persons suspected of crime or of some knowledge direct or indirect of the commission of a crime, are brought to headquarters and closely questioned by the police. They may be and often are detained for twenty-four hours, although there is no charge against them and no reasonable ground for suspicion. In cases of serious crime whole neighborhoods are sometimes treated in this fashion. Indeed, the aim of the police is by gradual elimination to discover the guilty man, to break down his defense and force him to confess either before or after arrest. For this purpose, " third-degree " methods are frequently resorted to. Sometimes these methods take the shape merely of threats; occasionally, at least, more drastic expedients are employed, and the stories which one hears — often uncorroborated, to be sure — of the operation of this system in certain German cities would not make pleasant reading. Certainly the system is one which, except in judicious hands, is capable of great abuse.[1]

In England the police have no such powers. A person cannot be detained until he has been arrested, and he can-

---

[1] Coercive methods, popularly known as " third-degree " methods, are strictly prohibited by Section 343 of the German Criminal Code (*Strafgesetzbuch*), which reads as follows: " An official who applies or permits the application of coercive measures in an inquiry to extort a confession or declaration shall be punished with penal servitude up to five years." The difficulty in the way of enforcing this section, of course, arises from the fact that the police invariably claim that no coercive measures were employed in obtaining a confession — and the word of a civilian has little weight against the word of an official.

European Police Systems

not be arrested until there is evidence to warrant it, evidence which must be satisfactory to a judge in open court. Neither judge, magistrate, jurymen nor police can interrogate an accused person. Indeed, the police are strictly forbidden to put any question to a person whom they have arrested, or are about to arrest, touching the crime of which he is accused, and the first statement made to a prisoner in a police station is in the nature of a caution that he is not bound to say anything to incriminate himself.[1]

In contrast with this practice, the German police make frequent use of what is called the *Razzia* system. Raids are made on certain classes of saloons or cafés, and even on lodging houses of a lower order, and all persons who cannot give a satisfactory account of themselves, or in regard to whose identity there is some suspicion, are taken wholesale to police headquarters, where they may be detained twenty-four hours. Here their employment cards are viséed,[2] their names, residences and changes of address are verified by the official regis-

[1] For a discussion of the relations between the police and arrested prisoners, see *An Address to Police Constables on Their Duties,* by the Right Hon. Lord Brampton, printed as a foreword in Sir Howard Vincent's *Police Code,* London, 1912.

[2] Employment cards are issued by the government under the state insurance plan; the employer attaches a stamp for each week's service by the employee. The card, therefore, not only constitutes a means of identification for the employee, but shows the police when and where he last worked. If it appears from the card that he has not had recent employment, he is served with a written order to find work, which, if disobeyed, and if no proper justification can be given for his failure, renders him liable to fine and imprisonment by the police.

Every German citizen, particularly among the lower classes, customarily carries papers of identification. These may be either employment cards, army discharge papers or other documents which can serve a similar purpose.

ters, and the records are searched to ascertain whether in any German city they are wanted for crime. Any infraction of the minute police regulations renders them liable to punishment, and the careful scrutiny made of each individual record frequently results in the discovery of criminals guilty of serious offenses.

Similarly the powers of the German police in the matter of the right of search simplify the detective problem. Section 102 of the German Code of Criminal Procedure gives wide scope to the exercise of this authority. It reads as follows: " The dwelling or other premises of any person suspected of being the perpetrator or accomplice of any culpable act, or of having countenanced such act, or received stolen goods, as well as the person of any such individual and all his property, may be searched, either with the purpose of arresting him, or *when it is believed that such search will lead to the discovery of evidence.*" The right to order a search rests with the courts, or in case of urgency, with the public prosecutor and his assistants. Under the German law,[1] however, the entire detective force is an auxiliary to the public prosecutor's office, with the result that the right of search, as far as practical purposes are concerned, lies entirely within the discretion of the police, and elaborate searches for evidence, in a manner and to a degree unheard of in England, are customary accompaniments of German criminal cases. In Berlin any police lieutenant in charge of a precinct, or officer of equal or higher rank, can order a house searched and property seized. No authority is required in the shape

[1] *Gerichtsverfassungsgesetz.'* § 153.

of a writ or a warrant. All that is necessary is a suspicion that incriminating evidence exists. If a seizure is made, the police official must, within three days, apply to the court, through the office of the prosecuting attorney, for authority to keep the evidence in question. If the application is denied, the seizure must be returned, but the victim whose house has been searched is without redress. "I can search my neighbor's house and lock him up for twenty-four hours, although he may be as innocent as a lamb," a Berlin lieutenant told the writer.

Other comparisons could be made between the powers of the English and German police with a view to showing the increased difficulties of detective work under the liberal British laws, and the correspondingly larger requirements in the way of ingenuity and resourcefulness demanded of Scotland Yard's representatives as compared with those of the *Kriminal-Abteilung* of Berlin. Indeed, if we had space, the comparison could be enlarged to include Austria, Italy, France and other Continental countries, for, in the matter of the limited powers of the police in apprehending criminals, British practice has no parallel on the Continent.

The extensive legal powers of the German police are, to a large extent, responsible for their success in detecting criminals. But there is another reason equally important. The German detective bureau is far better equipped than the average English bureau. Its office methods are greatly superior. A Berlin detective in Scotland Yard would find none of the thoroughly elaborated mechanical aids in the way of criminal indexes and registers to which he has been accustomed to re-

The Detective Force

sort in his own country. He would find a rule-of-thumb method in place of the scientific attention to details which characterizes the work of his own bureau. All the more elaborate appliances for the apprehension of criminals, such as the use of chemical and physical analyses, the extensive application of photography, the infinite number of devices for establishing identification, are missing. Indeed, such is the difference between England and Germany in this respect that a quiet, little city like Stuttgart, with 300,000 population, has better crime indexes than Scotland Yard, while Dresden, with 550,000 is so far ahead of Scotland Yard in mechanical contrivances of this kind that comparison is almost out of the question. In the scientific aspects of detective work, Germany has developed beyond England. In the former country it has become a progressive science to which each of the larger cities has contributed its share. In Great Britain, on the other hand, all the provincial cities have followed Scotland Yard, and Scotland Yard, after taking the lead in the introduction of fingerprints, has been passed and outclassed in the further extensions of criminal identification and crime detection by its more scientific and painstaking neighbors across the North Sea. For the last ten years there seems to have been a deep-rooted opposition at Scotland Yard to change and innovation, an opposition which, with the recent shift in the head of the detective bureau,[1] shows encouraging signs of weakening. It is in these ten years that Germany's constructive additions have largely been accom-

[1] In 1913 Basil Home Thompson, formerly of the Prison Commission of the Home Office, was appointed head of the detective organization.

plished, and it is in part due to their assistance, as I have already suggested, that the German detective succeeds where, because of his limited training, he might fairly be expected to fail.

The subject of detective methods and systems is of such importance and bears so directly upon the efficiency of a plain-clothes force that I shall devote the following chapter to its discussion.

CHAPTER IX

METHODS OF CRIME DETECTION

Criminal record files.— Necessity for such files.— Chief problem of detective bureau furnished by professional or habitual criminals.— Berlin's elaborate records.— Criminal records dependent upon accurate method of identification.— Anthropometry and dactyloscopy. — History of the two systems.— Their rivalry.— Advantages of dactyloscopy.— Dactyloscopic bureaus.— Necessity for coöperation in the exchange of finger-prints.— Scotland Yard the clearing house for Great Britain.— The national identification service of Italy.— Unsatisfactory conditions in Germany.— Necessity for international coöperation.— Crime indexes.— Various classification of photographs.— Tattoo and deformity register.— Nickname and alias register.— Handwriting classifications.— Newspaper clipping classifications.— Classifications of crimes by methods.— The " M. O." system.— The German *Meldewesen* or registration system.— Its operation and uses.— Its relation to the detection of crime.— The new science of crime detection.— Criminal laboratories in European universities.— The results of their work.

THE detection of crime involves two sorts of investigation, one having to do with inquiries made at the scene of a crime or in the actual pursuit of an offender, and the other dealing with the methods by which the results of these inquiries are sorted, classified and compared. In this chapter we shall discuss the latter. Our discussion will include consideration of criminal record files, of the two main systems of identification and the operation of dactyloscopic bureaus, of the various arrangements of criminal registers and indexes, of the advantages afforded by the German system of registration (*Meldewesen*), and finally, of the new movement, spring-

315

ing from the universities, to create a definite science of crime detection.

Criminal Record Files.

The prime requisite in the office equipment of a detective bureau is a criminal record file. The police must be acquainted with the criminal propensities of specific individuals; they must be armed with accurate knowledge of the past records of those whom they arrest or suspect. Such knowledge is not only essential to successful detective work in providing a basis for action, but it furnishes a guide to magistrates in pronouncing sentence. The bulk of crime, certainly of crime against property, is committed by those who have previously been in the hands of the police. The chief problem of a detective bureau is furnished by the professional or habitual criminal, by the man upon whom the possibility of another prison sentence exercises no restraint. Of the 159,747 criminals received in the prisons of England and Wales during the year 1911, 100,605 had been previously convicted.[1] During the same period, of the 10,646 persons

[1] *Judicial Statistics, England and Wales, Part I.—Criminal Statistics,* 1911, p. 138. The following table is compiled from these statistics:

Number of persons convicted.	Number of times previously convicted.
23,023	Once
12,154	Twice
9,104	Three times
7,057	Four times
5,474	Five times
17,431	Six to ten times
13,783	Eleven to twenty times.
12,579	Above twenty times

Total, 100,605

sentenced for serious offenses in the Courts of Assize and Quarter Sessions, 7,474 had been previously convicted.[1] Of the 2,881 persons sentenced for offenses against property with violence, 2,306 had had previous convictions.[2] For twelve years, the proportion of convicted persons in England and Wales, recognized as having previous convictions, has averaged between 60 per cent. and 70 per cent.[3] Similarly in Scotland, in 1911, of 2,898 persons sentenced for crimes against the person, 1,556 had been previously convicted; of 980 persons sentenced for crimes against property with violence, 499 had been previously convicted.[4] The same proportion of previous convictions is shown in the judicial statistics of practically every nation in Europe.

To enable the police to meet this situation intelligently criminal record files have become the principal part of the equipment of every detective bureau in Europe. In Berlin and Vienna these records are perhaps most completely developed. Comprising a number of card indexes, large and small, they show the records and sentences of all criminals who have at any time been in the hands of the police, classified phonetically rather than alphabetically, and cross indexed to other registers where papers, documents, and personal statistics are filed relating to each particular crime. If the police of Berlin wish to ascertain the early criminal record of Carl Schmidt, they have at hand not only the minute details of each offense with which he was connected, but a reg-

[1] *Judicial Statistics,* etc., p. 52.
[2] *Ibid.*
[3] *Ibid.,* p. 10.
[4] *Judicial Statistics of Scotland,* 1911, p. 66.

ister of his companions, friends and accomplices, of his family relations and his employers, all classified in such fashion that the information is available at a moment's notice. The German genius for arrangement and detail is nowhere shown to better advantage than in the criminal files of the Berlin department.[1]

Such records as these, however, classified by names, do not in themselves furnish an infallible instrument for the use of the police. Without an accurate method of

[1] In the Vienna department are filed the records of all criminals convicted in lower Austria. Budapest has the criminal records for all of Hungary. Police departments, however, are not the only depositories of criminal records. Throughout Germany such records (*Strafregister*) are filed in the city, town or village where a man was born, either in the office of the public prosecutor, as in Prussia, or in the office of the Magistrates' Courts (*Amtsgericht*) as in Saxony and Baden. In fact, one of the chief duties of the criminal courts in Germany is to forward to the place of birth, for the purposes of the *Strafregister,* the record of any sentence imposed upon a prisoner. In France, criminal records for the entire nation were formerly filed in the office of the Ministry of Justice in Paris. As the number of sentences began to assume large proportions, however, it was deemed advisable to decentralize the system and to establish a series of local bureaus (*casiers judiciaires*), one for each *arrondissement* of France. Criminal records, therefore, are now filed in the *arrondissement* of birth.

Other countries maintain national or centralized bureaus of criminal records, notably Belgium and Italy. The system in the latter country is perhaps the most complete of its kind in Europe. In the office of the Minister of Justice in Rome are filed the records of all crimes, large and small, committed in Italy or by Italian subjects abroad. Each crime is listed on a card which is classified according to the tribunal in which the commune of birth of the criminal is located, the secondary classification being the name of the criminal and his parents' names. At the present time, the file contains 1,200,000 cards, and is growing at the rate of 160,000 cards a year. Criminal records in Italy are also maintained at the tribunal in which the commune of birth is located. Each court in Italy, therefore, sends out two records of the result of a conviction, one to the office of the Minister of Justice in Rome, and the other to the tribunal in which the commune of birth of the prisoner is located. If the criminal is a foreign subject, a third record is sent to the Foreign Office of his country through diplomatic channels. (See p. 329.)

Methods of Crime Detection

identification, the simple invention of an alias or any other disguise will, if undetected, invalidate the entire system. Indeed, the usefulness of criminal records depends upon the ability of the police to fasten upon each human being an identity from which he cannot escape. Criminals must be differentiated from the rest of the population as well as from each other. Means must be discovered to prevent a person guilty of crime from losing or destroying his identity. Formerly the police were forced to depend on descriptions and photographs, but these methods proved by no means reliable, for the modern criminal is an adept in altering his personal appearance. More reliable methods were essential, and for years the science of crime detection concerned itself solely with the search for an infallible system of identification. When to-day, therefore, we speak of criminal records, we cannot readily differentiate them from the identification methods by which they are made practicable. Indeed, in most police departments, criminal records and identification devices are but parts of one huge interrelated system, approachable from many angles. In order to comprehend the system, however, we must study it from the point of view of the identification methods which control it.

Anthropometry and Dactyloscopy.

Within thirty years, two scientific systems of criminal identification have been developed in Europe — anthropometry, the science of bodily measurements, and dactyloscopy, the use of finger-prints. The former is the creation of the late Alphonse Bertillon, head of the Criminal

European Police Systems

Identification Department of Paris; the latter is largely the work of Sir William Herschel and Sir Francis Galton, although the means of classification by which this system was first made practicable was perfected by Sir Edward Henry, now Commissioner of the Metropolitan Police Force of London.[1]

Anthropometry, introduced in France by M. Bertillon in 1883, is based on the fact that the dimensions of certain bony portions of the human frame do not vary during the period between adolescence and extreme old age. M. Bertillon selected certain specific measurements, each primary classification being successively subdivided. On this basis he built up a system of identification which was adopted by most of the countries of Europe.[2]

---

[1] Finger-prints appear first to have been scientifically studied in Europe by Purkinje, of the University of Breslau. In 1823, he read before the faculty a Latin thesis on finger-print impressions, which, however, attracted no particular attention.

The Chinese seem to have used finger-prints for identification purposes from very early times. Indeed, M. Bertillon always insisted that this method represented an old idea even in Europe. Shortly before he died he sent me as a proof of his contention a photograph of the title page of an English book on which the original owner had inscribed the date, " January 1, 1824," followed by the print of his forefinger and the words: " Thomas Bewick, his mark."

[2] M. Bertillon selected head length, head breadth, middle finger length, foot length, and cubit, and distributed them as belonging to one of three equally numerous classes: " Small," " Medium," and " Large." Each of these primary headings is subdivided on the same general principle according to height, span, length and breadth of ear, the height of the bust and the eye color, this last providing seven divisions.

To these measurements he added, as sub-classifications of his system, his famous descriptive photography (*portrait parlé*) and his method of grouping colors and characteristic marks. Later, as we shall see, he added finger-prints. The Bertillon criminal card, there-

Methods of Crime Detection

Dactyloscopy, first tried by the English authorities in India, was introduced at Scotland Yard in 1901. It is based on the fact that the papillary lines on the surface of the finger tips form certain typical patterns capable of accurate classification. These patterns have been shown by experiment to make their appearance three months before birth and to disappear after death only with the dissolution of the body. Furthermore, the ridge characteristics in each set of finger tips are distinctive. No two impressions have ever been discovered that are exactly identical. On this basis, therefore, it is possible to establish an absolute system of identification. When Sir Edward Henry devised a method of classifying finger-print impressions so that their position in a file could be accurately determined, the system became immediately practicable.[1] Other methods of classification have since

fore, while classified under measurements, involves other methods of identification.

[1] Sir Edward Henry's book, *Classification and Uses of Finger Prints* (Fourth Edition, London, 1913), is the leading text-book on the subject. The details of the Henry system of classification are so generally understood that I have not thought it necessary to elaborate them here. To the uninitiated, however, the following facts may be of interest:

Finger-print impressions are divided into four types, namely: arch, loop, whorl, and composite. In the primary classification, arches are classed with loops and composites with whorls, so that only two patterns are dealt with. The ten impressions are divided into five pairs: right thumb and right index, right middle and right ring, right little finger and left thumb, left index and left middle, and left ring and left little finger.

Of the two patterns, only the whorl is given a numerical weight, no numerical value being attached to the loop. When a whorl appears in the first pair, it counts 16, in the second pair, 8; in the third pair, 4; in the fourth pair, 2; and in the fifth pair, 1. The value of each of the first fingers of the five pairs is totaled and to this 1 is added. This gives the denominator. A total is taken of each of the second fingers of the five pairs and 1 is added. This

been devised, although the Henry method is still the one most widely used. It is employed in Great Britain, Holland, Belgium, Austria-Hungary, Switzerland, and in Germany, with the exception of Hamburg and Berlin. In these two cities a modification of the Henry system has been adopted.[1] Rome and the other Italian cities use the "Argentine system," invented by Vucetich, and widely employed in South America. Modifications of this system are used in Madrid and Copenhagen. In Paris, finger-prints of women and children, to whom the anthropometric system cannot successfully be applied, are classified after a method devised by Bertillon.[2]

Between these two systems of identification, the Bertillon and the Finger-print, a bitter struggle has developed, with the result that some of the European cities, uncertain of the merits of the controversy and unwilling to lose the advantages of either method, have, at the cost

gives the numerator. Primary classifications arrange themselves in fractions from 1 over 1 to 32 over 32, as follows:

$$\frac{1}{1}, \frac{2}{1}, \frac{3}{1} \text{ to } \frac{32}{1}; \frac{1}{2}, \frac{2}{2}, \frac{3}{2} \text{ to } \frac{32}{2}, \text{ and so on up to } \frac{1}{32}, \frac{2}{32}, \frac{3}{32}, \text{ to } \frac{32}{32};$$

making the total number of combinations obtainable 1,024, which is the square of 32.

The secondary or sub-classification is required further to identify large accumulations of primary classification numbers. The details of this secondary classification cannot here be considered.

[1] Dr. Gustav Roscher, Police President of Hamburg, has devised a method which he describes in his pamphlet, *Handbuch der Daktyloskopie für Selbstunterricht bearbeitet*. The method used in the Berlin department is scarcely more than a modification of the Henry system.

[2] In a paper read before the Congress of International Judicial Police, in 1914, Professor Reiss, the well-known director of the Institute of Scientific Police of the University of Lausanne, urged the universal adoption of the Vucetich system of finger-print classification on the grounds of its simplicity. (*Premier Congrès de Police judiciaire internationale*, pp. 38 ff.)

of convenience and at great expense, adopted both. The Bertillon anthropometric system, however, has gradually lost ground. In London and the English provincial cities, in Amsterdam, Rotterdam, Dresden, Munich, Vienna, Budapest, and Rome, it has been altogether discarded for the finger-print method.[1] In Berlin and Hamburg, it is employed only for international or " roving " criminals who may have records in France. For all other purposes dactyloscopy is used.[2] It is only in the French cities and in Russia and Switzerland that the Bertillon system has a foothold. Even Bertillon was obliged to admit the value of dactyloscopy, and after many years of resistance, made it a part of his own system, producing the so-called *Parisian fiche,* which is made up partly of bodily measurements and partly of papillary line patterns. Of the ten fingers, Bertillon utilized at first only four of the left hand. Only recently did he consent to use all ten.

Since M. Bertillon's death in 1913, it has become exceedingly doubtful whether the anthropometric system will be continued even in France. It is fast losing ground everywhere. As a means of identifying criminals it is distinctly inferior to dactyloscopy. It cannot successfully be applied to women or children;[3] the instru-

[1] London discarded the Bertillon system in 1902 after several years of unsatisfactory experiment in combining the two systems. Vienna began with the Bertillon system in 1899; in 1902 the finger-print method was introduced and both systems were employed until 1907, when the anthropometric method was dropped. Similar illustrations could be given from other cities.

[2] Thus in 1912 the Hamburg department measured sixteen persons and took finger-prints of 11,231 (*Jahresbericht,* etc., p. 13).

[3] M. Bertillon was obliged to supply this gap in his system by a separate finger-print file for women and children.

ments required for its work are liable to get out of order; a margin for error must always be allowed, as no two officials make exactly the same measurements; men in charge of the system must be specially trained for the work; the method of classification frequently causes delay and uncertainty in searching the files. Finally, it is by no means proven that advancing age and pathological alteration of the organs will not frequently produce a change of bodily measurements. On the other hand, the only accessories needed to take finger-prints are a piece of tin and some printer's ink. Any person, whether educated or not, can perform the function with half an hour's practice. There is no possible margin of error, as finger-prints are absolute impressions taken from the body itself. Moreover, the ordinary system of classification is so simple as to facilitate ready search.[1] Finally the finger-print method is advantageous in affording the police frequent opportunity to discover the perpetrator of a particular crime through marks which he leaves behind him.[2]

[1] See *Report of Committee to Examine into Identification by Impressions,* submitted to the Government of India, March 31, 1897, printed as an appendix in Sir Edward Henry's book, *The Classification and Use of Finger Prints.* See also, *Mona Lisa und die Daktyloskopie* in *Die Woche,* Number 3, 1914, by *Polizeirat* Robert Heindl of the Police Department of Dresden.

As an example of the speed with which a search can be made under the Henry system of classification, my finger-prints were taken at Police Headquarters in Vienna, properly classified and filed with perhaps a hundred and fifty thousand others. An official who had not been present was called in and after taking my finger-prints afresh, was able, after a three minutes' examination, to find my card in the files. This experiment was repeated for me in perhaps a dozen cities in Europe.

[2] The finger-print system is, therefore, available for two purposes: first, *after* arrest to identify a prisoner with a previous criminal record; second, to discover the author of a particular crime be-

Methods of Crime Detection

The inability of the Parisian police authorities to discover the author of the theft of *Mona Lisa* was due not to any fault in the finger-print system, but to Bertillon's peculiar method of classification. The thief, Perugia by name, had been in the hands of the Paris police on a previous occasion, when his finger-prints were taken. Finger-print impressions were left on the frame of the picture, but his record in the file was not found, because *measurements, rather than finger-prints,* constitute the

fore any arrest is made by comparison of finger-prints left behind him with finger-print cards on file at headquarters. The system is, of course, employed primarily in carrying out the first function. Remarkable illustrations of its efficacy in respect to the second function are given in Sir Edward Henry's book cited above, pp. 54 ff. Many illustrations of a similar kind were obtained by the writer in Continental cities.

The extensive uses to which the finger-print system may be put are shown in Sir Edward Henry's book, pp. 6-8. He says:

"In India the employment of the new system has not been restricted to the police department, but has been introduced into all branches of public business, being particularly well suited to the requirements of a country where the mass of the people are uneducated and where false personation is an evil which even the penalties provided by the penal laws are powerless to control. All military and civil pensioners are now required to give their finger impressions and this precaution is effective against fraud. In the registration offices of the Province of Bengal, and in all the provinces of India, persons who, admitting execution, present documents for registration, are required to authenticate their signature or mark by affixing the impression of their left thumb both on the document and in a register kept for that purpose. In the Opium Department, employers who make advances to laborers, or pay them salaries, or enter into contracts with them, now protect themselves by taking their finger-prints on the receipt or agreement. All emigrants signing contracts under the Emigration Act are required to give the impression of their left thumb on the contract and on the registers. With large establishments, such as are employed by the Survey of India, this system is used to prevent the reëmployment of undesirable persons whose services have been dispensed with. The system has also been adopted by the Director-General of the Post Offices in India and by the Medical Department. In the latter case, the local medical officer and the Medical Board, when giving certificates, invariably take the thumb impression of the person examined." (Quotation abridged.)

325

primary classification. Under a pure dactyloscopic system, such as is employed in Rome, Vienna, Berlin, Munich, Dresden, London, or any of the provincial cities of England, the identity of the thief could have been established in half an hour.

In terms of actual results, the superiority of the finger-print system can be readily established. In England and Wales, for the year ending December 31, 1911, the number of identifications made by the finger-print system was twenty times greater than the largest number effected in previous years by the anthropometric method. A study of the identifications made by the anthropometric and finger-print systems in Scotland Yard shows similar results. Beginning with 1898, when the Bertillon system was in force, there were, for the year, 152 identifications; in 1899, 243; in 1900, 462; in 1901, 503, which included 93 identifications by the finger-print method. In 1902, when finger-prints had completely superseded the Bertillon system, the figures jumped to 1,032. In 1903, there were 2,062; in 1904, 2,611; in 1905, 2,853, since which time they have been steadily mounting as the number of cards on file at Scotland Yard has become annually larger. In 1912, 10,677 identifications were made, that is, 10,677 people were identified with previous criminal records. Statistics of a similar nature were obtained in Vienna and elsewhere.[1]

---

[1] Professor Reiss of the University of Lausanne urges that the Bertillon system be not discarded but be worked in conjunction with dactyloscopy. In his paper before the International Congress (above referred to) he argues that the *Parisian fiche* of M. Bertillon possesses means of identification, such as the *portrait parlé* and the color and characteristic scar or mark classification, by which a system of pure dactyloscopy may well be supplemented.

(*See next page*)

Methods of Crime Detection

Dactyloscopic Bureaus.

With the finger-print system of identification firmly established in most of the European police departments, the next step has been to devise some system either of centralization or of distribution by which the records of one city can be available for all. For, under modern conditions of life, the traveling criminal has come to play a predominant part in the police problem. The same man will commit burglaries in London, Manchester and Carlisle. The same footpad will terrorize Worcester and Hereford. A man arrested for vagrancy in Dresden may be wanted for picking pockets in Berlin and Hamburg. For the lack of certain finger-prints filed in Lyons, the Paris police may allow a well-known counterfeiter to go free. No single department by itself can cope successfully with the traveling criminal. The problem calls for wide coöperation, and cities, districts, and even countries must combine in their efforts to solve it.

To this end various methods have been adopted. In Great Britain, Scotland Yard has been made the clearing house for all information relating to identification. In England and Wales the permanent dactyloscopic records are taken by prison officials; in Scotland, by the police.[1] In all cases, however, they are sent to the Finger

In effect, he says that it is the duty of the police to employ *all* methods of identification available. Outside of France this point of view finds little support. In London, Liverpool, Vienna, Rome, Rotterdam, Dresden and Munich, not to mention smaller cities, the idea of operating these two systems in the same department is ridiculed, although, as we shall see, photographs, scars, marks and other factors are often used as separate rather than supplementary classifications.

[1] In Great Britain, finger-prints are taken *after* appearance be-

Print Branch of Scotland Yard, where all dactyloscopic impressions taken in the United Kingdom are on file. Several cities, to be sure, such as Liverpool and Manchester, maintain their own registers for local or immediate reference, but, for important cases — indeed, we may safely say, for all cases — Scotland Yard is consulted. For example, a man is arrested in Leeds on the charge of burglary. His finger-prints are immediately forwarded by the police of Leeds to Scotland Yard to ascertain who he is and whether he has had a previous record. The files of Scotland Yard, which contain 200,000 records, may show that he is an habitual criminal who, perhaps, is wanted in other cities for the same offense. In any case an answer is at once returned by wire. By means of this centralized system, the county and borough forces of England, Scotland and Wales,

fore a magistrate, during "remand," in cases requested by the police, or after conviction in the case of all persons sentenced at Quarter Sessions or Assizes to not less than a month's imprisonment or at Petty Sessions to more than a month's imprisonment without the option of a fine. The statement that the prints are taken by prison officials in England and Wales needs some qualification. This is true in London. It is also true of the *permanent* records taken after conviction. In the provincial cities, however, the police themselves take finger-prints (after appearance before a magistrate) either for their own files or for those at Scotland Yard, but in the latter case, these records are supplanted by the permanent records taken later by the prison officials. If a prisoner who has been finger-printed during "remand" is acquitted on his trial, his prints are ordinarily destroyed, but to this there are "occasional exceptions,"— somewhat reluctantly admitted by officials at Scotland Yard.

At the race tracks at Epsom and Ascot finger-prints of sharpers are taken on the spot, although not until the prisoners have been arraigned before a magistrate sitting at the track. This is the only case in which members of the Metropolitan Police Force themselves take finger-prints. In all other cases, as I have pointed out, they are taken by prison officials.

Methods of Crime Detection

and the Metropolitan force of London are able to present a united front against the professional criminal.

Even more complete is the identification service in Italy, where special advantages are afforded by the national police system. The finger-print bureau, under the well-known Dr. Gasti, is a branch of the Ministry of the Interior and is located at Rome.[1] In this central bureau are filed the finger-prints for the entire detective service of Italy, sent in from 550 police offices and prisons throughout the Kingdom. Prints are taken, under uniform rules, of all persons charged with committing dangerous crimes, of all foreigners under arrest, of those in regard to whose nationality there is doubt, and of the unidentified dead.[2] " When in doubt, take finger-prints," Dr. Gasti told the writer. Instituted on the present scale in 1908, the bureau has rapidly become one of the most complete in Europe. Its records are increasing at the rate of 1,500 a month. A record card includes not only the criminal's finger-prints, which constitute, of course, the major classification, but his photograph and his description. In this respect, and in respect to the uniform conditions under which finger-prints are taken through-

---

[1] This bureau is located in the *Scuola di Polizia Scientifica*. As we have already observed (Chap. V, p. 192), Italy combines her school for the training of police executives with the national identification service. This identification bureau should not be confused with the criminal record file maintained at the Ministry of Justice (See note 1, p. 318). The two are quite distinct. The latter contains the records of all crimes and misdemeanors, classified by the place of birth of the delinquents. The former has to do with serious offenses only, and is classified dactyloscopically. The two bureaus continually coöperate and unsuccessful searches in one are prosecuted in the other.

[2] The finger-prints of Italian subjects arrested for crime in foreign countries are also filed here whenever such records can be obtained.

out the country, the system is superior to Great Britain's. The latter system is a coöperative arrangement between local forces; the former is a national service covering the entire country.

In Germany, conditions are not so satisfactory. The division of the Empire into self-governing states has prevented the fullest coöperation. Five cities maintain independent registries — Berlin, Dresden, Hamburg, Munich and Stuttgart — and each operates for itself and the surrounding territory.[1] Most of the cities appeal to Berlin in cases of doubt, and Berlin has, indeed, the largest finger-print file. But hitherto, there have been no established rules for the whole of Germany governing either the taking of finger-prints or the conditions under which they shall be sent to Berlin. As a result, therefore, there has been no extensive coöperation, and, of course, no complete file as in Great Britain and Italy.[2]

German officials have not been slow to see the disadvantages of this arrangement. In 1912 an inter-state police congress (*Deutscher Polizeikongress*) was called at Berlin by the Prussian Minister of the Interior in which the police bodies of every state of the Empire were represented. The object of this gathering was to bring about, through uniform methods, systematic coöperation in the identification of criminals. Its program included questions relating not only to the exchange of finger-prints and the possibility of establishing a central

[1] Thus Dresden operates for Saxony, Munich for Bavaria, Stuttgart for Württemberg.

[2] In Prussia, however, where the principal police forces are under the direction of the Minister of the Interior, Berlin has been made the central bureau to which all finger-prints must be sent.

Methods of Crime Detection

bureau for Germany, but to other coöperative measures, such as a common telegraph code and a national criminal newspaper. The Congress appointed a commission of representative officials to work out the details of these suggestions, and their results will be submitted for approval or disapproval to another Congress to be summoned later. If out of this movement uniformity in method and procedure can be achieved, Germany will undoubtedly have an identification service as effective as that of Great Britain or Italy.[1]

In France, where, as we have seen, the anthropometric system is in vogue, the Paris police department is the central bureau of criminal identification. All measurements taken, not only by the municipal police and prison officials throughout the Republic, but by the agents of the

[1] The German finger-print files, such as Berlin, Dresden and Hamburg maintain, are much more elaborate than those in England. Scotland Yard, for example, has two dactyloscopic files, one classified according to the Henry system, and the other (a finger-print index) according to the names of prisoners. This latter file contains the Henry formula for each prisoner, and is cross-indexed to the regular file.

Dresden, to use as an illustration a typical German city, has four files:

1 — The regular Henry classification file.

2 — A finger-print index system, differing from the London file in that it shows the right forefinger print of a prisoner for each time he is arrested, together with date and cause of arrest. Classified according to names, as in London, this file reveals at a glance the number of times that a prisoner has been in the hands of the police, and his previous record, making unnecessary a further consultation of other classifications and documents.

3 — A finger-print file for housebreakers, the impression of only one finger being placed on a card. Each convicted burglar has thus ten cards in this file. The file is used to expedite comparisons with impressions left behind by housebreakers on glass, metal or woodwork.

4 — A finger-print file of all police officials, so that prints found at the scene of a crime may be distinguished from those inadvertently made by the officers in the course of their investigations.

national *Brigade mobile* [1] as well, are sent here to be filed, and the *Service de l'identité judiciaire,* organized by Bertillon, performs the same functions for France that the Finger Print Branch of Scotland Yard performs for Great Britain.

A national system of identification, although highly serviceable, is not as effective as would appear at first glance. The criminal world is to-day characterized by a remarkable solidarity. Crime has become a career, an industry, an art, with established customs and practices and a recognized technique. The professional criminal is a cosmopolitan. He knows no national boundaries. He can counterfeit French money as easily as Austrian or English. He can work a commercial fraud in Germany as well as in Italy. If his record precludes further operation in one country, if his methods become too well known, or the police too active, he can quietly slip to another. The problem of the criminal is thus no longer national but international. It is not enough that the cities of England or of Germany should form a union for their own protection. England and Germany themselves must coöperate with France and Italy and the other nations of Europe. The struggle against crime and the criminal is the struggle of civilized society rather than of individual nations or states.

[1] See note 2, p. 288. The central office of the national *Brigade mobile* in Paris maintains an extensive file of photographs and descriptions of French criminals. Indeed, it was M. Hennion's plan, when he was head of the *Sûreté générale,* to create a national identification bureau for France. It was found impracticable and unnecessary, however, to maintain a separate Bertillon file, and the identification department of the Paris police force is, therefore, used for that purpose.

Methods of Crime Detection

The attempts to approximate this ideal by systematic methods have hitherto been far from successful. There has been no consistent international action worthy the name. To be sure, criminal records are often exchanged between nations on the basis of special treaties and a few cities coöperate in reference to certain cases or classes of cases. Thus, Stuttgart sends finger-prints to Zurich, and Berlin to Vienna, or Paris sends descriptions to London, and Hamburg to Copenhagen. But of broad coöperation on a systematic basis there is none. Indeed, the difficulties in the way of such action are not to be minimized. Diplomatic usage and the prescribed formalities of official communication between nations have greatly complicated the task. If a thief operating in Berlin is thought to have made his escape to England, the Berlin police may not communicate directly with Scotland Yard. The information must first be sent to the Prussian Minister of the Interior, by him to the Minister of Foreign Affairs, by him to the German Ambassador in London, by him to the British Secretary for Foreign Affairs, by him to the Home Secretary, and by him to Scotland Yard. If Scotland Yard requires further information in regard to the thief before action can be taken, the request and answer must both travel through these same diplomatic channels. Effective coöperation is obviously impossible under such conditions. Nor is such formality peculiar to Germany and England. It is the common practice among civilized nations everywhere. To be sure, some of the police departments, particularly Paris and London, occasionally communicate directly with each other, leaving the diplomatic formalities to fol-

European Police Systems

low in their own good time, but this practice is irregular and is generally frowned upon in high places.

Another obstacle to international coöperation in criminal matters has hitherto been the lack of a uniform system of identification. The Bertillon system, as we have observed, is still used in France and is necessary in other countries when French criminals are involved. It is scarcely too much to say that the adherence of the Bertillon School to the anthropometric system of classification has been the greatest single obstacle to international coöperation. With the passing of the Bertillon tradition, however, the way is open to uniformity, and it will probably not be long before all criminal registers in Europe are classified on a dactyloscopic basis. With this effected, the path will be clear for an International Bureau of Identification, located perhaps at The Hague, to which the finger-prints and records of all convicted criminals considered dangerous from an international standpoint will be sent for filing. Such a proposition is not a utopian dream. It was seriously discussed at the last International Police Congress, held in Monaco,[1] and while its establishment may be indefinitely postponed, it is the only feasible solution of the difficulties arising from the present unsystematized arrangement.

An international identification bureau is not the only step necessary to thorough coöperation in police matters. Simplification of diplomatic routine is, as we have seen, equally essential. So, too, a common police code or

---

[1] *Congrès de Police judiciaire internationale,* April 14-20, 1914. This subject was ably handled by M. Maurice Yvernès, Chief of Statistics and Judicial Records in the Ministry of Justice, Paris.

Methods of Crime Detection

cipher is necessary to enable the officials of one country to communicate accurately and rapidly with the officials of another.[1]   A universal extradition treaty is also needed. Again, a uniform method of distributing information relative to crimes committed and criminals wanted would add greatly to the efficiency of international police work. At present, each force or each country has a publication or group of publications relating to these subjects.   Germany has more than twenty such notification journals (*Steckbriefregister*).   The Berlin force alone has three. No recognized principle, however, governs the use of these publications.   There is nothing to guide officials in determining the papers in which " wanted " notices shall be inserted.   Moreover, out of the mass of such journals coming regularly to every police office, there is no way of ascertaining which shall be regularly and systematically read.   An international notification service, perhaps an international criminal newspaper would remedy this situation.[2]   These suggestions and others looking toward uniformity in police method, are receiving earnest attention from European officials, particularly on the Continent.   There can be little doubt that these various steps, slowly and perhaps reluctantly adopted, will lead in time to complete coöperation between nations in the prevention and detection of crime.

[1] M. Lucien Mouquin, *Directeur général honoraire* of the Paris police, argues strongly for the use of Esperanto in international reports. (Report of the *Congrès*, etc., pp. 14, ff.)
[2] This subject is fully discussed by Dr. Robert Heindl of the Dresden police department in *Der Nachrichtendienst der Kriminalpolizei* prepared for the *Deutscher Polizeikongress*. It was also treated by several speakers before the International Judicial Congress held at Monaco in 1914.

European Police Systems

Crime Indexes.

So far, we have spoken principally of the dactylo-scopic system of identification and its use, local and national. It is important to remember, however, that this system has its limitations. It is effective only where the finger-prints of a criminal are already on file. It merely establishes the identity of a man under arrest and serves to connect him with a previous criminal record. In the discovery of an unknown criminal or of one known only by description, it offers no assistance. As Professor Reiss pertinently remarked, " It is not easy to run in the streets after every suspicious man and beg him to be kind enough to let his finger-prints be examined." [1] Further indexes, based on other means of identification, are therefore necessary. The police must be equipped with instruments which will expedite their search for criminals whose identity is unknown. They must have ready access to all information bearing upon their subject, classified for immediate reference to cases in hand. It was with this idea in mind that Bertillon incorporated the *portrait parlé* and the characteristic marks or scars of criminals as sub-classifications of his anthropometric system. This idea, too, led the Italian police to add the photograph and description of a criminal to his finger-print card. These additions, serviceable in themselves, are nevertheless open to objection in that they are subsidiary to a major key or classification, which must be discovered before they can be made practicable. It is useless to search the Italian records for the picture of a

[1] In his address before the *Congrès de Police judiciaire internationale.*

Methods of Crime Detection

burglar without having his finger-print formula. Similarly, it is wasted effort to look through a Bertillon file for the characteristic scars of a pickpocket without knowing his measurements. Additional classifications rather than sub-classifications are necessary. Sub-classifications furnish no new clues; they serve only to supplement the major key.

Much ingenuity has been expended by European authorities in devising new criminal files and indexes. Indeed, this phase of police activity has become a distinct science to which many police forces in various countries have contributed. Perhaps the most widely employed classification, certainly the oldest, is furnished by photography. Until the inauguration of Bertillon's system in 1883, photographs supplied the only means of identification known to the police. Even to-day their importance in detective work cannot be overstated. There is scarcely a police department in Europe which does not maintain some kind of a photograph file either as a subdivision of its main system of identification, or as an independent index to aid in the discovery of unknown criminals. In carrying out this latter purpose, photographs were originally classified by crimes. A man who complained that he had been robbed on the street, for example, was given the opportunity to look through the gallery of highwaymen to see whether he could identify his assailant. As the number of photographs increased, however, this method became impracticable.[1] A man untrained in the science of identification may correctly pick

[1] It is still employed, however, in Berlin, where through its use 245 criminals were accurately identified by victims in 1912.

his assailant from fifty or perhaps a hundred photographs, but when the number runs into thousands, as it often does in the Continental departments, the feat is practically impossible.[1] A system was thereupon devised which subdivides crimes by methods on the theory that a criminal will always commit his special offense in the same manner. That is, the tendency of criminals is to specialize, not only in a particular crime, but in a particular method of committing it. The burglar who forces a back window with a " jimmy " usually confines himself to that method. Similarly, there are such specialties as stealing scarf-pins in theaters or snatching pocketbooks on lonely streets. In many departments, therefore, the photographs are divided and subdivided according to crimes and methods respectively.[2]

---

[1] The Budapest authorities claim to have the photographs of over a million criminals, although this is probably an exaggeration.

[2] This specialization is carried to an amazing extreme. In Austria and Hungary there are pickpockets who confine themselves to the following method: Consuming enough garlic strongly to taint the breath they board a crowded street car and stand close to some prosperous looking passenger. In his endeavors to escape the odor breathed in his face, the victim presents an easy opportunity to the pickpocket.

In this connection Lieutenant Colonel Sir Henry Smith, K. C. B., Ex-Commissioner City of London Police, writes as follows:

" Criminals, if they will pardon me for saying so, show a strange want of originality. The streets of London have thousands of pickpockets: they began to pick pockets, and they continue to pick pockets. The omnibus thief remains the omnibus thief; and the stealer of milk-cans steals milk-cans and nothing else. The stealer of dogs might surely diversify his program by occasionally stealing a cat; but no, the feline race concerns him not. With strange stupidity they frequent the same line of omnibuses, return to the same streets, and, till Nemesis overtakes them, steal the same articles. In the higher walks of the profession these peculiarities are still more striking. The bank robber and the forger are fascinated by their own style of business. They never have an idea in their heads beyond bank robbery and forgery. The coiner is always severely dealt with; but who ever saw him take

Methods of Crime Detection

In Berlin, Vienna, Dresden, Munich and other cities in Germany and Austria, still another system is in force. The photographs are arranged primarily according to crimes and the height of criminals, the former constituting the horizontal classification and the latter the vertical. Thus, pickpockets approximately five feet, six inches tall, have a separate file, or burglars five feet, eight inches tall. These files are further classified according to age, shape of nose and shape of ear lobe, the whole system including five distinct classifications. This arrangement furnishes a valuable aid to a detective force in following minute clues.[1]

In many cities the photographs of criminals wanted by the police are mounted on separate cards for the pocket use of individual detectives. Hamburg issues a small folder, three inches by four inches, containing not only the front and profile views of a criminal, but his full description as well. This serves to keep the features of a man wanted for crime constantly before the detectives. In some cities, too, each member of a detective squad is furnished with the photographs of all the more important criminals coming within his specialty. Thus each

to a less dangerous pursuit? The ruffian who robs with violence, uniformly knocks his victims down as the slaughterer poleaxes an ox; the good old-fashioned 'stand and deliver' would in the vast majority of cases be quite sufficient, entailing possibly only six weeks or two months instead of five years or ten."—(*Blackwood's Magazine*, May, 1906. Quotation slightly abridged.)

[1] This classification is described in Gross' *Archiv für Kriminal-Anthropologie und Kriminalistik*, Vol. 33, ("*Kriminalphotothek*"). It originated in the Munich department. In the Dresden department, where it has perhaps been most fully developed, the horizontal classification includes thirty-three species of crime, while the vertical height classification runs from approximately five feet, two inches, to six feet, two inches.

member of a burglary squad maintains a small " rogues' gallery " of the well-known criminals in this particular line who might reasonably be expected to repeat their offenses.

Photography furnishes the opportunity for an extensive series of indexes, but like finger-prints, it has its limitations, and further classifications have been found necessary. One of the most interesting of these is the so-called " Tattoo and Deformity Register," in use in most of the Continental departments. This classifies all criminals according to characteristic physical features such as marks, scars, and other disfigurations. The basis of the classification is furnished by various parts of the anatomy — right arm, left arm, cheeks, lips, eyes, ears, legs, etc. A citizen complains that he has been robbed by a man with a scar on his left cheek or perhaps a tattoo mark on his right hand. A search of the file reveals all criminals known to the police answering that description. The file is cross-indexed to the photograph and criminal record classification and a speedy identification often follows. Or again, the police arrest as a suspicious person a man who is found to have a design tattooed on his arms or body. A reference to the index may show him to be an old offender. For this latter purpose, however, the tattoo registry has been generally superseded by the finger-print file.

Another effective index is the " Nickname and Alias Register " of criminals, classified according to appellations used in the underworld. The fact that " Iron Billy " is the name given by his confederates to William Smith may prove the means of connecting him with a

Methods of Crime Detection

series of crimes. This classification has been especially well developed in Berlin and Stuttgart.

Berlin has originated, too, an extensive handwriting file classified after a system devised by Dr. Schneickert, the well-known head of the *Kriminal Archiv* of the Berlin department.[1] In this file are catalogued specimens of the handwriting of criminals whenever and wherever they can be obtained. Letters, bank checks, signatures in hotel registers and documents of various kinds representing the handwriting of over six hundred criminals are here classified for immediate reference. The system has been especially effective in the detection of blackmailers and the international hotel thieves.[2]

The Berlin department maintains a catalogue of newspaper clippings relating to crime and criminals in Germany.[3] These clippings, which are carefully classified and filed, serve to keep the department informed as to the state of crime throughout the country. An unusual

[1] Dr. Schneickert's position in the Berlin department is an example of the desire of Continental police departments to secure the services of trained men for particular tasks. A university graduate in law, he studied handwriting in Munich, becoming one of the best known handwriting experts in Germany. Appreciating the value of his work in the detection of crime, the Berlin police authorities made a placé for him in the department.

[2] This classification has been copied by the Dresden department. It is described in Gross' *Archiv,* Vol. 39. Dresden has another interesting file which I did not find in any other city. It consists of a classification of criminal slang and jargon, new words being added as they are discovered. It includes also the cabalistic signs used in the criminal world and often chalked upon houses and sidewalks. Dr. Hans Gross has made quite a study of this phase of crime life in his *System der Kriminalistik.*

[3] The department is a regular subscriber to a clipping bureau. Dresden has a similar system. In Berlin, the clippings are filed by crimes after a system devised by Dr. Schneickert. Indeed, the system forms part of his bureau, operated in connection with the handwriting file.

European Police Systems

burglary in Munich, a swindle in Stuttgart, a murder in Frankfort-on-Main, are thus immediately brought to the attention of the Berlin authorities. It is possible that the Munich burglar gained admittance by completely cutting away the lock of a door with a fine saw. This may suggest the work of a particular criminal known to the police of Berlin, and the Munich authorities are immediately informed. Or again, a man is arrested for swindling in Stuttgart under circumstances which suggest to the Berlin police that he has a criminal record in other cities, perhaps in Berlin itself. They thereupon write to Stuttgart for further particulars of the crime and for the picture and finger-prints of the defendant. In this fashion they keep in daily touch with crime conditions throughout the Empire. The clipping index has proved especially serviceable and is rapidly growing in usefulness.

We have already observed that European authorities are beginning to classify their so-called "Rogues' Galleries" according to the methods by which crime is committed on the theory that professional criminals tend to commit their special offenses in certain regular modes. One house-breaker will always help himself to wine or food while robbing a dwelling; another will bathe and change his clothes after the task is done, robing himself in garments which he finds in the house; another will operate only at certain hours or in connection with certain classes of dwellings; still another will gain entrance by deceitfully describing himself as a gas inspector or an agent. Such facts as these often furnish important clues to the discovery of a

342

Methods of Crime Detection

criminal. Indeed, in the investigation of a crime there is no point too trivial to be overlooked. In view of this fact, Dresden has initiated the experiment of a separate file for burglars and thieves, classified by their methods. The information for this index is obtained from prisons, newspapers, and police officials all over Germany. Here is the file of sneak thieves who enter a window by way of the veranda roof; here are the men who use skeleton keys; here are those who pry off a latch. Each such specialization has its own separate file. In addition to this arrangement by methods which, of course, forms the major classification, each card in the index contains the front view and profile photographs of the criminal, his name and prison sentences, including the dates of entrance and release. The last-named item is of peculiar importance. During the term of his sentence a criminal cannot be suspected of contemporary crimes. If, on the other hand, certain crimes break out in a locality following the release from prison of a convict who formerly adopted the same methods now again employed, there is reasonable ground for suspecting that he may be the guilty party. The information regarding prison sentences is furnished to the Dresden department by the prison authorities;[1] and the records in the file are sub-

[1] The idea of using the dates of release of convicts from prison as an asset to detective work was borrowed from England, where it has been employed since 1896. On the basis of information furnished by the governors of every prison in England and Wales, a *Weekly List of Habitual Criminals* is published by Scotland Yard, giving notice of convicts about to be released from prison and the locality to which they are expected to return. This list is sent to every police force in the country. It contains the names of those habitual offenders who come within the provisions of Sections 5, 7 and 8 of the Prevention of Crimes Act of 1871 relating to sec-

European Police Systems

ject to continual modifications. The success of this classification has been so pronounced that the Dresden authorities are now at work on similar files for other crimes than burglary and theft.[1]

What is probably the most ambitious plan of crime classification by methods has been initiated in some of the counties and boroughs of England. I refer to the so-called "M. O." or *Modus Operandi* system devised by Major L. W. Atcherley, Chief Constable of the West Riding of Yorkshire Constabulary.

His system is more than an index for a single department. It is a coöperative arrangement by which habitual or traveling criminals can be traced from community to community by a comparison of their methods of work. Hitherto information relating to the modes and peculiarities of criminals has been recorded in the memory of some particular policeman or on the books of some particular force. No systematized arrangement has existed by which this information could be placed at the service of

ond offenders and police supervisees. In addition to the above information, the *Weekly List* contains a full description of each such convict, including height, complexion, hair, eyes and characteristic marks, his aliases, the offense for which he was committed and his "office number," corresponding to his record file and finger-print form at Scotland Yard. The various police forces in the country, therefore, have at hand a complete record of the habitual criminals released in their neighborhoods.

[1] The idea of classifying criminals by their methods of committing crime was developed as early as 1896 at Scotland Yard, although the classification was exceedingly cumbersome. It consisted merely of a printed index to huge books published from time to time, containing the names of criminals sentenced for various offenses. Not until 1913, long after the card index system had superseded the unwieldy book index in nearly every city on the continent, did Scotland Yard consent to alter its arrangement. As a result, the *Crime Index* which it started in 1913 is, in point of completeness and extensiveness, far behind the indexes of such cities as Vienna, Berlin, Dresden, Munich and Stüttgart.

Methods of Crime Detection

all police bodies operating in a given district. It is true that " alarms " are constantly being exchanged between departments, and each country has two or more official criminal journals devoted exclusively to the publication of crime news. But the information contained in these papers is not classified; indeed much of it is not subject to classification. Most of the notices inserted in these " alarms " or journals consist of long lists of stolen property and occasionally a general description of a suspect. The serviceability of this information depends on the retentiveness of memories already overloaded with routine work and local requirements. Indeed the ordinary attitude of a detective force is that it has more than enough of its own to deal with, without attempting to apprehend the criminals of neighboring cities. Meanwhile the brotherhood of traveling criminals, profiting by the shortcomings of the police system, continues to flourish.

Major Atcherley's system is designed to meet this condition. Briefly, it involves the establishment of a number of coöperative clearing-houses of information for certain areas comprising a number of counties or boroughs. In these clearing houses facts relating to crime methods are collected, sifted, sorted, and stored for future reference and use in the investigation of subsequent offenses. This plan necessitated a new classification, a difficulty which was successfully met by the adoption of Dr. Mercier's arrangement of offenses employed in his well-known book, *Crime and Insanity*.[1] Inasmuch as offenses against property constitute approximately 90 per cent. of criminal work in England, the system has

[1] New York, 1911, Chap. VIII.

been limited for the time being to this category, although it is capable of expansion to include other phases of crime. Ten subdivisions or headings have been adopted, each relating to a phase of the method employed by the criminal in the perpetration of his crime.[1] These headings are so arranged that they can be expressed in numerical figures, and the whole crime can be accurately and minutely described in a formula.[2] For example, a burglary is committed in Wakefield by an unknown person who pasted a piece of sticky fly-paper over a window glass, so that it would not fall when broken, then smashed the glass and slipped the latch. The formula for this crime and the necessary particulars are sent to the clearing house

---

[1] The ten headings are as follows:

1 — *Classword;* kind of property attacked, whether dwelling house, lodging house, hotel, etc.

2 — *Entry;* the actual point of entry, front window, back window, etc.

3 — *Means;* whether with implements or tools, such as a ladder, jimmy, etc.

4 — *Object;* kind of property taken.

5 — *Time;* not only time of day or night, but whether church time, market day, during meal hours, etc.

6 — *Style;* whether criminal to obtain entrance describes himself as mechanic, canvasser, agent, etc.

7 — *Tale;* any disclosure as to his alleged business or errand which the criminal may make.

8 — *Pals;* whether crime was committed with confederates, etc.

9 — *Transport;* whether bicycle or other vehicle was used in connection with crime.

10 — *Trademark;* whether criminal committed any unusual act in connection with crime, such as poisoning a dog, changing his clothes, leaving a note for the owner, etc.

For full particulars of this system of classification see *"M. O."* (*Modus Operandi*) in *Criminal Investigation and Detection,* Major L. W. Atcherley, M. V. O., West Riding of Yorkshire, 1913.

[2] Thus a theft from a place used for public worship is "M. O. 2, 3," or a misapplication of money in a confidential relationship is "M. O. 1."

of the district. Here, by comparison it is shown that similar burglaries have been committed under exactly the same circumstances in other towns in the vicinity. Perhaps in one town the burglar was seen and a description obtained. Perhaps the police of another place know his identity. Gradually by comparison and elimination, crime is linked with crime, offender with suspect, until finally the case is brought to a point where an arrest can be effected and the finger-print register employed to show connection with previous sentences.

Major Atcherley's system is daily growing in usefulness as its operation becomes more widespread. At the present time it is confined practically to the Northern District of England, where it is employed by both county and borough forces. It is highly probable, however, that it will soon be adopted in the Southern District.[1] So far, Scotland Yard has regarded it with some suspicion. Indeed the London detective organization, as we have already noticed, has been exceedingly slow in adopting improvements relating to its office methods. The advantages of the " M. O." system, however, or of some similar system, will ultimately compel attention. Classification of crimes by methods, operated through clearing-houses over a wide territory, is bound to become a permanent feature of detective work. Just as the invention of a formula has made identification by finger-prints a method of practical utility by connecting the pris-

---

[1] For favorable opinion of the operation of the " M. O." system, see Mr. Leonard Dunning's comment in his report on the condition of the constabulary of the Southern District of England, published in the Home Office pamphlet, *Police, England and Wales,* 1913.

European Police Systems

oner with his past record, so the application of a formula to these other peculiarities of the criminal will be of enormous value in facilitating his apprehension.[1]

In considering the various systems in use in the Eu-

[1] Space is lacking in which to describe the details of various other indexes and registers used in connection with detective work. Mention should be made, however, of the elaborate *Missing and Dead* files maintained in Berlin and Dresden. All persons reported missing and all unidentified dead are classified in parallel files. The cards in both files are equipped with projecting tabs or flaps in such manner that the height, age, color of eyes and hair and condition of teeth are shown at a glance. On the face of each card is a description of the clothes and personal effects found on the body in the case of unidentified dead or upon the person reported missing at the time he disappeared. An elaborate physical description is also given. The cards are arranged in the files according to dates — date of discovery of body or date of disappearance. When an alarm is sent to headquarters in regard to a missing person, a search is immediately made of the files to determine whether any unidentified dead have been reported answering to the description. Similarly the attempt to identify dead bodies begins with a search of the "missing" file. The Berlin and Dresden systems both operate for all of Germany, although each of the two cities pays particular attention to its own state. The information for the files is obtained from newspapers, police officers, courts, etc.

Many Continental police departments maintain elaborate card index systems of property reported stolen. In this respect, Berlin and the German cities easily lead the way. The cards are grouped according to classes — men's gold watches, men's silver watches, women's gold watches, women's silver watches, plain gold rings, various classes of jeweled rings, bicycles, passports, etc. To be classified the property must be capable of exact identification, that is, it must bear some number, monogram, or distinctive mark. Otherwise, it cannot be entered in the files. Lists of suspicious property found in pawnshops, "fences," etc., are referred to the index to determine the question of ownership. Hitherto, this index has been comparatively local in scope. A plan is now on foot in Berlin, however, to extend the system to cover all of Prussia and eventually the entire Empire, and to include every kind of property which can be stolen.

Many departments maintain elaborate Lost and Found Bureaus. In London and Vienna, these bureaus are the object of particular care and attention from the authorities. For the year 1912, the London office returned 36,865 lost articles to their owners; in 1911, 32,499. During the same period, the Vienna office returned approximately 25,000 articles a year. *(See next page)*

348

Methods of Crime Detection

ropean departments, the progressiveness of the German cities is at once apparent. Police administration in Germany in all its phases appears to be more nearly a science than in any other country. The departments are keenly alive and eager to experiment with fresh ideas. There seems to be little of the apathy and instinctive resistance to the introduction of new methods which one often finds in England. The friendliest rivalry pervades the departments in the different cities, each eager to surpass the other. To accomplish their purposes they freely borrow ideas from one another. Munich introduced the classification of photographs by crimes and height, subdivided by age, shape of nose and ear; Dresden and Stuttgart borrowed it from Munich, Berlin borrowed it from Dresden. So, too, Dresden originated the file system of newspaper clippings; Berlin immediately adopted it. On the other hand, Berlin's handwriting classification was borrowed by Dresden. Dresden's method of classifying the missing and dead was copied by Berlin. The German detective works with better tools than are ordinarily employed in England or even in France. In everything that pertains to mechanical equipment the German bureaus easily take first rank.

Berlin has an index of police presidents and commissioners throughout Europe, cross indexed to a file of envelopes, stamped and addressed, so that alarms can immediately be dispatched to police departments over the entire continent. In connection with this file a *telegraph register* (*Fahndungskartothek*) is maintained on the card catalogue plan containing information as to train service and train points north, south, east and west of Berlin, together with the police authorities located at those points. Alarms for criminals escaping from Berlin can be telegraphed to these authorities without delay.

European Police Systems

The Meldewesen.

No discussion of detective methods in Germany and Austria would be adequate without an understanding of the *Meldewesen* or registration system, by which each community, large and small, keeps track of the movements of its residents. This system affords a basis for detective work which deserves extended consideration. Continental countries, as is well known, exercise a closer supervision over the private affairs of their citizens than is practised in England. In no respect is this more clearly illustrated than in the diverse ideas concerning the registration of inhabitants. In Great Britain, there is no official registration of any kind. In France, Holland, Belgium, and Italy, the system, as far as the police are concerned, is confined to foreigners, who, if they intend to remain for any length of time, are obliged to file their names with the department.[1] In Germany and Austria, however, the system includes citizens as well as foreigners. All inhabitants of a community, of whatever nationality, must report their coming and going to the police.

This system has reached its greatest development in Germany and to its operation in that country our discussion is confined. Briefly, the laws [2] oblige all persons

[1] In France, Belgium, Holland and other Continental countries the citizens of a community are generally required to file their names and addresses with the civil officials at the city hall. This, however, is not a police measure, being required solely for the purposes of taxation and the census.

[2] Under Par. 10 of the Law of Freedom of Removal (November 1, 1867) the registration of new arrivals is left to the discretion of the states which make up the Empire. In some states, therefore, the matter is handled by municipal ordinances, as in Alsace-Lorraine; in others by local police regulations, as in Prussia, Saxony,

Methods of Crime Detection

in a community to report their arrival, departure or change of dwelling within the police boundaries. A citizen who moves, for example, from Coblentz to Berlin must, within twenty-four hours after arrival, file with the police of the latter city his *Anmeldung* or announcement of appearance.[1] This gives his name, his business, the day, month and year of his birth, place of birth, his religion, his former residence, and whether he is married, single or widowed. If he is a foreigner or a transient and stops at a hotel, the hotel proprietor must notify the police of his appearance. A man of any nationality who spends a single night at a hotel or lodging house in any German town or city has his name filed at police headquarters, although in the case of foreigners, it is not customary to procure the detailed information required of German citizens.

Not only must a new arrival in a German city announce

Bavaria, Baden and Hessen; while in other states it is a matter of state-wide legislation, as in Württemberg, Brunswick, Mecklenburg-Schwerin, etc.

In spite of these divergences in source, the announcement laws are largely similar. The efforts of the Imperial Chancellor in 1904 to coördinate them terminated without result in view of the objections raised by the various states. Plans have from time to time been suggested looking to a national system of registration with a central bureau for all names in Berlin. The great cost of such a system has hitherto prevented its adoption. At the present time a plan is being developed to have a single bureau for Berlin and its environs (Greater Berlin) instead of separate bureaus in each of the suburbs as well as in the city. Even this plan will not be completed for three or four years, so great is the clerical work involved.

[1] In most cities, the announcement is sent to the precinct station and by the precinct sent to headquarters. In Berlin, in addition to the headquarters file, each precinct station (*Revier*) has a file of the inhabitants in its own district. Strictly speaking each precinct has two files, one with the names arranged alphabetically, and the other with the names classified according to addresses. An *Anmeldung* sent to the precinct station is, therefore, copied on two cards, one for each of the files.

himself to the police but in many places he must present a certificate of character (*Abzugsattest*) from the police of the locality which he left. He is also generally required to produce other documents of identification, such as his birth certificate, his marriage certificate, or his army discharge papers. In many towns and cities the police of the community from which he comes are communicated with and an inquiry made as to whether he has a past criminal record. Similarly, if there is a birth in his family, if he employs a new servant, if he has a visitor from out of town, or if he changes his residence within the city limits (*Ummeldung*) the police must be notified.[1] If he moves away from the city, he must not only announce the fact (*Abmeldung*) but must obtain from the police a character certificate to be presented to the police of his new residence.[2]

No laws in Germany are more rigidly enforced than those relating to the *Meldewesen*. Evasion is difficult and when detected is severely punished.[3] The police-

---

[1] The law in Bremen requires the announcement of the beginning, change, or termination of any business or calling.

[2] In hotels or lodging-houses the obligation of giving notification rests upon the proprietor.

[3] In 1912, there were 26,876 penalties imposed by the police of Hamburg for violations of the announcement law. These violations for the most part concerned the failure or neglect of householders to notify the police of the arrival of newcomers within the required time. *Jahresbericht der Polizeibehörde Hamburg*, 1912, p. 11.

Under an opinion handed down by Imperial Court (*Reichsgericht*), false announcements to the police are punishable under section 366 of the Penal Code. This is the section which, as we have seen, has been used as the basis of the right of the police to assess fines and penalties. False announcements, therefore, are ordinarily punishable directly by the police rather than by the courts. (See *Entscheidungen des Reichsgerichts in Strafsachen*, Vol. 12, p. 228.)

Methods of Crime Detection

men on their beats are continually checking up new arrivals and special squads of detectives cover hotels and lodging-houses. In most cities hotel registers must be sent to police headquarters every month for examination and comparison. It is difficult for any one successfully to conceal his identity. Residence can easily be traced. Attempts to evade debts or escape the attentions of friends or foes can be defeated. In so far as names and addresses are concerned, the information at police headquarters is at the disposal of any citizen. A small fee of a few *pfennigs* will secure the address of any person living within the police jurisdiction.[1] The Vienna police headquarters in 1912 furnished the addresses of 983,025,[2] while Hamburg furnished 954,550 out of 1,025,551 asked for.[3] In Berlin, where the system has been in operation since 1836, 12,000,000 cards are now on file, and the bureau, employing 200 men and occupying 130 rooms, is one of the principal branches of the department. Its size is evidenced by the fact that the letter " H " alone fills ten rooms, while the letter " S " occupies fifteen. Indeed the enormous detail involved in this system is perhaps its most striking point. The cards give the names of all persons who were born in Berlin or who have at

[1] Wishing to test the efficacy of the system, I inquired at police headquarters in Berlin for an American friend who had sometime previously been traveling in Germany. Within a few minutes I was informed that two months before he had stopped for three days at the Hotel Bristol and had then departed for places unknown. Had he been a German citizen I could have learned his destination in Germany, and an application to the police of that place would quickly have disclosed his address.

[2] Personally communicated.

[3] *Jahresbericht,* etc., p. 11. The difference, 71,001, or 6.92 per cent., represents inquiries for people who it was assumed might be in Hamburg.

any time been in Berlin.[1] For example, a card shows the name of Carl Schmidt, his place and date of birth, his parents' names and the successive residences where he has lived in Berlin, with the date of moving from each, the date of his marriage and his wife's maiden name (cross-indexed to his wife's family card) ; the names of his servants; the names of his children, and dates of birth and death;[2] religion, if any,[3] and finally his criminal record if he has one. Throughout Germany, as we have seen, criminal records (*Strafregister*) are filed in the city, town and village where a man is born. When, therefore, Carl Schmidt, moving to Berlin from Düsseldorf, registers at police headquarters, the police authorities write to the police of Düsseldorf, to ascertain not only the truth of the statements which Herr Schmidt makes in his *Anmeldung* but to determine whether he has a criminal record. It is possible that Herr Schmidt was not born in Düsseldorf, but his criminal record, on file in the town of his birth, follows him from place to place, and the Berlin authorities are free to refuse to allow him to live in Berlin in case his record is not desirable.[4] If a citizen wishes a certificate of character for an employer he can obtain one from the police that is authentic as far as the criminal record is concerned.[5] Or if he wishes to know

[1] The file for foreigners (*Fremdenliste*) is kept distinct. There is also a " dead file." People moving from Berlin are kept on the " active " list for twenty years. No cards are ever destroyed.
[2] A child moving away from home has his own card.
[3] Required for the collection of church taxes.
[4] Prussian law of December 31, 1842. This law, as we have seen, gives to the *Landespolizei* authorities the right to exclude individuals from sojourn in case they have been sentenced to imprisonment in a penitentiary or house of correction. See note 5, p. 110.
[5] A charge of two or three marks is usually made for a character

Methods of Crime Detection

where his father was living sixty years ago or the name of a servant in his mother's family twenty-five years before, he can obtain the information in three or four minutes at police headquarters.[1]

The *Meldewesen,* maintained at great cost and often great personal inconvenience, is used by the officials for many purposes. The police department notifies the tax board of new arrivals subject to taxation; it informs the school board of children who should be in school under the compulsory system of education; it notifies the military authorities of inactive officers, or of men between the ages of 20 and 45 who have not served in the army; it informs medical authorities of unlicensed practitioners; it makes up lists of children to be vaccinated under the compulsory vaccination law; it compiles the election lists and furnishes information for the purpose of the state insurance act; it works in close cooperation with the post office and has charge of making up the annual city directory. In 1912, the Vienna police headquarters furnished the post office with 151,899 addresses which were missing; it furnished the tax office with 191,376 addresses. The Hamburg police department in the same year furnished the Board of Education with 3,166 notices of arrival of children of school age, and gave the municipal department for the care of ju-

certificate. The annual income of the Berlin department for supplying addresses and certificates averages 100,000 marks.

[1] These records at police headquarters are not all open to public scrutiny. Any one may obtain an address upon application, but criminal records are closely guarded. Thus it is not possible for private citizens to obtain the police records, if any, of their neighbors, although a man may secure his own record in the shape of a character certificate.

veniles the addresses of 8,780 who, under the law, were required to be vaccinated. The application of this system to the problem of crime detection, however, is our particular interest. It is no exaggeration to say that in Germany and Austria the *Meldewesen* constitutes the core of the detective department. Through its agency the police can put their hands on any citizen when they want him. A change of name is the only way by which the system can successfully be evaded and even this is a doubtful expedient in view of the pains taken by the police to verify the details of the *Anmeldung*.

The connecting link between the *Meldewesen* and the detective department is furnished by the *Steckbrief*. This is a notice or warning of men wanted for crime. Each important police jurisdiction in Germany and Austria publishes a daily or weekly paper or journal (*Fahndungsblatt*) containing the names or descriptions of such men, and neighboring police bodies are constantly on the watch to identify and arrest them.[1] The names

[1] Of the *Fahndungsblätter*, the *Deutsches Fahndungsblatt* is perhaps the best known. Published daily by the Berlin department it is circulated in Germany, France, Austria, England and other European countries. Every German department sends news of its important cases to this paper. The *Königliches Preussisches Zentral-Polizei-Blatt*, published three times a week by the department, is circulated in Prussian cities only. Other important police papers in Germany are the *Internationales Kriminal-Polizei-Blatt*, the *Königliches Sächsiches Gendarmerieblatt*, the *Königliches Bayerisches Zentral-Polizei-Blatt*, and the *Fahndungsblatt des Königlichen Württembergischen Landjäger-Korps*. Another important paper is the *International Criminal Record*, published at Frankfort-on-Main in three languages — English, German and French. This deals only with international criminals. The principal police papers in Austria are the *Zentral Polizei-Blatt* of Vienna, printed three times a week, and the *Zentral Polizei-Anzeiger* for Lower Austria.

Methods of Crime Detection

published in these journals are transcribed on cards which in most of the German states form an integral part of the *Meldewesen*.[1] That is, the card containing the name of a fugitive from justice is entered alphabetically in the *Meldewesen* file exactly as if the man in question had registered his appearance with the police. For this purpose red ink is used instead of black. The name of a man wanted by the Berlin police, therefore, will appear in the *Meldewesen* file of perhaps fifty towns and cities. If the man ever registers in any of these places, even twenty years later, the fact that he is wanted by the Berlin police is immediately discovered, for a red-inked card bearing his name and the particulars of his case is found in the alphabetic file. Through this means many men are arrested in Berlin who are wanted by the police not only of other German cities but of the cities of France, Austria and Hungary, for it is customary to enter in the file the names of all international criminals of importance for whom alarms have been sent out by foreign countries. In Vienna in 1912, 15,726 people were thus caught.[2] Similarly, whenever a man is arrested for any cause, the *Meldewesen* file is used to determine whether he is wanted for crime elsewhere. Or again, suspicious persons or persons inhabiting disorderly resorts are brought to headquarters pending a search of the files. This latter method, indeed, under the name of the *Razzia* system,[3] is broadly employed. Lodging houses of the poorer class, restaurants and cafés frequented by

[1] In Berlin these alarm notices are also printed each on a separate card, for handy reference in the different brigades and bureaus.
[2] Personally communicated by police officials.
[3] See Chap. VIII, p. 310.

suspicious persons, and even entire districts of an undesirable character are frequently raided by the police and
the *Steckbrief* system is used to determine whether any
of the men thus gathered in are wanted for crime. Thus,
on the evening of July 19, 1913, the Berlin police raided
the *Jungfernheide,* an amusement park of questionable
character in North Berlin. Over 300 persons who could
give no satisfactory account of themselves were taken
to police headquarters. Sixty of these were found to be
criminals for whom the police had for some time been
searching.[1] A false name is the only way by which this
system can be defeated, and even this is of little avail in
the case of German citizens, who must satisfy the police
as to their identity by means of their military papers or
their employment and insurance cards. In cases of
doubt, men are held pending further investigation.

The *Meldewesen,* and its complement, the *Steckbrief*
system, together form an intricate network. Every town
and city has its files, maintained with the greatest care
and scrupulous attention to detail. In the smaller villages and country districts, the files are kept by the *Gendarmerie.* A farmer settling in Bavaria or a blacksmith
taking up his calling in a small hamlet of Saxony must
report his presence to the police, for the *Gendarme* on his
patrol has sharp eyes for newcomers. In city or country
the system is difficult to evade. A resident of Chemnitz,
for example, wanted for a crime, escapes to Berlin. His
name is immediately entered in *Steckbrief* files all over
Germany. He cannot stay at a lodging house or hotel

[1] Personally communicated by police officials. The details of
this raid appeared in the *Berliner Tageblatt* of the following day.

Methods of Crime Detection

for his name would appear on the list of newcomers sent to the police each night. He cannot remain in a private house without incurring great risk both to himself and his host. The individual policeman is trained to know the members of every family on his beat, and a new face immediately attracts attention. Nor can the fugitive hope to escape by living as a vagrant, sleeping in parks and under bridges. Such a course may gain him time, but the police are vigilant in their search for these cases, and sooner or later the *Razzia* system will catch him. Even the assumption of an alias will not avail him permanently, for, as we have seen, the police are careful to verify the details of each newcomer's announcement not only by his military papers and his *Abzugsattest,* but by personal communication with the police of his former residence.[1]

From a detective standpoint the *Meldewesen* is not,

[1] A striking example of the operation of the *Meldewesen* and *Steckbrief* systems upon the vagrant classes is afforded by the activities of the police at the *Asyl der Obdachlosen,* a large public charitable institution in *Fröbelstrasse,* Berlin. This institution provides lodging, supper and breakfast for unfortunate men and women. It opens to receive its inmates at five o'clock every afternoon and turns them out at 7.30 the next morning. A man is allowed to come five times in one year without question. If on his sixth appearance he cannot show that he has tried to obtain work, he is handed over to the police to be dealt with as a vagrant. The average nightly attendance at this institution is 2,300 in summer and 5,700 in winter. To this institution a small force of detectives is continually assigned. Every man passing out in the morning is obliged to identify himself by his military papers, his working card, his insurance certificate, or in some other equally conclusive manner. Those in regard to whom some suspicion exists, and those who cannot satisfactorily establish identification are held for further examination. The *Steckbrief* system is used to determine whether any of the men thus detained are wanted for crime in Berlin or elsewhere, and criminals are continually being discovered for whom the police have been searching.

of course, complete. It is immediately effective only when men wanted for crime are known *by name*. In the apprehension of unknown criminals or of criminals known only by description it offers no assistance. Further, it is of little avail against foreign criminals or Germans with criminal records in foreign states. In this respect its effectiveness is hampered both by the lack of international coöperation and the absence of the identification papers carried by all German citizens. Its chief utility centers around the advantage which it affords the police of knowing where each citizen in a community can be found and what his past history has been.

That the *Meldewesen* or anything resembling it could ever be successfully adopted in England or in any country whose political philosophy is less paternal than Germany's is difficult to believe. To a German or Austrian there is nothing offensive in the fact that the coming and going of a private citizen in the ordinary routine of his life should be recorded at police headquarters. It is simply indicative of the solicitude of the state for its own. It is a systematic, domestic arrangement, representing internal order and discipline. It is part of the German passion to have everything in its place. Indeed, to a German, the failure of a State to keep an accurate record of every citizen implies disorder. Utter amazement was expressed by more than one German official when informed by the writer that England has no such system. " How do the English keep track of each other? How would you find a person whose address you had lost? How do the police know where anybody is living? "— these were their invariable questions.

Methods of Crime Detection

To an Englishman, on the other hand, the right to be let alone, to go his way without the knowledge of any one, if he so pleases, is part and parcel of his conception of liberty. A system which made necessary a police record of his coming and going and which gave friends or foes an opportunity to find him when he desired not to be found would be intolerable.

This divergence of opinion finds its basis, of course, in national character, and it is unnecessary to do more than mention it here. The *Meldewesen* is typically German. Even in France and Italy, where police surveillance is comparatively rigid, it could not easily be installed.

Other Methods of Crime Detection.

Appliances based on indexes and registers by no means exhaust the methods which can be employed by a detective office in its search for the author of a crime. The camera, the yard-stick, the microscope, the physical and chemical laboratory, and a vast assortment of special criminal apparatus, growing year by year in variety and extent, are also serviceable. As we have learned, the detection of crime has become a profession involving scientific methods and specialized tools. The old-time rule-of-thumb procedure which depended only on a good memory for faces and a superficial knowledge of criminals has been superseded by the scientific spirit. In recent years great impetus has been given to the movement in Germany, Austria, France and Italy. The study of criminology has been broadened to include crime detection. The subject has been approached as medicine and biology have been approached

European Police Systems

— from the standpoint of facts. A burglary is a fact, the tools with which it was accomplished are facts, every incident surrounding its commission is a fact. The science of crime detection springs from the analysis and systematization of these facts. It is interesting to observe that this new movement originated not in police departments, but in the universities. Dr. Hans Gross of the University of Graz, Dr. R. A. Reiss of the University of Lausanne, and Dr. Alfredo Niceforo of the University of Rome, are its prophets and sponsors. At these universities and at Bucharest and Sienna, special chairs have been established and men who ultimately become lawyers, magistrates, and prison and police officials are being trained in criminal laboratories exactly as chemists or biologists are trained. In Austria, where the influence of the University of Graz is especially marked, Dr. Gross's students and the laboratories of his department are called to aid in the solution of every complex crime.

The extraordinary work accomplished not only in these laboratories but in the police departments where their influence has been felt is worthy of more attention than can be given in these pages. Every assistance that science affords has been brought to bear on the mysteries of crime. Dentistry, medicine, chemistry, physics, psychology and anthropology have been enlisted in the work. No fact connected with a crime is too trivial to escape attention. The marks of teeth on pipes and cigar-ends are examined; blood stains are analyzed; hair is the object of minute study. The results of these examinations are often little short of astonishing. For example, Dr. Gross tells of a cigar-holder with an amber mouthpiece,

362

Methods of Crime Detection

found near the scene of a murder, which was so shaped that it could be held only in one position. A close examination showed that it had two marks which must have been made by two teeth of unequal length. While the murdered man had no such irregular teeth, it was discovered that his nephew had. The suspicions of the authorities were aroused by this simple but important fact and they soon learned enough to arrest the nephew on the charge of murder.[1] Or, again, a razor was identified as the instrument used by a murderer through finding in the dried blood on its edge a shred of cotton identical with the material of the murdered man's nightcap, which had been cut through.[2] Again, a man was gravely wounded at night by an unknown person, who dropped his cap in his flight. Inside the cap two hairs were found which were subjected to microscopic examination. As a result, the authorities were provided with the following description of the criminal which enabled them ultimately to apprehend him: "A man of middle age, of robust constitution, black hair intermingled with gray, recently cut; commencing to grow bald."[3]

The range of topics covered by these analytic methods is wide and varied. The practices of a criminal in disguising his face, in using false names, in pretending illness or insanity, in shamming blindness, deafness, epilepsy, or paralysis; the customs of the underworld in the employment of ciphers, graphic signs, and calls and cries of warning; the use of invisible inks, the decipher-

[1] *System der Kriminalistik,* Chap. V, § 2.
[2] *Ibid.,* Chap. XIV, § 6.
[3] *Ibid.,* Chap. V, § 3.

ing of burnt paper, the piecing together of torn paper, the interpretation of footprints, the forgery of documents, the action of poisons — these subjects are being studied in university laboratories and the results applied in practical form in the detective bureaus of the Continent.

Clues are often discovered, for example, by a chemical and microscopic examination of dirt and dust. To use Dr. Gross's words: " The coat of a locksmith contains a different kind of dust from that on the coat of a miller; the dust accumulating in the pocket of a schoolboy is essentially different from that in the pocket of a chemist; while in the groove of a gentleman's pocketknife a different kind of dirt and dust will be found than that in the pocketknife of a tramp. . . . For instance, upon the scene of a crime a garment was found from which no information could be obtained as to its owner. The coat was placed in a strong and well gummed paper bag which was vigorously beaten with sticks for as long a time as could be done without tearing the paper. The bag was then opened, the dust collected and submitted to a chemical examination. The examination proved that the dust was composed of wood fibrous matter finely pulverized. The deduction drawn was that the coat belonged to a carpenter, joiner or sawyer. But among the particles of dust, gelatine and powdered glue were found and as these are not extensively used by carpenters and sawyers, the further deduction was drawn that the garment belonged to a joiner — a fact which was subsequently substantiated." [1]

[1] Gross, *loc. cit.,* Chap. V, § 3.

Methods of Crime Detection

Again, the examination of a man's teeth may betray his occupation. By the callous spots on his hands it is possible to tell the kind of tools he has customarily worked with. Long, delicate fingers, kept supple by the application of glycerine and cold cream, indicate to a trained observer the pickpocket's profession. Footprints will often afford a description of a criminal adequate enough to warrant arrest.

Particular attention has been given in the laboratories to the methods by which theft and fraud are perpetrated. The equipment of burglars, the use of accomplices, the operations of gangs, the infinite variety of ways by which entrance is effected, the artifices of sneak-thieves, the tricks of counterfeiters, the methods of horse-frauds and card-sharps, the manufacture of spurious antiquities and works of art — on each of these subjects a distinct literature has developed, brought about largely through the influence of the universities.[1] Not only are crimes and crime methods the subject of study and analysis but the pathology and psychology of criminals as well, including such subjective phenomena as lying, hysteria, suggestion, defective mentality and self-deception. The criminal impulses that sway the epileptic, the effect of suggestion upon neurotic men and women in the commitment of hideous sexual crimes, the delusions that prompt the mentally defective to confess offenses that they did

[1] Probably the three best known books on the general subject of crime detection are Niceforo's *La Police et l'enquête judiciaire scientifiques,* Gross' *System der Kriminalistik,* and Reiss' *Manuel de Police scientifique.* Dr. Gross' book has been translated into English by John Adam and J. Colyer Adam, and is published in Madras, India. It contains an extensive bibliography with references to over 1,200 books and pamphlets.

not perpetrate, or to swear to the truth of incidents they never saw are factors for the consideration of a trained investigator. So, too, the superstitions of criminals, the belief in divination and fortune telling, the use of oaths and chiromancy, the influence of omens, form a phase of study not to be overlooked in an intelligent search for clues.

In the last ten years the laboratory methods of the universities have been adopted in many of the detective departments of the Continent. In Italy twenty-seven criminal research bureaus or laboratories have been established under the direction of the Division of Public Safety in the office of the Minister of the Interior. These bureaus, located in different cities, are equipped with the latest apparatus, both physical and chemical, employed in the detection of crime, such as appliances for micro-photography, instruments by which footprints may be molded and cast, and the ingenious mechanical devices perfected by the late M. Bertillon in connection with his system of metric photography.[1] Each bureau is in charge of trained investigators who assume responsibility for the work in the territory in which they are located, although the more serious cases are referred to the bureau in Rome.

Berlin has for years had a large chemical and physical laboratory at headquarters, although until recently it was

[1] *Photographie métrique* — the system by which pictures of the scenes of crime may be reproduced so as to show mathematical distances. See Bertillon's *La Photographie judiciaire,* translated under the title, *Legal Photography,* by P. R. Brown, New York, 1897. The most recent publication on this subject is, *Photographie métrique de Alphonse Bertillon,* a descriptive book published by La Cour-Berthiot, Paris, 1912.

Methods of Crime Detection

used for testing foods and supplies rather than for crime research. Under the inspiration of the work of Professor Reiss and Dr. Gross, however, a large section of the laboratory is now given over to this latter use. To this bureau many interesting problems are presented. Bloodstains, ink-spots and hand-writing are made the subject of micro-photography. By the use of chemicals the authorities examine finger-prints on anonymous letters sent to the Kaiser. By magnified photographs they determine whether blackmailing letters sent to a newspaper were written on the same typewriter, or whether a forgery was written in the same ink as the original. Again by physical tests they ascertain whether a certain grade of wire was manufactured in a given place. In 1913 a successful clue to the discovery of a murderer was furnished by the microscopic analysis of the ends of burnt matches found at the scene of the crime. The matches had been torn from a block, and thus were left with ragged ends. A close comparison of these ends with a block discovered in the pocket of a suspect led to his arrest and conviction.[1]

In other German cities work of a similar nature is carried on, although in many cases it is done by experts retained by the department rather than by the officials themselves. In Dresden twenty-four burglaries were identified as the work of one man through clay impressions made of the marks left by his burglary tools. Similar incidents have occurred in Munich and Stuttgart.

In England the influence of Dr. Gross and his disciples is not yet perceptible. Indeed there are but few English

[1] Personally communicated by officials.

officials who know anything of the work that is being done on the Continent. To be sure, many of Dr. Gross's methods are adapted to that peculiar phase of Continental criminal procedure known as the interrogatory system, under which those suspected of crime may be subjected to cross-examination before arrest — the " sweating system," as it is often called. This system, as we have seen, is illegal in England, and that part of the new method which deals with the psychology of the criminal and the means by which his defense may be broken down and a confession obtained would have little or no applicability in Great Britain. But there remains a great field of criminal research, as valuable in England as on the Continent, to which the police officials of the former country have not yet opened their eyes. As a result, Germany and Austria, with their scientific temper and their love of detail, are developing a method of criminal research which, in spite of the handicap imposed by the poor quality of their detectives, will inevitably give them front rank in dealing with crime.

CHAPTER X

THE INTEGRITY OF THE EUROPEAN POLICE

Special temptations of the police.— Question of integrity a fair question.— Excellent reputation of the European police.— Police have the confidence of the public.— Glasgow's public key office.— Report of the Royal Commission on the Metropolitan Police.— No " system " in European police forces.— Existence of individual cases of corruption.— Examples.— Integrity of police due to careful training of commissioners and their unrestricted powers of selection and removal.— Effect of the Continental class system on integrity.— The class system and tipping.— Corruption diminished by character of laws affecting public morality.— European police not called upon to enforce personal standards of conduct.— The excise law in London. — System of rewards and gratuities a deterrent to corruption.— Conclusion.

In the preceding chapters, we have studied the organization, management and work both of the uniformed forces and the detective bureaus. We have noted the various administrative systems by which their functions are controlled. We have seen that the term of office of the commissioner is in no way limited or defined and that officers and men alike are selected and trained with scrupulous care. We have observed the precautions taken to avoid associations prejudicial to disinterested service. It is only fair, therefore, in conclusion, to ask how far such factors as these succeed in preserving the integrity of the police. For this is a question of more than local interest and importance. Everywhere there are special pitfalls for the policeman, peculiar tempta-

tions to which he is continually exposed. The prostitute
who walks the streets, the bookmaker who plies his trade
on the sidewalk, the public-house proprietor who would
keep open after hours, the prisoner on his way to a cell,
in short, every man or woman who would escape the
operation or the penalty of the law and is ready to pay
for immunity constitutes a menace to the integrity of
the policeman. From the very nature of his work, he
is surrounded by temptation. With a salary modest,
if not inadequate, he is placed in positions of peculiar
responsibility and confronted with opportunities to add
to his income by merely refraining from positive action.
For a policeman who desires to make money need not do
anything affirmatively. All that is necessary is that he
should turn his head. How does the European policeman stand this strain? To what extent is his integrity
impaired?

On the whole, the police forces of Europe bear an
excellent reputation. Scandals are infrequent. With
few exceptions, both officers and men have the confidence of the public. It is only occasionally that one
hears of dishonesty. Even suspicions of dishonesty are
not common. The police are not associated with dishonesty in the public imagination. The citizens of a
community are confident of the ability of the commissioner both to discover corruption if it exists and to deal
with it effectively when found. With a trained commissioner, whose personal character is above suspicion,
and whose powers of action are large, the public is satisfied that the integrity of the rank and file will be rigidly
maintained. A European city, therefore, is inclined

The Integrity of the European Police

to take the honesty of its police force as a matter of course.

This confidence is shown in the relations of the public to the police. In many cities, for example, it is customary for a citizen leaving his house for any period to give the key to the patrolman who walks the beat so that ready entrance may be had in case of fire or accident. Similarly shopkeepers often give duplicate keys to their premises to the policemen on beat. In Glasgow a Public Key Office is maintained by the police in the center of the city, where warehousemen and storekeepers voluntarily leave their keys for emergency use by the officials. Again, the Lost and Found Bureaus operated by the London department and by those of Continental cities often contain articles of great value. Suggestions made in two or three of these cities that these bureaus be placed directly under the control of the municipalities have been rejected on the ground that ordinary municipal clerks cannot be trusted to handle these articles with the same care and honesty as the police.

Public confidence in the integrity of the police is not undeserved. In Dresden, the officials were able to remember, after some thought, the case of a policeman who, ten years before, had been discharged for dishonesty. Apart from his case, however, there have been no other removals for like cause within the memory of the authorities. Similar conditions were reported in Amsterdam and Rotterdam. In the larger cities, where the police forces are numerically stronger, it is not possible, of course, to present so clean a record. Yet even London, with 20,000 men in the police force, is surprisingly free from extensive corruption, although instances of individual dishonesty occasionally develop. In 1906, as a result of certain charges lodged against the Metropolitan police in connection with their activities in making arrests, a Royal Commission was appointed under sign manual of the Crown, and clothed with full power by special act of Parliament to investigate the duties of the force.[1] Complaints were invited from all sources, the testimony of many witnesses was heard, and full opportunity was extended to the public to present its opinions of the police. Particular attention was paid by the Commission to the charge that constables had made a practice of accepting fees from prostitutes. The finding of the Commission on this point is most interesting:

> " We have come to the conclusion that there is no ground for believing that there has existed, or that there at present exists any widespread or systematic bribery of the police by prostitutes in any part of London. Although we cannot believe that isolated instances of constables having received money gifts from women have never occurred, we believe that they have been and· are very infrequent." [2]

Mr. William A. Coote, Secretary of the National Vigilance Association, testified before the Commission as follows:

> " During the twenty-one years that I have acted as Secretary of the National Vigilance Association, I

[1] 6 Edw. VII, c. 6.
[2] *Report of the Royal Commission*, Vol. I, p. 130.

The Integrity of the European Police

have interviewed hundreds of women of questionable character with the view of ascertaining how they became such, how they maintained themselves as such, and what treatment they received from the police in the various districts in which they plied their calling. I have not in one instance had a charge made against the police as a body or against an individual policeman of levying blackmail, or of exacting bribes of any amount from these unfortunate women." [1]

The testimony of Sir Edward Henry, the Commissioner, was in similar vein. "I have not received a single letter," he said, "and no complaint, oral or written, has been made to me during the three and a half years I have been Commissioner, charging the police with levying blackmail from women of the unfortunate class. From what I know of the tone of the men themselves, I am satisfied that if any individual man were to take money from these women it would certainly come to the knowledge of his comrades, and I am also certain that his comrades would look upon him as an unmitigated blackguard and that he could not remain on the force for long." [2]

The point to be emphasized is that in the European police organization there is no "system," to use the word in its evil association. No organized connection exists between the police department and the underworld. No official collects for another or shares his plunder with a group. There is no passing of money

[1] *Report of the Royal Commission,* Vol. I, p. 83. (Quotation slightly abridged.)
[2] *Ibid.,* p. 81.

European Police Systems

to "men higher up." Dishonesty, where it occurs, is an individual matter between a particular officer and an outsider seeking a favor. The London department, for example, has had considerable trouble in protecting the integrity of its constables against the advances of street bookmakers. During the ten years ending December 31, 1906, thirty-two members of the force were found guilty of receiving money from these gamblers or of sustaining improper relations with them.[1] The matter was exhaustively investigated by the Royal Commission above referred to, but no facts were found pointing to "an extensive or effectual corruption of the men engaged in the work of putting down street betting." To continue in the words of the Commission: "We have considered the matter in all its bearings, and have come to the conclusion that there is no reason for believing that bribery of the police by bookmakers has been carried on according to any organized system."[2]

While it is true that the police forces as a whole possess the confidence of the public, and that systematic corruption is rarely if ever encountered, it would be idle to maintain that there is no corruption at all. At some

[1] *Report of the Royal Commission*, Vol. I, p. 81. During this period, 548 complaints were received from private persons in regard to the relations of the force with bookmakers. Of these complaints, 340 were against the police generally and 208 against particular constables. Every complaint was investigated by the Commissioner of Police. In only twenty cases, however, was it discovered that any foundation for the allegation existed. In addition to these twenty cases, twelve complaints were preferred by superior officers against members of the force, all of which were found to be well based. During this ten-year period the total amount of fines imposed by magistrates upon bookmakers for betting in the streets within the Metropolitan Police District was £127,276. (*Ibid.*, p. 100.)
[2] *Ibid.*, p. 131.

374

The Integrity of the European Police

time or other in every department, human weaknesses are bound to make their appearance, and to this rule the European departments constitute no exception. As we have already noted, within a year the Chief Constable of Carlisle, England, and the assistant to the Police President of Kiel, Germany, have been removed on charges of dishonesty, the latter official being sentenced to a long prison term. Early in 1914, the Police President of Cologne was forcibly retired when in the trial of a libel case three *Inspektors* and two *Kommissars* of his department refused to testify because they feared to incriminate themselves. In Paris, in 1913, nearly a dozen officials were removed for manufacturing evidence. In the same year, three members of the plain-clothes force of Berlin were arrested, and one was sentenced to prison, for blackmailing the prostitutes under their supervision. During the year just past, this offense has also led to disciplinary action in Frankfort-on-Main and Mülheim-on-Rhine. Indeed, wherever the control of prostitution by regulation has been attempted it has been accompanied, if not by open corruption, at least by grave suspicions that such corruption exists.[1] Similarly, in 1914, two members of the Prussian *Gendarmerie* corps were sentenced to prison for accepting bribes from bookmakers at the Berlin race-tracks.[2] Several years ago, a *Polizeirat* of the Budapest force committed suicide following revelations of extensive dishonesty. In the English provincial cities, as I have al-

[1] For full treatment of this point see Flexner, *loc. cit.*, Chap. VIII.
[2] At the Hoppegarten and Karlshorfe tracks.

ready pointed out, flagrant examples of corruption have from time to time developed. In Manchester, particularly, a condition was disclosed fifteen years ago denoting widespread demoralization.

It is important to remember, however, that these instances are individual and exceptional. They by no means represent typical or general conditions. They are incidental to the employment of large groups of men in responsible positions. Considering the number of men involved and the character of their duties, the police forces of Europe must be adjudged to be singularly free from corruption.[1]

I have already emphasized the factors to which the integrity of the European police is, in my judgment, to be attributed. Primarily it is due to the careful training of the heads of the departments and their freedom in selecting and removing their subordinates. On no other basis can the integrity of a police force be permanently maintained. *"Choose the head of your force with scrupulous care; clothe him with full power; make him responsible."* This maxim was repeated by officials all over Europe. A commissioner who is not free to take direct action when reasonable suspicion falls on particular policemen cannot be held ultimately responsible for evil conditions in his force. In so far as the European authorities have recognized this fact — and the recognition has been all but universal — they have placed their fingers upon the main key to the situation.

There are other factors, however, which simplify the European problem. The rigid class distinctions of Con-

[1] But see note I, p. 243.

The Integrity of the European Police

tinental society serve to erect barriers not only to class advancement but to class ambition. The German *Schutzmann* coming from the under class is troubled by no tempting dreams of wealth or promotion, because he knows that his position not only in the department but in the whole social scheme is definitely established. Lacking the opportunities materially to better his lot in life, he lacks the impulse to push ahead. With no dreams of advancement to disturb his vision he is content. He can live as well as any of his class; his position in the department is secure; at the end of faithful service, he can retire on a pension. Indeed, in point of permanent work and ultimate security, to say nothing of the authority incidental to his official position, he is in a more fortunate situation than his neighbors. He is therefore unwilling to run risks which will jeopardize his established lot.

Continental class distinctions serve also to minimize temptation among the higher officers of a police force. The official class, particularly in Germany and Austria, is sharply defined. It has its own traditions, organizations and distinct points of view. It is socially cohesive. Believing itself superior to the " citizen class," it holds aloof from their interests and their aims. Indeed, between the so-called bureaucracy of Germany and the burgher class a gulf is fixed, with no basis for mutual sympathy or understanding. The higher officers of a police department, therefore, have no general acquaintances among the commercial classes of a city. The merchants, the trades people and the shop keepers are un‐ known to them. As a result, the basis for understandings of a pernicious character between representatives of the two classes is wholly lacking. No easy avenue of approach is afforded a police officer to drive a corrupt bargain or to sell immunity from interference to those who for reasons of commercial advantage might desire to avoid the law.

Class distinctions afford a background for another characteristic of the European policeman which is not so creditable. We have already noticed the widespread practice in the rank and file of the police forces of accepting tips. This practice is by no means confined to Germany. It is prevalent in London and the English provincial cities, in France, Holland, Belgium and Italy, while in Austria and Hungary it has reached startling proportions. In this chapter, I have not considered tipping in the same class as bribery for the reason that tips are given generally for special but usually legitimate services rendered by the policeman, and not to secure immunity from interference or punishment. The London " Bobby " who calls a cab upon request, the Amsterdam *Agent* who points out the location of a street, or the Vienna *Wachmann* who awakens a household at a certain hour every morning will all gratefully receive a bit of silver, although the practice is strictly forbidden by the police rules. Incidents such as these would have no special significance, indeed would be scarcely worth mentioning, if it were possible to confine them within altogether harmless limits. The difficulty of drawing a sharp line, however, between what is proper and what is improper is at once apparent. A policeman who accepts a tip for giving a stranger a bit

The Integrity of the European Police

of useful information may not readily see the impropriety of a Christmas gift from the public-house keeper on his beat. From this latter practice to something worse is an easy step, even though it be rarely taken. The only position which the police authorities can afford to take on this matter, therefore, is against the entire practice of tipping in any form.

It is here that class distinctions exercise a pernicious influence. The subservience which they tend to breed, the feudal conception of society upon which they are based, make them formidable bulwarks of the tipping system. The increase of the salaries of the policemen may, to some extent, curb the further extension of the practice, but the fact that it is a social custom, based on social laws, will make impossible its complete eradication.

However, perhaps the most important safeguard against police corruption is negative in character. The European police are not called upon to enforce standards of conduct which do not meet with general public approval. There is little attempt to make a particular code of behavior the subject of general criminal legislation. The high moral standards of a few people are not the legal requirements of the state. Only occasionally is there any movement to place upon the statute books laws which serve only to satisfy the consciences of those responsible for them. This is a subject worthy of more attention than can be given in these pages. It strikes deep into the heart of the police problem. For example, the public houses of London, within a four-mile radius of Charing Cross, are allowed to open on Sundays, by act of Parliament, between the hours of 1 and 3 P. M.

European Police Systems

and 6 and 11 P. M.[1] This particular provision, which from personal investigation I know to be generally enforced, meets with the approval of London's citizens.[2] It is a fair approximation to the tastes and standards of the majority. I asked a high official at Scotland Yard whose name in this connection I am not at liberty to mention, what would be the effect on the Metropolitan Police Force if Parliament passed a law prohibiting the sale of liquor on Sunday. "It would mean the demoralization of the force," he replied. "We cannot guarantee the integrity of the police against the vicious influences arising from unenforceable laws." In Berlin, where, as in most Continental cities, no distinction is made in the sale of liquor between week-days and Sundays, a similar question propounded to a police official of high rank was greeted with a stare of amazement. "Preposterous!" he exclaimed. "The entire German army could not enforce such a regulation."[3]

[1] Licensing (Consolidation) Act of 1910. Elsewhere in the Metropolitan District, or in any town in England with a population of at least 1,000, saloons may be open on Sunday between 12:30 and 2:30 P. M. and between 6 and 10 P. M.

The week-day hours of saloons within the County of London or within a four mile radius of Charing Cross are 5 A. M. to 12:30 A. M. except on Saturday nights, when they must close at midnight. Elsewhere in the Metropolitan District, or in towns of England, with a population of at least 1,000, saloons may be open between 6 A. M. and 11 P. M. In towns of less than 1,000 population, saloons must close at 10 P. M. Scotland has its own special excise laws.

[2] The effect of having the saloons closed on Sunday in England during specified hours is somewhat vitiated by the so-called *bona fide traveler* provision of the law under which a licensee is permitted to sell liquor to persons who can show that during the preceding night they lodged at least three miles away by the nearest public thoroughfare. Under this provision, hotels often succeed in doing considerable business during prohibited hours.

[3] Excise questions in Germany are determined on the basis of *" Die Gewerbeordnung für das Deutsche Reich"* of July 1, 1883.

The Integrity of the European Police

These illustrations are not intended as an argument for open saloons on Sunday. That is a separate question to be determined on the basis both of national habits and local conditions. The point is that a police department cannot be used to enforce standards of conduct which are widely disapproved or to regulate the private habits of a population contrary to its wishes. Attempts to enforce laws of this type which are not representative of public opinion invariably breed corruption.

"It would be idle to pass laws curbing the gambling instincts of our people," a Swiss official told me, "because there is no public demand for such regulation. It could not be enforced." Indeed, according to the testimony of police officials all over Europe, it is not enough that laws relating to public morality shall have the support of some elements in the community. They must have the substantial support of the entire community. They must represent the standards which most people desire to see enforced. "The thing that we dread," said a Scotland Yard official, "is the passage of laws making a crime of actions which a great many people regard as innocent." Fortunately, Parliament and other European assemblies are not much given to legislation

This law lays down certain general principles in connection with the granting of licenses, leaving the local regulations to be framed by the police. Thus in Berlin the police fix the closing hours of each saloon. Ordinarily, under the first concession, the closing hour is established at II P.M. This may be extended to 12 P.M., and ultimately to 2 A.M. Some public houses are allowed to keep open even later. The police may also regulate the kind of drink to be sold in public houses, whether beer, or spirits, or both.

In Vienna, the closing hour is generally 2 A.M. Places wishing to keep open longer must apply for special permission from the police. As in Germany, the police of Austria are given wide discretion in the matter of licenses.

of this kind. The distinction between what is criminal and what is merely vicious is on the whole clearly drawn, and the penal laws are not encumbered with provisions the only purpose of which is to enforce by threat a given standard of morality. The functions of the police are not confused with those of the church, the school and other organizations and influences by which civilization is advanced. M. Lépine's definition of police which we have already noted exactly expresses the European point of view —" an organized body of officers whose primary duties are the preservation of order, the security of the person and the safety of property." [1] With the personal morals of private citizens the European police have little to do. In short, the police are not confronted at the start with an impossible task. To this fact, perhaps more than to any other, their integrity is ascribable.

Our consideration of this question could not properly be brought to a conclusion without noticing one of the methods by which the members of a force are encouraged not only to avoid dishonesty, but to do effective work. Nearly every department in Europe maintains a system of financial rewards for meritorious service. These rewards are not large — they seldom exceed five dollars — but they are eagerly sought by the police. Typical items taken from Liverpool's weekly list are as follows: Promptly extinguishing small fire, 2 shillings, sixpence. Special vigilance in detective work, 15 shillings. Clever first aid to the injured, 3 shillings, sixpence. Stopping runaway horse, 10 shillings. Assaulted in the performance of duty, 20 shillings. In Berlin, the rewards are

[1] See p. 4.

slightly higher, running occasionally to 50 marks in cases of extreme merit. London spends approximately $5,000 a year in rewards of this kind, the discretion resting in each case, of course, with the Commissioner.

Not only are rewards given by the department as a stimulus to efficiency, but gratuities are allowed from outside parties to individual members of the force provided they are reported to the commanding officers and approved by the Commissioner. This is generally true throughout Europe. A detective, for example, who has been assiduous in the recovery of stolen property is given five dollars by the owner to whom the property is returned. If the officer keeps it without reporting it, he is dismissed if the fact is discovered. If he reports it, however, the chances are that he will be allowed to keep it, although it is possible that the Commissioner may decide that the sum is out of proportion to the service rendered. In the latter case, part of the gratuity is returned to the owner. No member of a force is allowed to ask for a gratuity under penalty of dismissal. If it is voluntarily given to him, he is obliged to turn over the money to his commanding officer pending the decision of the Commissioner.[1] In case the Commissioner allows it, the beneficiary receives it with his regular salary at the next pay day. European authorities are generally impressed with the results of this system. It distinguishes between graft and gratuities given for

---

[1] In London and elsewhere regular printed forms are filled out by the beneficiary of the gratuity showing amount received, by whom given, for what service rendered, and with spaces for remarks by the commanding officers and the Commissioner. See Metropolitan Police Forms Nos. 360, 361, and 362.

special or meritorious service. It lifts the ban from rewards which are perfectly proper. It affords an opportunity to an honest policeman to profit by his good work without exposing him to the temptation of becoming underhanded and deceitful. "A very serviceable system," the Head Constable of Liverpool called it.

If the foregoing pages may be assumed to portray the leading features of European police systems, it is scarcely necessary, in bringing our study to a conclusion, to elaborate the points that have been made. It must be clear that the European police department is, on the whole, an excellent piece of machinery. To its construction a high order of creative intelligence has been devoted; in its operation an equally high order of intelligence is constantly employed. In the last resort, the police problems of a modern city make a large demand upon intelligence, and Europe has succeeded in formulating and solving its police problem because, discarding all inferior persons and agencies, it has utilized in this work a superior type of intelligence.

Beneath all the variations which we have from time to time commented on, there are certain common principles on the basis of which the efficiency of the European police department can be explained. First, the police are not called upon to compel conformity to moral standards which do not meet with general public approval. They are not asked to enforce laws which from the standpoint of accepted public habit or taste are fundamentally unenforceable.

384

The Integrity of the European Police

Second, control is centered where responsibility can be definitely fixed — in a single official. This official, thoroughly trained for his work and chosen with painstaking deliberation, is clothed with independent authority. Secure in his position and free from external interference, he enjoys the widest powers in dealing with his subordinates. Perhaps the most striking fact in connection with the European police commissioner is not only the absence of checks and balances by which a possible abuse of power may be curbed or minimized, but the sustained faith of the people that power will be wisely employed.

Finally, the rank and file of the European police forces are selected and trained with the same care and attention shown in the case of their superior officers. Indeed, in all ranks the character of the personnel is the essential constant factor of efficiency. On this and on no other basis is it possible to secure an effective organization. Other features can indeed produce better conditions, but without these fundamental human values there can be no real or permanent efficiency.

APPENDICES

APPENDICES

APPENDIX I.

AN ACCOUNT OF MONIES EXPENDED FOR THE SERVICE OF THE METROPOLITAN POLICE OF LONDON DURING THE FISCAL YEAR FROM APRIL 1, 1911, TO MARCH 31, 1912.[1]

I. ADMINISTRATIVE EXPENSES.

	£	s.	d.	£	s.	d.
Commissioner's office.						
One Commissioner (including £100 horse allowance)	2,600					
Four assistant Commissioners (including 2 horse allowances of £100)	5,030					
18 clerks, 14 assistant clerks, 20 temporary clerks and writers	12,606	3	1			
79 police officers employed on clerical duty	11,264	15	5			
13 police officers employed as messengers	1,444	11	3			
Receiver's office.						
One Receiver	1,200					
14 clerks, 11 assistant clerks and writers	6,537	5	5			
Legal expenses	155	13	6			
Surveyors, draftsmen, assessors, technical clerks and a Consulting Sanitary Adviser	4,112	8	10			
Store-keepers, examiners of clothing, tailors, inspectors and messengers	2,935	12	7			
Legal expenses	5,017	9	10			
Cost of police printing office..	3,118	16	9			
Amount carried forward..	56,022	16	8			

[1] Compiled from the published expenditures of the Metropolitan Police Force, London, 1912.

	£	s.	d.		£	s.	d.
Amount brought forward.	56,022	16	8				
Newspapers and advertisements	1,200	17	3				
Postage	2,237	8	10				
Books and stationery, porters, charwomen and miscellaneous	13,663	15	3				
					73,124	18	

II. Office Expenses.

					£	s.	d.
Maintenance of headquarters, rates, taxes, erection of additional offices, repairs, etc....................					19,084	5	8

III. Police Courts, Administrative Expenses.

	£	s.	d.		£	s.	d.
29 clerks, 13 assistant clerks...	14,410	14	6				
83 ushers, assistant ushers, jailers, office keepers, etc....	9,514	18	8				
Printing, stationery, traveling expenses, etc.	5,256	1	3				
					29,181	14	5

IV. Pay, Clothing and Equipment of the Force.

	£	s.	d.		£	s.	d.
Six Chief Constables..........	3,843	0	9				
31 divisional and other superintendents	12,365	9	9				
Pay of inspectors, sergeants and constables 1,749,882		16					
Allowances for rent..........	51,565	19	6				
Gratuities, rewards and extra duty pay	1,424	8					
Clothing and plain clothes allowances and accoutrements.	105,325	15	10				
					1,924,407	9	10

V. Medical and Funeral Expenses.

	£	s.	d.		£	s.	d.
Salaries of Chief Surgeon and divisional surgeons	8,842	16	9				
Amount carried forward..					2,045,798	7	11

Appendices

	£	s.	d.	£	s.	d.
Amount brought forward.				2,045,798	7	11
Medical attendance, medicines, etc., for prisoners and poor persons injured in public thoroughfares	8,848	12	10			
Funeral expenses of police officers	160	10				
				17,851	19	7

VI. Horses, Vans and Carts.

Purchase of horses, forage, police vans and carts				24,925	8	6

VII. Erection and Maintenance of Police Stations.

Expenses incidental to erection	115,154	16	7			
Expenses incidental to maintenance	46,736	18	4			
				161,891	14	11

VIII. Police Courts.

Erection and maintenance of premises and incidental expenses				18,975	10	

IX. Incidental Expenses in Connection with Police Stations.

Coal, gas, cleaning, etc.				55,334	8	1

X. Miscellaneous Charges.

Contingent expenses for refreshments supplied to destitute prisoners, expenses incurred in the pursuit, apprehension and conveyance of prisoners, duties performed beyond the Metropolitan Police district, telegraph and telephone service, steam launches and boats, etc.				101,393	3	4
Amount carried forward.				2,426,170	12	4

XI. Public Carriage Office Expenses.

	£	s.	d.	£	s.	d.
Amount brought forward................				2,426,170	12	4
Pay of clerks, office rent, stationery, plates and badges, etc.				44,334	19	3

XII. Retired Allowances.

	£	s.	d.
Under special act of Parliament (This does not include pensions)	7,461	5	6

XIII. Special Expenses.

	£	s.	d.	£	s.	d.
Expenses in connection with the Coronation of His Majesty the King...............	43,513	3	6			
Incidental expenses	1,830	14	6			
				45,343	18	

XIV. Repayments.

	£	s.	d.
Deductions for lodgings, etc., paid to Admiralty and War Departments, repayments to parishes of police rate on valuations reduced on appeal...............	6,650	17	10

XV. Pension Fund Deficiency.[1]

	£	s.	d.
Transfer to police pension fund	300,627	17	11
Grand Total	2,830,589	10	10

[1] The Metropolitan Police Pension Fund is kept separately from the expenses above set forth. During the year April 1, 1911, to March 31, 1912, the total payments from this fund were £571,590, 5s., 6d.

APPENDIX II.

AN OUTLINE OF THE BUDGET FOR THE PREFECTURE OF POLICE OF PARIS FOR THE FISCAL YEAR 1914.[1]

Francs

I. Administrative Expenses 2,391,297
II. The Commissariats of Police, Inspection of the Stock Exchange and weights and measures.... 2,510,317
III. Uniformed and Detective Forces. Salaries of 8,314 of the Uniformed Force and 1,236 of the Detective Force, including Executive Officials, together with various expenses, equipment, etc..34,946,258.60
IV. Horses and Vans 466,389
V. Supervision of Navigation and Ports........... 114,661
VI. Building Department 80,967
VII. Public Health and Hygiene.................... 117,315
VIII. Medical Dispensary 56,020
IX. Public Ambulance and Medical Service........ 201,095
X. Supervision of Markets, Market-places and Slaughter-houses 367,773
XI. Pensions and Relief.......................... 882,421
XII. Miscellaneous Expenses, including postage, telegraph and telephone, printing, office furniture, books, transportation of prisoners, etc........ 582,192
XIII. Fire Department 3,543,483
XIV. Chemical Laboratory 334,862

Total .... [2] 46,595,050.60

1 Compiled from the *Budget de la Préfecture de Police,* Paris, 1914.
2 Of this sum, 13,980,744 francs was paid by the national government, the balance by the city upon vote of the Municipal Council.

APPENDIX III.

AN OUTLINE OF THE BUDGET FOR THE POLICE DISTRICT OF BERLIN FOR THE FISCAL YEAR JANUARY 1, 1913, TO DECEMBER 31, 1913.[1]

I. HIGHER ADMINISTRATIVE SALARIES.

	Marks	Marks
One Police President......................	13,000	
Three *Oberregierungsräte* and 18 *Regierungsräte*	123,000	
Extra allowances	8,100	
		144,100

II. OTHER ADMINISTRATIVE SALARIES.

Salaries of 69 officials of various ranks.............	330,800

III. CLERICAL FORCE.

741 clerical and telegraphic officials.................	2,184,600

IV. AUDITING FORCE.

Salaries of 14 officials..............................	51,800

V. CARE-TAKERS, MESSENGERS AND PRISON HELPERS.

Salaries of 137.....................................	199,470

Amount carried forward	2,910,770

1 This budget includes a small part of the expenses of the five police forces presided over by the Police President of Berlin,— the city of Berlin, Charlottenburg, Lichtenberg, Neukölln and Schöneberg. No budget of the police force of the city of Berlin is separately obtainable. The above outline is compiled from the budget of the Minister of the Interior, *Etat des Ministeriums des Innern, Anlagen Bd. II, Nr. 28*, Berlin, 1913.

Appendices

VI. Executive Officials of the Uniformed Force.

	Marks	Marks
Amount brought forward		2,910,770
One police Colonel	7,700	
Three majors	18,200	
25 captains, 9 criminal inspectors, 2 telegraphic engineers and one police prison inspector	192,600	
210 police lieutenants, 82 criminal commissioners (*Kommissars*)	1,137,700	
		1,349,200

VII. Uniformed Force.

	Marks	Marks
22 first sergeants...........................	54,050	
739 sergeants	1,517,600	
7,807 policemen 13,156,140		
		14,727,790

		Marks
VIII.	Rent Allowances in Addition to Salaries..	5,126,640
IX.	Additional Personal Allowances and Payment of Supplementary Employees........	697,335
X.	Miscellaneous Expenses, Maintenance of Morgue, Postage, Etc.	1,007,901
XI.	Maintenance of Police Stations, Including a Few New Erections.....................	59,470
XII.	Rent of Buildings for Police Purposes......	60,109

XIII. Personal Expenses.

	Marks
Horses, traveling expenses, miscellaneous rents.......	1,751,030

		Marks
XIV.	Clothing and Equipment of the Uniformed Force	910,440

XV. Miscellaneous Expenses.

	Marks
Substitutes, feeding of prisoners, medical inspection of prostitutes, etc.	1,093,030
Grand Total	29,693,715

APPENDIX IV.

AN OUTLINE OF THE BUDGET FOR THE POLICE DEPARTMENT OF VIENNA FOR THE FISCAL YEAR, JANUARY 1, 1913, TO DECEMBER 31, 1913.[1]

I. HIGHER ADMINISTRATIVE SALARIES.

	Kronen	Kronen
One Police President	22,000	
One *Hofrat*	11,933	
14 *Oberpolizeiräte*	116,627	
		150,560

II. OTHER ADMINISTRATIVE SALARIES.

151 officials of various ranks........................	768,605

III. CLERICAL FORCE.

Salaries of 373 officials	877,369

IV. SANITARY FORCE.

Examination of prostitutes, etc., salaries of 49 physicians of various ranks....................	227,300

V. CARE-TAKERS.

Salaries of 25 officials...............................	97,826

VI. MISCELLANEOUS.

Remuneration of occasional employees, rewards, traveling expenses, printing, telegraph and telephone, etc........................	892,817
Amount carried forward	2,972,044

[1] Compiled from the budget of the Minister of the Interior, *Staatsvoranschlag für die im Reichsrate vertretenen Königreiche und Länder für das Jahr 1913*, Vienna, 1912.

Appendices

VII. Detective Force.

	Kronen	Kronen
Amount brought forward		2,972,044
Salaries of 679 men, including officials......	1,589,180	
Miscellaneous, including clothing, rewards, traveling expenses, etc. ....·.....	352,899	
		1,942,079

VIII. Executive Officers of the Uniformed Force.

Salaries of 68 officials............................	263,380

IX. Uniformed Force.

Salaries of 1,846 non-commissioned officers and 2,668 policemen......................	9,090,139	
Salaries of occasional employees, extra pay, rewards, traveling expenses, rents, allowances, equipment, etc.	2,598,986	
		11,689,125
Total		16,909,061
Deductions for pension purposes		42,433
Grand total		16,866,628

397

APPENDIX V.

TABLE I.

SUMMARY OF ANNUAL EXPENDITURES AS SHOWN IN PRECEDING APPENDICES.[1]

	London	Paris	Berlin	Vienna
Total Annual Expenditure	$13,784,971.03	$8,992,844.77	$7,067,104.17	$3,423,925.48
Cost per capita of Population	$1.91	$2.16	$1.87	$1.69

[1] In comparing these expenditures the extended functions of the Continental police must necessarily be taken into consideration.

APPENDIX V.

TABLE II.

COMPARISON OF COSTS OF SALARIES, ALLOWANCES, AND EQUIPMENT OF UNIFORMED AND DETECTIVE FORCES.[2]

	London	Paris	Berlin	Vienna
Annual Cost of Uniformed and Detective Forces	$9,371,864.45	$6,744,627.91	$5,048,296.54	$2,820,600.55
Cost per capita of Population	$1.29	$1.63	$1.34	$1.33

[2] The variations in bookkeeping methods between the cities named make these figures approximate only.

Appendices

APPENDIX V.

TABLE III.

AREA OF POLICE JURISDICTION.

	Area in Square Miles
London	699.42
Paris (Department of the Seine)	185
Berlin (City of Berlin proper)	24
Vienna	104.75

APPENDIX VI

ANNUAL BUDGETS OF THE POLICE DEPARTMENTS OF THE PRINCIPAL CITIES OF EUROPE [1]

City	*Year*	*Amount*
Amsterdam	1913	$ 651,280
Barcelona	1913	430,765
Berne	1913	95,000
Christiania	1911	245,364
Constantinople	1913	871,156
Copenhagen	1913	661,020
Dresden	1912	794,118
Glasgow	1913	1,069,610
Hamburg	1912	3,060,605
Leipzig	1912	672,247
Lisbon	1913	476,000
Liverpool	1912	1,182,438
Madrid	1913	561,348
Manchester	1913	443,549
Moscow	1909	713,944
Oporto	1913	240,000
Rotterdam	1913	450,550
St. Petersburg	1913	1,717,793
Stockholm	1913	650,623
Stuttgart	1913	591,837
Zurich	1913	202,650

[1] Exclusive of London, Paris, Berlin and Vienna, which have been given in the foregoing tables.

APPENDIX VII

STRENGTH OF THE POLICE FORCES OF THE PRINCIPAL CITIES OF EUROPE

City	Population	Number of officers and men
Amsterdam	580,960	1,416
Barcelona	560,000	1,531
Bergen	72,251	143
Berlin	2,071,257	6,374
Berne	85,264	129
Brussels	176,947 [1]	817
Budapest	880,371	3,000
Christiania	241,834	459
Constantinople	1,200,000	2,500
Copenhagen	462,161	806
Dresden	548,308	1,238
Edinburgh	320,318	624
Glasgow	784,496	2,020
Hamburg	931,035	1,697
Lisbon	356,009	1,680
Liverpool	746,421	2,148
London:		
City of London	19,657 [2]	1,183
Metropolitan District	7,231,701	20,540

[1] Includes only the City of Brussels. " Greater Brussels " including the city and suburbs has a population of 660,000.
[2] Night population. The day population is 364,061.

European Police Systems

City	Population	Number of officers and men
Madrid	571,539	2,103
Manchester	714,333	1,350
Moscow	1,533,400	4,500
Oporto	167,955	763
Paris	2,888,110	8,597
St. Petersburg	1,962,400	5,726
Rome	542,123	2,619
Rotterdam	436,018	995
Stockholm	346,599	840
Stuttgart	286,218	442
Vienna	2,031,498	4,596
Zurich	189,088	320

APPENDIX VIII

EUROPEAN POLICE COMMISSIONERS—QUALIFICA-
TIONS AND MODE OF APPOINTMENT [1]

Amsterdam — *Hoofd-Commissaris* (Chief Commissioner) appointed by the Crown upon recommendation of the Minister of Justice. An army officer generally chosen.

Barcelona — *Jefe superior de Policia* (Chief of Police) appointed by the Minister of the Interior. No definite position or rank of life taken into consideration in making the appointment.

Berlin — *Polizeipräsident* (Police President) appointed by the Crown upon recommendation of the Minister of the Interior. An official from some other branch of the government service is usually appointed.

Berne — *Polizeidirektor* (Director of Police) elected by popular vote. He is one of the members of the City Commission (composed of nine members in all) charged with the administration of municipal affairs.

Bremen — *Polizeipräsident* (Police President) appointed by the *Burgershaft* or State Senate. He is usually promoted from among the subordinate officers of the force.

Brussels — Burgomaster, appointed by the Crown, acts as the Chief of Police, although the commander of the Central division performs many of the functions of the Chief.

Budapest — *Fökapitámy* (Police President) appointed by the Crown upon recommendation of the Minister of the Interior. He is always a university graduate in law who has spent his life in the government service.

Christiania — *Politimester* (Police Master or Chief) appointed by the Crown. He must be a university graduate in law, and for not less than five years must either have practised law or have been a deputy judge.

Constantinople — Chief of Police appointed by the Sultan upon recommendation of the Minister of the Interior. He may be

1 For some of the material included in this table, I am indebted to the Department of State at Washington, which obtained it for my purposes through the American Consular offices.

promoted from among the subordinate police officers, or may be appointed from among the governors or sub-governors, or from among judiciary officials.

COPENHAGEN — *Politidirektor* (Police Director) appointed by the Crown. He must be a jurist. He is usually, though not always, promoted from among the subordinate officers of the force.

DRESDEN — *Polizeipräsident* (Police President) appointed by the King of Saxony upon recommendation of the Minister of the Interior. Usually he is promoted from among the subordinate officers of the force.

GLASGOW — Chief Constable appointed by the joint action of the Magistrates Committee of the Town Council and the Sheriff of the County. A man experienced in police work is usually appointed. Occasionally he is taken from the Royal Irish Constabulary.

HAMBURG — *Polizeipräsident* (Police President) appointed by the *Burgershaft* or State Senate. He is usually promoted from among the subordinate officers of the force.

LISBON — *Commandante* of Police appointed by the government through the Minister of the Interior from among officers of the regular army of the rank of Major or higher.

LIVERPOOL — Head Constable appointed by the Watch Committee of the Town Council. Usually called from similar position in a smaller town.

LONDON, CITY OF — Commissioner appointed by the City with the approval of the Crown. Army officer preferred.

LONDON — Metropolitan District. — Commissioner appointed by the Crown upon recommendation of the Home Secretary. Civilian preferred, usually one who has had some previous governmental experience.

MADRID — *Inspector de Seguridad* (Inspector of Police) appointed by the Director General. This latter official controls all the police forces of Spain save the *Guardia Civil,* an organization corresponding to the French *gendarmerie.* He is appointed by the Crown upon recommendation of the Minister of the Interior. Generally a governmental official of high rank.

MANCHESTER — Chief Constable appointed by the Watch Committee of the Town Council. Usually called from similar position in a smaller town.

MOSCOW — *Gradonachalnik* (Prefect of Police) appointed by the Emperor. He is always a high ranking officer of the army.

MUNICH — *Polizeidirektor* (Police Director) appointed by the Crown upon recommendation of the Minister of the Interior. A high governmental official usually chosen.

Appendices

OPORTO — *Commandante* of Police appointed by the government from among the civil or criminal judges.

PARIS — Prefect of Police appointed by the President of the Republic upon recommendation of the Minister of the Interior. Army officer or high governmental official usually appointed.

ROME — *Questore* (Chief of Police) appointed by the Crown upon recommendation of the Minister of the Interior. The *Questori* of the various municipalities and their assistants enter the police service as *delegati* by competitive examination, being promoted as their abilities warrant.

ROTTERDAM — *Hoofd-Commissaris* (Chief Commissioner) appointed by the Crown upon recommendation of the Minister of Justice. An army officer generally chosen.

ST. PETERSBURG — *Gradonachalnik* (Prefect of Police) appointed by the Emperor upon recommendation of the Minister of the Interior. Usually a prominent general of the army.

STOCKHOLM — *Polismästare* (Chief of Police) appointed by the Crown upon recommendation of the Governor General of Stockholm and the Civil Minister. Of late years it has been customary to appoint an assistant in the department who has had legal training.

STUTTGART — *Polizeidirektor* (Police Director) appointed by the *Gemeinderat* (Council). Usually promoted from among subordinate police officials of other towns.

VIENNA — *Polizeipräsident* (Police President) appointed by the Crown upon recommendation of the Minister of the Interior. Always a university graduate in law who has spent his life in the government service, being gradually promoted through the operation of the Austrian official system.

ZURICH — *Polizeidirektor* (Police Director) appointed by the City Council from among officers holding the rank of lieutenant in the Swiss army.

BIBLIOGRAPHY

BIBLIOGRAPHY

THE list of books which follows makes no pretense of being exhaustive. It is merely a suggestive list to assist those who desire to pursue further the study of certain phases of the police problem. It should be said at once that there are but few books dealing directly with the subject of police organization and management. In fact, in the English language, McAdoo's *Guarding a Great City* (New York, 1906) and Fuld's *Police Administration* (New York, 1910) are practically the only books relating to the question, and even these are limited in scope and treatment. Much has been written in German, French, Italian, and Swedish on special phases of police activity, particularly the detection of crime; but no comparative study of police organization on broad lines has hitherto been attempted. The following list, therefore, is made up for the most part of books which either treat the police problem indirectly, or concern themselves with specific phases of it.

GENERAL — GOVERNMENT, STATE AND LOCAL

Under this heading, I have included only a few of the better known books and encyclopedias for reference purposes.

ATKINSON, MABEL. *Local Government in Scotland.* Edinburgh, 1904.

BLOCK, MAURICE. *Dictionnaire de l'administration française.* 2 vols. Paris, 1905.

European Police Systems

DAWSON, WILLIAM H. *Municipal Life and Government in Germany.* London, 1914.
A sympathetic study of German cities at work.

GOODNOW, FRANK J. *Municipal Government.* New York, 1909.

Handwörterbuch der Kommunalwissenschaften. Jena, 1914.
This encyclopedia of local government in Germany is not yet completed. Made up of the contributions of eminent Continental scholars, it promises to be the most important work of its kind.

HOWARD, BURT ESTES. *The German Empire.* New York, 1913.

JAMES, HERMAN GERLACH. *Principles of Prussian Administration.* New York, 1913.

LOWELL, A. LAWRENCE. *The Government of England.* 2 vols. New York, 1912.

MUNRO, WILLIAM BENNETT. *The Government of European Cities.* New York, 1909.

OGG, FREDERIC AUSTIN. *The Governments of Europe.* New York, 1913.

POLLARD, J. *The Corporation of Berlin; A Study in Municipal Government.* 2d ed. London, 1894.
An elementary study, of service chiefly because there is little else in English on the subject.

REDLICH, JOSEF. *Das Wesen der österreichischen Kommunalverfassung.* Leipzig, 1910.
A very engaging picture of Austrian local government by an eminent Austrian scholar.

REDLICH, JOSEF, and HIRST, F. W. *Local Government in England.* 2 vols. London, 1903.

SHAW, ALBERT. *Municipal Government in Continental Europe.* New York, 1906.

SHAW, ALBERT. *Municipal Government in Great Britain.* New York, 1898.

WEBB, SIDNEY and BEATRICE. *English Local Government from the Revolution to the Municipal Corporations Act.* 2 vols. London, 1908.

WILSON, WOODROW. *The State.* New York, 1898.

Bibliography

COLLECTIONS OF LAWS AND GENERAL REFERENCE WORKS

Strafgesetzbuch für das Deutsche Reich vom 15. Mai 1871.
German Imperial Penal Code. The only English translation of the Imperial Code of the German Empire is by Geoffrey Drage, London, 1885. Unfortunately, the book is now out of print.

Strafprozessordnung.
German Code of Penal Procedure. There is no English translation of this code. Both the Penal Code and the Code of Penal Procedure have been published in handbook form (C. H. Beck, München, 1911-12).

Straf-Gesetz das allgemeine vom 27. Mai 1852, bezüglichen im Reichsgesetzblatte enthaltenen Gesetzen und Verordnung.
Austrian Penal Code.

Strafprocess-Ordnung vom 23. Mai 1873. Gesetz über die zeitweilige Einstellung der Wirksamseit der Geschwornengerichte.
Austrian Code of Penal Procedure. There is no translation in English of the Austrian Penal Code or of the Code of Penal Procedure.

RAULT, J. and PHELIPOT, H. *Manuel de Police.* Paris, 1911.
This includes the *Code Pénal* and the special laws and decrees relating to crime in France.

VINCENT, SIR HOWARD. *The Police Code.* London, 1912.
A general manual of the English criminal law.

STONE'S JUSTICES' MANUAL. Edited by J. R. Roberts. London, 1910.
This is probably the most useful reference book on English criminal law and procedure.

RENTON, ROBERT WEMYSS, and BROWN, HENRY HILTON. *Criminal Procedure According to the Laws of Scotland.* Edinburgh, 1909.
A critical commentary on the peculiar criminal procedure under the laws of Scotland.

HIPPEL, ROBERT VON. *Handbuch der Polizeiverwaltung.* Berlin, 1910.
Police administration — chiefly a collection of laws — but in systematic arrangement.

411

European Police Systems

EIBEN, H. *Die Ortspolizei.* Cologne, 1908.
> Handbook of laws, for officials and private citizens.

GRAIS, HUE DE, COUNT. *Handbuch der Verfassung und Verwaltung.* Berlin, 1912.
> Perhaps the best known handbook of German government in general, covering the imperial, state and municipal administration.

BRAYER, FELIX. *Dictionnaire général de police administrative et judiciaire.* 4 vols. Paris, 1886-90.

MEYER, GEORG. *Lehrbuch des deutschen Verwaltungsrechts.* 3d ed. Leipzig, 1910.

MAYER, OTTO. *Deutsches Verwaltungsrecht.* 2 vols. Leipzig, 1895-96.

STENGEL, KARL VON, FREIHERR. *Wörterbuch des deutschen Staats- und Verwaltungsrechts.* 2d ed. Tübingen, 1911-13.
> A very useful reference work.

ARNSTEDT, OSKAR VON. *Das Preussische Polizeirecht.* Berlin, 1905.

CARMICHAEL, EVELYN G. M. Compilation of " The County and Borough Police Acts." London, 1900.
> A collection of all the acts relating to the county and borough police forces of England and Wales.

ALEXANDER, G. GLOVER. *The Administration of Justice in Criminal Matters* (in England and Wales). Cambridge (Eng.), 1911.
> An excellent outline of the English machinery of justice.

KENNY, C. S. *Outlines of Criminal Law.* Cambridge (Eng.), 1902.

HISTORIES AND COMMENTARIES

ANDERSON, SIR ROBERT. *The Lighter Side of My Official Life.* London, 1910.
> Sir Robert Anderson was for some time Assistant Commissioner of the Metropolitan Police Force. His book is interestingly written, but shows decided bias at certain points.

Bibliography

CURTIS, R. *The History of the Royal Irish Constabulary*. Dublin, 1871.

EUVRARD, F. *Historique de l'institution des commissaires de police; son origine. . . . leurs prérogatives*. Montpellier, 1910.

LEE, CAPTAIN W. L. MELVILLE. *A History of Police in England*. London, 1901.
> A well written account of the various steps which led to the reformation of the English police forces by the Municipal Corporations Act of 1835 and the Rural Police Act of 1856.

MACNAGHTEN, SIR MELVILLE. *Days of My Years*. London, 1914.
> Sir Melville MacNaghten was for many years the head of the Criminal Investigation Department of the London Metropolitan police. He resigned in 1913.

REY, ALFRED and L. FERON. *Histoire du corps des gardiens de la paix*. Paris, 1896.

SMITH, LIEUTENANT COLONEL SIR HENRY. *From Constable to Commissioner*. London, 1910.
> Sir Henry Smith was formerly Commissioner of the City of London police.

POLICE ORGANIZATION AND ADMINISTRATION

ASSESSOR. (pseudonym). *Die Berliner Polizei*. Berlin, 1907.
> A sketchy account of police organization in Berlin.

BLAND, J. P. *The Metropolitan Police*. (A pamphlet). London, 1909.
> Largely a summary of the findings of the Royal Commission appointed to investigate the Metropolitan Police. The articles in this pamphlet were originally written for the London *Times*.

BUDDING, C. *Die Polizei in Stadt und Land in Grossbrittanien*. Berlin, 1908.
> Dr. Budding's book was written after an intimate personal study of police conditions in England. It is descriptive rather than critical.

European Police Systems

Encyclopedia of Local Government Law. 6 vols. London, 1906-1908.
> Containing an article on *Police* by H. B. Simpson, Principal Clerk in the Home Office, London.

FRIEDEL, C. *Die Polizeiliche Strafverfügung.* Berlin, 1905.
> A guide in the application of police punishments.

GUYOT, I. *La Police.* Paris, 1884.

LAUFER, FRANZ. *Unser Polizeiwesen.* Stuttgart, 1906.
> A serviceable handbook on police organization in Germany.

MOREL, PIERRE. *La Police à Paris.* Paris, 1907.
> A vigorous and rather biased attack on the Paris police organization.

MOUNEYRAT, E. *La Préfecture de police.* Paris, 1906.
> A serviceable, though not exhaustive, study of the office of police Prefect in Paris.

Police, La. Paul Dupont, editor. *Notions générales de police, organisation de la police en France, police administrative, préfecture de police.* Paris, 1905.

Police en France, La. Published by the Minister of the Interior, *Direction de la Sûreté générale.* Versailles, 1913.
> An excellent descriptive account of police organization in France.

ROSCHER, GUSTAV. *Grossstadtpolizei; ein praktisches Handbuch der deutschen Polizei.* Hamburg, 1912.
> Dr. Roscher, the well known President of the police organization of Hamburg, has written perhaps the most complete book on the subject of police organization in large cities. Unfortunately, the book is confined to conditions in Germany. He gives a very interesting and detailed account of police activity in German municipalities.

WEIDLICH, DR. KARL. *Die Polizei als Grundlage und Organ der Strafrechtspflege in England, Schottland und Irland.* Berlin, 1908.
> Dr. Weidlich, who is a judge of the county court, or *Amtsgericht,* of Württemberg, is a well known student of local government. His book contains an interesting comparison of the powers and functions of English and German police.

Bibliography

CRIME AND THE CRIMINAL

In this list, I have included a few of the more important books which deal in a general way with crime and the criminal.

Bosco, Augusto. *La delinquenza in vari Stati di Europa.* Rome, 1903.

Ferri, Enrico. *L'omicidio nell'antropologia criminale.* Turin, 1895.

Ferri, Enrico. *Das Verbrechen in seiner Abhängigkeit von dem jährlichen Temperaturwechsel. (Zeitschrift für das gesammte Strafwesen,* Vol. II).

Mercier, C. A. *Crime and Insanity.* New York, 1911.

Niceforo, Alfredo. *La delinquenza in Sardegna.* Palermo, 1897.

Niceforo, Alfredo. *Italia barbara contemporanea.* Milan and Palermo, 1898.

Ripley, W. Z. *Races of Europe.* New York, 1910.

Wright, Carrol D. *The Relations of Economic Conditions to the Causes of Crime.* Philadelphia, 1900.

Special attention is called to the following books, which have been translated into English and published under the auspices of The American Institute of Criminal Law and Criminology. In their field, they represent the best thought of foreign scholars.

Aschaffenburg, Gustav. *Crime and Its Repression.* Translated from the Second German Edition by Adalbert Albrecht. Boston, 1913.

Bonger, W. A. *Criminality and Economic Conditions.* Translated from the French by Rev. Henry P. Horton. Boston, 1914.

Ferri, Enrico. *Criminal Sociology.* Translated from the Fifth Italian and Second French Edition by Joseph I. Kelly and John Lisle. Boston, 1914.

Garofalo, Raffaelle, Baron. *Criminology.* Translated from the First Italian and Fifth French Edition by Robert W. Millar. Boston, 1914.

European Police Systems

GROSS, HANS. *Criminal Psychology.* Translated from the Fourth German Edition by Dr. Horace M. Kallen. Boston, 1911.

LOMBROSO, CESARE. *Crime, Its Causes and Remedies.* Translated from the French and German Editions by Rev. Henry P. Horton. Boston, 1912.

QUIRÓS, C. BERNALDO DE. *Modern Theories of Criminality.* Translated from the Second Spanish Edition by Dr. Alfonso de Salvio. Boston, 1912.

SALEILLES, RAYMOND. *The Individualization of Punishment.* Translated from the Second French Edition by Mrs. Rachael Szold Jastrow. Boston, 1911.

TARDE, GABRIEL. *Penal Philosophy.* Translated from the Fourth French Edition by Rapelje Howell. Boston, 1912.

METHODS OF CRIME DETECTION

Archiv für Kriminal-Anthropologie und Kriminalistik. (Periodical.) Vols. 1-50. Leipzig, 1899-1914.
> This periodical, edited by Dr. Hans Gross, furnishes current information in regard to new methods of crime detection, new ideas of criminology, etc.

ATCHERLEY, MAJOR L. W. *"M. O." (Modus Operandi) in Criminal Investigation and Detection.* West Riding of Yorkshire, 1913.

BERTILLON, ALPHONSE. *Instructions for taking Descriptions for the Identification of Criminals by the Means of Anthropometric Indications.* Translated by Gallus Miller with a historical introduction by the translator. Chicago, 1889.

BERTILLON, ALPHONSE. *Signaletic Instructions, Including the Theory and Practice of Anthropometric Identification.* Translated from the latest French edition, edited under the supervision of R. W. McClaughry. Chicago, 1896.

BERTILLON, ALPHONSE. *La Photographie judiciaire.* Translated under the title *Legal Photography* by P. R. Brown. New York, 1897.

Bibliography

BERTILLON, ALPHONSE. *Photographie métrique de.* Published by La Cour-Berthiot. Paris, 1912.
A well illustrated book, edited under the supervision of M. Bertillon, outlining his system of metric photography.

GROSS, DR. HANS. *Criminal Investigation.* A Practical Handbook for Magistrates, Police Officers and Lawyers. Translated and adapted to Indian and Colonial Practice from the *System der Kriminalistik* of Dr. Hans Gross, by John Adam and J. Colyer Adam. Madras, India, 1906.
Dr. Gross's book is well known in Europe and India. It is perhaps the best text-book on the subject of crime detection.

HENRY, SIR EDWARD R. *Classification and Uses of Finger Prints.* 4th ed. London, 1913.
This book has been translated into many languages. It describes in detail the advantages of the finger-print system of identification and the Henry system of classification.

NICEFORO, ALFREDO. *La Police et l'enquête judiciaire scientifiques. Avec préface du docteur Lacassagne.* Paris, 1907.
This well known book ranks with Dr. Gross's *System der Kriminalistik.* It is a practical handbook for detective officers.

OTTOLENGHI, SALVATORE. *L'estensione del "Bertillonage" e la lotta contro gli anarchici. (Rivista d'Italia, anno 4, Vol. II, p. 304-316. Roma, 1901).*

REISS, R. A. *Manuel de police scientifique.* Preface by M. Louis Lépine. Lausanne, 1911.
This book is comparable with Dr. Niceforo's book, cited above.

REISS, R. A. *La Photographie judiciaire.* Paris, 1903.

REISS, R. A. *Le Portrait parlé.* Paris, 1905.

ROSCHER, GUSTAV. *Handbuch der Daktyloskopie für Selbstunterricht bearbeitet.* (A pamphlet.) Leipzig, 1905.
An outline of Dr. Roscher's system of classifying finger-prints.

SCHNEICKERT, HANS. *Polizeiliche Handschriftensammlungen. (Archiv für gerichtliche Schriftuntersuchungen und verwandte Gebiete,* p. 361-387. Leipzig, 1909.)

THROL, F. *Das polizeiliche Meldewesen.* Berlin, 1897.
Describes in detail the system of police registration and the forms in use in the Berlin department.

European Police Systems

VUCETICH, JUAN. *Dactiloscopia comparada del nuevo sistema argentino.* La Plata, 1904.
An outline of the Vucetich system of classifying finger-prints.

WINDT, KAMILLO, and KODICEK, SIEGMUND. *Daktyloskopie. Verwertung von Fingerabdrücken zu Identifizierungszwecken.* Vienna, 1904.

POLICE REPORTS.

MANY of the European police departments, particularly in England and Scotland, publish annual reports of their activities. Perhaps the most comprehensive is the one published by the Metropolitan Police of London, called *Report of the Commissioner of Police of the Metropolis.* Similar reports are published annually by the Chief Constables of English and Scottish cities. In Paris, the activities of the preceding year are included in a document which accompanies the budgetary estimate (*Rapport. Conseil Municipal de Paris*). Berlin no longer publishes an annual report, but annual statistics relating to convictions are presented in the *Statistisches Jahrbuch der Stadt Berlin.* Perhaps the most complete annual police report in Germany is the one published by the Hamburg department (*Jahresbericht der Polizeibehörde Hamburg*). The statistics in this report give a vivid picture of the manifold activities of a German police department.

In addition to the departmental reports, there are the compilations of judicial statistics in various countries, relating to crime and criminals. Among these compilations, *Judicial Statistics, England and Wales,* published by the Home Office, is perhaps the most nota-

418

Bibliography

ble. These statistics, printed annually, include the criminal returns from every county and criminal court in England and Wales. A similar annual report is published by the Scottish office relating to the counties and courts of Scotland.

Attention should also be called to the annual reports of the Inspectors of Constabulary attached to the Home Office, relating to the maintenance and condition of the borough and county police forces of England and Wales (*Police, England and Wales*). A similar return is published annually by the Scottish office, relating to the county and borough forces of Scotland.

The budgetary estimates and expenditures of the various state controlled police departments, such as those of Berlin and other Prussian cities, Dresden, Munich, and Vienna, can be found in the annual estimates of the respective Ministers of the Interior. Similarly the annual expenditures of the Italian *Carabinieri* appear in the budgets of the Minister of War and the Minister of the Interior of Italy. The expenditures of the London Metropolitan Force are printed each year in a report to Parliament. The Paris police budget appears each year in pamphlet form for the use of the Paris Municipal Council.

The reports of commissions appointed to investigate the activities of police bodies often furnish extensive information. Perhaps the best known is the *Report of the Royal Commission on the Metropolitan Force*, London, 1908. Attention should also be called to the *Final Report of Her Majesty's Commissioners on the Opera-*

European Police Systems

tion and Administration of the Laws Relating to the Sale of Intoxicating Liquors, London, 1899, and to the *Report of the Committee on Inquiry, 1901,* Dublin Metropolitan Police, Dublin, 1902.

POLICE INSTRUCTION BOOKS.

Nearly every police department in Europe has its instruction book for the use of the police. Many departments, notably in Vienna, Dresden, and Hamburg, have an elaborate series of such books, dealing with all phases of official activity. In Hamburg, these books are published in pocket editions, one for each branch of the service, as, for example, *Harbor Police, Detective Bureau, Political Police,* etc. In Vienna, three large text-books (*Organisation und Instruktion der Wiener k. k. Sicherheitswache,* Vienna, 1910) are published for the use of the police. The London Metropolitan Police book (*Instruction Book for the Guidance of the Metropolitan Police Force,* London, 1912), although small, is very serviceable. Liverpool's book (*Liverpool City Police — Instructions,* Liverpool, 1911), edited by former Chief Constable Leonard Dunning, is perhaps the most complete in England. In Sweden, a guide to the police has been published in the shape of three elaborate volumes, dealing with the theoretical and practical aspects of police work (*Polishandbok,* R. von Schultz, Upsala and Stockholm, 1912-13). These books, unfortunately, have not yet been translated into any other language. They represent an excellent attempt to present the modern point of view of the police problem.

INDEX

INDEX

423

European Police Systems

Austria, administrative provinces, 79
constructive control system, 267
criminal record files, 318
gendarmerie corps, 73
illegitimate births in, 13
police management in, 79–83
registration system, 350
state control of police, 79
suicides in, 11
system of police punishment, 33
Austrian criminal procedure, 17, 33
official promotion system, 154, 190
police, analysis of, 82–83
censorship, 83
public assembly law, 83
Statthalter, 83

Barcelona, Chief of Police, qualification and appointment, 403
patrolmen, salaries of, 238
police, budget, 400
number of, 401
Barmen, municipal police system, 69, 71
Barracks, of London police, 240
of Vienna police, 241
Bavaria, police control, 68
Beats and transfers, 269
Belgian burgomasters, appointment of, 67
police powers of, 66
Belgium, criminal record files, 318
gendarmerie corps, 73
illegitimate births, 13
police system, 66
registration of foreigners, 350

Belgium, suicides in, 11
Bergen, patrolmen, salaries of, 238
police, number of, 401
Berlin, area of police jurisdiction, 399
character of detective force, 306
classification of electors, 75
criminal record files, 317
decentralization experiments, 113
department's mechanical equipment, 270, 271
detective officers, training of, 301
detective system, 279
detectives, promotion of, 300
training of, 301, 302
extent of police district, 110
Greater, 110, 111
hours of service, 256
Inspektor of police, 118
Kriminalkommissar of the detective force, 283, 301
murder commissions, 282
homogeneous population of, 7
newspaper clippings file, 341
Oberwachtmeister, appointment, training, salary, 184
officer's personal record books, 270
patrolmen, promotion of, 245, 250
salaries of, 238
"bèat control book," 268
pension system, 254
personnel of police department, 115
photograph classification, 339
police, annual expenditures, 398
blackmail, 375
budget, 45, 394

424

Index

425

European Police Systems

Brussels, burgomaster, qualification and appointment, 403
chief of police, 67
"Greater," 137
patrolmen, salaries of, 238
police, administrative sections, 137
organization of, 136, 137
number of, 401
ratio of police to population, 138
requirements for police service, 210
Brzesowsky, Karl Ritter von, 151
Budapest, burgomaster, method of electing, 82
city government, 82
hours of service, 257
methods of control, 267
Oberkommandant and his duties, 125
patrolmen, promotion of, 245
salaries of, 238
photographs of criminals, 338
police, barracks, 242
budget, 45
exchequer, 81
number of, 401
organization, 124
president, 152, 403
system of, 80, 124
requirements for police service, 210
salary of commissioner, 179
selection of detectives, 297
training system, 216
Budgets of police departments, 400
Bureau of identification, international, proposed, 334
Burgomasters, Belgian, appointment of, 67

Burgomasters, Belgian, police powers of, 66
Budapest, choice of, 82
Dutch, police powers of, 65, 66
German method of appointment, 76
German, police powers of, 70
Rotterdam, police powers of, 260
Vienna, choice of, 82

Carabinieri, of Italy, 73, 92–95
budget of, 93
school of, 213
Rome, 134
Cassel, state police force, 68
Castaldi, Dr. Domenico, 152
Centralized vs. decentralized detective organization, 289–293
Charlottenburg, police system, 110
Chemnitz, municipal police system, 69
Chief Constables, candidates, advertising for, 163
English, 53–55, 163
methods of appointing, 160–163
Glasgow, 55
London, appointment and duties, 105
Christiania, patrolmen, salaries of, 238
police budget, 400
master, qualification and appointment, 403
number of, 401
salary of commissioner, 179
Citizen, private, police powers of, 15
City Guards of Italy, 94, 95

426

Index

Index

England, illegitimate births in, 133
Municipal Corporations Act,
48, 49
"one-day-rest-in-seven" law,
225
"Permissive Act" of 1839, 61
police, organization in provincial cities, 107
powers of Home Secretary,
174
provincial cities, police discipline in, 262
Rural Police Act of 1856, 49
suicides in, 11
English detective system, 275
conception of police duties, 9,
18
county police, 61
Home Secretary's police supervision powers, 64
methods of appointing chief
constables, 162-163
methods of employing finger-
print system, 327
penal procedure, 17
police, powers of, 310
system, defects of, 147
status of, 15
"Standing Joint Committees,"
62, 63
training system, 159, 182
vs. Continental police organization, 140
promotion system, 246
recruiting system, 199, 200
vs. German penal procedure,
17, 308-312
system of training detec-
tives, 306-308
Equipments, 239
Esperanto, proposed use of in international reports, 335
Essen, classification of voters, 75
state police force, 68

European cities, homogeneity of,
6-8
European police forces, state
control of, 38, 39
European states, comparative
criminality, 10
Excise regulation, 379-381
Extra-police work, 245
Extradition treaties, 335

Factory laws, 19
Ferri, Enrico, classification of Eu-
ropean criminality, 10
Files, criminal record, 316
Finger-print files, German, 331
Finger-print identifications at
Scotland Yard, 326, 328
Finger-print records, England,
when taken, 327
Finger-print system, Argentine
method, 322
Bertillon method, 322
Dresden, 331
English methods, 327
growth of, 326
Henry method, 321, 324
Roscher's method, 322
Finger-prints, early study of, 320
Finland, illegitimate births in, 13
suicides in, 11
France, administrative departments, 85
commissaires de police, 86
criminal record depositories,
318
gendarmerie corps, 73, 86, 87
homicides in, 11
identification methods, 332
illegitimate births in, 13
Minister of the Interior, head
of police system, 87
police, budget, 87
management in, 84-90
powers of the *Maire,* 85

429

Index

Hennion, M., 152
plan of reorganizing Parisian
police, 144
Henry, Sir Edward, 150, 165,
171, 320, 321
Henry finger-print system, 321,
323, 324
Herschel, Sir William, origina-
tor of finger-print sys-
tem, 320
Herzegovina, suicides in, 12
Holland, "agents," 199
gendarmerie corps, 23
illegitimate births in, 13
Marachausses of, 73
police, administration, 158
powers of burgomasters, 65,
66
system of, 65
registration of foreigners, 350
selecting and training *inspecteurs*, 188
Homicide and climate, 14
economic conditions, 14
Homicides in European countries, 11
Home Secretary of England, police supervising pow-
ers, 64, 174
Hours of service, 255–257
Hungarian Press Law, 83
state control of police, 81
Hungary, administrative counties, 80
illegitimate births in, 13

Identification Bureau, International, 334
of Paris, 288
Identification methods, English,
327
French, 332
German, 330

Identification methods, international, 333
Italian, 329
papers of German cities, 310
photographic, 337
Illegal police action, procedure
after, 16
Illegitimate births, comparative
statistics, 13
Index of nicknames and aliases,
340
photographs, 337–339
police, of stolen property, 348
police presidents and commissioners, 349
system of "Missing and
Dead," 348
tattoos and deformities, 340
India, employment of the finger-
print system, 325
Integrity of police, 370
International criminal newspaper, 335
Identification Bureau proposed, 334
notification service, 335
Ireland, homicides in, 11
illegitimate births in, 13
Royal Irish Constabulary, 4, 65
recruiting system of, 161
suicides in, 12
Italian police administration, 157
Italy, administrative provinces, 91
Carabinieri organization, powers and budget, 92–95
City Guards, 94, 95
commissari of police system,
96
criminal identification methods, 329
criminal record files, 318
delegati of police system, 96
gendarmerie corps. See *Carabinieri*

Index

433

Index

London, salary, police commissioner, 178
  of superintendent, 195
  Sunday Observance Bill, 176
  superintendents of police, duties, 104
  training detectives, 298
  vs. Vienna training system, 194, 195
Lost and Found bureaus, 348
Lyons, police budget, 88
  police system of, 87, 88
  salary of commissioner, 179
Luxemburg, suicides in, 12

Magdeburg, state police force, 68
Madrid, Inspector of Police, qualification and appointment, 404
  patrolmen, salaries of, 238
  police, budget, 400
  number of, 401
  salary of commissioner, 179
Maire, head of French *communes,* 84
  police powers of, 85
Malstatt-Burbach, state police system, 71
Manchester, Chief Constable, qualification and appointment, 404
  patrolmen, salaries of, 238
  police, budget, 400
  court cases, 35
  number of, 401
  organization, 109
  requirements for police service, 210
  salary of commissioner, 178
  selection of patrolmen, 205
  Watch Committee, 52
  investigation, 56

Marachausses, the, of Holland, 73
Marseilles, police, budget, 88
  system of, 88
  salary of commissioner, 179
Massard, M., on lack of coherency in Paris police system, 143
Mayne, Sir Richard, police commissioner of London, 164, 176
Medical service, 242
Meldwesen, Germany, 350–355
Mercier's classification of crimes, 345, 346
Metropolitan Police Force of London, 40
  expenditures, 389–392
  management of, 45–48
  organization of, 100–107
  regulations concerning class distinction, 233
Military discipline of Continental police, 228
Modus Operandi system of classification, 344
Mona Lisa theft, the, 325
Monaco, suicides in, 11
Monro, James, police commissioner of London, 165, 167, 174
Moscow, police, budget, 400
  number of, 401
  Prefect of Police, qualification and appointment, 404
Munich, finger-print records, 330
  photograph classification, 339
  Police Commissioner Van der Heydt, 152
  police department branches, 117
  police director, qualification and appointment, 404

435

European Police Systems

Index

European Police Systems

438

Index

439

European Police Systems

Index